LOSING MY

Virginity

LOSING MY

How I've Survived, Had Fun, and Made a Fortune Doing Business My Way

RICHARD BRANSON

THREE RIVERS PRESS • NEW YORK

Published by Three Rivers Press, New York, New York.
Member of the Crown Publishing Group.

Random House, Inc. New York, Toronto, London, Sydney, Auckland www.randomhouse.com

THREE RIVERS PRESS is a registered trademark and the Three Rivers Press colophon is a trademark of Random House, Inc.

Originally published in the United States in hardcover by Times Books, a division of Random House, Inc., and in the United Kingdom by Virgin Publishing Ltd, London, in 1998.

Printed in the United States of America

Design by Helene Wald Berinsky

Library of Congress Cataloging-in-Publication Data
Losing my virginity : how I've survived, had fun, and made a fortune doing business my way / Richard Branson.
Contents: v. 1. 1950–1993
1. Branson, Richard.   2. Businesspeople—Great Britain—Biography.
3. Virgin Group.   4. Airlines.   5. Music trade.   I. Title.
HC252.5.B73   1998
338′.04′092—dc21
[B]

ISBN 0-8129-3229-3

10

Dedicated to Alex Ritchie and his family

A special thank-you to Edward Whitley
for helping me pull this project together. Edward spent
two years in my company, practically lived in my
house, waded through twenty-five years of
scribbled notebooks, and helped me bring them to life.

Contents

LOSING MY
Virginity

Prologue

"Oh, screw it, let's do it."

January 1997

Tuesday, 7 January 1997, Morocco

5:30 A.M. • I woke before Joan and sat up in bed. From across Marrakech I heard the wavering cry of the muezzins calling people to prayer over the loudspeakers. I still hadn't written to Holly and Sam, so I tore a page out of my notebook and wrote them a letter in case I didn't return.

Dear Holly and Sam,

Life can seem rather unreal at times. Alive and well and loving one day. No longer there the next.

As you both know I always had an urge to live life to its full. That meant I was lucky enough to live the life of many people during my 46 years. I loved every minute of it and I especially loved every second of my time with both of you and Mum.

I know that many people thought us foolish for embarking on this latest adventure. I was convinced they were wrong. I felt that everything we had learned from our Atlantic and Pacific adventures would mean that we'd have a safe flight. I thought that the risks were acceptable. Obviously I've been proved wrong.

However, I regret nothing about my life except not being with Joan to finally help you grow up. By the ages of 12 and 15 your characters have already developed. We're both so proud of you. Joan and I couldn't have had two more delightful kids. You are both kind, considerate, full of life (even witty!). What more could we both want.

Be strong. I know it won't be easy. But we've had a wonderful life together and you'll never forget all the good times we've had.

Live life to its full yourselves. Enjoy every minute of it. Love and look after Mum as if she's both of us.

I love you,

Dad

• • •

I folded the letter into a small square and put it in my pocket. Fully clothed and ready, I lay down beside Joan and hugged her. While I felt wide awake and nervous, she felt warm and sleepy in my arms. Holly and Sam came into our room and cuddled into bed between us. Then Sam slipped off with his cousins to go to the launch site and see the balloon in which I hoped shortly to fly around the world. Joan and Holly stayed with me while I got dressed and spoke to Martin, the meteorologist. The flight, he said, was definitely on; we had the best weather conditions we'd had for five years. I then called Tim Evans, our doctor. He had just been with Rory McCarthy, our third pilot, and had bad news: Rory couldn't fly. He had mild pneumonia, and if he was in a capsule for three weeks, it could get much worse. I immediately called up Rory and commiserated with him.

"See you in the dining room," I said. "Let's have breakfast."

6:20 A.M. • By the time Rory and I met in the hotel dining room, it was deserted. The journalists who had been following the preparations for the launch over the previous twenty-four hours had already left for the launch site.

Rory and I met and hugged each other. We both cried. As well as becoming a close friend as our third pilot on the balloon flight, Rory had been joining forces with me recently on a number of business deals. Just before we had come to Morocco, he had bought a share in our new record label, V2, and had invested in Virgin clothes and Virgin Vie, our new cosmetics company.

"I can't believe I'm letting you down," Rory said. "I'm never ill—never, ever."

"Don't worry," I assured him. "It happens. We've got Alex, who weighs half your weight. We'll fly far further with him on board."

"Seriously, if you don't come back," Rory said, "I'll carry on where you left off."

"Well, thanks," I said, laughing nervously.

Alex Ritchie was already out at the launch site, supervising the mad dash to get the capsule ready with Per Lindstrand, the veteran hot-air balloonist who had introduced me to the sport. Alex was the brilliant engineer who had designed the capsule and the pressurizing system. Until then, no one had succeeded in building a system that could sustain balloon flights at jet-stream levels. Although he had built both our Atlantic and Pacific capsules,

I didn't know him, and it was too late to find out much about him now. Despite having no flight training, Alex had bravely made the decision to come with us. If all went well with the flight, we'd have about three weeks to get to know one another—about as intimately as any of us would want.

Unlike our crossings of the Pacific and Atlantic Oceans by hot-air balloon, on this trip we would not heat air until we needed to; the balloon had an inner core of helium, which would take us up. Per's plan was to heat the air around that core during the night; this in turn would heat the helium, which would otherwise contract and grow heavy and sink.

Joan, Holly, and I held hands and the three of us embraced. It was time to go.

8:30 A.M. • We all saw it at the same time. As we drove along the dirt road out to the Moroccan air base, it looked as if a new mosque had sprouted overnight. Above the bending, dusty palm trees, a stunning white orb rose like a mother-of-pearl dome. It was the balloon. Men on horseback galloped along the side of the road, guns slung over their shoulders, heading for the air base. Everyone was drawn to this huge, gleaming white balloon hanging in the air, tall and slender

9:15 A.M. • The balloon was cordoned off, and around the perimeter railing was an amazing collection of people. The entire complement of the air base stood off to one side in serried ranks, dressed in smart navy-blue uniforms; in front of them was the traditional Moroccan collection of dancing women, wearing white shawls, hollering, wailing, and whooping. Then a group of horsemen dressed in Berber costume and brandishing antique muskets galloped into view and lined up in front of the balloon. For an awful moment, I thought they would fire a celebratory salvo and puncture the balloon. Per, Alex, and I gathered in the capsule and completed a final check of all the systems. The sun was rising rapidly, and the helium was beginning to expand.

10:15 A.M. • We had done all the checks and were ready to go. I hugged Joan and Holly and Sam one last time. I was amazed at Joan's strength. Holly had been by my side for the last four days, and she too appeared to be totally in control of the situation. I thought that Sam was as well, but then he burst into tears and pulled me toward him, refusing to let go. I almost started crying too. I will never forget the anguished strength of his hug. Then he kissed me and let go and hugged Joan. I ran across to kiss Mum and Dad good-bye.

Mum pressed a letter into my hand. "Open it after six days," she said. I silently hoped that we would last that long.

10:50 A.M. • There was nothing left to do except to climb up the steel steps into the capsule. For a second I hesitated and wondered when and where I would put my feet back on solid ground—or water. There was no time to think ahead. I stepped in through the hatch. Per was by the main controls; I sat by the camera equipment; and Alex sat in the seat by the trapdoor.

11:19 A.M. • 10, 9, 8, 7, 6, 5—Per counted down and I concentrated on working the cameras. My hand kept darting down to check my parachute buckle. I tried not to think about the huge balloon above us, and the six vast fuel tanks strapped around our capsule—4, 3, 2, 1 . . . and Per threw the lever that fired the bolts that severed the anchor cables, and we lifted silently and swiftly into the sky. There was no roar of the burners; our ascent was like that of an enormous party helium balloon. We just rose up, up, and away, and then as we caught the morning breeze we headed over Marrakech.

The emergency door was still open as we soared up, and we waved at the by then little people below. Every detail of Marrakech—its square pink walls, the large town square, the green courtyards and fountains hidden behind high walls—was laid out beneath us. By 10,000 feet it became cold and the air grew thin. We shut the trapdoor. From then on we were on our own. We were pressurized, and the pressure would mount.

Our first fax came through the machine just after midday.

"Oh God!" Per handed it over. "Look at this."

"Please be aware that the connectors on the fuel tanks are locked on."

This was our first mistake. The connectors should have been locked off so that if we got into trouble and started falling, then we could jettison a one-ton fuel tank by way of ballast.

"If that's our only mistake, we're not doing badly," I said, trying to cheer Per up.

"We need to get down to five thousand feet, and then I'll climb out and unlock them," Alex said. "It's not a problem."

It was impossible to lose height during the day because the sun was heating the helium. The only immediate solution was to release helium, which, once released, would be impossible to regain. We couldn't afford to lose any helium, so we agreed to wait for nightfall to bring the balloon down. It was a nagging worry. We didn't know how this balloon would fly at night, and with our fuel tanks locked on, our ability to escape trouble was limited.

Although Alex and I tried to brush off the locked canisters, it sent Per into a fierce depression. He sat slumped by the controls in a furious silence, speaking only when we asked him a direct question.

We flew serenely for the rest of the day. The views over the Atlas Mountains were exhilarating, their jagged peaks capped with snow, gleaming up at us in the glorious sunshine. The capsule was cramped, full of supplies to last us eighteen days. However, locking off the connectors was not the only thing we'd forgotten to do. We'd also neglected to pack any lavatory paper, so we had to wait to receive faxes before we could go down the tiny spiral staircase to the loo. And my Moroccan stomach was in need of a lot of faxes. Per maintained his glowering silence, but Alex and I were just grateful that we knew then rather than finding out later the hard way.

As we approached the Algerian border we had a second shock when the Algerians informed us that we were heading straight for Béchar, their top military base, and told us that we could not fly over it. "You are not, repeat *not,* authorized to enter this area," said the telex.

We had no choice.

I spent about two hours on the satellite phone to Mike Kendrick, our flight controller, and tried various British ministers. Eventually André Azoulay, the Moroccan minister who had ironed out all our problems for the launch in Morocco, came to the rescue again. His explanation to the Algerians that we could not change our direction and that we did not have powerful cameras on board was accepted, and they relented. As the good news came through, I scribbled down all the notes and turned over another page in my logbook. There was a handwritten note from Sam, in thick black ink and Sellotaped to the page: "To Dad, I hope you have a great time. Safe journey. Lots and lots of love, your son Sam." I recalled that he'd slipped into the capsule without me last night, and now I knew why.

By five o'clock in the afternoon we were still flying at 30,000 feet, and Per started firing the burners to heat the air inside the envelope. Although we burned steadily for an hour, just after 6 P.M. the balloon started losing height steadily.

"Something's wrong with the theory here," Per said.

"What's the matter?" I asked.

"I don't know."

Per was firing the burners continuously, but the balloon was still heading down. We lost 1,000 feet, and then another 500 feet. It was getting colder all the time as the sun disappeared. It was clear that the helium was rapidly contracting, becoming a dead weight on top of us.

"We've got to dump ballast," Per said. He was frightened. We all were. We pulled levers to dump the lead weights that were on the bottom of the capsule. These were meant to be held in reserve for about two weeks. They fell away from the capsule and I saw them on my video screen, dropping like bombs. I had a horrible feeling that this was just the start of a disaster. The capsule was bigger than the Atlantic and Pacific ones, but it was still a metal box hanging off a giant balloon, at the mercy of the winds and weather.

It was now getting dark. Without the lead weights, we steadied for a while, but then the balloon started falling once more. This time the fall was faster. We fell 2,000 feet in one minute, 2,000 feet the next. My ears went numb and then popped, and I felt my stomach rising up, pressing against my rib cage. We were at only 15,000 feet. I tried to stay calm, focusing intently upon the cameras and the altimeter, rapidly going through the options available. We needed to jettison the fuel tanks. But as soon as we did so, the trip would be over. I bit my lip. We were somewhere over the Atlas Mountains in darkness, and we were heading for a horrible crash landing. None of us spoke. I made some rapid calculations.

"At this rate of fall we've got seven minutes," I said.

"Okay," Per said. "Open the hatch. Depressurize."

We opened the trapdoor at 12,000 feet, dropping to 11,000 feet, and with a breathtaking rush of freezing air, the capsule depressurized. Alex and I set to work and started throwing everything overboard: food, water, oil cans, anything that wasn't built into the capsule. Everything. Even a wodge of dollars. For five minutes, this stalled our fall. There was no question of continuing. We just had to save our lives.

"It's not enough," I said, seeing the altimeter drop to 9,000 feet. "We're still falling."

"Okay, I'm going out on the roof," Alex said. "The fuel tanks have got to go."

Since Alex had practically built the capsule, he knew exactly how to undo the locks. In the panic I realized that if Rory had been on board, we'd have been stuck. We would have had no choice but to parachute. Right now we'd have been tumbling out into the night over the Atlas Mountains. The burners roared overhead, casting a fierce orange light over us.

"Have you parachuted before?" I shouted at Alex.

"Never," he said.

"That's your rip cord," I said, pushing his hand to it.

"It's seven thousand feet and falling," Per called out. "Sixty-six hundred feet now."

Alex climbed through the hatch, onto the top of the capsule. It was difficult to feel how fast we were falling. My ears had blocked. If the locks were frozen and Alex wasn't able to free the fuel cans, we'd have to jump. We had only a few minutes left. I looked up at the hatch and rehearsed what we would have to do: one hand to the rim, step out, and jump into the darkness. My hand instinctively checked my parachute. I also checked to see that Per was wearing his. Per was watching the altimeter. The numbers were falling fast.

We had only 6,000 feet to play with and it was dark—no, 5,500 feet. If Alex was up there for another minute, we'd have 3,500 feet. I stood with my head through the hatch, paying out the strap and watching Alex as he worked his way around the top of the capsule. It was pitch-dark below us and freezing cold. We couldn't see the ground. The phone and fax were ringing incessantly. Ground control must have been wondering what the hell we were doing.

"One's off," Alex shouted through the hatch.

"Thirty-seven hundred feet," Per said.

"Another one," Alex said.

"Thirty-four hundred feet."

"Another one."

"Twenty-nine hundred feet; twenty-four hundred."

It was too late to bail out. By the time we'd jumped, we'd be smashing into the mountains rushing up to meet us.

"Get back in," Per yelled. "Now."

Alex fell back through the hatch.

We braced ourselves. Per threw the lever to disconnect a fuel tank. If this bolt failed, we'd be dead in about sixty seconds. The tank dropped away, and the balloon jerked to an abrupt halt. It felt like an elevator hitting the ground. We were flattened into our seats; my head crammed down into my shoulders. Then the balloon began to rise. We watched the altimeter: 2,600; 2,700; 2,800 feet. We were safe. In ten minutes we were up past 3,000 feet and the balloon was heading up into the night sky.

I knelt on the floor beside Alex and hugged him.

"Thank God you're with us," I said. "We'd be dead without you."

They say that a dying man reviews his life in the final seconds before his death. In my case this was not true. As we had hurtled down toward becoming a fireball on the Atlas Mountains and I thought that we were going to die, all I could think of was that if I escaped with my life, I would never do this again. As we rose toward safety, Alex told us a story of a rich man who had set out to swim the English Channel: he went down to the beach, set up his deck chair, laid his table with cucumber sandwiches and strawberries, and then announced that his man would now swim the Channel for him. At this moment, it didn't sound like such a bad idea.

Throughout that first night, we fought to control the balloon. At one point it started a continuous ascent, rising for no apparent reason. We finally realized that one of the remaining fuel tanks had sprung a leak and we had been unwittingly jettisoning fuel. As dawn approached, we made preparations to land. Below was the Algerian desert, an inhospitable place at the best of times, more so in a country in the middle of a civil war.

The desert was not the yellow sandy sweep of soft dunes that you expect from *Lawrence of Arabia*. The bare earth was red and rocky, as barren as the surface of Mars, the rocks standing upright like vast termites' nests. Alex and I sat up on the roof of the capsule, marveling at the dawn as it broke over the desert. We were aware that this was a day that we might not have survived to see. The rising sun and the growing warmth of the day seemed infinitely precious. Watching the balloon's shadow slip across the desert floor, we found it hard to believe that it was the same contraption that had plummeted toward the Atlas Mountains in the middle of the night.

The still-attached fuel tanks were blocking Per's view, so Alex talked him in to land. As we neared the ground, Alex shouted out:

"Power line ahead!"

Per shouted back that we were in the middle of the Sahara and there couldn't possibly be a power line. "You must be seeing a mirage!" he bawled.

Alex insisted that he come up and see for himself: we had managed to find the only power line in the Sahara.

Despite the vast, barren desert all around us, within minutes of landing there were signs of life. A group of Berber tribesmen materialized from the rocks. At first they kept their distance. We were about to offer them some water and the few remaining supplies, when we heard the clattering roar of gunship helicopters. They must have tracked us on the radar. As quickly as they had appeared, the Berber vanished. Two helicopters landed close by, throwing up clouds of dust, and soon we were surrounded by impassive soldiers holding machine guns, apparently unsure where to point them.

"Allah," I said encouragingly. For a moment they stood still, but their curiosity got the better of them and they came forward. We showed their officer around the capsule, and he marveled at the remaining fuel tanks. As we stood around the capsule, I wondered what these Algerian soldiers thought of it.

Looking back at the capsule, I saw it for a moment through their eyes. The remaining fuel tanks were painted like huge cans of Virgin Cola and Virgin Energy in bright red and yellow. Among the many slogans on the side of the capsule were ones for Virgin Atlantic, Virgin Direct, Virgin Territory, and Virgin Cola. It was probably lucky for us that the devoutly Muslim soldiers could not understand the writing around the top of the Virgin Energy can: DESPITE WHAT YOU MAY HAVE HEARD THERE IS ABSOLUTELY NO SCIENTIFIC EVIDENCE THAT VIRGIN ENERGY IS AN APHRODISIAC.

As I looked at the capsule standing in the red sand, and relived the harrowing drop toward the Atlas Mountains, I renewed my vow that I would never attempt this again. Likewise, in perfect contradiction to this, at the back of my mind I also knew that as soon as I was home and talked to the other balloonists who were trying to fly around the world, then I would agree to have one last go. It's an irresistible challenge, and it's now buried too deeply inside me for me to give up.

The two questions I am most often asked are, Why do you risk your neck ballooning? and Where is the Virgin Group going? In some ways the sight of the ballooning capsule standing in the middle of the Algerian desert, with its cluster of Virgin names plastered over it, summed up these prime questions.

I knew that I would attempt another balloon flight because it's one of the few great challenges left. And as soon as I've banished the terrors of each actual flight, I once again feel confident that we can learn from our mistakes and achieve the next one safely.

The wider question of where the Virgin Group will end up is impossible to answer. Rather than be too academic about it all, which is not how I think, I have written this book to demonstrate how we made Virgin what it is today. If you read carefully between the lines, you will, I hope, understand what our vision for the Virgin Group is and you will see where I am going. Some people say that my vision for Virgin breaks all the rules and is too wildly kaleidoscopic; others say that Virgin is set to become one of the leading brand names of the next century; others analyze it down to the last degree and then write academic papers on it. As for me, I just pick up the phone and get on with it. Both the series of balloon flights and the numerous Virgin companies I have established form a seamless series of challenges that I can date from my childhood.

The Virgin Cola launch in New York in May of 1998 exemplifies the type of business challenge I love. The cola market is dominated by one huge, established competitor—Coke. It's the ultimate brand and one of the world's most profitable and biggest companies. Coke has one weak competitor around the globe, Pepsi, and I like to think that Virgin will be able to use the experience we've built up during the first half of my life to give Coke its first proper competition. Coke's size doesn't intimidate me—the dinosaurs didn't last forever either. If any brand can give Coke a serious run, it's Virgin.

To show Coke that Virgin meant business, I commandeered a tank and drove it into Times Square, the crossroads of America. With the help of some clever pyrotechnicians, we rigged the Coke sign in Times Square with fireworks, and I aimed the tank's gun squarely at the sign and it went up in a burst of false flames. It was all great fun, something I want to see in every Virgin business, but it had its serious side as well. We've made a major financial and corporate commitment to the cola market, and at the very least over the next couple of years I want to see Virgin Cola edge ahead of Pepsi in America, just as we've done in the United Kingdom, where Virgin has 11.9 percent of the diet and regular cola market, ahead of Pepsi's 11.3 percent.

Our base of operations for the Coke "attack" was the Virgin Megastore in Times Square, a location, I was repeatedly advised several years ago, that should not be the one from which to launch our retail business in New York. Times Square was a squalid mess and not the right image for Virgin. But we obtained the space at very reasonable rates. Times Square is undergoing a renaissance. The Virgin Megastore not only survived, it is performing beautifully, and megastores have sprouted everywhere.

If there is a theme in this book, it is survival. Most people who start from scratch don't survive, and although I have, this is not a book of "lessons" about what I've learned. I don't want to pontificate about what you can learn from my life. Rather, I want to tell my story and use these experiences to convey my own thoughts and ideas about both business and life. While the many businesses I've started play an important role in this book, equally as important is my belief that every minute of every day should be lived as wholeheartedly as possible and that we should always look for the best in everyone and everything. Some will say, though, my greatest fault is that I can't say no. But it's led to an enjoyable, open life, and the best thing I wish readers is that they have fun reading this book.

• • •

This book is Volume One of my autobiography. It covers the first forty-three years of my life. Having come so close to dying over the Atlas Mountains, I thought that I should write this book now in case my guardian angel deserts me on our next attempt. Rather like the balloon flight, the first forty-three years of my life and my business career were all about survival. This volume ends in January 1993, the year after I was forced to sell Virgin Music, the low point of my business life, but also the year that ended in Virgin Atlantic's extraordinary victory over British Airways. This was the turning point for Virgin. Against the odds, I had survived for forty-three years, I had money at my disposal for the first time in my life, we had lots of dreams that we wanted to fulfill, and I was free to see what we could create at Virgin. How we set about putting these ideals into practice will be the material for the next book. This book is about how we managed to cling on by our fingertips and survive and get to that point.

A final chapter does bring the Virgin story up through 1998, albeit in very brief form. Since 1993 the Virgin brand has proliferated into a great many businesses. I suspect that telling the story of each business would be terribly dull and repetitive. But during the past five years Virgin has developed some unique ways of thinking about business development, and the concluding chapter develops a sketch of our current thinking.

When I was searching for titles, David Tait, who runs the American side of Virgin Atlantic, suggested that I call it *Virgin: The Art of Business Strategy and Competitive Analysis.*

"Not bad," I told him. "But I'm not sure it's catchy enough."

"Of course," he said. "The subtitle would be: *Oh, Screw It, Let's Do It.*"

Chapter 1

My childhood is something of a blur to me now, but there are several episodes that stand out. I remember that my parents continually set challenges for us. My mother was determined to make us independent. When I was four, she stopped the car a few miles from our house and made me find my own way home across the fields. I got hopelessly lost. My youngest sister Vanessa's earliest memory is being woken up in the dark one January morning because Mum had decided that I should cycle to Bournemouth that day. She packed some sandwiches and an apple and told me to find some water along the way. Bournemouth was fifty miles away from our home in Shamley Green, Surrey. I was under twelve, but Mum thought that it would teach me the importance of stamina and a sense of direction. I remember setting off in the dark, and I have a vague recollection of staying the night with a relative. I have no idea how I found their house or how I got back to Shamley Green the next day, but I do remember finally walking back into the kitchen like a conquering hero, feeling tremendously proud of my marathon bike ride and expecting a huge welcome.

"Well done, Ricky," Mum greeted me in the kitchen, where she was chopping onions. "Was that fun? Now could you run along to the vicar's? He's got some logs he wants chopping, and I told him that you'd be back any minute."

Our challenges tended to be physical rather than academic, and soon we were setting them for ourselves. I have an early memory of learning how to swim. I was either four or five, and we had been on holiday in Devon with Dad's sisters, Auntie Joyce and Aunt Wendy, and Wendy's husband, Uncle Joe. I was particularly fond of Auntie Joyce, and at the beginning of the holiday she had bet me ten shillings that I couldn't learn to swim by the end of the fortnight. I had spent hours in the sea trying to swim against the freezing cold waves, but by the last day I still couldn't do it. I just splashed along, with one foot hopping on the bottom. I'd lunge forwards and crash beneath the waves before spluttering up to the surface, trying not to swallow the seawater.

"Never mind, Ricky," Auntie Joyce said. "There's always next year."

But I was determined not to wait that long. Auntie Joyce had made me a bet, and I doubted that she would remember it next year. On our last day we got up early, packed up the cars, and set out on the twelve-hour journey home. The roads were narrow, the cars were slow, and it was a hot day. Everyone wanted to get home. As we drove along I saw a river.

"Daddy, can you stop the car please?" I said. This river was my last chance; I was sure that I could swim and win Auntie Joyce's ten shillings. "Please stop!" I shouted.

Dad looked in the rear mirror, slowed down, and pulled up on the grass verge.

"What's the matter?" Aunt Wendy asked as we all piled out of the car.

"Ricky's seen the river down there," Mum said. "He wants to have a final go at swimming."

"Don't we want to get on and get home?" Aunt Wendy complained. "It's such a long drive."

"Come on, Wendy. Let's give the lad a chance," Auntie Joyce said. "After all, it's my ten shillings."

I pulled off my clothes and ran down to the riverbank in my underpants. I dared not stop in case anyone changed their mind. By the time I reached the water's edge I was rather frightened. Out in the middle of the river, the water was flowing fast, with a stream of bubbles dancing over the boulders. I found a part of the bank that had been trodden down by some cows and waded out into the current. The mud squeezed up between my toes. I looked back. Uncle Joe, Aunt Wendy, Auntie Joyce, my parents, and my sister Lindi stood watching me, the ladies in floral dresses, the men in sports jackets and ties. Dad was lighting his pipe and looking utterly unconcerned; Mum was smiling her usual encouragement.

I braced myself and jumped forward against the current, but I immediately felt myself sinking, my legs slicing uselessly through the water. The current pushed me around, tore at my underpants, and dragged me downstream. I couldn't breathe and I swallowed water. I tried to reach up to the surface but had nothing to push against. I kicked and writhed around, but it was no help. Then my foot found a stone and I pushed up hard. I came back above the surface and took a deep breath. The breath steadied me, and I relaxed.

I had to win that ten shillings. I kicked slowly, spread my arms, and found myself swimming across the surface. I was still bobbing up and down, but I suddenly felt released: I could swim. Not caring that the river was pulling me downstream, I swam triumphantly out into the middle of the current. Above the roar and bubble of the water I heard my family clapping and cheering. As I swam in a lopsided circle and came back to the riverbank some fifty yards below them, I saw Auntie Joyce fish in her huge black handbag for her purse. I crawled out of the water, brushed through a patch of stinging nettles, and ran up the bank. I may have been cold and muddy and stung by the nettles, but I could swim.

"Here you are, Ricky," Auntie Joyce said. "Well done."

I looked at the ten-shilling note in my hand. It was large, brown, and crisp. I had never held that amount of money before: it seemed a fortune.

"All right, everyone," Dad said. "On we go."

It was only then that I realized he too was dripping wet. He had lost his nerve and dived in after me. He gave me a massive hug.

I cannot remember a moment in my life when I have not felt the love of my family. We were a family that would have killed for each other—and we still are. My parents adored each other. In my childhood there was barely a cross word between them.

Eve, my mother, was always full of life and galvanized us. Ted, my father, was a quieter figure who smoked his pipe and enjoyed his newspaper. But both my parents had a love of adventure. Ted had wanted to be an archaeologist, but his father, a High Court judge, had wanted him to follow Branson tradition and enter the law. Three generations of Bransons had been lawyers. When Ted was at school, my grandfather engaged a careers officer to talk to him and discuss possible careers. When it emerged that Ted wanted to be an archaeologist, my grandfather had refused to pay the careers officer's bill on the grounds that he hadn't done his job properly. So Ted reluctantly went to Cambridge to read law and continued, as a hobby, to build up his collection of ancient artifacts and fossils, which he called his "museum."

When the Second World War broke out in 1939, Ted volunteered for the Staffordshire Yeomanry, a cavalry regiment organized around the Inns of Court. His regiment fought in Palestine, and Ted fought in the Battle of El

Alamein in September 1942 and subsequent battles in the Libyan desert. He was then involved in the invasion of Italy and fought at Salerno and Anzio. Before Ted went to war, he devised a code to let my grandparents know where he was: they agreed that in letters home, the cellar would be the world and certain drawers in the cupboards would represent certain countries. Ted would write and ask his mother to pull out his old riding gloves from the top left-hand shelf of the right-hand cupboard, which had been designated Palestine. Unsurprisingly, the censors never picked this up and my grandparents could tell where he was.

When Ted joined up, his uncle Jim Branson had already become quite notorious in the army because he advocated eating grass. Great-uncle Jim had owned an estate in Hampshire, which he finally split up among the tenants before moving to Balham, a distant suburb of London, in 1939. He was obsessed with eating grass, and *Picture Post* ran a story with a photograph of him in his bathroom in Balham, where he grew tubs of grass for making into hay. Whenever Jim was invited out to eat—which was increasingly often as he became a celebrity—he brought his nosebag with him and ate grass. In the army, everyone mocked my dad: "You must be Jim Branson's son! Here, have some grass! You're a sprightly-looking colt. When are they going to geld you?" And so on.

Ted hotly denied any involvement with Uncle Jim. However, as the war progressed, David Stirling set up the Special Air Service, a crack regiment designed to operate behind enemy lines. The SAS had to travel light, and soon it became known that Jim Branson was advising David Stirling and his elite troops on how to live off grass and nuts.

From then on, whenever Ted was asked, "Branson? Are you anything to do with Jim Branson?" he puffed out his chest with pride: "Yes, actually he's my uncle. Fascinating what he's doing with the SAS, isn't it?"

Ted actually enjoyed the five years away from home and found it quite difficult to knuckle down to the law again when he returned to Cambridge. A few years later as a young barrister, he arrived rather late at a cocktail party, where he was greeted by a beautiful blond girl called Eve, who swooped across the room toward him, picked up a tray of honeyed sausages, and said: "The way to a man's heart is through his stomach. Here, have some of these!"

Eve Huntley-Flindt had picked up some of her dazzling energy from her mother, Dorothy, who holds two British records: at the age of eighty-nine Granny became the oldest person in Britain to pass the advanced Latin American ballroom dancing examination, and at ninety she became the oldest person to hit a hole in one at golf.

Granny was ninety-nine when she died. Shortly before that, she had written to me to say that the previous ten years had been the best of her life. That same year, on her way round the world on a cruise ship, she had been left behind in Jamaica with only her swimming costume on. She had even read *A Brief History of Time* (something I'd never been able to manage). She never stopped learning. Her attitude was, You've got one go in life, so make the most of it.

Inheriting Granny's love of sports and dancing, Mum at age twelve appeared in a West End revue written by Marie Stopes, who later became famous for her work with women's health education. Sometime later Mum was almost obliged to strip for another stage job, dancing for the Cochran Show at Her Majesty's Theatre in the West End. Sir Charles Cochran's shows were notorious for having the most gorgeous girls in town, and they took their clothes off. It was wartime and work was scarce. Eve decided to take the job on the grounds that it was all a lot of harmless fun. Predictably, my grandfather violently objected and told her that he'd come storming up to Her Majesty's and pull her out of the show. Eve relayed this to Sir Charles Cochran, who allowed her to dance without stripping. Then, as now, she's been able to get away with pretty much anything.

During the day, Eve looked for other work and went out to Heston, where a gliding club taught the Royal Air Force (RAF) to glide before they became pilots. She asked for a job as a pilot but was told that these jobs were available only to men. Undeterred, she chatted up one of the instructors, who relented and secretly gave her the job so long as she pretended to be a boy. So, wearing a leather jacket and a leather helmet to hide her hair and adopting a deep voice, Eve learned how to glide and then began to teach the new pilots. In the last year of the war she joined the Women's Royal Naval Service (Wrens) as a signaler and was posted to the Black Isle in Scotland.

After the war Eve became an air hostess, a most glamorous job at the time. The qualifications were challenging: you had to be very pretty and unmarried and between the ages of twenty-three and twenty-seven, to speak Spanish, and to be trained as a nurse. Undaunted that she couldn't speak Spanish and wasn't a nurse, Mum chatted up the night porter at the recruitment center and found herself on the training course to be a hostess with British South American Airways, BSAA. BSAA operated two kinds of planes between London and South America: Lancasters, which carried thirteen passengers, and Yorks, which carried twenty-one. They had wonderful names—*Star Stream* and *Star Dale*—and the air hostesses were known as Star Girls. When the plane taxied down the runway, Mum's first job was to offer around chewing gum, barley sugar, cotton wool, and Penguin paperbacks and to explain to the passengers that they had to blow their noses before taking off and landing.

The cabins were not pressurized, and the flights were marathons: five hours to Lisbon, eight hours to Dakar, and then fourteen hours across to Buenos Aires. For the Buenos Aires–to–Santiago leg the York aircraft was exchanged for the more robust Lancaster, and everyone had to wear oxygen masks over the Andes. After she had been with BSAA for a year, it was taken over by BOAC and Eve began working on Tudor aircraft. *Star Tiger,* the first Tudor plane to leave for Bermuda, exploded in midair. Her plane was next and arrived safely. But the plane after hers, *Star Ariel,* vanished without a trace in the Bermuda Triangle and all Tudor aircraft were then grounded. It was later discovered that their fuselage was too weak to withstand the recently installed pressurization system.

By this time Ted probably thought that if he didn't marry Eve and thereby disqualify her from being an air hostess, she would most likely disappear somewhere over the Atlantic. He proposed to her as they roared along on his motorbike, and she shouted "Yes!" back at him at the top of her voice so that the wind wouldn't blow the word away. They were married on 14 October 1949, and I was conceived on their honeymoon in Majorca.

My parents always treated my two sisters, Lindi and Vanessa, and me as equals, whose opinions were just as valid as theirs. Before Vanessa's arrival, if my parents went out to dinner they took me and Lindi with them, lying on blankets in the back of the car. We slept in the car while they had dinner, but we always woke up when they started the drive back home. Lindi and I kept quiet and looked up at the night sky, listening to my parents talk and joke about their evening. We grew up talking as friends to our parents. As children we discussed Dad's legal cases and argued about pornography and the legalization of drugs long before any of us knew what we were really talking about. My parents always encouraged us to have our own opinions and rarely gave us advice unless we asked for it.

We lived in a village called Shamley Green in Surrey. Before Vanessa was born, Lindi and I grew up in "Easteds," a red-brick, ivy-covered cottage, which had tiny white windows and a white wicket gate leading out onto the village green. I was three years older than Lindi and nine years older than Vanessa. My parents had very little money during our childhood, and perhaps because Mum wasn't greatly interested in cooking or perhaps because she was saving money, I remember eating a good deal of bread and dripping. Even so traditions were still upheld, and we were not allowed to leave the table until we had finished all our food. We were also given onions, which grew in the garden, which I always hated, and which I used to hide in a drawer in the table. This drawer was never cleaned out until we moved house ten years later. The drawer was then opened and my pile of fossilized onions was discovered. Food was not so important at meals, but company was. The house was always full of people.

In order to make ends meet, Mum invited German and French students over to learn English in a typical English household. We had to entertain them, and Mum always had us working in the garden, helping her prepare meals, and then clearing up afterward. When I wanted to escape, I ran off across the village green to see my friend Nik Powell. At first the best thing about Nik was that his mother made amazing custard. So after a meal spent stuffing onions into the table drawer, I would slip away to Nik's house, leaving the Germans trying to speak English with my family laughing and helping them out. If I timed it right, which I made sure I did, pudding and custard were already on the table. Nik and I were best friends. He was a quiet boy with straight black hair and black eyes. Soon we started doing everything together—climbing trees, riding bikes, shooting rabbits, and hiding under Lindi's bed to grab her ankle when she turned the light out. I can't remember a time when Nik and I weren't friends.

At home Mum had two obsessions: she always generated work for us, and she was always thinking of ways to make money. We never had a television, and I don't think my parents ever listened to the radio. Mum worked in a shed in the garden, making wooden tissue boxes and wastepaper bins, which she sold to shops. Her shed smelled of paints and glue and was stacked with little piles of painted boxes ready to be sent off. Dad, who was inventive and very good with his hands, designed special pressing vices, which held the boxes together while they were being glued. Eventually Mum began supplying Harrods with her tissue boxes, and it became a proper little cottage industry. As with everything she did, Mum worked in a whirlwind of energy, which was difficult to resist.

There was a great sense of teamwork within our family. Whenever we were within Mum's orbit, we had to be busy. If we tried to escape by saying that we had something else to do, we were firmly told we were selfish. As a result we grew up with a clear priority of putting other people first. Once a boy whom I didn't particularly take to came for the weekend. During the church service I slipped out of our pew and went across the aisle to sit with Nik. Mum was furious. When we got home she told Dad to beat me, and we duly went into his study and closed the door. Rather than towering over me in a rage, Dad just smiled.

"Now make sure you cry convincingly," he said, and clapped his hands together six times to make great smacking noises.

I ran out of the room, bawling loudly. Mum adopted a severe look to imply that this was in my best interests and resolutely carried on chopping onions in the kitchen, my portion of which were duly stuffed into the kitchen drawer during lunch.

Great-Uncle Jim wasn't the only maverick: irreverence for authority ran on both sides of my family. I remember that we acquired an old Gypsy caravan, which we kept in the garden, and sometimes Gypsies came by and rang the doorbell. Mum always gave them something silver and let them rummage around in the barn for anything they needed. One year we were all taken to the Surrey County Show at Guildford, which was thronging with gleaming show jumpers and men in tweed coats and bowler hats. As we walked past one of the stalls, Mum saw a group of Gypsy children in tears and we went over to see what was the matter. They were all crowded around a magpie, which was tied to a piece of string.

"The RSPCA has ordered us to bring the bird in to be put down. They say it's illegal to own wild birds," they said.

Even as they told her what was happening, we saw a Royal Society for the Prevention of Cruelty to Animals official walking toward us.

"Don't worry," Mum said. "I'll save it."

She picked up the bird and wrapped it in her coat. Then we smuggled it out of the showground past the officials. The Gypsy children met us outside and told us to keep the magpie since they would only be stopped again. Mum was delighted, and we drove it home.

The magpie loved Mum. It sat on her shoulder when she was in the kitchen or working in her shed, and would then swoop out to the paddock and tease the ponies by sitting on their backs. It dive-bombed Dad if he sat down to read *The Times* after lunch, flapping the pages so that they scattered over the floor.

"Damned bird!" Dad would roar, waving his arms to shoo it away.

"Ted, get up and do something useful," Mum said. "That bird's telling you to do some gardening. And Ricky and Lindi, run along to the vicar and ask him if there's anything you can do to help."

Apart from spending summer holidays with Dad's family at Salcombe in Devon, we also went to Norfolk to stay with Mum's sister, Clare Hoare. I decided that when I grew up, I wanted to be like Aunt Clare. She was a close friend of Douglas Bader, the fighter ace who had lost his legs in a plane accident. Aunt Clare and Douglas owned an old biplane, which they flew together. Sometimes Aunt Clare would parachute out of the plane for fun. She smoked about twenty small cigars a day.

When we stayed with her, we swam in the millpond at the bottom of her garden. Douglas Bader would unstrap his legs and haul himself into the water. I used to run off with these tin legs and hide them in the rushes by the edge of the water. Douglas would then pull himself out of the water and come lunging after me; his arms and shoulders were immensely powerful, and he could walk on his hands. When he had been held a prisoner in Colditz, after two failed escapes the Nazis had confiscated his legs.

"You're as bad as the Nazis," he'd roar at me, swinging himself after me on his hands like an orangutan.

Aunt Clare was as much of an entrepreneur as Mum. Obsessed with Welsh mountain sheep, which were then endangered species, she bought a few of these black sheep in order to save them from extinction. She eventually bred a large flock and managed to bring them off the endangered list. She then set up a business, The Black Sheep Marketing Company, and started selling pottery decorated with pictures of black sheep. The mugs began to sell rather well with the nursery rhyme "Baa Baa Black Sheep" written around the sides. Soon Aunt Clare had all the old ladies in the village knitting her black wool into shawls and sweaters. She worked very hard to build up Black Sheep as a trade name, and she succeeded: forty years later it's still going strong.

Some years later, in the early days of Virgin Records, I received a call from Aunt Clare:

"Ricky, you won't believe this. One of my sheep has started singing," she said.

Initially my mind reeled, but it was the sort of thing I had come to expect from her.

"What does it sing?" I asked, imagining a sheep singing "Come on, baby, light my fire."

" 'Baa, Baa, Black Sheep' of course," she snapped at me. "Now, I want to make a recording. The sheep probably won't do it in a studio, so can you send some sound engineers out here? And they'd better hurry since it could stop at any time."

That afternoon a bunch of sound engineers headed to Norfolk with a 24-track mobile studio and recorded Aunt Clare's singing sheep. They also amassed an entire choir of sheep, ducks, and hens for the chorus, and we released the single "Baa Baa Black Sheep." It reached Number 4 in the Top Twenty.

My friendship with Nik was based not only on affection but also on a strong element of competition. I was determined to do everything better than he did. One summer Nik was given a brand-new bike for his birthday. We immediately decided to do the "River Run," a game where you raced straight downhill, braked at the last moment, then skidded to a halt as close to the edge of the riverbank as possible. This was an extremely competitive game, which I hated losing.

Since it was his bike, Nik went first. He did a highly credible skid, curving around so that the back wheel came to within a foot of the water's edge. Nik generally tried to spur me on to do even more outlandish things, but this time he tried to stop me.

"You can't do better than that skid," he said. "Mine was perfect." ·

I thought otherwise. I was determined to do a better skid than Nik. So taking his bike up the hill, I launched myself toward the river, pedaling madly. As I approached the river, it became apparent that I was out of control and had no chance of stopping. In a fast-moving blur I caught sight of Nik's open mouth and horrified expression as I hurtled past him. I tried to brake, but it was too late. I somersaulted head over heels into the water, and the bike sank beneath me. Swept downstream by the current, I finally managed to clamber back ashore. Nik was waiting for me, enraged.

"You've lost my bike! That's my birthday present!" Furious and sobbing with rage, he pushed me back into the water. Then he shouted, "You'd damn well better find it."

"I'll find it," I spluttered. "It'll be okay. I'll fish it out."

"You bloody well better had."

I spent the next two hours diving down to the bottom of the river and groping around the mud and weeds and stones trying to find his new bike. I couldn't find it anywhere. Nik sat on the bank, hugging his knees up to his chin, glaring at me. Nik was epileptic, and I'd been with him on a couple of occasions in the past when he'd experienced fits. Now he was furious, and I hoped his anger would not spur another one. But eventually, when I was so cold that I could barely talk and my hands were white, numb, and bleeding from bashing into rocks on the riverbed, Nik relented.

"Let's go home," he said. "You'll never find it."

We walked back home, and I tried to cheer him up. "We'll buy you another one," I promised him.

My parents must have groaned because the bike cost over twenty pounds, nearly a month's supply of tissue boxes.

When we were eight years old, Nik and I were separated and I was sent away to board at Scaitcliffe Preparatory School in Windsor Great Park.

On my first night at Scaitcliffe, I lay awake in my bed, listening to the snorings and snufflings of the other boys in the dormitory, feeling utterly lonely, unhappy, and frightened. At some point in the middle of that first night, I knew I was going to be sick. The feeling came on so fast that I didn't have time to get out of bed and run to the bathroom; instead, I vomited all over the bedclothes. The matron was called. Rather than being sympathetic, as my mother would have been, she scolded me and made me clean it up myself. I can still remember the humiliation I felt. Obviously, my parents thought they were doing the right thing by sending me there, but at that moment I could feel only confusion and resentment toward them, and a terrible fear of what lay in store for me. Within a couple of days another boy from the school had taken a liking to me and got me into his bed to play "feelies." On my first weekend home, I matter-of-factly told my parents what had happened under the sheets. My dad calmly said, "It's best not to do that kind of thing," and that was the first and last time such an incident happened.

My father had been sent to boarding school at the same age, and his father before him. It was the traditional way for a boy from my background to be educated and to cultivate independence and self-reliance—to teach someone to stand on their own two feet. But I loathed being sent away from home at such an early age, and have always vowed to myself that I would never send my children to boarding school until they were of an age to make up their own minds about it.

In my third week at Scaitcliffe I was summoned to the headmaster's study and told that I had broken some rule; I think I had walked onto a patch of hallowed grass to retrieve a football. I had to bend down, and I was caned across my bottom six times.

"Branson," the headmaster intoned. "Say 'Thank you, sir.' "

I couldn't believe my ears. Thank him for what?

"Branson," the headmaster said, lifting up his cane. "I'm warning you."

"Thank you . . . sir."

"You're going to be trouble, Branson."

"Yes, sir. I mean, no, sir."

I was trouble—and always in trouble. By age eight I still couldn't read. In fact, I was dyslexic and nearsighted. Despite sitting at the front of the class, I couldn't read the blackboard. Only after a couple of terms did anyone think to have my eyes tested. Even when I could see, the letters and numbers made no sense at all. Dyslexia wasn't deemed a problem in those days, or, put more accurately, it was a problem only if you were dyslexic yourself. Since nobody had ever heard of dyslexia, being unable to read, write, or spell just meant to the rest of the class and the teachers that you were either stupid or lazy. And at prep school you were beaten for both. I was soon being beaten once or twice a week for doing poor class work or confusing the date of the Battle of Hastings.

My dyslexia was a problem throughout my school life. Now, although my spelling is still sometimes phonetic, I have managed to overcome the worst of my difficulties through training myself to concentrate. Perhaps my early problems with dyslexia made me more intuitive: when someone sends me a written proposal, rather than dwelling on detailed facts and figures I find that my imagination grasps and expands on what I read.

However, my saving grace was that outside the classroom I was good at sports. It is difficult to overestimate how important sports are at English public schools. If you are good at sports, you are a school hero, the older boys won't bully you, and the masters won't mind you failing all your exams. I was intensely keen to succeed at sports, possibly because it was my only opportunity to excel. I became captain of the football, rugby, and cricket teams. Every sports day I won a series of cups for sprinting and hurdling. Just before my eleventh birthday in 1961, I won all the races. I even decided to go in for the long jump. I had never done a good long jump before, but this time I decided to just have a go. I sprinted down the track, took off from the wooden plank, and soared through the air. After I landed in the sand the master came up to me and shook me by the hand: it was a new Scaitcliffe school record. That summer day I couldn't put a foot wrong, and my parents and Lindi sat and clapped in the white marquee afterwards as I went up to collect every cup. I won the Victor Ludorum. Who cared if I couldn't spell? Not me.

The next autumn term I was playing in a football match against another local school. I was running rings around the defender and had already scored one goal. I put my hand up and yelled for the ball, which was booted upfield and bounced over both of us. I turned and sprinted after it, controlled it, and was bearing down on the goal when the defender caught up with me and floored me with a sliding tackle. My leg was caught beneath him, and he fell across me. I heard a ghastly scream, and for a split second I thought that he was hurt until I realized that it was me. He rolled off me, and I saw my knee twisted at a horrible angle. My parents had always told us to laugh when we were in pain, so half laughing but mainly screaming I was carried off the field to the school matron, who drove me to hospital. My agony stopped only after they gave me an injection. I had badly torn the cartilage in my right knee, and they were going to have to operate. At the hospital, I was given a general anesthetic and fell unconscious. I awoke to find myself out in the street. I was still in my hospital bed and a nurse was holding a drip above my head, but my bed, together with several others, was parked outside. I thought I was dreaming, but the nurse explained that there had been a fire in the hospital during my operation, and all the patients had been evacuated onto the street outside.

I went home for a few days to recover. Lying in bed I looked at my silver cups on the mantelpiece. The doctor told me that I would not play sports again for a very long time.

"Don't worry, Ricky," my mother said as she swept into the room after the doctor had gone. "Just think of Douglas Bader. He hasn't got any legs at all. He's playing golf and flying planes and everything. You don't want to be lying there in bed doing nothing all day, do you?"

The worst aspect of this injury was that it immediately revealed how bad I was in the classroom. I was bottom in every subject and would clearly not pass the common entrance exam.

I was sent to another school, a "crammer" on the Sussex coast called Cliff View House, which had no sports to distract boys from the grim and usually hopeless task of preparing for common entrance. If you couldn't spell or couldn't add or couldn't remember that the area of a circle is "pi r squared," then the solution was simple: you were beaten until you did. I learned my facts in the face of unflinching discipline and with a black-and-blue bruised backside. I may have been dyslexic, but I had no excuse: I couldn't get it right. When I gave the inevitable wrong answer, it was either more lines or a beating. I almost grew to prefer the beatings since at least they were quick. There were no games apart from an early-morning run, and as well as for any faults in the class, we were also beaten for almost anything outside such as not making our beds properly, running when we should be walking, talking when we should be quiet, or having dirty shoes. There were so many possible things to do wrong that although we learned most of them, we accepted that we would be beaten for some obscure misdemeanor almost every single week.

My only consolation was the headmaster's eighteen-year-old daughter, Charlotte. She seemed to take a fancy to me, and I was delighted that I, out of all the boys, should have caught her attention. We soon established a routine of nocturnal visits. Every night I would climb out of my dormitory window and creep over to her bedroom in the headmaster's house. One night, as I climbed back through the window, I was horrified to see one of my teachers watching my progress.

The next morning I was summoned to the headmaster's study.

"What were you doing, Branson?" he asked.

The only answer I could think of was the worst one I could possibly have given: "I was on my way back from your daughter's room, sir."

Not surprisingly, I was promptly expelled, and my parents were told to come and collect me the following day.

That evening, unable to think of any other way to escape the wrath of my parents, I wrote a suicide note saying that I was unable to cope with the shame of my expulsion. I wrote on the envelope that it was not to be opened until the following day but then gave it to a boy who I knew was far too nosy not to open it immediately.

Very, very slowly, I left the building and walked through the school grounds toward the cliffs. When I saw a crowd of teachers and boys beginning to run after me, I slowed down enough for them to catch up. They managed to drag me back from the cliff, and the expulsion was overturned.

My parents were surprisingly relaxed about the whole episode. My father even seemed quite impressed that Charlotte was "a very pretty girl."

Chapter 2

"Congratulations, Branson. I predict that you will either go
to prison or become a millionaire."

1963–1967

After the crammer had served its purpose by beating me into shape, I moved to Stowe, a big public school in Buckinghamshire for over eight hundred boys. There I faced a daunting prospect. Fagging was still in place—an archaic practice in which the young boys were expected to run errands and do minor chores for the older ones (in effect, to be their servants). Bullying was rife. Your reputation—and ability to avoid being picked upon—was helped enormously by your ability to score a goal or hit a six. But I could not play any games since my knee buckled whenever I tried to run. Since I was also unable to cope with the academic work, I was very quickly sidelined. Being out of the sports teams and at the bottom of the class was an unenviable double. It seemed as if all the challenges my parents had set me were now irrelevant.

I found refuge in the library, where I went every afternoon and started writing a novel. I sat in the most wonderful splendor surrounded by leather-bound books and two globes, overlooking the ornamental lake where the last Head Boy had dived in and never surfaced. I wrote the most lurid sexual fantasies I could conjure up, amazing erotic stories all about a young boy who couldn't play sports due to a knee injury, but who was befriended and then gloriously and expertly seduced by the young Scandinavian school matron. In my mind's eye she used to creep up behind him when he was working in the library. . . . But sadly for me, no matter what incredible sexual encounters I dreamed up, there wasn't a girl, let alone a Scandinavian, within miles of Stowe, and our matron was sixty years old.

As I sat in the library panting at my own prose and scribbling faster and faster, I became aware of another regular visitor to the library: Jonathan

Holland-Gems. By comparison with most of the boys at Stowe, Jonny was extremely worldly and sophisticated, widely read, and staggeringly knowledgeable about the arts. He came from London, where his parents knew journalists and writers. When Jonny read *Private Eye,* he knew half the people mentioned in it. His mother was a successful playwright. It was through Jonny that my interest in the world of newspapers began to grow and I began to think that I would like to be a journalist. Halfway through the term I read a school announcement about an essay competition called the Junior Gavin Maxwell Prize, which had been set up by the author, an old boy from Stowe. I momentarily put aside my pulsating pornography and wrote a short story, which won the prize. The complete absence of competition must have helped.

Gavin Maxwell, the author of *Ring of Bright Water,* came to present the prize at Stowe. He arrived with Gavin Young, the war correspondent from *The Observer* and later the author of *Slow Boat to China.* After the ceremony they drove back to Surrey and dropped me off at Shamley Green. I stayed in touch with them, and they remained good and helpful friends.

After I won the prize, my English began to improve and I soared up the class to third out of twenty-one. I was still eighteenth in Latin, bottom in math, physics, and chemistry: "He tries hard but has very great difficulty in understanding even the simplest mathematical process and in retaining any new topic covered," read one end-of-term report.

Over one Easter holiday, I decided to follow my mother's example and make some money. Undeterred by the school's lack of faith in my ability with numbers, I saw an opportunity to grow Christmas trees. We had just moved house from one side of Shamley Green to the other—from Easteds Cottage to Tanyards Farm, a rambling building with many barns and sheds and some land. I went round to talk Nik into the plan. He was also on holiday from his school, which was at Ampleforth in Yorkshire. We would plant four hundred Christmas trees in the field at Tanyards Farm. By the Christmas after next, they would have grown to at least four feet and we would be able to sell them. Nik and I agreed to do the work together and to share the profits equally.

That Easter we furrowed the ground and planted the four hundred seeds in the field above Tanyards Farm. We figured that if they all grew to six feet, we would make £2 a tree, a grand total of £800 compared with our initial investment of just £5 for the seeds. The following summer we investigated the trees. There were one or two tiny sprigs above ground, but the rest had been eaten by rabbits. We exacted dire revenge by shooting and skinning a lot of rabbits, which we sold to the local butcher for a shilling each, but it wasn't quite the £800 we had planned.

The following Christmas Nik's brother was given a budgerigar as a present. This gave me the idea for another great business opportunity: breeding budgies! For a start, I reasoned, I could sell them all year round rather than just during the fortnight before Christmas. I worked out the prices, calculating how fast they could breed and how much their food cost, and persuaded my father to build a huge aviary. In my last week at school I wrote to Dad and explained the financial implications:

> So few days now until the holidays. Have you ordered any material we might want for our giant budgerigar cage? I thought our best bet to get the budgerigars at reduced rate would be from Julian Carlyon. I feel that if the shops sold them for 30sh., he would get say 17sh. and we could buy them off him for 18 or 19sh. which would give him a profit and save us the odd 10sh. per bird. How about it?

My father reluctantly built the aviary, and the birds bred rapidly; however, I had overestimated the local demand for budgies. Even after everyone in Shamley Green had bought at least two, we were still left with an aviary full of them. One day at school I got a letter from my mother breaking the bad news that the aviary had been invaded by rats, which had eaten the budgies. It was only many years later that she confessed that she was fed up with cleaning out the aviary, so one day she left the cage door open and they all escaped. She didn't try too hard to recapture them.

Although neither of these schemes effectively made money, they did teach me something about math. I found that it was only when I was using real numbers to solve real problems that math made any sense to me. If I was calculating how much a Christmas tree would grow or how many budgies would breed, the numbers became real and I enjoyed using them. Inside the classroom I was still a complete dunce at math. I once took an IQ test where the questions seemed absurd. I couldn't focus on any of the mathematical problems, and I think that I scored about zero. I worry about all the people who have been classified as stupid by these kinds of IQ tests. Little do these people know that often these IQ tests have been dreamed up by academics who are absolutely useless at dealing with the practicalities of the outside world. I loved doing real business plans, even if the rabbits did get the better of me.

• • •

I think my parents must have instilled a rebellious streak in me. I have always thought rules were there to be broken, and Stowe had as many rules and regulations as the army. Many of them, it seemed to Jonny Gems and me, were completely anachronistic and pointless. There was the outmoded practice of fagging, for one thing. Then there was the Combined Cadet Force, in which boys dressed up as soldiers and paraded around with antiquated rifles. And there was compulsory church attendance on Sundays (I managed to dodge that one by skipping the first service of the new term; my name was left off the register, and I was never missed from then on).

During January and February 1966, Jonny and I began to talk about how to change the school rules. We were fifteen years old, but we believed that we could make a difference. My parents had brought me up to think that we could all change the world, so when I looked at how Stowe was run I felt sure that I could do it better. Stowe was actually reasonably liberal in encouraging boys of all ages to contribute to the running of the school.

Jonny and I were particularly incensed by the rule that anyone who wasn't playing games had to watch the school team when they were playing another school. Although we were able to go to the library during weekday afternoons, we were still forced to watch the school teams play most Saturdays. Given that I knew that if only I wasn't ruled out by my weak knee I would be on the teams, I felt doubly frustrated. I wrote to the headmaster: "I am against the utter waste of time that is spent in compulsory watching of matches. If one is unable to play for the First XI one should be able to spend one's time in better ways than that. I know this sounds a frightful break against tradition, etc., but I feel very strongly about this. If 450-odd people watching matches spent that time in Buckingham cleaning windows, for instance, they would gain at least something more than watching others achieving something."

I also tried to reorganize the system of school meals: "I feel that to improve Stowe one has first got to do it socially, even before religiously. There are many boys who are thirsting for knowledge through interesting conversations. One of the best times to talk is at meals, but at Stowe this is practically impossible. One goes into hall, sits down at one's allotted table next to the same boys every day. A canteen must be constructed in one of the dining rooms. Then boys could choose their own food, they would be free to sit down where they wish, and they could put their forks and plates in a box when they go out. The food waste at the moment is fantastic, and with a canteen system you could cut down on at least half the Italian and Spanish waiters.

"I would be very interested in your views on this, and any money saved could possibly be put towards my next plan . . ." and I went on to explore the idea of a sixth-form bar.

The headmaster suggested that I air my views in the school magazine, but Jonny and I wanted to set up an alternative magazine with a fresh attitude. We wanted to campaign against fagging, corporal punishment, compulsory chapel and games, and Latin. All these ideas were far too "revolutionary" to be aired in the school magazine, *The Stoic*—a name that seemed only too apt to its long-suffering readers. We then thought about linking up with other schools that had similar rules. Gradually the idea of an inter-school magazine was hatched. We would link up with other schools and swap ideas. I jotted down a few titles in a school notebook: "Today," "1966," "Focus!," "Modern Britain," and "Interview." Then I wrote out what I wanted to publish: "A new political magazine with the aim of getting every school boy more interested in politics and to know about the improvements and 'goings on' at every other School in the country. To be 100 pages long, 15" × 9" and on the same sort of paper as *The Economist* or *Punch*. To be 1/6 in price and strongly advertised before the first edition comes out on Saturday, 4th June (Stowe's Speech day). To be brought out every 4 months with the aim of cutting that down after a year. 4,000 copies to be published the first three months, and to have date ready for the next magazine as the first one comes out. To have three representatives from each school writing and headmasters and other masters. To have a large collection of MP's writing. To have famous authors writing. To have members of the public contributing."

I did some more sums where once again I enjoyed thinking about the implications of the math, as shown on the page opposite.

I wrote out a list of 250 MPs, whom I found in *Who's Who*, and a list of possible advertisers, which I found by going through the telephone book. I also wrote to W. H. Smith asking whether they would be prepared to stock the magazine. Thus with contributors, advertisers, distributors, and costs all in place—at least on paper—I had written my first business plan.

The numbers looked too small to work, so Jonny and I decided to involve other schools, technical colleges, and universities since it would open the magazine up to more people and encourage advertisers. We thought that if we aimed the magazine at university students, then sixth formers would buy it; but if we published a magazine for sixth formers, then older students wouldn't be interested.

We settled on the name "Student," which seemed a good one since at the time there was a great deal of talk about "student power." This was the pe-

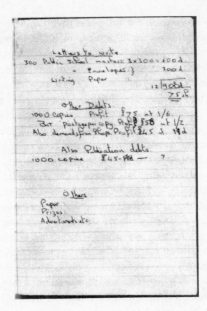

riod of student sit-ins, occupations, and demos at universities and polytechnics. It was an exciting time to be young. My mother lent me £4 as a float against the cost of telephone calls and letters, and Jonny's father arranged for headed notepaper to be printed up with the title STUDENT—THE MAGAZINE FOR BRITAIN'S YOUTH printed across the top with the symbol of a rising sun. We set to work writing to all the contributors and possible advertisers.

Student was a perfect vehicle; it gave us a new lease on life. There was so much to organize. I began to set up an office in my study at school and asked the headmaster for a telephone in my room, which he unsurprisingly refused. As a result I had to make telephone calls from the call box, but I quickly discovered a useful trick: if I called up the operator and told her that the machine had taken my money but my call had been disconnected, I was able to get a free call. As well as having a free call, I was also able to avoid the telltale "pip . . . pip . . . pip . . ." as the coins went in. Better still, the operator sounded like a secretary: "I have Mr. Branson for you."

I drew up lists and lists of people to call and slowly worked my way down them. Most of them rejected the idea of paying for advertising in an unpublished magazine, but gradually I began to see ways to attract their attention. I would call up National Westminster Bank and tell them that

Lloyds Bank had just taken out a full-page advertisement; would they want to advertise alongside Lloyds Bank? *Student* would be Britain's biggest magazine for young people, I added. I called up Coca-Cola and told them that Pepsi had just booked a big advertisement but that the back page was still free. I called up the *Daily Telegraph* and asked them whether they would prefer to advertise before or after the *Daily Express*. Another tack would be to ask an innocuous question that they couldn't easily refute: "Are you interested in recruiting the best-caliber school leavers and university graduates?" No personnel manager would ever admit that they're looking for mediocre recruits. "Then we're publishing just the magazine for you . . ."

In order to avoid the operator coming back on the line to cut me off, I learned how to pack all this into five minutes, and I started speaking faster and pushing harder. My voice had broken early, and nobody guessed that they were talking to a fifteen-year-old schoolboy standing at a public telephone box. I gave my address at Shamley Green, and when I sent out letters I wrote them by the dozen and sent them to my parents, who in turn asked Elizabeth, an old friend in the village, to type them.

My schoolwork was going from bad to worse, but I was receiving a wonderful education in confidence building. Had I been five or six years older, the sheer absurdity of trying to sell advertising to major companies in a magazine that did not yet exist, edited by two fifteen-year-old schoolboys, would have prevented me from picking up the phone at all. But I was too young to contemplate failure.

During the holidays I told Nik all about *Student*. He was equally excited and agreed to help distribute it in Ampleforth. He would also try to find contributors for it. Nik recognized that *Student* was really my and Jonny's creation, so he stood back a little bit, but he was as enthusiastic as we were about its potential. We were fifteen years old and felt we could do anything.

By April 1966 and the run-up to the O levels I was able to drop a number of subjects that I had no chance of passing at O level and put even more time into *Student*. To the mutual relief of myself and my Latin and science teachers, we went our separate ways: "He is a very weak candidate indeed at Latin and he has now given it up" and "His interest in Science was obviously minimal. Although I am far from convinced that he could not have done better than he did, it was quite evident that he was never going to make much progress." I was doing better at history, French, and English, but not at math, which was compulsory: "In spite of much apparent effort he is finding difficulty in retaining methods of attack on problems from one week to the next. He will need a lot of luck with the questions in July."

However, the main excitement in my life was writing the hundreds of letters that I started sending out from Stowe, and waiting on tenterhooks for the answers. For all my enthusiasm and newfound guile, it took a long time to find any advertisers willing to commit themselves to taking space in *Student*. Jonny and I sent letters out all summer term, and continued in the holidays and through the following autumn term. By April 1967, with my single ancient history A level looming up in the summer (I was to take it after only one year in the sixth form), we were still no nearer to pulling a magazine together. Jonny and I had been working on *Student* for over a year, and all we had to show for it were dozens of letters of support from various headmasters and teachers, and various vague promises to contribute from politicians, but no advertisements or hard copy. I refused to bow to the inevitable. My letter home dated 27 April 1967 apologized for the small amount of time I had spent with my family over Easter:

> It was a wonderful holiday these last four weeks and more was achieved than ever before. I only hope you do not feel too annoyed with me for not being home longer and for not making the time to do more in the garden. I, possibly wrongly, see a divided duty: one to my home, and one to "Student." It is a difficult decision. Anything I do in life I want to do well and not half-heartedly. I feel I am doing my best in "Student"—as well as the time allows. Yet that leaves little time for my other duty. To me I saw a danger of falling between two stools and still do. Of being a failure in everything I did and having to search for priorities if I am to get anywhere. I am also still only sixteen. Although it sounds a terribly "I" thing to say, and I only say it in defence, what do most sixteen year olds do? No one I know here did anything more last holidays than I used to do two or three years ago, flicks in the evening, mucking about during the day. What did you do when you were a boy of 16? Shoot, fish, swim, go out with girls on one side and possibly your museum and helping around the garden on the other side. You had time to help around the garden. You did not see the world as it is today when you were sixteen. Your career was almost lined up. Today it is one long struggle.
>
> You say "STUDENT" is selfish and self-centred of me. "Possibly" I say. But is it any more selfish than anything else one does in life? It is, in my opinion, a career like anything else. It could benefit many many more people than going to the films etc. It is a beginning to my life like university or your finals were to yours. It might sound really foul of me bringing this up in my first letter, but I've had little else on my mind over the last two weeks and felt it made sense to get it out on paper.

I was lucky. I always felt that I could speak to my parents as if they were my closest friends. Rather than closing down on me, they reacted very well to this letter, and we kept open our lines of communication. At about this time I noticed that a good many of my friends stopped confiding in their parents, but I never felt embarrassed by or rebellious against mine. They always encouraged me to go ahead and do whatever I wanted to do, and if they did not always praise my projects, they never expressed less than sympathy and support. The last thing my father wanted to do was to spend his weekends building a cage for my budgerigars, but he never told me. My mother was extremely keen to help me with *Student* and wrote articles, gave me pocket money that she could scarcely spare, and thought of people whom I should approach. Once when I told her that I wanted to get in touch with David Frost, she spent weeks asking all her friends whether they knew anyone who knew anyone who knew David Frost.

Then we had our first breakthrough: we received our first hard copy and a £250 check for an advertisement, and Gerald Scarfe agreed to draw a cartoon for us and be interviewed. *Student* was finally changing from a gleam in my imagination to a real magazine.

The other thing that changed from a bright gleam in my mind's eye to a reality was sex. I had a number of girlfriends during the holidays and came tantalizingly closer and closer to losing my virginity at parties when the lights went out and everyone lay around on cushions.

I finally found a girl who was reputed to go the whole way, and at one party we slipped upstairs into a remote bedroom. I was amazed when she let me push up her skirt and take off her knickers. As we began to make love, she started to moan and groan. She was clearly having a very erotic time. I was secretly pleased by how well I must be performing since she was panting and tossing her head from side to side as she fought to control her breathing. I put up a great show and finally came with equally impressive gusto, roaring and shouting and huffing and puffing. Then I rolled off her. To my astonishment she carried on panting, apparently having what I took to be ecstatic multiple orgasms. Just as I was beginning to feel a little bemused and somewhat redundant, I finally realized that she was panting for a reason.

"Asthma!" she wheezed in breathless panic. "Inhaler! Ambulance!"

Happily my first steady girlfriend was healthy and Dutch. Rudi was a Dutch "revolutionary," and in my last term I invited her to Stowe, where she slipped into the school grounds and secretly pitched her tent in the middle of the wood. For one glorious week I crept out every night and walked past the lake to the woods, where Rudi would be smoking pot and cooking over a tin stove. We lay out under the stars and talked about what we would do to change the world. Rudi was passionately interested in world politics. She became *Student's* grandly titled Dutch Overseas Correspondent and went on to write some powerful pieces about the Baader-Meinhof terrorist gang.

After dropping all subjects except ancient history, I had even more time for *Student* magazine. Soon Jonny and I were regularly taking the train to London to interview people. However, I had to take my A level, and I was having difficulty remembering facts that struck me as meaningless and abstract. I had bought some fact file cards on ancient history that contained all the necessary information about Greece and Rome. In preparation for the exam I cut the edges off these and put them in various pockets and even slid one under my watch strap. When I looked at the questions in the exam, the most difficult thing was remembering which pocket the relevant facts were in. Then I pulled them out of the pocket and held them curled in the palm of my left hand as I wrote with my right. As it happened, I was too preoccupied with *Student* to care about what grade I achieved. I was just intent upon leaving Stowe as quickly as possible and starting life as a journalist in London.

When I left Stowe in 1967 aged almost seventeen, my headmaster's parting words to me were: "Congratulations, Branson. I predict that you will either go to prison or become a millionaire."

The next and final time I heard from Stowe was six months later in a letter from the headmaster dated 16 January 1968:

> Dear Branson,
> I have been pleased to see that the Press have given you a good send-off and I was very interested to see a copy of your first issue. May I send you congratulations and all good wishes for the future.
> Yours,
> R. Drayson

The first issue of *Student* was published in January 1968.

Chapter 3

"I'm sorry to interrupt, Richard, but it's Mick Jagger for you and he says it's urgent."

1967–1970

At the end of the summer term of 1967, Jonny Gems and I moved into the basement of his parents' house in Connaught Square, just off Edgware Road in London. We managed to persuade Vanessa Redgrave to change her mind from merely sending us her best wishes for the success of *Student* to giving us an interview. The interview was a turning point for us since we could now use her name as a magnet to attract other contributors. As the list of contributors grew to include people like David Hockney and Jean-Paul Sartre, it became correspondingly easier for me to persuade some of the possible advertisers that *Student* would be a worthwhile place for them to appear.

Jonny and I lived in the basement all summer. The room was dark, dank, and sparsely furnished. Jonny and I slept on mattresses on the floor. The place quickly began to look a complete shambles, scattered with papers, dirty coffee cups, and fish-and-chip wrappers. We were always hungry. Sometimes we would slip upstairs to raid Jonny's parents' fridge. Mum would occasionally burst in through the door carrying a picnic hamper.

"Red Cross delivery!" she would shout. "When did you two last wash?"

We would laugh and spread a counterpane on the floor and pile into her picnic. One day she brought us £100 in cash.

Mum had found a necklace on the road near Shamley Green and taken it in to the police station. When nobody had claimed it after three months, the police had told her she could have it. She knew we had no money, so she came up to London, sold it, and gave us the money. Her £100 paid off our telephone and postage bills and kept us going for months. Without it we would have collapsed.

Peter Blake, who was famous for designing the Beatles' *Sergeant Pepper* album cover, drew a picture of a student for our first edition. It was a plain white cover with only two splashes of red, the title *Student,* and the red tie the student wore. As well as giving us this illustration, Peter Blake also gave us an interview. He began in arresting style:

"A very pretty girl with no clothes on is a marvellous subject, and one I'm particularly interested in. It is one of those things, along with perspective and anatomy, which teach you how to draw."

While I rapidly considered the advantages of becoming an artist, he went on to point out the dangers of student power—a point that struck a controversial note at the time: "I don't think the students should have any more power over the teachers than they have already. Just at the moment I don't really like students as a group of people. I think they rather overrate themselves. They seem to talk a lot and protest a lot, and have too many rights. I think one could get overinvolved in the activity of being a student. After all, students are not so important—they are really only there to learn how to be adults. Students shouldn't feel that they *have* to complain."

Perhaps because we were so young and not as aggressive as the usual professional interviewers they faced, some of our contributors made very revealing and graphic remarks. Gerald Scarfe described his work: "I'll always draw—it's a matter of energy. I could never stop. It's as much a part of me as eating. When I get an idea it has to come out—it is like being sick, a bodily function." When I asked Dudley Moore what he thought of students, he answered: "The only thing I hate about your generation is your age." He had been an organ scholar at Magdalen College, Oxford, but when I mentioned classical music, he said: "I'd much rather roll about in the mud with six women all day than sit down at the piano."

Mick Jagger and John Lennon also agreed to be interviewed. Both were demigods to the student population. *Student* gave a grandiose introduction to the Jagger interview: "Recently *Melody Maker* wrote: 'Jagger is rather like Dostoyevsky's brother Karamazov who, when told by his venerable brother that pain must exist so that we might learn of goodness, replied that if it was necessary that one small child should suffer in order that he should be made more aware, he did not deny the existence of God, but merely respectfully returned his ticket of admission to heaven. That is Mick Jagger's kind of rebellion.' " I can't imagine what we were thinking of when we quoted that; I certainly didn't understand it.

I nervously went along to his house on Cheyne Walk, and was shown into the living room by Marianne Faithfull, who then tantalizingly disappeared upstairs. Mick and I smiled at each other genially but were both equally at a loss for words:

RB: "Do you like giving interviews?"

MJ: "No."

RB: "Why did you ask *Student* to interview you?"

MJ: "I don't know. I've got no idea. I don't usually give interviews. I mean hardly ever."

RB: "You're not interested in politics?"

MJ: "No."

RB: "Why not?"

MJ: "Because I've kind of thought about it for a long time and decided that I haven't got time to do that and understand other things. I mean if you get involved in politics you get really fucked up."

RB: "Do you think people can be influenced by music?"

MJ: "Yeah, I think they probably can because it's one of those things—it's repetitive, the same thing over and over again. It gets into your brain and influences you."

Our interview with John Lennon was another classic. Jonny and I went along together, and Jonny tried to make a literary allusion:

JG: "A critic has written about 'A Day in the Life' as a kind of miniature *Waste Land*."

JL: "Miniature what?"

JG: "T. S. Eliot's poem, *The Waste Land*."

JL: "I don't know about that. Not very hip on me culture, you know."

Ironically, the interview with John was almost the end of *Student*. After Jonny and I had met him, I had the idea of asking whether John and Yoko would provide the magazine with an original recording, which we could distribute with *Student* as a flexidisc.

I contacted Derek Taylor, the Beatles' press officer. At that time, the Beatles had just set up the Apple Foundation for the Arts, with the idea of funding struggling artists and musicians. Most of Derek's day was spent sitting in his office in Savile Row, interviewing a long procession of supplicants, all with a hundred different reasons why they thought the Beatles should give them money. He was like a lord chamberlain at the court of the king. A sweet man, Derek would listen patiently to every request, no matter how far-fetched or nonsensical.

When I told him what we wanted to do, Derek agreed without a moment's hesitation. John and Yoko would delighted to provide something, he said. He introduced me to Ron Kass, the managing director of Apple, and to a manufacturer of flexidiscs, and we arranged a delivery date.

I rushed back to Connaught Square with the good news. Not only did we have a John Lennon interview, but also we would soon have an original, unreleased John Lennon song. It was a fantastic promotional coup for *Student*. We contacted Alan Aldridge, the most fashionable illustrator of the day, and commissioned him to design a special front cover, leaving a white space where the flexidisc would be attached. And we made plans to print 100,000 copies of the magazine—our largest run ever.

The weeks went by, and still no record arrived. In mounting anxiety I called Derek. "Don't worry, Richard," he said. "We've had a few problems. But I promise you'll get something." In fact, I could hardly have chosen a worse time to tax the Lennons' goodwill. Yoko had just lost the baby she was expecting, John had been busted for possession of cannabis, and the couple were lying low at their mansion in Weybridge.

I was in trouble myself. Our plans for the special issue had put *Student* on the brink of bankruptcy. I was getting desperate. For the first time in my life, I contacted a lawyer, Charles Levison, who wrote to Derek, threatening to sue Apple and the Lennons for breach of promise.

A few days later, I received a telephone call from Derek. "Come round to Apple, Richard," he said. "We've got something for you."

That afternoon I sat in the basement studio at Apple with Charles, Derek, John, and Yoko, listening to the recording they'd provided. The hiss of the tape recorder was followed by a steady, metronomic beat—like the sound of a human heart.

"What is it?" I asked.

"It's the heartbeat of our baby," said John.

No sooner had he spoken than the sound stopped. Yoko burst into floods of tears and hugged John. I didn't understand what was going on, but before I could speak John looked over Yoko's shoulder straight into my eyes.

"The baby died," he told me. "That's the silence of our dead baby."

I went back to *Student* with no idea what I should do. I felt unable to release this private moment as a record. Perhaps I was wrong because, as Derek said, "It's conceptual art," and it would have become a collector's piece. We had to scrap the covers and redesign the magazine. It cost a lot of money, but somehow we managed to scrape the money together. I considered taking legal action against the Lennons, but they'd had enough problems and, anyway, they'd honored the agreement in their own particular way, even if I couldn't see the value of it at the time. After our dispute over the recording, Derek wrote a note apologizing for all the trouble I'd been caused. His sign-off was a line he put on all his correspondence: "All you need is love . . ."

Jonny read extensively. I hardly read at all. I never seemed to have the time. I would spend the days on the telephone, trying to sell advertising space, persuading people to write for *Student* for nothing, or to be interviewed. Throughout my life, I've always needed somebody as a counterbalance, to compensate for my weaknesses and to work off my strengths. Jonny and I were a good team. He knew whom we should interview and why. I had the ability to persuade them to say yes and the obstinacy never to accept no for an answer.

In many of the interviews I conducted for *Student* I just turned the tape recorder on and let the people say whatever they wanted. Before meeting the psychiatrist R. D. Laing, I had tried to read his best-seller, *The Politics of Experience*. Like most people, I suspect, I had understood hardly a word of it. I aimed the microphone at him, and he spoke without stopping for an hour and a half, staring at a corner of the ceiling behind my head. I had no idea what he was rabbiting on about, I was just grateful that there wasn't any room for me to ask him a single question. At the end, when it became apparent that he had finished, I thanked him profusely, went back to the office, and transcribed what he had said. It turned out that he had just quoted pages from the *The Politics of Experience* almost verbatim.

After a few issues the number of people involved with *Student* began to grow. Jonny and I would sometimes go to nightclubs, where we chatted up girls; sometimes we could even persuade them to come back to the flat "for coffee." If they stayed the night, the next morning we would try to persuade them to help out; for some reason, they often seemed to take pity on us. Word of mouth spread. Old friends turned up from school, as well as friends of friends or people who had read the magazine and wanted to be involved. Increasingly, the basement began to resemble a squat. We all worked for no money, living off whatever was in the fridge and going out for cheap curries. All sorts of people helped to distribute the magazine. The basic idea was that they would take away bundles of magazines, sell them for two shillings and six pence a copy, and then give us half the proceeds—one shilling and three pence for each copy sold. Although they were meant to pay us in advance, it rarely seemed to work like that. But I never really worried about how much profit *Student* made. I was just determined to have enough cash in the kitty so that we could produce the next issue and pay our bills. I thought that the more copies we sold, the more word of mouth would spread and ultimately the more advertising we could attract.

Although I hardly realized it at the time, my ambitions to be a journalist were beginning to be pushed to one side by the imperatives of keeping the magazine afloat. Jonny ran the editorial side, while I ran the business and sold advertising space and argued with the printers. I was becoming an entrepreneur almost by default, although if anybody had mentioned the word to me then, I probably would have had to ask Jonny what it meant. I certainly didn't regard myself as a businessman. Businessmen were middle-aged men in the city who wore pin-striped suits, had wives and two to four children in the suburbs, and were obsessed with making money. Of course, we wanted to make money on *Student* too; we needed money to survive. But we saw it as much more a creative enterprise than a moneymaking one. Later, it became apparent to me that business could be a creative enterprise in itself. If you publish a magazine, you're trying to create something that is original and stands out from the crowd, something that will last and serve some useful purpose. Above all, you want to create something you are proud of.

That has always been my philosophy of business. I can honestly say that I have never gone into any business purely to make money. If that is the sole motive, then I believe you are better off not doing it. A business has to be involving, it has to be fun, and it has to exercise your creative instincts.

Running *Student* was certainly fun. Each day unfolded to the deafening strains of Bob Dylan, the Beatles, and the Stones blaring out of the hi-fi system, shaking the cramped walls of the basement. When Jonny and I went out to sell copies of the magazine, we would celebrate a single sale of the magazine for two shillings and six pence by going and buying two hamburgers for one shilling and three pence each. Every now and then I would look out of the grimy basement window and see that it was a beautiful day. I would turn off the music and tell everyone we had to go out for a walk. We would wander across Hyde Park, and then somehow someone would end up in the Serpentine and we'd all have a swim.

Tony Mellor was one of the main assistant editors, and we all respected him because he had been a trades union official. Tony was rather older than the rest of us and was extremely articulate about socialism. As everyone argued over the exact wording of some of the more political pronouncements in the magazine, I was becoming aware of a wider picture: the politics of survival. In some ways I became an outsider on the magazine. While the others would be talking about the "LSD guru" Timothy Leary, Pink Floyd, and the latest convulsions of student politics, I would be worrying about paying the printers and telephone bills. As well as spending time on the telephone trying to persuade leading figures of the day to write for Student just for the love of it, I also had to spend hours on the phone calling up companies such as British Leyland and Lloyds Bank, trying to convince them to buy advertising space. Without their money, Student would collapse.

The responsibility made me grow up fast. You might almost say that I was old before my time. While the others might happily sit around in the evening getting stoned, unconcerned about waking up late next morning with a hangover, I was always aware of the need to keep a clear head.

My parents and Lindi came up to help us sell copies of the magazine. Mum took a bundle to Speakers' Corner in Hyde Park and pushed them into the unsuspecting hands of tourists. Lindi and I walked up and down Oxford Street selling copies of Student to anybody we could stop. I was once with Lindi when a tramp came up and asked for money. We had no money—that's exactly what we were looking for too—but in a histrionic fit of idealism, I stripped off most of my clothes and gave them to him. I spent the rest of the day walking around in a blanket.

"Poor old tramp!" Dad chuckled when he heard the story. "That'll teach him. All he wanted was some loose change, and he got a set of infested clothes from you!"

Student began to develop a high profile, and one day a German television channel asked me whether I would make a speech at University College along with the activist Tariq Ali and student leader Daniel Cohn-Bendit. The brief was to talk about people's rights. A vast crowd welcomed these two firebrand revolutionaries. I stood and listened as Danny Cohn-Bendit made a brilliant speech full of intellectual depth and passion. Everyone around him was cheering and roaring their approval. Then Tariq Ali stood up, and he too made a passionate speech. The crowd stamped and shouted at the tops of their voices as if they were about to descend upon the Bastille. I began to feel a little queasy.

At Stowe there had been a very cruel tradition. Each boy had to learn a long poem and stand up in front of the entire school and recite it. If you made the slightest mistake or paused for a moment, the master hit a gong, and you had to leave the stage accompanied by great boos and jeers all round: you were "gonged" off. Since I was mildly dyslexic, I found it extremely difficult to learn anything by heart and for several years was gonged off with relentless regularity. As I watched Danny Cohn-Bendit and Tariq Ali making their inspiring speeches, surfing on the goodwill of the crowd, and milking the television camera for all it was worth, I felt the same sickening feeling in my stomach as I had felt when I was waiting to recite my Tennyson piece in the sure knowledge that I would be gonged offstage and loudly booed.

Finally Tariq Ali finished his speech. There was pandemonium. Everyone cheered, somebody hoisted him on their shoulders, pretty girls waved admiringly up at him, and the camera swiveled in his direction. Then somebody beckoned to me; it was my turn. I hopped up to the podium and nervously took the microphone. I had barely spoken in public, let alone made a speech before, and I felt chronically nervous. I had absolutely no idea what to say. I had prepared a speech, but under the scrutiny of a thousand expectant faces, which turned toward me like sunflowers, my mind had gone completely blank. Dry-mouthed, I mumbled a few words, gave a sick smile, and realized with a mounting feeling of panic that I could not do it. There was nowhere to hide. I gave a final inarticulate mumble, somewhere between a cough and a vomit, dropped the microphone, leaped off the podium, and disappeared into the safety of the crowd. It had been the most embarrassing moment of my life. Even now, whenever I am interviewed or have to give a speech, I feel the same trepidation and have to overcome the same sense of shyness. If I'm talking on a subject that is familiar to me or that I feel passionately about, then I can be reasonably fluent. But when I'm asked to talk on a subject I know very little about, I become uncomfortable—and it shows. But I take some comfort from this: I now accept that I will never have all the smooth, instant answers that a politician will have and I don't have to fight my stutters or inability to leap to a perfect answer. Instead, I just try to give the truthful answer. If it takes a little time to work out that answer, I hope that people will trust a slow, hesitant answer more than a rapid, glib one.

The wars in Vietnam and Biafra were the two leading issues of the late sixties. If *Student* was to be a plausible publication, we had to have our own reporters in both countries. We had no money to send any reporters out there, let alone pay for them to stay in hotels and telex back articles, so we had to think laterally. We finally came up with the idea that if we chose very young reporters, they might be a story in themselves. So I called up the *Daily Mirror* to ask whether they would be interested in running an exclusive story about a seventeen-year-old reporter going to Vietnam. They bought the story and paid for Julian Manyon, who was working with us at *Student,* to go to Vietnam. Julian went there, filed some great articles about the Vietnam War, and subsequently went on to become a famous ITN reporter. We managed to make the same arrangement with sending a sixteen-year-old reporter to Biafra. These two ventures were my first experience of leveraging up the *Student* name: we put in the name and the people, and the other side put up the money to fund it.

I felt passionate about the campaign to end American involvement in Vietnam. So in October 1968 all the *Student* staff joined Vanessa Redgrave on the student march to Grosvenor Square to protest outside the American embassy. I marched alongside Vanessa and Tariq Ali. It was tremendously exciting to be marching for something I believed in, along with tens of thousands of others. The mood of the crowd was exhilarating but at the same time slightly frightening. I felt that at any moment things could get out of control. And they did. When the police charged the crowd, I ran like hell. A photograph of the demonstration later appeared in *Paris Match.* It shows me, back arched, an inch away from the outstretched hand of a policeman who was trying to catch me as I sprinted across the square.

While I opposed Vietnam, I didn't feel as passionately left-wing on other issues as most of my fellow demonstrators.

"I suppose I am left-wing," I told a reporter from *The Guardian.* "Well, only to the extent that I think left-wing views are sane and rational."

Student was not a radical magazine in the political sense. Nor were we an underground magazine, like *Oz* and *It.* We weren't advocating putting LSD in the water supply, as they might have done from time to time—although I think there was just as much free love in our offices as there was in theirs.

I tried to maintain a balance between the views of the Left and the Right, but what I hoped was balance some people saw as prevarication. The writer and poet Robert Graves wrote to me from Deyá, Majorca: "Your hands seem tied tighter than students deserve. In the Biafra story, for instance, you don't once mention what the war is *really* about in the international context. But that is because you have to keep pals with the 'over-thirties' and the Big Business Boys, or the journal couldn't survive. Yet, you do your best."

In fact, "the Big Business Boys" weren't being as friendly as I'd hoped. The struggle to secure advertising was much more difficult than finding contributors. We were pleased to be able to interview the actor and director Bryan Forbes or to publish Gavin Maxwell's article, but they didn't bring in money to help us run the magazine and distribute it. We charged £250 for a whole-page advertisement down to £40 for one-eighth of a page. For example, after countless calls I managed to get nine companies—J. Walter Thompson, Metal Box, *The Sunday Times,* the *Daily Telegraph,* the Gas Council (the forerunner to British Gas), *The Economist,* Lloyds Bank, Rank Organisation, and John Laing Builders—to take out full-page advertisements in the first edition. These nine advertisements brought in £2,250 and had been wrung out of a list that had started off with over three hundred possible companies. But it was enough to cover the cost of printing the 30,000 copies of the first edition. I opened an account at Coutts, where my family had always banked, as our clearing bank. I must have been their only customer who walked in barefoot and asked for a £1,000 overdraft. Throughout the life of *Student,* selling advertising space was an uphill struggle.

For all our efforts, it was clear that *Student* wasn't making money. I began to think of ways to develop the magazine and the "Student" name in other directions: a Student conference, a Student travel company, a Student accommodation agency. I didn't see Student just as an end in itself, a noun. I saw it as the beginning of a whole range of services, effectively an adjective, a word that people would recognize as having certain key values. In 1970s language, *Student* magazine and everything Student promoted was hip. Student was a flexible concept, and I wanted to explore this flexibility to see how far I could push it and where it would lead. In this way I was a little removed from the rest of my friends, who concentrated exclusively on the magazine and the student politics that they wanted to cover.

In the end Peter Blake was right in saying that student revolution would go out of fashion—and students with it. Looking at the early editions of *Student* thirty years later, however, I'm amazed by how little has changed. *Student* then had cartoons of Ted Heath by Nicholas Garland; today he's still being caricatured by Nicholas Garland. David Hockney, Dudley Moore, and John Le Carré still make good copy; and Bryan Forbes and Vanessa Redgrave, or at least their daughters, are still in the news.

Life in the basement was the kind of all-embracing, glorious chaos in which I thrived and have thrived ever since. We never had any money, we were incredibly busy, and we were a close-knit team. We worked together because it was fun, because we felt that what we were doing was important, and because we had great lives together. Soon a number of journalists from the national papers came to interview me to see what all the buzz was about.

We developed a foolproof way of impressing them. I sat at my desk, the telephone ringing at my elbow.

"Great to meet you. Take a seat." I would wave the journalist down into the beanbag opposite me. As the journalist shuffled around trying to retain his or her dignity, get comfortable, and remove the drips of hummus and cigarette ash from the folds, the telephone would ring.

"Can someone take that, please?" I said. "Now." I turned my attention to the journalist. "What do you want to know about *Student*?"

"It's Ted Heath for you, Richard," Tony called across the room.

"I'll call him back," I said over my shoulder. "Now, what did you want to know about *Student*?"

By this time the journalist was craning round to watch Tony tell Ted Heath that he was sorry but Richard was in a meeting and he'd call him back. The telephone rang again, and Tony picked it up.

"David Bailey for you, Richard."

"I'll call him back, but will you ask if he can change that lunch date? I've got to be in Paris. Okay." I flashed an apologetic grin at the journalist. "Now, how are we doing?"

"I just wanted to ask you . . ."

The telephone rang again.

"I'm sorry to interrupt," Tony apologized, "but it's Mick Jagger for you and he says it's urgent."

"Please excuse me for a minute," I said, reluctantly picking up the phone. "Mick, hello. Fine, thanks, and you? Really? An exclusive? Yes, that sounds great. . . ."

And on I went until Jonny couldn't stop laughing from the call box opposite and the pips rang out.

"I'm sorry," I said to the journalist. "Something's cropped up and we've got to dash. Are we finished?"

The journalist would be ushered out in a daze, passing Jonny on the way, and the telephone would stop ringing.

Journalists swallowed our scam hook, line, and sinker: "Photographers, journalists, writers from papers throughout the world seem to have fallen over themselves in assisting *Student*," wrote the *Sunday Telegraph*, "and a massive voluntary distribution organisation has grown throughout schools and universities allowing, perhaps, over half a million students to read the magazine."

"An amazing number of top-class contributors. Its scope is limitless," said *The Observer*, while the *Daily Telegraph* said, "It seems probable that *Stu-*

dent, the glossy publication that has attracted a lot of well-known writers, will become one of the largest circulated magazines in the country."

By autumn 1968 Jonny's parents had understandably had enough of having almost twenty teenagers squatting in their basement and asked us to find somewhere else to live. We moved to Albion Street, just around the corner from Connaught Square. Jonny left to go back to school and take his A levels. He felt guilty about abandoning me, but he was under pressure to continue his education, and his parents sensibly worried that working on a small magazine from their basement was hardly the perfect foundation on which to earn much of a living.

Without Jonny, *Student* almost fell to pieces. There was too much for me to do and nobody else whom I could really trust to help me out. After a few weeks, I asked Nik to come and help. Nik had finished at Ampleforth but was due to go to Sussex University at Brighton. He agreed to delay going to university and to come instead to *Student's* aid.

With Nik's arrival, *Student* was put back on the rails. He started controlling the cash, and rather than having a large biscuit tin full of money, which anyone could dip into and buy food or drink or dope, Nik used our Coutts account properly. He started writing checks and then checking the stubs off against the bank statements. Nik had lost a front tooth, and with his long black hair he looked rather terrifying. I think he kept away a lot of debt collectors.

The commune, which had been very cramped at Jonny's basement, now spread up and down the new house. People made dens out of fabric, and there were mattresses and joss sticks everywhere. By now most of the people working with *Student* were nineteen or twenty, and there was lots of talk about "free love" and lots of practice of it. I installed a large brass bed on the top floor and a telephone, which ran off a long extension lead that looped down through the banisters. Some days I did all my business from bed. I put the house in my parents' name so that the owners—the church commissioners—would not think we were running a business from it. My parents loved the excitement of journalism, and although Dad was a barrister with short hair and he wore a blazer and tie to church on Sundays, they never had any problem talking to people who had hair halfway down their backs and hadn't shaved or washed for a month. Lindi came up every half term and during some of her holidays and stayed in Albion Street, where she helped distribute *Student* and fell in love with a series of men working on the magazine.

I had a short relationship with Debbie, one of the girls living at Albion Street and working on *Student*. One day she told me that she was pregnant. We were both very shocked and realized that a baby was the last thing we could cope with. Debbie decided that she wanted to have an abortion. After a few telephone calls it became clear that this would be very difficult to arrange. Debbie could not have an abortion on the National Health Service unless she had proven psychiatric or medical problems. We grew frantic phoning around all the different branches of the National Health hospitals trying to see if there was any way this could be overcome. When we tried to find a private doctor to help, we found it would cost over £400, money we didn't have. I was at my wit's end when I finally tracked down a kind doctor in Birmingham who told me that she would arrange the operation for £50.

After the procedure, Debbie and I realized that there must be a host of young people who had faced the same problem and had nowhere to turn for help. It would surely be much better if there was one telephone number that you could ring to be referred to the right doctor. It wasn't just unwanted pregnancies that were the problem. What if you needed psychological help, or had a venereal disease but were scared of admitting it to your nice family doctor, or had run away from home and had nowhere to live? We drew up a long list of the sorts of problems that students faced and decided to do something about it. We would give out our telephone number, work out a list of all the best and most helpful doctors, and see who called.

Give Us Your Headaches was the slogan for the Student Advisory Centre. We handed out leaflets along Oxford Street and advertised in *Student*. Soon the calls started coming in. A number of doctors both in the National Health Service and in the private sector agreed to give their services for free or for minimal charge, so we built up a network of professionals to whom we could refer people. Pregnancies and contraception were the subjects of many of the calls, but we also became quite a hangout for homosexuals and lesbians. It soon became clear that they were not as interested in asking our advice as in finding ways of meeting each other, another example of how difficult it was for gays to lead a normal social life.

The Student Advisory Centre began to take up more time than *Student* magazine. I would be talking to possible suicides for an hour at three in the morning, advising pregnant girls as to who was the nicest doctor they could go and see, writing to someone who was terrified that he had caught venereal disease but didn't dare tell his parents or go to a doctor—and in what little time was left, be trying to run the magazine. One of the biggest problems we found ourselves dealing with was that teenagers were unable to confide in their parents. Hearing others' stories made me realize how lucky I was in my relationship with my own parents. They had never judged me but had always supported me, always praised the good things rather than criticized the bad things, so I had no qualms about admitting my problems, worries, and failures. Our work was to try to help out those who were in trouble but had nowhere to turn.

With both the Student Advisory Centre and *Student* magazine, life at Albion Street remained frantic and the numbers of people coming in and out of the house at all times of day and night continued to drive our neighbors to distraction. Unfortunately, under the terms of the lease, we weren't allowed to use the house as an office because of the complaints from the neighbors. We were visited by the church commissioner inspectors on a regular basis to check that we were not carrying out any kind of business. These visits had all the clockwork tension of a West End farce. The commissioners had to give us twenty-four hours' notice before an inspection, and as soon as we received it the whole *Student* staff and my mum immediately wheeled into action. All the telephones were piled into a cupboard, and the desks and chairs and mattresses were covered by dust sheets. The *Student* staff would pull out paint pots and paintbrushes, put on overalls, and start painting the walls of the house. Mum would arrive with Lindi and eight-year-old Vanessa and an armful of toys from the country. By the time the commissioners arrived they would find a friendly crew of painters cheerfully decorating the house, the furniture all swathed in dust sheets, while a mother and her family huddled upstairs. The little girl would be playing with some toys in a rather bemused way while Lindi and I were engrossed in Monopoly. If Vanessa ever looked as if she might ask us what was going on, Mum would rapidly shoo everyone out of the room, saying it was time for Vanessa's bed.

The church inspectors would look at this happy domestic scene and wonder what all the fuss was about. They would scratch their heads and say what a lovely girl little Vanessa was, drink their tea, and have a nice chat with my mum. As soon as they had disappeared down the street, Mum went back home, we put away the Monopoly, yanked off the dust sheets, plugged in the telephones, and got back to work.

The end came on one fatal visit when we forgot to unplug the telephones. By then it was their fifth visit, and the inspectors must have suspected something. They stayed for their ritual cup of tea and were just about to leave when two of the telephones started ringing from inside the cupboard. A shocked silence fell.

"And just listen to that," I improvised quickly. "Can you hear that telephone? The walls are so thin in these houses that we can hear everything which goes on next door!"

The inspector strode forward and pulled open the cupboard door. Five telephones, a switchboard, and a tangle of wires all tumbled out on top of him. Not even a big family needed a switchboard. That was the end of 44 Albion Street. Vanessa and her collection of dolls and toys were taken down to Shamley Green for the last time, and Lindi and I packed up the Monopoly set. *Student* magazine had to find somewhere else to use as an office.

We scoured the neighborhood looking for somewhere to rent. The best deal, no rent at all, was offered by the Reverend Cuthbert Scott. He liked the work of the Advisory Centre and offered us the use of the crypt at Saint John's Church, just off Bayswater Road, for no rent. I put an old slab of marble across two tombs to make my desk, and everyone found themselves somewhere to sit. We even charmed the local post office engineer to connect our phone without having to wait the normal three months. After a while none of us noticed that we were working in the dim light of the crypt surrounded by marble effigies and tombs.

In November 1969 I received a visit from two plainclothes policemen from Marylebone Police Station. They had come to draw my attention to the 1889 Indecent Advertisements Act and the 1917 Venereal Disease Act in case I was unaware of them, which, not surprisingly, I was. They told me that it was illegal to advertise any help or remedy for venereal disease. These acts had been introduced to stop quack doctors around the turn of the century from exploiting the large numbers of people with venereal disease who came to them for expensive and ineffective cures. I argued that I was only offering a counseling service and that I passed on anyone who had venereal disease to qualified doctors at Saint Mary's Hospital. But the policemen were adamant: if the Student Advisory Centre continued to mention the words "venereal disease" in public, I would be arrested with the prospect of two years' imprisonment.

The week before we had successfully prosecuted a policeman at Marylebone Police Station for planting drugs on one of the Student Advisory Centre's clients. The policeman had been sent down, and so I suspected that this visit was connected. I was amazed that the police had trawled through this old legislation to find some obscure law that we were breaking.

We duly changed the mention of venereal disease in the leaflets that we distributed around London and started describing it as "social disease." Then we got a huge number of inquiries from people who were suffering from acne or pimples, and the number of people calling us for help over venereal disease dropped from sixty a week to ten. We decided that the police were bluffing and that helping the remaining fifty people a week was worth risking the metropolitan police's threats: we reinserted the mention of venereal disease. We were wrong. The police came back to the crypt again in December 1969 and arrested me.

John Mortimer, a barrister who was already establishing a reputation for his support of libertarian causes after his defense of the magazine *Oz* and his role in the *Lady Chatterley's Lover* trial, offered to defend me. He agreed that the law was ridiculous and that the police were merely being vindictive. John reminded us that every public lavatory carried a government notice on the inside of the door offering advice to those suffering from venereal disease. If I was guilty, then so was the government. I was duly prosecuted on two accounts: under the Indecent Advertisements Act 1889, which prohibited advertisements of an "indecent or obscene nature" and which deemed references to syphilis and gonorrhea to be indecent, and the Venereal Disease Act 1917, which banned advertisements offering treatment or advice or mentioning the words venereal disease.

At the first hearing on 8 May 1970 at the Marylebone Magistrates Court, Tom Driberg, the flamboyant Labour MP, gave a dramatic plea on my behalf. Chad Varah, the founder of the Samaritans, also gave evidence pointing out how many people the Student Advisory Centre had referred to his charity. John Mortimer made his argument that if I was found guilty, then I would have no option but to prosecute the government and all the local authorities since they had also put up notices in public lavatories. The magistrate dismissed the charge under the Venereal Disease Act on the grounds that the Student Advisory Centre did not offer to cure people but referred them on to other qualified doctors. He adjourned the other charge until 22 May.

Even as the court case was proceeding, statistics were released that revealed that the number of people with venereal disease had risen dramatically in the last year to a postwartime peak. Lady Birk, the chairman of the Health Education Council, used the statistics together with the example of my prosecution to try to amend the 1889 Indecent Advertisements Act in the House of Lords.

"It's ludicrous that outmoded laws should restrict responsible efforts to stop the spread of these serious diseases," she said.

By the time of the second court case, a number of newspapers had declared how idiotic it was that I was being prosecuted. There was a strong movement to change the law. The magistrate reluctantly found me guilty under the strict letter of the law, but he made it clear that he considered that the law was absurd by fining me just seven pounds, some way short of the two years' imprisonment with which the police had been threatening me. John Mortimer made a statement to the press outside the court in which he called for the law to be changed or we would have no alternative but to prosecute the government for mentioning venereal disease on the doors of public lavatories. The newspapers all joined forces behind us, and Lady Birk's amendment to the law was incorporated into government legislation at the next sitting of Parliament. Reginald Maudling, the home secretary, sent me a personal letter apologizing for the Crown prosecution.

That court case taught me that although I was young and wore jeans and a sweater and had very little money behind me, I need not be afraid of being bullied by the police or the Establishment, particularly if I had a good barrister.

One day in 1970 I came back to my desk and found that Nik had been sitting at it. By mistake he had left a draft of a memo, which he was writing to the staff. It was a plan to get rid of me as publisher and editor, to take editorial and financial control of *Student,* and to turn it into a cooperative. I would become just part of the team, and everyone would share equally in the editorial direction of the magazine. I was shocked. I felt that Nik, my closest friend, was betraying me. After all, *Student* had been my and Jonny's idea. We had started it at Stowe, and against all odds we had managed to publish it. I knew what I wanted to do with *Student,* and it seemed to me that everyone was happy working there. We all drew equal salaries, but ultimately I was the editor and publisher and it was up to me to make the decisions.

I looked around at everyone working. They all had their heads bent down studiously over their desks. I wondered how many were part of this. I put the memo in my pocket. When Nik came back, I stood up.

"Nik," I said, "will you come outside for a quick chat?"

I decided to bluff my way through the crisis. If Nik had already whipped up support from the ten other people, it would be difficult for me to stop them. But if they were undecided, then I could drive a wedge between Nik and the rest of them and cut Nik out. I had to put our friendship to one side and get rid of this challenge.

"Nik," I said as we walked down the street, "a number of people have come up to me and said that they're unhappy with what you're planning. They don't like the idea, but they're too scared to tell you to your face."

Nik looked horrified.

"I don't think that it's a good idea for you to stay here," I went on. "You're trying to undermine me and the whole of *Student*. I think that we should remain friends, but I don't think you should stay here anymore."

I still don't know how I managed to say those words without blushing or my voice cracking. Nik looked down at his feet.

"I'm sorry, Ricky," he said. "It just seemed a better way to organize ourselves . . ." He trailed off.

"I'm sorry too, Nik." I folded my arms and looked straight at him. "Let's see each other down in Shamley Green, but *Student* is my life."

Nik left that day. I told the rest of the people that Nik and I had disagreed over how to run *Student,* and they were free to leave or to carry on, whatever they wished. They all decided to stay with me, and life at the crypt went on without Nik.

This was the first real disagreement I ever had, and although I felt great anguish, I knew that I had to confront it. I hate criticizing people who work with me, and I always try to avoid doing so. Ever since then I have always tried to avoid the issue by asking someone else to wield the ax. I admit that this is a weakness, but I am simply unable to cope with it.

Nik was my best friend, and I deeply hoped that he would remain so. When I was next down in Shamley Green, I went round to see Nik and found him eating one of his mum's puddings. We sat down together and polished it off.

Apart from the fact that he was my oldest friend, Nik had taken charge of the distribution of the magazine and made sense of it. I missed him terribly. Until Nik arrived, the distribution had been only casually handled with bundles being sent out to volunteers in schools and universities. For over a year *Student* carried on without Nik and we put out four more editions. When Nik told me that he was standing for some student election at Sussex University, I used *Student's* purchasing power with the printers to run off some cheap campaign posters. Nik won the election, but later he was disqualified because he had got outside support for his campaign.

One thing I knew from everyone who came in to chat or to work for us was that they spent a good deal of time listening to music and a good deal of money buying records. We had the record player on constantly, and everyone rushed out to buy the latest Rolling Stones or Bob Dylan or Jefferson Airplane album the day it was released. Music was tremendously exciting: it was political, it was anarchic, it summed up the young generation's dream of changing the world. And I also noticed that people who would never dream of spending as much as forty shillings on a meal wouldn't hesitate to spend forty shillings buying the latest Bob Dylan album. The more obscure the albums were and the more they cost, the more they were treasured.

Up until this point I had been interested in making money only to ensure *Student's* continuing success and to fund the Student Advisory Centre, but it struck me as a very interesting business opportunity. When I heard that despite the government's abolition of the Retail Price Maintenance Agreement, none of the shops was offering discounted records, I began to think about setting up a record distribution business.

The number of people working on *Student* had grown to around twenty, and we all still lived together in 44 Albion Street and worked in the crypt.

I thought about the high cost of records and the sort of people who bought *Student* magazine, and wondered whether we could advertise and sell cheap mail-order records through the magazine. As it turned out, the first advertisement for mail-order records appeared in the final edition of *Student* magazine. Without Nik to manage *Student's* distribution, it was floundering, but the mail-order offer for cheap records brought in a flood of inquiries and more cash than we had ever seen before.

We decided to come up with another name for the mail-order business, a name that would be eye-catching, that could stand alone and not just appeal to students. We sat around in the church crypt trying to choose a good name.

"Slipped Disc" was one of the favorite suggestions we toyed with for a while until one of the girls leaned forward:

"I know," she said. "What about 'Virgin'? We're complete virgins at business."

"And there aren't many virgins left around here," laughed one of the other girls. "It would be nice to have one here in name if nothing else."

"Great," I decided on the spot. "It's Virgin."

Chapter 4

"We sat down and had some lunch, and before we knew what we were doing we were lying on the bed making love."

1970–1971

And so we became Virgin. Looking back at the various uses to which we've since put the Virgin name, I think we made the right decision. I'm not sure that Slipped Disc Airline, Slipped Disc Brides, or Slipped Disc Condoms would have had quite the same appeal.

Our tiny sample of market research proved correct: students spent a good deal of money on records, and they didn't like spending thirty-nine shillings at W. H. Smith when they found out that they could buy them from Virgin for thirty-five shillings. We started giving out leaflets about Virgin Mail Order Records along Oxford Street and outside concerts, and the daily post increased from a bundle of letters to a sack. One of the best things about mail order for us was that the customers sent their money in first, which provided the capital for us to buy the records. Our bank account at Coutts started to build up a large cash balance.

As Virgin Mail Order grew, I tried to sell *Student* to another magazine group. IPC Magazines emerged as the only interested buyer, and we had long negotiations that culminated in a meeting where they asked me to stay on as editor. I agreed to do so but then made the mistake of telling them all about my future plans. Fantasizing about the future is one of my favorite pastimes, and I told them at the meeting that I had all sorts of other plans for *Student*: I felt that students were given a raw deal by banks, and I wanted to set up a cheap student bank. I wanted to set up a string of great nightclubs and hotels where students could stay, perhaps even offer them good travel—like student trains or even, who knows, a student airline. As I warmed to my theme, I saw that their eyes had glazed over. They thought that I was a madman. They decided that they did not want to keep such a lunatic on as editor of *Student,* and in the end they decided that they did not even want to buy it. *Student* died a quiet death, and my plans for the future had to be shelved for the time being.

We switched all our attention to Virgin records. One look at the huge numbers of orders coming in and the need to organize where to buy the records from and send them out to the customers persuaded me that I needed someone to help me.

Although we all had great fun at Albion Street, I was increasingly aware that I was the only one who had to worry about paying all the wages. Even though these were small amounts of money, it was difficult to make sufficient profit even to cover that cost. There was only one person I could turn to: Nik. I wanted my old friend back again. I buried the episode when Nik had tried to throw me out and offered him 40 percent of the newly formed Virgin Mail Order Records company if he would come to work with me. He agreed immediately. We never negotiated over the 60/40 percent split. I think that we both felt that it was a fair reflection of what we would each put into the business.

Although Nik was not a trained accountant, he was meticulous at counting the pennies. He also led by example: he never spent any money, so why should any of us? He never washed his clothes, so why should any of us? He scrimped and saved every penny, he always turned lights off when he left a room, he made only rapid phone calls, and he handled our bills with great skill.

"It's fine to pay bills late," he said. "So long as you pay them regularly."

So we paid our bills on the nail, except that it was always the last nail. Apart from Nik and me, there were no other permanent employees in the crypt. A rotating band of casual workers came in and were paid £20 a week before drifting on. Throughout 1970 Virgin Mail Order Records thrived.

Then in January 1971 we were almost ruined by something entirely out of our control: the post office workers went on strike. Led by Tom Jackson, the general secretary of the Union of Post Office Workers, the postmen went home and the Post Office taped up the letter boxes. Our mail-order business was set to go bust: people couldn't send us checks, and we couldn't send out records. We had to do something.

Nik and I decided that we should open a shop to carry on selling the records. We had to find a shop within a week, before we ran out of money. At the time we had no idea about how a shop works. All we knew was that we had to sell records somehow or the company would collapse. We started looking for a site.

In 1971 the record shops were dominated by W. H. Smith and John Menzies, both of which were dull and formal. The record departments were generally downstairs and staffed by people in drab brown or blue uniforms who appeared to have no interest in music. Customers chose their records from the shelves, bought them, and left within ten minutes. The shops were unwelcoming, there was little sympathetic service, and prices were high. Although rock music was very exciting, none of that feeling of excitement or even vague interest filtered through to the shops that sold the records. The dowdy staff registered no approval or interest if you bought the new Jefferson Airplane; they just rang it up on the till as if you had bought Mantovani or Perry Como. It was all the same to them. Nor did they seem particularly enthused about putting in a special order for the Van Der Graaf Generator or Incredible String Band record that had been reviewed in *Melody Maker* that week. None of our friends felt at home in record shops, they were just a rather functional place where they had to go to buy their favorite records. Hence the appeal of a cheap mail-order business.

We wanted the Virgin record shop to be an extension of *Student,* a place where people could meet and listen to records together, somewhere where they weren't simply encouraged to dash in, buy the record, and leave. We wanted them to stay longer, chat to the staff, and really get into which records they were going to buy. People take music far more seriously than many other things in life. It is part of the way in which they define themselves—like the cars they drive, the films they watch, and the clothes they wear. Teenagers spend more time listening to music, talking about their favorite bands, and choosing records than almost anything else.

Virgin's first record shop had to incorporate all these aspects of how music fits into people's lives. In exploring how to do this, I think we created the conceptual framework of what Virgin later became. We wanted the Virgin record shop to be an enjoyable place to go at a time when record buyers were given short shrift. We wanted to relate to the customers, not patronize them, and we wanted to be cheaper than the other shops. To achieve all this was a tall order, but we hoped that the extra money that went on creating the atmosphere and the profits we forfeited by selling cheaply would be more than made up for by people buying more records.

Nik and I spent a morning counting people walking up and down Oxford Street compared with people walking along Kensington High Street. Eventually we decided that the cheaper end of Oxford Street would be the best site. We knew that we couldn't rely upon people knowing about the Virgin record shop and making a special trip to buy a record, so we had to be able to attract passersby into the shop on impulse. At the exact point where we counted the most people walking along the street, we started looking for an empty property. We saw a shoe shop with a stairway leading up to what looked like an empty first floor, so we went upstairs to see what it was like.

"What are you doing?" a voice called up to us.

"We're looking to set up a shop," we said.

"What kind of shop?"

Nik and I came back down the stairs and found the owner of the shoe shop blocking our way.

"A record shop," we said.

The owner was a large, square Greek called Mr. Alachouzos.

"You'll never pay the rent," he said.

"No, you're right," I said. "We can't afford any rent. But we'll attract lots of people past your window, and they'll all buy shoes."

"What kind of shoes?" Mr. Alachouzos's eyes narrowed.

"Jesus sandals are out," Nik said. "Do you sell any Doc Martens?"

We agreed that we would fit out the record shop and that we could occupy it for no rent until somebody else came along and wanted it. It was, after all, just an empty space. Within five days we had built shelves, put piles of cushions on the floor, carried a couple of old sofas up the stairs, and set up a till. The first Virgin record shop was ready for business.

We handed out hundreds of leaflets along Oxford Street on the day before opening, offering cut-price records, and on the first Monday a queue over a hundred yards long formed outside. I was on the till when the customers started coming through. The first customer bought a record by Tangerine Dream, a German band that we had noticed selling very well through mail order.

"Funny bloke you've got downstairs," he said. "He kept trying to sell me a pair of Doc Martens as I waited in the queue."

At the end of the day I took the money to the bank. I found Mr. Alachouzos hovering outside the shop.

"How's business?" I asked, trying to make light of the heavy bag of cash I was carrying.

He looked at me and then back at his shop window, which was still piled high with unsold Doc Martens.

"Fine," he said firmly. "Couldn't be better."

During 1971 Nik was running the Oxford Street record shop, Debbie was running the Student Advisory Centre from Piccadilly, and I was generally looking to do anything I could to expand the business. We were in the process of changing from *Student* ideas to Virgin, and in due course we renamed the Student Advisory Centre as a new charity called Help! It continues to operate to this day.

I knew very little about the record industry, but from what I saw at the record shop I could see that it was a wonderfully informal business with no strict rules. It had unlimited potential for growth: a new band could suddenly sweep the nation and be a huge hit, as the sudden craze for the Bay City Rollers, Culture Club, or the Spice Girls' shows. The music business is a strange combination of real and intangible assets: pop bands are brand names in themselves, and at a given stage in their careers they can practically guarantee hit records. But it is also an industry where the few successful bands are exceptionally rich and the bulk of the bands remain obscure and impoverished. The rock business is a prime example of the most ruthless kind of capitalism.

As a record retailer, Virgin was immune to the success or failure of an individual band just so long as there were bands whose records people were keen to buy. But we were restricted to living off our retail margin, which was small, and I saw that the real potential for making money in the record industry lay in the record companies.

For the time being Nik and I concentrated on building up the image of our shop. We continued to work on different ideas to make our customers as welcome as possible. We offered them headphones, sofas and beanbags to sit on, free copies of *New Musical Express* and *Melody Maker* to read, and free coffee to drink. We allowed them to stay as long as they liked and to make themselves at home.

Word of mouth began to spread, and soon people began to choose to buy records from us rather than from the big chains. It was as if they thought that the same album by Thin Lizzy or Bob Dylan somehow had a greater value if bought at Virgin rather than Boots. I felt enormous pride whenever I saw people carrying Virgin paper bags along Oxford Street. Our staff began to report that the same people were coming back every couple of weeks. With a loyal customer base, Virgin's reputation began to grow.

At the other end of the spectrum from buying records—the recording studios—I heard that conditions were extremely formal. Bands had to check in at an appointed time, bring all their equipment and set it up, and then leave according to the set timetable, taking all their equipment with them.

Since the studios were so overbooked, they would often have to record straight after breakfast. The idea of the Rolling Stones having to record "Brown Sugar" straight after finishing their bowls of cornflakes struck me as ridiculous. I imagined that the best environment for making records would be a big, comfortable house in the country where a band could come and stay for weeks at a time and record whenever they felt like it, probably in the evening. So during 1971 I started looking for a country house that I could convert into a recording studio.

In one copy of *Country Life* I saw a fairy-tale castle for sale in Wales for just £2,000. It seemed a bargain. I drove off to see it with Tom Newman, one of the early recruits to the Virgin mail-order company. He was a singer who had already released a couple of records, but was more interested in setting up a recording studio. When we arrived at the castle, we realized that the sales details had inexplicably forgotten to point out that this castle was actually in the middle of a housing estate.

Feeling tired and disappointed, Tom and I turned back and set off on the five-hour drive back to London. Thumbing through *Country Life* on the way home, I saw an advertisement for another property: the old manor house at Shipton-on-Cherwell, some five miles north of Oxford. We turned off the motorway and followed the signs to Shipton-on-Cherwell, drove through the village, and turned down a dead end that led to the Manor. The gates to the Manor were locked, but Tom and I climbed over the wall and found ourselves on the grounds of a beautiful seventeenth-century manor house built with the yellow Cotswold stone, which glowed in the late-afternoon sunshine. We walked around the outside of the house and both realized that this would be perfect.

When we called the estate agent the next morning, we discovered that the Manor had been on the market for a long time. With over fifteen bedrooms it was too big for a family house but too small to be converted into a hotel. The asking price was £35,000, but he agreed on £30,000 for a quick sale. I went to see Coutts, this time wearing a suit and a pair of black shoes, and asked for a loan. I showed them the sales figures that Virgin Mail Order and the Virgin shop on Oxford Street were achieving. I don't know how impressed they were by them, but they offered me a mortgage of £20,000. Some years later Coutts told me that if I ever came to see them looking remotely smart, they knew that I was in trouble.

The Coutts loan was a breakthrough for me: it was my first large debt, and I could see that I was almost in a position to buy the Manor. Although I had no money myself, my parents had put £2,500 aside for me, Lindi, and Vanessa, respectively, for when we were thirty, and I asked them if I could draw it down early and use it to buy the Manor. They both agreed, even though there was a risk that if the recording studio went bust, the bank would sell the Manor over my head at a knockdown price and the money would be lost. I was still looking at a shortfall of £7,500.

We were talking about the Manor over Sunday lunch at Shamley Green when my dad suggested that I should go and see Auntie Joyce. Auntie Joyce had no children of her own and had always been devoted to us. Her fiancé had been killed in the war, and she had never fallen in love again. She lived in Hampshire, and I drove over to see her that afternoon. As always she was both very straightforward and very generous. She had arranged everything.

"Ricky, I've heard about this Manor," she told me. "And I gather that Coutts have lent you some money."

"Yes."

"But not quite enough."

"No."

"Well, I'll step in with the balance. I want the same interest as Coutts," she said. "But you can delay paying it to me until you are able to."

I knew that Auntie Joyce was being extraordinarily kind to me and had probably accepted that she would never see the money again. What I didn't know was that she had remortgaged her house to raise the £7,500 to pass on to me and was having to pay interest on it herself. When I started thanking her, she brushed me aside.

"Look," she said, "I wouldn't lend you the money if I didn't want to. What's money for anyway? It's to make things happen. And I'm sure you'll make things happen with this recording studio just as you won that ten shillings off me when you learned to swim."

I promised myself that whatever happened, I would repay that money to Auntie Joyce with interest on top.

I had dealt with the estate agent only over the telephone, but after the money was transferred and I had bought the Manor, I went to his office to pick up the key.

"Can I help you?" he said, no doubt wondering what a scruff like me could possibly want in a smart estate agent's office.

"I've come to pick up the key to the Manor," I said. "I'm Richard Branson."

He looked astonished. "Yes, Mr. Branson," he said, pulling out a large iron key. "Here you are. The key to the Manor. Please sign here."

And with a flourish on his paper I picked up the key and drove off to take possession of the Manor.

Tom Newman, together with his friend Phil Newell, immediately set about converting the Manor outhouse into a recording studio. He wanted to install a state-of-the-art 16-track Ampex tape machine together with the best of everything else he could think of: a 20-channel desk, quadraphonic monitoring, phasing and echo facilities, and a grand piano. We both wanted to ensure that everything was as good as at the best studio in London. The Manor gradually took shape. Every weekend I drove up with Nik, and we would camp on the floor and knock out the partitions that had been put across the fireplaces, strip off the lino to get down to the original flagstone floors, and paint the walls. Lindi also came up and helped, as did most of the people involved in Virgin. Mum arrived one day with a grandfather clock, which she had just bought at Phillips.

"You'll need this," she said.

We put it in the hallway, and we kept our money in the casement. It's now standing in the Virgin upper-class lounge at Heathrow but without the money stuffed inside.

When the lease on Albion Street expired, I moved in with some friends around Notting Hill for a while as we carried on working in the crypt. Soon we were too crowded to stay in the crypt, and we found an old warehouse in South Wharf Road, near Paddington Station, which became the base for Virgin Mail Order. Although the mail-order business was busy and we had sacks of mail each day, we weren't actually making any profits.

One day I found myself driving beneath the Westway and into Maida Vale. As I drove over a humpback bridge, I saw a line of houseboats moored along the canal. With the water, lines of trees, boats brightly painted in reds and blues with flower beds on their rooftops, and various ducks and swans nosing around, it felt as if I was suddenly in the countryside.

Since I was brought up running wild in the country, I never really liked living in London and often felt that I never saw the sunshine or breathed any fresh air. Ever since our summer holidays in Salcombe I had always loved the water and the smells of boats—oil, tar, and ropes. I drove around to the local council office to inquire about houseboats and was told to go to the water board, which was responsible for allocating houseboats. They warned me that there was a long waiting list. If I applied now, I might eventually be allocated one in about five years' time. I didn't bother to apply but drove back to Little Venice and drove along Blomfield Road, hoping to find somebody on a houseboat who could tell me how to rent one. I felt sure that there must be a way round the system.

As I drove down Blomfield Road along the canal, my car broke down. This was not unusual. I got out and stared hopelessly at the bonnet.

"Do you want a hand with that?" someone called out in an Irish accent.

I turned around and saw an old Irishman on top of a houseboat fiddling with the stovepipe chimney.

"It'll be all right," I said, wandering over toward him. "What I'd really like a hand with is how to live on one of these boats."

Brendan Fowley straightened up.

"Well, now," he said. "There's a thing."

He took out a pipe and lit it, obviously delighted to have an excuse to stop work.

"You should go along to that boat over there," he said. "I've just sold it to someone, and that young lady has moved in. Now I don't know, but there are two bedrooms and she might be looking for a lodger. You'll have to go through a little wooden gate and along the towpath. She's the last boat before the bridge, and she's called *Alberta*."

I walked along the road, pushed open the leaning wooden door, and walked along the narrow towpath. At the last boat I peered into a round porthole and saw a fair-haired girl bent over in the kitchen.

"Hello," I said. "You must be Alberta."

"Don't be silly," she said, turning around. "That's the name of the boat. I'm called Mundy."

"Can I come in?" I asked. "My car's just broken down and I'm looking for somewhere to live."

Mundy was beautiful. Not only was she beautiful, but she had just moved a bed on board. We sat down and had some lunch, and before we knew what we were doing we were lying on the bed making love. Her name was Mundy Ellis, and I stayed the night with her and moved my suitcase on board the next morning. She had a Labrador called Friday, so with Mundy and Friday I had the week pretty well sewn up. We had the most romantic affair on *Alberta*, having dinner out on the roof in the summer nights, watching the ducks and other boats slip up and down the canal.

Mundy and I lived together for almost a year. She helped out with the Student Advisory Centre and then with the Manor. At that time everyone was taking drugs, and soon Mundy had taken a couple of LSD trips up at the Manor with Tom Newman. She brought some LSD back to London for me to try, and one evening she and two other friends, Rob and Caroline Gold, settled down on *Alberta* to have a trip. Rob decided that he wouldn't take any in case anything went wrong. I lived by the dangerous (and sometimes rather foolish) maxim that I am prepared to try anything once, and I took the little paper square. After a while my mind began to race. At first everything was fine. We listened to some music and went outside to watch the evening sky. But when we went back inside, everything started to go wrong: my vision began to tilt, and Mundy loomed in and out like a tiny eight-year-old child. I looked around the room at everyone else, smiling and chatting and laughing. But whenever I caught sight of Mundy, all I saw was a wizened creature rather like the red-coated dwarfish murderer in the movie *Don't Look Now*.

I hate being out of control, and I had no idea what to do. Although everyone else at *Student* and then later at Virgin took lots of drugs, I never really joined them. I prefer to have a great time and to keep my wits about me. I know that I've got to get up early the next morning, and so I've rarely been able to get smashed the night before. Utterly unused to this kind of thing and with the LSD charging through my system, I couldn't think straight. I finally went back outside and lay looking up at the sky. Mundy came out and hauled me into bed. When we started making love, I kept my eyes tightly closed, dreading what I would see if I opened them.

By the time the LSD trip was over, it became clear that my relationship with Mundy was also over. Even though she no longer looked like a murderous dwarf the next morning, I was never able to look at her in the same way again. Soon afterward, Mundy left *Alberta* and went up to the Manor, where she moved in with Tom Newman.

Chapter 5

"You look great just as you are. I wouldn't bother with any more clothes."

1971

Throughout the spring of 1971 Virgin Mail Order Records attracted many more customers. And although the company was growing, we were losing money. We offered large discounts on all records, but after spending time on the telephone ordering the records, paying for the postage, and paying for the staff and the shops, we weren't keeping up. Sometimes our customers pretended that they hadn't received the records, so we would have to send out a second copy, and often a third and so on. All in all we were gradually losing money, and before long we were £15,000 overdrawn.

In the spring I received an order for a large number of records from Belgium. Going to the companies that had published the requested records, I bought them directly from the companies, less the purchase tax that we had to pay on records sold in the United Kingdom. I then borrowed a van and drove down to Dover to take the ferry across to France and then drive on to Belgium. Some papers were stamped at Dover to confirm that so many records had been exported, but when I arrived at Calais I was asked for another document, a carnet that proved that I wasn't going to sell them en route in France. The British and the French tax authorities both charged purchase tax on records, while Belgium charged nothing, so the records in my van were effectively bonded stock. I did not have this carnet and to my disappointment was forced to return by ferry to Britain with the records still in my van.

As I drove back to London, however, it dawned on me that I was now carrying a van load of records that had apparently been exported. I even had the customs stamp to prove it. The fact that the French customs had not allowed me through France was unknown. I had paid no purchase tax on these records, so I could still sell them either by mail order or at the Virgin shop and make about £5,000 more profit than I could have done legally. Two or three more trips like this, and we would be out of debt.

As well as the £15,000 debt of Virgin Records, I had taken on the £20,000 mortgage on the Manor and the cost of converting the outbuildings into a recording studio. It seemed like the perfect way out. It was a criminal plan, and I was breaking the law. But I had always got away with breaking rules before. In those days I felt that I could do no wrong and that even if I did, I wouldn't be caught. I had not yet reached my twenty-first birthday, and somehow the normal everyday rules of life didn't seem to apply. On top of all this exuberance, I was about to fall head over heels in love with a beautiful American girl called Kristen Tomassi.

One day at the Manor I was looking for Bootleg, our Irish wolfhound. Unable to find her anywhere, I went upstairs along one of the corridors, opening all the bedroom doors and calling out "Bootleg! Bootleg!" In one tiny bedroom I flung open the door and found a lovely, tall American girl getting changed. Not only was she considerably more attractive than Bootleg, with a rather quizzical, naughty face, but she was by herself, wearing only an old pair of skintight jeans and a black bra.

"You look great just as you are," I said. "I wouldn't bother with any more clothes."

"Whatever are you shouting out about bootlegs for?" she asked.

"Bootleg's my dog. She's an Irish wolfhound," I said, adding rather irrelevantly, "and we've also got Beatrice."

Sadly, Kristen did put on a shirt, but I managed to keep her chatting for almost an hour before someone started shouting for me. She had come to England for a summer holiday and had met a musician who was doing some backing work at the Manor. She had come along with him for the ride.

We drove back to London in different cars. Kristen was with her musician boyfriend, I was by myself. As I followed her along the road, I wondered if we would ever see each other again. I followed them all the way down to London and finally decided to write a note to her. As I drove along I scrawled a note on a scrap of paper asking her to call me at seven o'clock. I waited until we reached the traffic lights at Acton, then jumped out of my car and ran up to theirs. I tapped on Kristen's window, and she rolled it down.

"I just wanted to say good-bye," I said, leaning in to give her a kiss on the cheek. "Have a good trip back to the States."

As I said this I secretively slipped my hand inside the car, reached down, and pushed my note into her left hand. As Kristen's fingers closed around mine, I let go of the note and smiled across at the boyfriend.

"Hope the recording went well," I said to him.

The lights changed and the cars in the traffic jam behind us started hooting. I tried to catch Kristen's eye, but she was staring straight ahead. My note was in her hand. I hopped back into my car and drove back to *Alberta*.

I sat by the telephone, refusing to make any calls, which was most unlike me, and waited until seven o'clock. Then Kristen called.

"I'm calling from a pay phone," she said. "I didn't want John to overhear."

"Can you step out of the phone box and catch a taxi?" I asked. "Come on around and see me. I live on a boat called *Alberta*. Ask the taxi driver to take you to Blomfield Road in Little Venice. There's a little wooden door in the fence which leads to the towpath."

There was a measured pause.

"It sounds like *Alice in Wonderland*," Kristen said. "I'll see you in ten minutes."

And with that Kristen came around and I had my second whirlwind romance on *Alberta*.

The next morning I was due to make what I hoped would be my final trip to Dover to pretend to export records. By this time I had made three trips, and we had clawed back the tax and made £12,000 profit. This last trip would provide enough money to pay off our overdraft. I could then give up the scam and concentrate on the business. It is impossible to know whether we really would have stopped, since making such easy money is addictive, but that was our intention. That morning I loaded up the van once again with records and set off for Dover. This time I was even more casual than normal, and after my papers were stamped I didn't even bother going on the ferry but simply drove around the dock and headed back for London. I was anxious to get back to *Alberta* to reassure myself that Kristen was still there. At Little Venice I walked along the towpath to the boat. It was the last week of May 1970, and the apple trees along the towpath were all in blossom.

Kristen had gone. In a panic I called her at her boyfriend's flat and put on an American accent when he answered the telephone.

"I'm looking for a Miss Kristen Tomassi," I said. "This is American Airlines."

"I'll just get her."

"Kristen," I hissed, "it's Richard. Pretend you're talking to a travel agent. And then call me back as soon as you can. Go to a pay phone."

"Thank you very much. I'll do that," Kristen said and rang off.

Fifteen minutes later the telephone rang. It was Kristen.

"Just hold the line a minute," I told her.

"Okay, Eddy," I said, holding my hand over the receiver. "Time to go."

Eddy was the Virgin driver who picked up all our record deliveries. He set off to the boyfriend's flat.

"Kristen," I said, "what's your number there? This is going to take some time."

I called her back, and we had a long chat about what we were doing. I spun every yarn I could think of. Twenty minutes later Eddy returned from the flat. He had all Kristen's clothes in a suitcase. He had told the boyfriend that Kristen was moving in with me.

"Kristen," I said, "you'd better come round here. I've got something to show you. It belongs to you."

I refused to reveal what it was. Her curiosity kindled, Kristen came around to *Alberta*. She was set upon saying good-bye to me and returning to America.

When she arrived, I held up her suitcase. She tried to grab it from me, but I opened it and threw her clothes all around the boat. Then I picked her up and carried her to the bedroom.

As Kristen and I spent the afternoon in bed, the customs and excise officials were planning to raid Virgin. It had never occurred to me that I wasn't the only person who had stumbled across this tax evasion scam. Many other much larger record shops were doing it, and they were being much more sophisticated than I. I was simply putting the records that should be exported for sale in our Virgin record shop on Oxford Street and stocking up the new shop in Liverpool, which was due to open the next week. The big operators were distributing their illegally "exported" records right across the country.

Later that night the telephone rang at around midnight. The caller refused to give his name, but what he had to say was terrifying. He warned me that my bogus trips to the Continent had been noticed and that I was about to be raided by the customs and excise office. He said that if I went out and bought an ultraviolet sunlamp from a chemist's shop and shone it on the records that I had bought from EMI, I would notice a fluorescent *E* stamped on the vinyl of all the records that were meant to have been exported to Belgium. He told me that I would be raided first thing tomorrow morning. When I thanked him, he told me that he was helping me because I had once stayed up late talking to a suicidal friend of his who had called me at the Student Advisory Centre. I suspected that he was a customs officer.

I called Nik and Tony and rushed out to buy two sunlamps from a late-night chemist on Westbourne Grove. We met at South Wharf Road and quickly pulled the records out of their sleeves. The ghastly truth was revealed: an E shone up at us from all the records we had bought from EMI for export. We began to run in and out of the warehouse, carrying piles of records into the van. We then made a terrible mistake: we assumed that the customs and excise officers would raid just the South Wharf Road warehouse. We therefore drove all the records around to the Oxford Street shop and put them on the racks to be sold. We had no idea that customs and excise officers have more powers of immediate search than the police. I had had the similar attitude to the church commissioners coming to Albion Street. It was all some great game, and I found it difficult to take very seriously. By the early hours of the morning we had taken all the E-stamped records to the Oxford Street shop and substituted some bona fide records for the warehouse stock.

Kristen and I set off early the next morning and walked from *Alberta* along the Grand Union Canal to South Wharf Road. I wondered when the raid would be. We crossed over the footbridge beside Saint Mary's Hospital and walked along the path. As we walked by the hospital there was a scream above us, and a body fell out of the sky and hit the railings beside us. I caught a glimpse of an old man's gray, unshaven face as he hit the railings. It was horrific. His body seemed to explode and a huge amount of entrails fell onto the ground or hung dripping in red-and-white shiny rings from the railing. He was naked apart from his white dressing gown, which quickly began to soak up the blood. Kristen and I were too shocked to do anything other than stop and stare. He was clearly dead on impact, his neck hung off from his body, and his back seemed to be broken in half. As we stared at the corpse, a hospital nurse came running over from the side door. There was nothing she could do. Someone else came rushing out with a white sheet and covered the body and the bits in the street. Kristen and I stood there, enveloped by silence until we became aware of the noises of everyday life—traffic, horns blowing, and birdsong.

"Are you all right?" the nurse asked us. "Do you want a cup of tea?"

We shook our heads and walked on. We were shaken, but it was another surreal twist to the start of our relationship. Two days ago we had met for the first time and I had slipped a clandestine note into her hand. We had enjoyed a fabulous night together on the boat. I had then driven to Dover and back, and had arranged for her suitcase to be stolen. All last night I'd spent scrabbling about with the records. Now somebody had killed himself right in front of us. Like me, I think Kristen must have simply suspended her disbelief about what was going on. We were living off adrenaline and bewilderment. At the South Wharf Road warehouse, we unlocked the doors and walked upstairs. But before we could reach my office there was a knock on the door. I opened it to find seven or eight men in brown macs.

"Are you Richard Branson?" they said. "We're customs and excise and we've got a warrant to inspect your stock."

These men were rather different from the two dowdy little accountants I had been expecting. They were bulky, tough men and very threatening. Some of my cocksure confidence evaporated, and I showed them into the warehouse.

"You're meant to have gone to Belgium yesterday," one of them said. "You can't get back this quickly."

I tried to laugh this off, and I watched as they began to check all the records with their sun-ray lamp. They grew increasingly worried when they couldn't find any illegal records. I enjoyed their bewilderment and tried to conceal my hope that we would get away with it. We began helping check all the records, handing them the records from the sleeves for them to inspect and restocking them on the shelves.

What I didn't realize until it was too late was that they were simultaneously busting our shops in Oxford Street and Liverpool and finding hundreds of illegal records.

"All right," the officer said, coming off the telephone. "They've found them. You'd better come with me. I'm arresting you. Come down to Dover with us and make a statement."

I couldn't believe it. I had always thought that only criminals were arrested and couldn't accept that I had become one. I had been stealing money from Customs and Excise. It wasn't some great game that involved my getting one up on the customs and excise office and getting off scot free: I was guilty.

At Dover I was charged under Section 301 of the Customs and Excise Act 1952: "That on 28th May, 1971 at Eastern Docks, Dover, you caused to be delivered to an officer a ship's manifest being a document produced for the purpose of an assigned matter, namely Customs, which was untrue in a material particular in that it purported to show the exportation of 10,000 gramophone records . . ."

And so on. I spent that night in a cell lying on a bare, black plastic mattress with one old blanket. The first part of my Stowe headmaster's prediction had come true: I was in prison.

That night was one of the best things that has ever happened to me. As I lay in the cell and stared at the ceiling, I felt complete claustrophobia. I have never enjoyed being accountable to anyone else or being out of control of my own destiny. I have always enjoyed breaking the rules, whether they were school rules or more general rules such as the idea that no seventeen-year-old can edit a national magazine. As a twenty-year-old I had lived life entirely on my own terms, following my instincts.

But to be in prison meant that all this freedom was taken away. I was locked in a cell and utterly dependent upon somebody else to open the door. I vowed to myself that I would never again do anything that would cause me to be imprisoned, or indeed do any kind of business deal that would embarrass me.

In the many different and varied business worlds I have inhabited since that night in prison, there have been many times when I could have succumbed to some form of bribe or could have had my way by offering one. But ever since that night in Dover prison I have never been tempted to break my vow. My parents had always drummed into me that all you have in life is your reputation: you may be very rich, but if you lose your good name, then you'll never be happy. The thought will always lurk at the back of your mind that people don't trust you. I had never really focused on what a good name really meant before, but that night in prison made me understand.

The next morning, Mum arrived to meet me at the court. I applied for legal aid, since I had no money to pay for a lawyer. The magistrate told me that if I applied for legal aid I would have to stay in prison, since I obviously had no money to pay for bail. If I wanted to be released, I would have to put up bail of £30,000. Virgin itself had no money that we could put up as security. The price of the Manor was £30,000, but using that wasn't an option since it was financed mainly by a mortgage. I had a pile of debt and no real money.

Mum told the magistrate that she would put up Tanyards Farm, her home, as security. I was overwhelmed by the trust she showed in me. We stared at each other across the court and both started weeping. The trust that my family had shown me had to be repaid.

"You don't have to apologize, Ricky," Mum said as we took the train back up to London. "I know that you've learnt a lesson. Don't cry over spilt milk, we've got to get on and deal with this head-on."

Over the summer I confronted the problem with far less shame than I would have done if my parents had added to the burden. I kept a clear head, I was sorry, I wouldn't do it again, and I negotiated an out-of-court settlement with the customs and excise office. The tax authorities in the UK are more interested in extracting money than in going through expensive court cases. On 18 August 1971, I agreed to pay £15,000 as an immediate payment with £45,000 to be paid in three installments over the next three years. The total was calculated as being three times the illegal profit that Virgin had made from avoiding the purchase tax. If I paid off the sums agreed, I would avoid a criminal record. But if I failed to pay it, then I would be rearrested and tried.

From that night in prison and the subsequent negotiations with the customs and excise office, I needed to work twice as hard to make Virgin a success. Nik, Tony, my South African cousin Simon Draper, and Chris Stylianou (who had both just joined Virgin) resolved to help keep me out of prison. They knew it could have been them and were grateful to me for carrying the can: we were all in it together, and it bound us ever closer together. In a desperate attempt to earn money to repay the settlement, Nik started opening Virgin record shops across the country, Simon began to talk about a record label, and Chris started exporting records for real. Incentives come in all shapes and sizes, ranging from a pat on the back to share options, but avoiding prison was the most persuasive incentive I've ever had.

The next two years were a crash course for us in how to manage cash. From being a completely relaxed company, which ran on petty cash from the biscuit tin and a series of unpaid IOU notes, we became obsessively focused. We used every penny of the cash generated from the shops, knowing that every pound we earned was another pound toward opening up another shop, which in turn was another pound toward paying off my customs and excise debt.

Eventually I was able to pay everything and relieve Mum of the bail she had put up. Three years later I was also able to repay Auntie Joyce her £7,500 with £1,000 on top for interest. If I had been unable to make these payments, the rest of my life could have been ruined: it is unlikely, not to say impossible, that someone with a criminal record would have been allowed to set up an airline or would have been taken seriously as a contender to run the national lottery.

We knew that we had to sell more records through the shops, overseas, and through mail order; to attract important artists like Cat Stevens or Paul McCartney to record at the Manor; and to set up a record label. What we didn't know was that even as we set out to do this, our first fortune was quietly making its way up the graveled drive to the Manor in the form of another van, this time carrying not illegal records but a young composer and his folk-singer sister up from London to act as backing musicians for a band. He was the third reserve guitarist on the musical *Hair*, and she was a folk singer who sang in pubs. At the back of their minds was the hope that they might be able to record some esoteric instrumental music when the rest of the band wasn't using the studio. Their names were Mike and Sally Oldfield.

Chapter 6

"There was a thin dividing line between what was hip and what wasn't, and Simon made Virgin the hippest place to be."

1971–1972

Before the postal strike nearly ruined us in January 1971, someone my age with a South African accent walked into my office at South Wharf Road and introduced himself as my cousin. Simon Draper had graduated from Natal University and come over to London with just £100 and the idea of staying over in London for a while. He was thinking of doing a postgraduate degree, perhaps following his brother, who had been a Rhodes scholar at Oxford, but in the meantime he was looking for a job.

Simon had sat next to my mother at a family dinner party over Christmas, and she had told him to get in touch with me. After Simon had exhausted the hospitality of both sides of his family over Christmas and New Year, he moved into a flat in London and tracked down the Virgin record shop in Oxford Street. Sandy O'Connell, the manager, told him to go over to see me at South Wharf Road, where he arrived just before lunch.

We went off to have something to eat at the Greek restaurant around the corner in Praed Street, where, over lukewarm meatballs, chips, and peas, Simon explained what he wanted to do. While he had been at Natal University, he had also worked on the South African *Sunday Times*. He told me stories of sitting up through Saturday night until the first edition was ready and then leaving work to go to a jazz club with the first edition tucked under his arm. We swapped stories about journalism and then moved on to music.

Simon was obsessed by music. Because I had left school so young and had never been to university, I had missed out on those long evenings spent lying around listening to music. Even though music was playing constantly in the *Student* basement, I was too busy calling up advertisers and negotiating with printers to absorb it. If I heard a record, I knew whether I liked it or not, but I couldn't compare it with some other band or recognize that it had been influenced by the Velvet Underground. It seemed to me that Simon had listened to every record released by every band. He didn't just casually enjoy the latest Doors album, he thoroughly understood what they were doing and how they had developed from their previous album and how this album compared with a whole catalog of music. He had hosted his own half-hour show on Natal Radio, and I soon realized that he knew more about music than anyone else I'd ever met.

We also talked about politics. Although I had been involved in various political demonstrations, such as the anti–Vietnam War march to Grosvenor Square, this was nothing compared with the brutality of South African politics. Simon, steeped in both music and politics, saw music as one way to make a political protest. One of Simon's fellow students was Steve Biko, who was then leading the all-black South African Students Organisation, and his tutor, a Marxist, had been shot by government-backed vigilantes in front of his own children. The South African government at that time did not tolerate any form of political dissent. Simon was not allowed to play any song with political or sexual connotations, like songs by Jimi Hendrix or Bob Dylan.

By the time we were drinking coffee I had persuaded Simon to work at Virgin. There was no awkward salary negotiation since everyone at Virgin was paid the same, £20 per week, and Simon agreed to be the record buyer for the Virgin record shop and the Virgin mail-order list.

Tony Mellor had moved from working on *Student* to compiling the record mail-order list. We were trying to sell *Student* to another magazine company, and although it had not been published for over a year, Tony kept producing dummies of the next issue for the purpose of impressing potential buyers. He was therefore happy to hand the record buying to Simon and to revert to the more political question of *Student*'s future. Tony simply gave Simon the one golden, unbreakable rule: "Virgin doesn't ever, ever stock Andy Williams!" And then he handed over the first joint of the morning.

"You don't need to worry," Simon said. "I'd be the last person to break that one."

From then on Simon was on his own, and I rather left him to it for the first few months. I was falling in love with Kristen and was trying to prevent her from going back to finish her architectural course in America. I offered her the job of further renovating the Manor:

"Come on!" I said. "You don't have to study for six years to qualify as an architect. Just start doing it!"

After not too much persuading she eventually agreed with me and set to work. She was a natural with perfect taste. With her long blond hair and fine, almost elfin face, Kristen soon became a familiar figure at all the auction rooms around London as she bid for large remarkable pieces of furniture for the Manor.

While Nik managed the costs of the mail-order company and the Virgin record shops, Simon began to define the mail-order list and the Virgin record shops themselves by choosing which records to stock. Simon's taste in music quickly became the single most critical element of the Virgin ethos. A record shop is not just a record shop, it is an arbiter of taste itself. I had no idea what music to promote, but Simon was full of wonderful plans to bring in unknown foreign albums unavailable elsewhere. There was a thin dividing line between what was hip and what wasn't, and Simon made Virgin the hippest place to be. He started importing records directly from America, flying them in to beat the competition. We only ever dealt in albums because singles either were crass or were loss leaders to promote albums. In the 1970s serious bands such as Pink Floyd, Yes, and Genesis rarely released singles. An album was seen as a combination of political statements, art, and a way of life. The serious bands didn't produce dance music; theirs was music to savor while lying down. There was a good deal of discussion about different recordings of the same songs, something that became especially interesting when the American albums arrived that had different covers from the British versions, sometimes even different versions of the same songs. These days CDs have been standardized to be mass marketed around the world.

As well as imports, notably from Germany, France, and America, and a furtive trade in live bootleg recordings, we also made a lot of money by dealing in deletions—recordings that had gone out of stock and were being sold off by the record company. Since we operated a mail-order business, we had hundreds of letters every day asking for special recordings. We thus knew which of these deletions actually had some residual demand, and it was comparatively simple for us to pick up the popular ones cheaply and sell them.

Most people assume that a record shop's skill lies in selling records. In fact, Virgin's success both in mail order and in the record shops lay in Simon's skill at buying records. He was able to pick out bands that did not sell through the mainstream shops and sell large numbers of them through Virgin. He knew so much about music that he knew which bands would sell even before they were a proven success. To that extent he was already using the antennae that enabled us to set up the record label two years later. Without Simon such a move would have been a blind step in the dark. Our other genius was John Varnom, who did all the promotion for the records and wrote the advertising slogans for the shops.

Virgin began to gather a broader reputation: with the best music playing in the shop and the warehouse all day, both the staff and the customers lying around smoking dope and talking about how to get hold of the highly prized American recording of *Aerosol Grey Machine* by Van Der Graaf Generator, and everyone enjoying plenty of sex, there was no better place for any self-respecting twenty-year-old to be.

But beneath that there was a business to run. At the Manor, building work dragged on. I dreaded every call from Tom Newman, who was fitting all the equipment, since he always asked for more money to buy some other piece of recording equipment. At the same time I had the customs fine, the mortgage, and the thought of prison hanging over me.

The mail-order business was doing well but mainly seemed to attract the serious music buyers who were looking for quite rare records, and it seemed difficult to expand it further. We realized that if we were going to make money, then it would have to come from opening up more Virgin record shops.

Nik and I began a program of serious expansion. Toward the end of 1971 and throughout 1972, we aimed to open a shop every month until by Christmas 1972 we had fourteen record shops—several in London and one in every big city across the country. As well as organizing all the records that the shops would stock, advertising the shops, choosing and training the staff to run them, and setting up the accounting systems to keep control of the money, we found that the timing of shop openings was crucial. After negotiating the lease until we were sure that the landlord would go no lower, we would push for a rent-free period for the first three months. This was the single most crucial element. We would not agree to open the shop unless this was in place, and as a result we walked away from a great many opportunities. When we opened, however, we knew that the record sales in the first three months would help pay for the rent on the previous shop that we had opened. The sales also demonstrated, without committing a huge overhead, whether the site we had chosen would attract enough people off the streets to make the shop viable.

As we opened these shops we learned all sorts of lessons that stood us in good stead for the future. We always looked for the cheaper end of the high street, where we might attract shoppers to come a few extra yards off the beaten track without us having to pay an exorbitant rent. We also chose areas where the teenagers hung out, such as near the Clock Tower in Brighton or Bold Street in Liverpool. We always asked the local teenagers where the best place for a record shop would be. There are many invisible lines in a town that people will not cross, and a street can change character in the space of twenty yards.

The other unique thing about record retailing is the speed with which records move. When a big release is out, like the latest David Bowie record, you can measure its sales in hours. You therefore need to keep right on top of the shop to find out what's selling that day. You can then use that information to rearrange the record displays in the other shops. If you run out of the key records that are selling that day, then you of course lose the opportunity to sell them, and the buyer will head off to the next shop to pick it up. And once you've lost that chance to sell a copy of *Hunky Dory,* you never get it back again. There are no repeat sales of the same record. So although you will always stock *Hunky Dory,* up to 70 percent of its sales will happen in the first two weeks of its release.

At first Virgin promoted its image as a place where people could come and spend time listening to and choosing their records, with a distinct emphasis on elitist, hip taste. As well as the more mainstream records, we wanted to show them more interesting ones. Our shops flatly refused to sell the mass-market teenybopper records such as the Osmonds and the Sweet, which were storming the charts. Despite Simon's persuasive arguments about style, our refusal to stock Gary Glitter and all the glam rock stars always slightly worried me since I could see the short-term income we were turning away. Simon assured me, however, that if we stuck to our image we would keep our integrity and build up more customers: "It's the Andy Williams rule," he told me. "We're not in that market."

The shop at 130 Notting Hill Gate became one of the best Virgin record shops. Simon started working above it, and in the shop we laid our cushions on the floor so that people could lie there all day. We knew that we were successful when people started coming up to London just to go to a Virgin record shop. If we could have sold marijuana, we would have done so. In fact, I suspect that some of the staff did. Selling records, chatting up the customers, recommending which music to buy, reaching under the counter for the latest bootleg, heading off to pubs and clubs to hear more bands play— it became a way of life.

When we opened our Virgin record shop in Bold Street, Liverpool, in March 1972, I proudly saw that we took £10,000 in the first week. A week later the figure was £7,000, and then the following week the takings were down to £3,000. By the middle of the summer they had dropped to £2,000, so I went up there to see what was going wrong. The shop was packed. There were rockers all jammed into one corner, mods in another, and hippies draped all over the floor near the till. All kinds of music were playing. But nobody was buying anything. Everyone was happily stoned and having a great time, but nobody could get to the till, and they were keeping other shoppers out of the store. The policy of treating our shops like clubs was out of control. For the next month we had someone at the door who gently warned people as they went in that they were going into a shop, not a night-club; we put in brighter lights and moved the counter and the till nearer the window. It was a narrow line between maintaining the shop's atmosphere and keeping it profitable. The takings at last recovered.

Throughout this expansion, one of our main difficulties was getting hold of the records to sell. Some record companies, including PolyGram, refused to supply us because we were discounting and therefore offending the main retailers. Equally, other record companies refused to supply us since they doubted our ability to pay. Nik and Chris Stylianou ("Chris the Greek," who had joined as our sales manager) called all the possible suppliers and eventually found an extraordinary solution: a tiny record shop in Ealing called Pop In, run by Raymond Laren. Raymond was prepared to use his account to buy records on our behalf. It was good business for him since he would order all our records on top of his own orders, charge a 5 percent margin, and pass them on to us.

When we first struck this deal with Raymond, we would give him the list of records to add to his orders, Tony or Simon would drive around and pick them up, and we'd drive them to the three or four Virgin shops. Pop In was a tiny shop with matte-black walls and peeling posters of *Sergeant Pepper* and Neil Young. It was difficult to squeeze in and out with the boxes of records, but we managed to cope. Over the next year as we opened up more and more shops, the number of records passing through Raymond's shop grew. Soon Raymond was ordering thousands of records from the record labels and we were sending a van to collect them.

We kept trying to deal with the record labels directly, but they continued to ignore us. Soon Virgin became one of the largest record chains in the country. The scenes at Raymond's shop were farcical: a line of vans unloaded hundreds of cases of records at the front door, and people staggered with them through the shop to the back door, where they were loaded onto another line of vans to take them around to the Virgin shops. Something had to give. We were still having to pay an extra 5 percent to buy our records through Raymond. Finally Nik and I went back to the record labels and pointed out what was happening. They agreed to sell records to us directly, and Raymond Laren's Ealing-comedy earner was over. His record shop reverted to selling a few dozen records each week, and his accountants were left to puzzle over what had gone wrong with his amazing record shop.

During 1972 Simon fell in love with a South American girl and told me that he was going to leave Virgin and live in Chile with her. The Manor was at last open for artists to record in, there were twenty Virgin record shops, and the mail-order business was doing well. Simon had been working with me for a year, and although neither of us had ever expected him to stay for more than a few months, I suddenly realized how vital he was to Virgin. His choice of music had established the Virgin record shops as *the* place to go and buy records. It was hip to spend an afternoon mooching around the Virgin record shops, whereas no self-respecting teenager would spend an afternoon hanging around Woolie's.

The credibility that Simon had always talked about and the sales of the Osmonds, which we had forgone, had worked. The music press now discussed which artists Virgin was promoting. When we put an eclectic German band called Tangerine Dream in our shop windows, it became a talking point. Record labels started contacting us and asking whether the Virgin record shops could run special promotions on their bands.

I tried to persuade Simon to stay, but he was set on leaving. His girlfriend went to Chile first, with Simon poised to join her in a month's time. During that month he suddenly received a "Dear Simon" letter from her, which called everything off. He was desperately disappointed, but at the same time it became clear that his future lay in London rather than either South America or even South Africa. Since Virgin now had the record shops and the recording studio, we started talking about the third part of the grandiose dream that we had originally discussed over our first lunch at the Greek restaurant: the Virgin record label.

If Virgin set up a record label, we could offer artists somewhere to record (for which we could charge them), we could publish and release their records (from which we could make a profit), and we had a large and growing chain of shops where we could promote and sell their records (and make the retail profit margin). The three businesses were mutually compatible and would also benefit the bands we signed since we could reduce prices at the Manor, the manufacturing end, and increase promotion at the shops, the retail end, while still making our own profit.

Simon and I drew up an agreement whereby he would set up and run the new Virgin record label, Virgin Music. He would own 20 percent of the company, which would henceforth be separate from the Virgin record shops. And the first person whom Simon and I wanted to sign up was that third reserve guitarist from *Hair:* Mike Oldfield.

Mike Oldfield had had a difficult childhood with an alcoholic mother, and he had often locked himself up in his room in the attic, where he taught himself how to play all kinds of instruments. At the age of fourteen he had made his first recording with his sister Sally, singing folk music. He and his sister formed a folk duo called Sallyangie and signed to Transatlantic Records. By fifteen he had left home and had become a guitarist alongside Dave Bedford with Kevin Ayers's group, the Whole World.

For a couple of weeks in October 1971, Mike was signed as a session guitarist to a singer called Arthur Louis who was recording at the Manor. Mike soon started chatting to Tom Newman and one day finally screwed up the courage and gave him a tape of his own music. Mike had recorded this tape himself, laboriously overdubbing many different instruments onto the same tape. It lasted eighteen minutes, was untitled, and had no vocals. Tom listened to it and described it as "hyper-romantic, sad, poignant, and brilliant." Tom then played it to Simon when he was next up at the Manor. Astonished by it, Simon tried to help Mike approach some record companies, but they all turned him down.

A year later Simon and I were sitting on the houseboat, and we finally decided to start a record company. We called up Mike. To our delight he had still not signed with anyone. Feeling completely rejected by the record industry and overwhelmed that we seriously wanted to release his music, he came straight over to the houseboat to see us. I suggested that Mike should go back to the Manor and live there, and then whenever the recording studio was free, he and Tom Newman could get together and work on his record.

"I'll need to rent some instruments, though," Mike warned me.

"Like what?" I pulled out my diary and prepared a list.

"A good acoustic guitar, a Spanish guitar, a Farfisa organ, a Fender precision bass, a good Fender amplifier, a glockenspiel, a mandolin, a mellotron."

"What's that?" I drew a circle around it.

"It's not absolutely necessary," Mike conceded. "A triangle, a Gibson guitar. Oh, and some chimes, of course."

"What are chimes?" I asked.

"Tubular bells."

I wrote down "tubular bells" and set about finding all these instruments in a music magazine. The guitar cost £35, the Spanish guitar was £25, the Fender amplifier £45, the mandolin £15, and the triangle a bargain at £1. The tubular bells cost £20.

"Twenty pounds for tubular bells?" I said. "They'd better be worth it."

Above: My fetish for sweaters started at an early age.
Left: I have never liked desks. *Both Private Collection.*

Above: First edition of *Student*, with cover designed by Peter Blake. *Private Collection.*
Left: Speakers' Corner, Hyde Park, 1968. Debating the decade away on a soap box with Jane Butters. *Peter Pearson Lund.*

Above: Kristen and me at the Manor
Studios with Bootleg, who was named after
those albums in white sleeves we sold
under the counter.

Above right: Just what exactly was it that the
incredibly handsome Nik saw in Kristen's sister Meryll? *Both Private Collection.*

Above: Roger Dean's original design
for our record label—Virgin Records.
© *Roger Dean 1972.*

Left: Listening to an early tape of
The Rolling Stones with a very young
Mick Jagger. *Private Collection.*

Right: *Tubular Bells*—the first release on Virgin Records. It made Mike Oldfield (left) the biggest-selling artist of the 1970s and us our first fortune—to lose. *Private Collection.*

Below: *Tubular Bells* and *Never Mind the Bollocks* record sleeves.

Right: With Boy George before heroin nearly destroyed his life and his musical career. *Rex Features.*

Above: After years of trying, we finally manage to sign The Stones. *Rex Features.*

Above: Making the best of a sad day, Friday March 4, 1992. Signing the deal with Colin Southgate and Jim Fifield of Thorn EMI. *Rex Features.*

Right: I take Janet Jackson on a balloon trip and threaten to use her as ballast. She signs with Virgin instead. *Mark Lockwood/Virgin Airship and Balloon Company.*

Right: I am lucky to share many of my experiences with my long-suffering parents.
Below Right: With father, Ted.
Both by Thierry Boccon-Gibod.

Above: Family album. *Roberta Booth.*
Below: Two loyal sisters, Lindi and Vanessa. *Private Collection.*

Above and left: Family album.
Above by Thierry Boccon-Gibod/left by Frank Spooner Pictures/Thierry Boccon-Gibod.

Below: Our lovely houseboat—home and headquarters.
Rex Features.

Right: Our own Virgin Island. Necker is one of the most beautiful jewels in the Caribbean and, with its great room **(above)** in the house on the hill, it remains my favorite getaway. *Both by Thierry Boccon-Gibod.*

Below: Impressing only the children and a couple of passing sea gulls, I arrive for our wedding with a box of chocolates in my teeth. *Private Collection.*

Left: Our wedding on Necker. A week later Sam said of a friend's wedding, "But they can't be getting married. They haven't had any children yet." *Private Collection.*

Right: Meeting the man I most admire in the world.

Below: With Princess Diana. *Both by Thierry Boccon-Gibod.*

Above: Richard and Per after rescue. *HMS Gannet, Royal Navy, Crown Copyright*

Right: Painful good-bye to Sam. *Thierry Boccon-Gibod*

Above: Balloons, balloons, balloons . . . Inflating the world's biggest balloon is a 48-hour project and a lot can go wrong. *Thierry Boccon-Gibod.*
Left: With Per on yet another photo shoot while we were waiting for the weather to come good for our round-the-world flight. *Rex Features/ Cam II/Virgin.*
Below: A day of contrasts—the beauty of the Atlas Mountains followed by a night of terror. *Thierry Boccon-Gibod.*

Above: Learning the tricks of the trade that Alex Ritchie had used to save our lives. *Frank SpoonerPictures/Thierry Boccon-Gibod.*

Right: Seconds before liftoff on our Atlantic crossing in 1987. *Private Collection.*

Above: Passing Bishop Rock Lighthouse off the Scilly Isles and bringing the Blue Riband back to Britain. *Private Collection.*

Right: Triumphant trip up the Thames with Margaret Thatcher and the crew. *Zoom Photographic.*

Above: Randolph Fields and me at a press conference before the inaugural flight to New York.

Left: Playing a prank during our inaugural flight with cricketers Ian Botham and Viv Richards.

Below: Liftoff! *All by Alan Davidson*

Right: Talking to and learning from passengers. *Thierry Boccon-Gibod.*

Below: Sir Freddie wishes us better luck than he had. *Arthur L. Field.*

Below right: Informal press conference on the plane about BA's dirty-tricks campaign. *Thierry Boccon-Gibod.*

Below: Outside the court. A moment to savor. *Rex Features/Today.*

Left: Lord King of BA and I bump into each other a few days after Virgin's victory. *Rex Features/Richard Young.*

Below: Dave Gaskill's view of our assault on the Iraq's president's stronghold. *Dave Gaskill.*

Above: Former British prime minister Edward Heath and King Hussein helped us to get the hostages out of Iraq. They celebrated in style on the flight home. *Mirror Syndication International.*

Above: Sometimes in the line of duty you have to make a fool of yourself. *Frank Spooner Pictures/Thierry Boccon-Gibod.*

Above right: Launching Virgin Brides—what a drag! *Rex Features/Julian Makey.*

Left: The "pirate" attacks Concorde at Heathrow. *Virgin Atlantic Press Office.*

Below left: Launching Virgin Vie. *Virgin Vie.*

Below: On the South Africa inaugural this friendly cat nearly removed my beard permanently. *Thierry Boccon-Gibod.*

Above: Two acres of Times Square, New York, 1992. How things have moved on since the Notting Hill pillows of 1972. *Thierry Boccon-Gibod.*

Left: On top of the world! *Mark Greenberg/ Visions.*

Chapter 7

"It's called Tubular Bells. I've never heard anything like it in my life."

1972–1973

S ince Mike Oldfield was the first artist we signed, we had no idea what sort of a contract to offer him. Luckily Sandy Denny, originally a singer with Fairport Convention who had now gone solo, had recently recorded at the Manor. She had become a friend of mine, and I asked her for a copy of her contract with Island Records. This was apparently a standard Island Records deal, and we retyped it word for word, changing "Island Records" to "Virgin Music" and "Sandy Denny" to "Mike Oldfield." It set out that Mike would make ten albums for Virgin Music and receive a 5 percent royalty on 90 percent of the wholesale value of the record (10 percent was kept by the record company to pay for packaging costs and breakages). Since Mike had no money, we put him on the standard Virgin salary we all received, £20 a week, which we would deduct from any future royalties if they ever materialized. Although Simon and I loved Mike's music, we never thought that we'd make any money from it.

It took Mike well into 1973 to record what became known as *Tubular Bells*. It was a fantastically complicated sequence of recordings to make, and he and Tom Newman went over it again and again in the recording studio, mixing, dubbing, and fine-tuning all the different layers of music. Mike played over twenty different instruments and made over 2,300 different recordings until he was happy. In the meantime we were still trying to rent out the Manor to any band we could find, so Mike was often interrupted and had to clear his kit out of the recording studio to make way for the Rolling Stones or Adam Faith.

Frank Zappa had made his reputation as one of the most original, innovative, and irreverent performers in rock music. His albums, like *We're Only* in It for the Money and Weasels Ripped My Flesh, were filled with biting satire, and when he came up to the Manor to investigate the possibilities of recording there, I felt sure he would appreciate a joke.

I drove Frank up from London, enthusing him with a description of the wonderful manor house in which the studio was situated. But instead of taking the road to Shipton, I made a detour to nearby Woodstock. I turned off the road under a majestic arch and drove down a long gravel driveway to the door of a magnificent house. "I'll park the car," I told Frank. "Just knock on the door and tell them who you are." The door was opened by a uniformed footman. Funnily enough, he didn't recognize Frank Zappa and was not amused to be told the long-haired musician had come to stay. Did Zappa know, the footman asked, that he was knocking at the door of Blenheim Palace, the ancestral seat of the Dukes of Marlborough?

Frank got back into the car, swearing that he could see the funny side of it. But he never did record at the Manor.

Throughout that summer our neighbor tried to close the Manor down. Although we had planning permission to use the recording studio during the day, we couldn't use it at night, which was when all the artists really wanted to play. By definition a recording studio is soundproof, but one of our neighbors reckoned that he could hear the music, which kept him awake, and kept appealing against our application to record at night. Unless we could record at night, the Manor would have few attractions over the other recording studios, and bands would stop coming out of London.

We engaged in clandestine warfare against this neighbor. We rigged up a pile of tin cans in the recording studio, looped a long piece of string around them at the bottom of the pile, and then ran it along the drive and down to the road. We took it in turns to sit in the hedge and hold the string. We sat there all night, and I remember the smell of the cowslips and grass and the heavy rustling of the badgers. But it was the rubbery squeaking of our neighbor's shoes as he walked along the road and came up our drive we were really listening out for. When we heard him coming, we yanked the string, which sent all the cans in the recording studio clattering to the floor. No matter what the musicians were doing, they had all to run into the Manor and start drinking cups of coffee. By the time the neighbor arrived, all he could see was a group of people sitting around the kitchen table. When he started calling the police, the same trick worked. We pulled the string as soon as the police car came around the corner. After several apparent false alarms, the police stopped coming, but the neighbor was still blocking our application to record at night.

We were still using this trick when Paul and Linda McCartney came to the Manor to record *Band on the Run*. It was June and the nights were still and hot, heavy with the smell of jasmine coming across the courtyard. Linda McCartney kept opening the door to the recording studio to let in fresh air. I was on watch in the hedge outside, and every now and then I heard snatches of music, so I ran back to shut the door. When I was settled back in the hedge I heard Linda McCartney throw open the door and shout, "Who keeps shutting this damned door?" Luckily our neighbor didn't come out that week, because I doubt whether the McCartneys would have appreciated a pile of tins cascading onto them as they recorded, followed by a mad dash to the kitchen.

One day the front doorbell rang, and I found an elderly couple standing there. They asked me whether I was having trouble with Mr. Sawtell, the neighbor. When I told them that he was the only person who was appealing against our planning permission, they told us that he had done the same to them when he moved in. They had wanted to convert a barn for their elderly mother to live next to them, but Mr. Sawtell had blocked it until one day he had asked for some money. When they gave him £500, he withdrew his appeal.

"He's just after a backhander," the elderly couple said. "Somebody should stop him."

The next day I bought a small tape recorder with a microphone, which I stuck to the inside of my shirt. I went around to see Mr. Sawtell and asked him whether there was any way in which he would withdraw his appeal since it was in danger of putting me out of business.

"Well, I've incurred heavy costs while I've been doing this," he said. "If you pay them, then I'll consider withdrawing my complaint."

"How much would that be?" I asked.

"Five thousand pounds."

"That's a vast figure," I said. "You must have had a whole law firm working on the case."

"It's been expensive," Mr. Sawtell said.

"Should I make the check payable to your lawyers?"

"No, no. Just make it payable to me."

I promised to think about what he had told me, and that afternoon I wrote to him enclosing a copy of the recording and suggesting that he might like to withdraw his complaint. I heard no more from him, and the Manor was granted the right to record at night.

• • •

On 22 July 1972 Kristen and I were married at the tiny church at Shipton-on-Cherwell. I had just turned twenty-two, and Kristen was still twenty. We had known each other only since May of the previous year. I still have a copy of the invitation that we sent out for the party before the wedding. It reads: "Kristen and I have decided to get married, and we thought that this would be a good excuse for a party. There will be a pig on a spit, so please come since the pig will not last. The Scaffold will be playing." One of the best things about the Manor was that it lent itself to having wonderful parties. We had bands who were happy to play, a river in which to swim, huge rooms with ancient fireplaces, and a cloistered courtyard, which caught the sun.

I have always enjoyed parties, and I love throwing the Virgin staff together. It's an important part of life at Virgin. After all, if the receptionist gets to meet the A&R person face-to-face, people will help each other out more if there's a problem. Likewise, if the shop staff get to know the record staff and so on. At Virgin we've always had staff parties, and we often get away for the weekend where people can really let off steam. Over the years the parties have got bigger and bigger, but the theme is always the same: glorious irresponsibility for the night. In our early days most of the hotels around Brighton and Bournemouth banned us after one party when my staff handcuffed me naked to some railings outside. I managed to knock the handcuffs off with a brick. I then charged into the dining room with a fire hose, pumping water at full volume.

Our wedding barbecue was a great feast with all the villagers from Shipton-on-Cherwell mixing with the Virgin staff and a great many of the rock bands around at the time. The wedding day was extraordinary throughout. As we were waiting at the church for Kristen to arrive, a huge articulated lorry started to squeeze its way down the narrow lane toward us. Nobody could understand what it was doing, until a tiny old lady in a blue suit with a blue hat jammed on her head climbed out.

"I'm not too late, am I?" Granny called out.

The lorry had crashed into her car coming through Oxford, and she had insisted that the driver take her to our wedding.

My parents gave us a beautiful old Bentley with red leather seats and a walnut dashboard as a wedding present. Although it tended to break down as much as my Morris Minor, it was supremely comfortable to sit in while we were towed along.

One of Kristen's bridesmaids was her sister Meryll, and Nik was my best man. At the reception afterward it became clear that there was a certain chemistry between them, and late that night they headed off toward a room in the Manor. By the time Kristen and I returned from our honeymoon, Nik and Meryll had announced that they too were getting married.

Nik and Meryll were married even faster than Kristen and I: their wedding was in the winter of 1972, just five months after they had met. Kristen and I found Nik and Meryll's marriage a little claustrophobic: I would spend all day with Nik at South Wharf Road, and then I would also see him and Meryll together in the evenings. Unfortunately, one of the reasons why Kristen had come to England was to escape from her family, and now she found that she and her sister had married two men who practically lived in each other's pockets. "Incestuous" wasn't the word for it. On top of that, Nik and I, who had run Virgin very much as a singles company, suddenly found ourselves both married, which was something of a culture shock.

Throughout the winter of 1972 and the spring of 1973 Mike Oldfield was living at the Manor and recording *Tubular Bells*. I think this was the happiest time of his life. He was there with Tom Newman, who was obsessed by the technology of recording and with whom he could endlessly refine the recordings; and Mundy was still there. When Kristen and I drove up to the Manor on a Friday night, we would find Mike, Tom, and Mundy sitting on cushions on the floor, stoking up the vast fire and listening to the latest tapes. They were oblivious to the outside world. *Tubular Bells* was finally ready for release in May 1973.

We knew that we had something extraordinary on our hands when we started selling *Tubular Bells* into the trade. Simon took the recording along to the sales conference at Island Records, who planned to distribute the album. They were all in a large conference room at a hotel near Birmingham. They had already had to listen to hours of music. These men had heard it all before—literally. Simon put on *Tubular Bells*, and they listened to the first side in its entirety. When it finished, there was an outburst of applause. This was Simon's first sales conference, and so he had no idea that it was unprecedented. He never again heard a room full of world-weary salesmen applauding a new record.

On 25 May 1973 Virgin Music released its first four albums: Mike Oldfield's *Tubular Bells; Flying Teapot* by Gong; *Manor Live,* a jam session from the Manor led by Elkie Brooks; and *The Faust Tapes* by Faust, a German band.

Nineteen seventy-three was an extraordinary year for rock and pop music. The summer saw the singles chart dominated by the glam rock of

Suzi Quatro, Wizzard, Gary Glitter, and the Sweet. But there was also a large Motown contingent with Stevie Wonder, Gladys Knight and the Pips, the Jackson Five, and Barry White. At the other end of the spectrum from these singers were Lou Reed with "Take a Walk on the Wild Side" and 10cc with "Rubber Bullets."

The album charts were headed by David Bowie at Number 1 with *Aladdin Sane,* the first proof of how he could reinvent himself to stay at the top. Below him were the Beatles with their 1962–1966 and 1967–1970 double albums, Pink Floyd with *Dark Side of the Moon,* Lou Reed's *Transformer,* and Roxy Music's *For Your Pleasure.*

In the face of this competition, we had to fight hard to attract attention for Virgin's first four releases. Apart from *Manor Live,* which was really just a regular jamming session, the other three did very well. Faust won great praise in the press. "Faust are probably the most exciting and original band to emerge from Europe in a long time," wrote *Melody Maker. New Musical Express* (*NME*) picked out Faust as the coolest band around. We offered their album at the price of a single, which immediately fired sales, and it went straight into the charts at Number 28. This marketing ploy also won attention for the new Virgin record label, although probably more on the grounds of foolhardiness than good judgment.

At forty-eight pence a record, Faust sold 40,000 copies in the first week and 100,000 copies after a month. They made esoteric music. The fact that they had previously been signed to the German classical music label Deutsche Grammophon gives some idea of their sophistication. For their album cover, Simon went to the Rowan Gallery in the West End with Uwe Nettelbeck, their manager (a leading political writer for *Der Spiegel*), where they chose a Bridget Riley painting called *Rise.* In short Faust carried a lot of intellectual clout: they were a band for people who were serious about their music, about as far away on the music spectrum from Donny Osmond or David Cassidy as it was possible to get. At one of their concerts in London they stopped by the side of the road and picked up a construction worker who was using a pneumatic drill. They took him along to the concert with them and set him up on stage, where he drilled through lumps of concrete as they played.

The other three albums we released were priced at the normal retail price of £2.19. Gong's *Flying Teapot* did quite well. *Melody Maker* wrote: "Once they stop chanting about Radio Gnome and cups of tea it's really excellent; flowing rock themes, punctuated by weird effects. It's a great pity that much of the music is hidden behind the silly lyrics." Gong's guitarist was Steve

Hillage, one of the best guitarists in the world, who some people thought was somewhat wasted within Gong. It was clear that Gong would never threaten Pink Floyd in the charts.

But of Virgin's first four albums it was *Tubular Bells* that really captured people's imaginations: it was completely original and immediately spellbinding. People found it addictive and played it again and again not only to listen to the music but also to marvel at how Mike had woven it all together. I remember reading a review in *NME* that I had to reread several times before I realized that although I would never understand what the critic was actually saying, he was clearly raving about it. *NME* was the single most influential music paper, and for it to praise *Tubular Bells* meant that everyone would look out for it.

Aside from the reviews, I knew that as soon as we could get people to listen to *Tubular Bells* once, it would take off. As one critic correctly said, "One hearing should provide sufficient proof." The problem was getting that hearing. I called up every radio producer I could to try to persuade them to play *Tubular Bells*. But at that time three-minute singles dominated radio music, and there was no room for a forty-five-minute piece of music without words. Radio 3 turned it down because it wasn't Mozart, and Radio 1 turned it down because it wasn't Gary Glitter.

For the first two weeks, sales of *Tubular Bells* were stillborn. Then I invited John Peel, a respected British DJ, over to *Alberta* for lunch. We had known each other since *Student,* when I had interviewed him, and he had also started his own record label, Dandelion. He was the only person who played serious rock music on the radio, and his show was our only chance of winning airtime for *Tubular Bells*. We all had lunch on *Alberta* and then settled down on the sofas. I put on *Tubular Bells*. He was amazed.

"I've never heard anything like it," John finally said.

Later that week we listened to John Peel's laconic voice coming out of the radio. I was sitting on the deck of the houseboat with Mike Oldfield and everyone from Virgin:

"Tonight I'm not going to play a whole lot of records. I'm just going to play you one by a young composer called Mike Oldfield. It's his first record, and it's called *Tubular Bells*. I've never heard anything like it in my life. It's released by Virgin, a brand-new record label, and it was recorded at Virgin's own studios in Oxfordshire. You'll never forget this."

With that *Tubular Bells* started. I was lying on the sofa. Everyone was lounging around in deep armchairs or on the rug, and we passed around beer and wine, cigarettes, and joints. I tried to relax. I could see everyone else lying there totally spellbound by the music. But I kept worrying. I find it impossible to stop my brain from churning through all the ideas and possibilities facing me at any given moment, and then I wondered how many people were listening to the *John Peel Show*. How many of those would go out and buy *Tubular Bells* the next day? Would they wait until Saturday, or would they have forgotten about it by then? Would they come to the Virgin shops or order it from Smith's? How fast would we receive the royalties? How many copies would we have to reprint? How should we break it in America? On one level I was absorbed in the music, but I felt like an outsider. I couldn't lose myself in it like Simon or Nik or my lovely new assistant, Penni, a real beauty with long black wavy hair and a generous smile. I was too aware that Virgin needed to sell a lot of copies to make money for next month's Customs and Excise repayment. I knew that *Flying Teapot* and *The Faust Tapes* were hardly going to knock the Rolling Stones or Bob Dylan off the charts. But *Tubular Bells* was extraordinary: something must happen from tonight's broadcast. Virgin would never be able to afford to buy such a length of radio time to advertise it.

Mike Oldfield sat in silence. He leaned against Penni and stared straight at the radio. I wondered what was going through his head. I had wedged above one of the picture frames a sleeve of *Tubular Bells,* which showed a giant tubular bell suspended over the sea with a wave breaking in the foreground. Mike stared at it as if he were staring out to sea. A greedy thought swam in the murky depths of my mind: perhaps he was already dreaming up another album.

All the next day the phones rang with orders from record shops for *Tubular Bells*. As well as choosing to break all tradition by playing it in its entirety, John Peel also reviewed *Tubular Bells* for *The Listener:*

On the all too frequent occasions when I'm told that a record by a contemporary rock musician is a work of "lasting importance" I tend to reach for my hat and head for the wide open spaces. Today these experts would probably tell you that in 20 years' time collectors will still be enthusing over the records of such weighty bands as Yes and Emerson, Lake & Palmer. I'm ready to bet you a few shillings that Yes and ELP will have vanished from the memory of all but the most stubborn and that the Gary Glitters and Sweets of no lasting value will be regarded as representing the true sound of the Seventies.

Having said that, I'm going to tell you about a new recording of such strength, energy and real beauty that to me it represents the first breakthrough into history that any musician regarded primarily as a rock musician has made. Mike Oldfield . . .

John Peel had an enormous following, and what he said was picked up by thousands of people across the country.

We arranged for both Gong and Faust to tour the country, but it was the grand *Tubular Bells* concert planned for 25 June that I hoped would bring the national press to witness the music celebrity of the moment. We made the *Tubular Bells* concert into an unmissable event. We managed to have Mick Taylor, then the Rolling Stones' guitarist, and Steve Hillage and Hatfield and the North all agree to play various instruments, and Viv Stanstall from the Bonzo Dog Doodah Band agreed to be on stage and announce the instruments as he did on the record.

On the day of the concert Mike came around to see me on the houseboat.

"Richard," he said quietly, "I can't go through with this concert tonight."

"But it's all arranged," I said.

"I simply can't go ahead," he repeated in a deathly whisper.

I felt a wave of despair. I knew Mike could be as stubborn as I when he wanted to be. I tried to forget that the whole concert was arranged, the tickets sold, and even television coverage agreed. I couldn't use any of that as leverage since it would only strengthen Mike's resolve. I had to be cunning.

"Let's go for a drive," I said innocuously, and led the way along the towpath and to my old Bentley parked outside. I knew that Mike had always admired this battleship gray car with its faded red leather seats. I hoped that a soothing drive past the Queen Elizabeth Hall would put Mike in a different frame of mind. We drove off with Mike sitting bolt upright. After a monosyllabic drive we reached the Queen Elizabeth Hall and I slowed down. Mike Oldfield posters were everywhere, and already a crowd of people were making their way to the concert.

"I can't go onto the stage," Mike repeated.

I couldn't tell him that it was in his best interests, that this concert might catapult him into a different league and put him up alongside Pink Floyd. I stopped the car.

"Do you want to drive?"

"All right," Mike said cautiously.

We drove on, over Westminster Bridge, past Victoria Station. I watched Hyde Park flash past the passenger window. Mike turned down Bayswater Road and drove near to the church where I had edited *Student* magazine.

"Mike," I said. "Would you like to have this car? As a present?"

"A present?"

"Yes. I'll get out here and walk home. You just keep on driving, and the car's yours."

"Come off it! It was your wedding present."

"No, all you have to do is then drive it around to the Queen Elizabeth Hall and go up onstage tonight. It's yours."

A silence fell between us. I watched Mike as he held the steering wheel and imagined himself driving this car. I knew he was tempted, and I hoped he would agree.

"It's a deal," Mike agreed.

I would have to tell Kristen and then my parents what I had done with our Bentley, but I knew they wouldn't mind too much. For all its charm and sentimental value, the Bentley was just a car. It was vital to get Mike onstage and sell copies of *Tubular Bells*. If he was successful, then I would be able to pick up any car I wanted. My mother would have approved.

As the last bars of *Tubular Bells* died away at the Queen Elizabeth Hall, there was a momentary silence as people digested what they had just heard. They seemed mesmerized, and nobody wanted to break the spell. Then they leaped to their feet in a standing ovation. I was sitting between Kristen and Simon, and we stood up and cheered and applauded. Tears ran down my cheeks. Mike stood up in front of the organ, a tiny figure, and just bowed and said thank you. Even the band applauded him. He was a new star.

That night we sold hundreds of copies of *Tubular Bells*. Mike was too shattered to speak to the press. Looking at all the people cheering and crowding around to buy his record, he said, "I feel as if I've been raped," and disappeared off in his new Bentley. Mike refused to go back onstage for many years afterwards. Kristen and I walked home. From that night onward, Mike Oldfield's *Tubular Bells* was set to become the most celebrated album of the year. Virgin Music was on the map, and the money started rolling in.

By the next week word of mouth had spread, and on 14 July *Tubular Bells* entered the album charts at Number 23. By August it was Number 1. For the next fifteen years, whenever Mike Oldfield released an album it reached the Top Ten. *Tubular Bells* eventually sold over thirteen million copies, making it the eleventh best-selling album ever released in Britain. The sacrifice of my Bentley was worth it; I never got around to buying another one.

Although overnight Virgin was an established record label, we were a tiny company with a staff of seven and no ability to distribute records to all the record shops across the country. We had two options open to us. The first was to license our records to another larger record label. This option would work only for fairly successful bands, and the other company would pay us an up-front payment for the right to promote the record, distribute it, and keep the bulk of the profits. If the record recouped its advance, the record company would pay us a royalty, typically around 16 percent. This arrangement was traditional for a fledgling record company like Virgin.

The second option was more risky. Virgin would forego the up-front payment and the royalties and simply pay another record label to manufacture and distribute the records as and when they were ordered by shops around the country. Virgin would be responsible for all the promotion of its records and carry all the risk if a record failed. Correspondingly, we would have all the upside if a record sold well.

Most small record labels licensed their records since it was easy money: they received 16 percent royalties from the other company and paid out whatever they had agreed to the artist, say 5 percent or 10 percent. But Simon and I decided that we would go for a manufacture-and-distribution deal (called press and distribute, or P and D). It was a bold move but even then I knew that it is only by being bold that you get anywhere. If you are a risk taker, then the art of a good risk is to protect the downside. It seemed to us that *Tubular Bells* was so good that we could promote it ourselves. I felt sure that it would sell enough copies to pay back our investment. With the idea of asking for a P and D deal rather than a straight licensing agreement, we went to see Island Records.

I had first come across Island Records when I was editing *Student* magazine. It had been set up by Chris Blackwell, who had been brought up in Jamaica and had almost single-handedly introduced reggae into Britain. Island had released Bob Marley, the first reggae superstar, and among others they also produced Cat Stevens and Free.

Predictably, at first Island refused to do a P and D deal. They already licensed Chrysalis and Charisma (which had Genesis), and they wanted Virgin, too. So they offered us a highly attractive licensing deal with royalties of 18 percent. We were paying Mike 5 percent, which meant that if we accepted Island's offer we could collect 13 percent of the sales of *Tubular Bells* for ourselves. At £2.19 this was 28.5p a record, which would mean a total profit to us of around £171,000 if *Tubular Bells* did astoundingly well and sold, say, 600,000 copies—that is to say, reached double platinum. A record goes "gold" at 200,000 copies and "platinum" at 300,000 copies. If it reached a million, then Virgin would make £285,000 without having to pay for any of the costs of promoting and marketing the record. To a seasoned eye Island were far better placed than Virgin to promote this record to all the shops across the country. Most small record companies in our place would have accepted it, and certainly both Island and our own lawyers urged us to do so.

But Simon and I felt differently. We had fourteen Virgin shops across the country, which could promote *Tubular Bells* in Liverpool, Manchester, Leeds, Newcastle, Sheffield, Edinburgh, Glasgow, Birmingham, and across the south of England down to Bristol, Bath, and Southampton. We also felt that we could do the promotion in the national press and the music press ourselves. The experience of selling 100,000 copies of *Student* across the country had given me confidence that we could get this record out in quantity. Of course our job was made so much easier because *Tubular Bells* was so good that people wanted to buy it as soon as they had heard it.

To an outsider this looked like an enormous gamble. If sales of *Tubular Bells* had faded, Virgin Music would have been dead in the water. But if we managed to sell 600,000 copies, total sales worth £1.3 million, Virgin would receive around £920,000 after the shops' retail margin, of which we would pay £65,700 to Mike Oldfield as the artist and £197,100 to Island Records for pressing and distributing the record, leaving us with £660,000 to divide between promoting the record and keeping as profit to reinvest in other artists. This was the upside.

The intellectual copyright of *Tubular Bells* was our birthright, and we were determined to build on it. So we turned down Island's offer and insisted that we stick to a P and D deal. They would press and distribute the record, and we would pay them between 10 and 15 percent for this. Island Records were still holding out for a licensing deal until we threatened to go to a rival record company, CBS. We signed a P and D deal and sacrificed an immediate cash payment, which would have been welcomed by Coutts since the Manor was still in debt. We committed ourselves to selling *Tubular Bells* with our own resources. Island unwittingly fostered a cuckoo that grew up in their nest: Virgin Records, rich beyond our dreams as the sales of *Tubular Bells* shot through silver, gold, platinum, double platinum, and then up over one million copies, grew into a major force in the record industry and eventually became a dominant rival to Island Records. Although the royalty rates we paid Mike Oldfield and Island changed over time, as did the price of the record, *Tubular Bells* went on to sell millions of copies and still sells around the world today. Our gamble that we could promote it ourselves made us our first fortune.

The next step was to try to sell our records overseas. I flew to New York to see Ahmet Ertegun, the head of Atlantic Records and one of the most influential men in the entertainment business.

Ahmet was the grand old man of the American music industry, and I was twenty-three years old. I was shown up into his office with a stunning view of the Manhattan skyline. Ahmet rose up from behind a huge desk and shook my hand. He was a tremendously suave man, Turkish by origin, and a smooth talker. He made it clear to me that he was very busy, that he had a long list of other pressing engagements, but that he could definitely set aside fifteen minutes to reach an agreement on the Mike Oldfield deal. He told me that he was interested in Mike Oldfield because he was so original, but he rather viewed the deal as a one-off. He made me an offer of $180,000 and smiled at me encouragingly. I knew that he expected me to ask for more and that we could agree on $200,000 within fifteen minutes. I shook my head. Ahmet smiled again and admitted that he too would have refused such an offer, but now his real offer was $200,000. That had to be his final offer. I was expected to sign without question. I allowed a silence to fall between us.

"What do you have in mind?" Ahmet asked.

"I'm not going to tell you," I said. "But considerably higher."

By the evening we had still not agreed on a deal. His diary had been extensively rearranged, and he now offered to take me out to a nightclub where we would have to agree on a deal before we went home. As his long limousine drew up at my seedy hotel, my spirits soared when I looked inside and saw that Ahmet was sitting in the back of the limo with two stunningly beautiful black girls. I thought that if he had gone so far as to provide such lovely company, then he must want *Tubular Bells* pretty badly. I was on cloud nine: not only was I going to have a great night with one of these girls, but Ahmet must surely be about to offer over $500,000 for *Tubular Bells*.

We chatted away in the back of the limo and Ahmet opened a bottle of champagne from the fridge as we drove along. We pulled up at the nightclub, and a couple of flashbulbs went off in Ahmet's face as he stepped out of the limo. I followed him and the girls into the club.

"Can I have a word in your ear?" Ahmet took me to one side as we stood waiting for our table.

"Of course," I smiled. This was the moment. He was going to offer me one million dollars for *Tubular Bells* with a massive royalty. I could then accept without further ado, and we could enjoy the rest of the night.

"Can you hear me?" Ahmet raised his voice above the music.

"Yes," I told him, grinning across at one of the girls.

"I'd just like to make one thing clear. I don't mind whether I sign Mike Oldfield or not," he said, patting my arm. "But I don't want any misunderstanding: both these girls are for me."

Chapter 8

"It seemed that we were destined to be forever the second choice, and in music, like so many other things, the second choice means nothing."

1974–1976

When Mike Oldfield drove away in my old Bentley after the concert at the Queen Elizabeth Hall, he was already spinning out of orbit. During all the months in which he had been incarcerated up at the Manor with Tom Newman, working in complete privacy and achieving his perfect album, he had been dreaming about everyone buying *Tubular Bells*. But when he stood up at the Queen Elizabeth Hall and saw the audience giving him a standing ovation, something inside him gave way. He found that although this adulation was something he had yearned for, now that he had it, he couldn't cope with it.

The music industry can make people rich beyond their dreams in a matter of months—whether they like it or not. Mike was now caught in that spiral, which would make him one of Britain's wealthiest men. The success was devastating to him, and I had to learn to live with that responsibility. I found it impossible to answer the question as to whether I should have pushed him into doing that concert. Mike went to live in a remote part of Wales and refused to talk to anyone except me.

When I first drove down to visit him, I could hardly find the house. It was a tiny stone cottage built up on a range of hills called Hergest Ridge. The house had its back to the prevailing winds, but it was so remote that it was like Wuthering Heights. Mike had moved in with a girlfriend, and the whole of the front room was taken up by a grand piano. He took me up onto Hergest Ridge, bringing along a six-foot balsa-wood glider he had made. I watched him as he ran carefully down the hill and then gently launched the huge plane. It hardly seemed to move at first, appearing suspended above

Mike's head, but then the wind caught it and it banked and soared up and flew away from us, down the ridge toward the fields below. Mike watched it, the wind blowing his hair back from his eyes, and for the first time I saw him smile.

I drove back to London and left Mike living on Hergest Ridge. In a sad mirror image of my having Kristen's clothes brought around to *Alberta* so that she would have to move in with me, Mike went to the local pub one night and asked a friend to pack up his girlfriend's clothes and take her to the station. For the next ten years, Mike lived as a recluse and did no promotion for any of his albums. Fortunately, we had made a film of Mike playing *Tubular Bells,* which we made into a documentary and intercut with pictures of abstract William Pye sculptures, which the BBC showed three times. Each time this film was broadcast, the sales of *Tubular Bells* and Mike's other records soared. Had Mike spent the next ten years touring like Pink Floyd, I am sure that he would have become one of the biggest rock stars in the world and John Peel's prediction would have come true. As it was, *Tubular Bells* became more famous than Mike Oldfield, and although he recorded many other beautiful albums such as *Ommadawn,* my own favorite, none of them matched the success of *Tubular Bells.*

The other record companies were mystified by Mike's reticence to perform. Ahmet Ertegun, whom I had left with his two beautiful black girls but who had eventually after much negotiation licensed *Tubular Bells* in America, couldn't understand it:

"You're telling me that you have a film of sculptures for the promo?" he snarled at me. "I don't get it. I'm not sure anyone over here will get it either. We can all visit the Met if we want to."

As usual Ahmet managed to come up with a solution: he sold *Tubular Bells* as the sound track for the film *The Exorcist.* As the film became a hit, so did the album, which finally reached the top of the American charts a year after it had done so in Britain.

One of the things every record company aims for is to transform their bands into household names. When a band has reached a certain stature, they are more like a brand name, and people start buying their new albums on faith. Although two bad albums will dent almost any star's career, once you have built up a following it is easy to predict how many copies the next record will sell. New artists have a high failure rate, but once they have crossed a threshold, the upside has far greater potential than book publishing or films, or indeed selling almost anything else that I can think of. If a record takes off, it can go through the roof: one week nobody has heard of "Karma Chameleon," the next week everyone across the world is humming it.

Alongside this astonishing potential for growth, music is more international than almost any other business. Some countries such as France and Japan remain quite parochial, but the big stars such as Stevie Wonder, Paul McCartney, and Fleetwood Mac sell globally in a way that most industrial companies can only dream about. Pushing exports is difficult for any company, but music is one business that soars over most boundaries: it is carried on the airwaves and by word of mouth, and when a band becomes successful there is no limit. It is also easier for an English language song to sell around the world because German and Scandinavian audiences are quite happy listening to the Beatles, whereas with the dubious exceptions of "Je T'aime" or "Viva España" we rarely tolerate listening to a pop song sung in a foreign language.

With this background in mind, Simon and I developed three key aspects of our negotiation for Virgin Records when dealing with bands. We never formally articulated them to each other, but our negotiations over Mike Oldfield taught us the following general principles.

We set out to own copyright for as long as possible. We tried our hardest never to agree to a deal where the copyright reverted to the artist because the only assets a record company has are its copyrights. We also tried to incorporate as much of an artist's back catalog into our contract, although this was often tied up with other record labels. Beneath all the glamour of dealing with the rock stars, the only value lay in the intellectual copyright of their songs. We would thus offer high initial sums but try to tie the artist in for eight albums. Over the life of Virgin Records, we prided ourselves that we had never lost a band. We never lost a band because we always renegotiated their contracts after a few albums, although ironically Mike Oldfield was one case where I was too slow to renegotiate and I almost lost him. The vital thing with a new band was if you built them up, it would often be their third or fourth album that would be the most valuable. The last thing we wanted was to lose them after a couple of albums only to see them become successful with another record label. One good example of this was the Human League, who had made two albums, each of which had sold progressively better, but who then broke into the big time with their third album, *Dare*, which sold over two million copies. After we signed the artist up, we would soon try to extend the contract, and although we might give away two or three percentage points in royalties, it was a small concession in comparison with the potential of adding another two albums onto the end of the contract.

Right from the start Simon and I tried to position Virgin as an international company, and the second thing we always insisted on was incorporating worldwide rights to the artists' copyright in our contracts. We would argue that there was less incentive for us to promote them in Britain if they then used their success here to sell well overseas.

Our last negotiating point was to ensure that Virgin owned the copyright of the individual members of the band as well as the band themselves. It was sometimes difficult to define a band; for example, the Rolling Stones included Mick Jagger, Keith Richards, Bill Wyman, and Charlie Watts, but a number of other people came and went. The record industry finally defined the Rolling Stones as "Mick Jagger plus two others." Some bands split up and players in them became individually successful. Genesis is perhaps the prime example, as Peter Gabriel and Phil Collins both became bigger stars outside Genesis than they had been within the band. We had to ensure that Virgin didn't sign a band only to be left with an empty shell while the lead guitarist went on to succeed as a solo artist on another label.

The only other great truth we found was that if we wanted a band, we had to sign it almost no matter how high the bidding went. An artist on another label remains just that: nothing to do with us. Part of the secret of running a record label was to build up a great sense of momentum, to keep signing new bands, and to keep breaking them into the big time. Even if a high-profile band lost us money, there would be other intangible benefits, such as attracting others to sign with us or opening doors to radio stations for our newer bands.

With these principles at the back of our mind, Virgin began to sign up new bands on the back of Mike Oldfield's success, the bulk of which would inevitably fail. We still paid ourselves tiny wages, we still all lived in each others' pockets, and we reinvested all the money we earned from *Tubular Bells* into new artists and building up the company.

Kristen and I had been married for two years when we went on holiday to Mexico. We were having some difficulties together. After our marriage, Kristen had insisted that we sell my houseboat and move into a house. She wanted more space to paint, and she found *Alberta* too cramped. At first we tried to compromise, and I bought another, larger houseboat just along the towpath called *Duende*. But that was still no good, so I sold *Duende* to the singer Kevin Ayers. Kristen found a small house on Denbigh Terrace, which was directly off the Portobello Market and just two streets away from our offices at Vernon Yard, and we moved onto dry land.

We both found that life at Denbigh Terrace was rather claustrophobic. Kristen never had any peace from the constant stream of Virgin staff and bands, which came in and out of the house every evening, nor did she have any peace from the continuous ringing of the telephone. I have always given out my home telephone number and address to everyone at Virgin, so that they can tell me of any problems they might have before the problems escalate into something more damaging. Ever since my time with the Student Advisory Centre I have spent a great deal of time on the telephone. And since, as far as I was concerned, the Virgin staff were the most important thing about Virgin, I wanted them to be as happy as possible. Consequently, Kristen and I never had any privacy. She grew increasingly frustrated that I spent all my life working and saw no distinction between our own lives and my working life. Whenever I came home, the telephone would ring as soon as I shut the front door behind me. Wherever I am, I always pick up the phone. I've seen other businessmen say "I'll call them back," but I've never been able to do that. In many ways I wish that I could, but I always feel that I have to talk to people: one call leads to another, which leads to the next opportunity. As I was always struggling to make ends meet, I was always fighting to win the next contract. So while picking up the telephone may have been good for business, it wasn't always good for our marriage.

Kristen and I also had a bizarre sexual allergy to each other. Whenever we made love, a painful rash spread across me, which would take about three weeks to heal. We went to a number of doctors, but we never resolved the problem. I even had a circumcision to try to stop the reaction. Being circumcised at age twenty-four is not a good idea, particularly if the night after your operation you find yourself watching Jane Fonda's erotic film *Barbarella*. Before I could stop myself, I had burst my stitches. Hearing my screaming, Kristen came running to see what the matter was. When she found out what had happened, she was in stitches. I no longer was.

Our love life was incredibly frustrating and difficult, and as a result the rest of our relationship began to flounder. We took a weekend trip to Paris to get away from Virgin and stayed in a poky little hotel near the Place des Vosges. That night Kristen refused to make love with me. I felt like a leper and never forgot the rejection.

By 1974 our marriage was falling apart and we were both having a number of affairs. I was happy living this nomadic life, but Kristen wanted a more secure relationship. It is strange looking back on those years because I think that I loved Kristen more than she loved me. I would not spend more than a night with another woman, but Kristen's affairs turned into relationships. I remember driving her to one man's house where she was having an affair and begging her not to go inside. Then I would come and pick her up the next morning and plead desperately for her not to go back.

In the summer of 1974 we decided to go on holiday to get away from it all and try to patch up our marriage. Kristen chose Cozumel off the coast of Mexico on the grounds that the telephones wouldn't work there and that nobody at Virgin could get hold of me. We spent two wonderful weeks and ended up on the Yucatán peninsula. I had never done any deep-sea fishing before, but one night in the bar of a small port we started talking to some other tourists who told us that this was the best place in the world for marlin and sailfish. We agreed that we would ask a fisherman to take us out the next day.

Although the next day seemed bright and clear to us, the fishermen were wary about going out. In bad English and with Kristen's broken Spanish interpreting, they explained that there was a possibility of a storm.

"Come on," I pleaded. "We've only got a couple more days here. We'll pay you double."

They accepted the incentive, and together with the two other tourists from the bar, who also paid the double fare, we set out. We started fishing and took turns at manning the rods. Soon Kristen caught a large sailfish, which jumped about eight feet out of the water and took almost forty minutes to wind in. We released it and started fishing again. Both the tourists caught marlin before one came for my bait. Marlin often knock fish up out of the water with their spikes and then catch them in the air. We watched the fin come up behind my bait, and then the bait spun up in the air and the huge black-and-silver side of the marlin rose above the water to take it.

As I played the marlin, we suddenly noticed that it was growing dark and cold. Behind us the clouds were gathering, and it soon became clear that we were going to be caught up in the predicted storm. Large drops of rain hit the deck. Without warning one of the fishermen pulled out his knife and cut my line. The abrupt loss of my fish and the thought of it swimming around trailing two hundred yards of nylon from its gullet sickened me. We had released the other fish we had caught, but this marlin was being consigned to certain death attached to this length of line.

The fishermen started up the engine to head home, but rather than heading back to the shore, the boat started drifting around in circles. The rudder had jammed. The sea rose around us, and the waves started breaking over the stern. Kristen was shaking uncontrollably. We were soaked through and freezing cold. The storm clouds completely blocked out the sun and it became dark, so dark that it might have been night. We went down into the tiny cabin, which was full of smoke from the engine. One of the tourists was sick. I tried to open the window, but the smell of vomit and diesel remained. The boat was being so badly smashed up that we were sure that she would sink.

After an hour of the worst storm any of us had ever experienced, the wind and rain abruptly stopped. The sea was still running very high, and the waves towered over ten feet above us. It was eerily still. We must have been in the eye of the storm. For a while there was bright sunlight. Then we saw the other side of the storm coming, a solid black line above the horizon, growing more threatening as it came nearer.

"Richard, I think we should swim for it," Kristen said. "This boat won't take another storm."

"You're mad," the other tourists said. "Stay on board."

Kristen and I agreed that the boat wouldn't survive another pounding. We argued with the fishermen and the tourists, who disagreed. The shore was about two miles away. The sea around us was an ugly matte-black color, swelling high and boiling with white foam flecked across the surface. I was terrified, but I decided that Kristen was right. She had been a good long-distance swimmer at school, and she gave me the only pair of flippers on board. We stripped off to our underwear, and the fishermen gave us a plank of wood from the bottom of the boat. We all wished each other the best of luck and then jumped overboard. Almost immediately the current swept us past the boat and up the coast. We lost sight of the boat and concentrated on kicking out for the coast, which we could see only from the tops of the waves. Kristen led the way, and I tried to keep up with her. As well as fishing for marlin, we had also been on the lookout for sharks. As we swam I started imagining that the first thing I would feel would be a vast fish rearing up beneath me, knocking me sideways in the same way that the marlin had dealt with my bait, and ripping into my stomach and legs.

"Don't kick too hard," Kristen shouted in my ear. "You don't want to get cramps."

We swam across the current, not worrying that we were being carried up the coast just as long as we weren't being taken out to sea. Slowly we came closer. We had been in the water for almost two hours before I knew that we would definitely make land. The coast was at first just a smudged green line, then we could see the trees, and finally a mud beach. Even after we could see the beach it took us another hour to get there. We hauled our way through the surf and collapsed onto the sand. We had swum in the stormy sea for almost three hours. We were freezing cold, and our hands and feet were white and wrinkled. Clinging onto each other, we told ourselves that after that we would always be together.

"We've got to get back down to the port," she said. "We've got to get a rescue party out to save the boat. They might have a lifeboat."

We started running down the peninsula. Fighting our way through some mangrove swamps, we finally arrived in the tiny port after an hour, half-naked, trembling with shock and exhaustion, and with our feet bleeding.

At the port Kristen explained to the captain of the local car ferry that there was a boat out at sea in trouble with a jammed rudder. He agreed to try to rescue the fishing boat. He lent us some clothes, and at once we set out to sea. Within fifteen minutes the second storm hit. It was far worse than the first one, and it picked up the car ferry, a big heavy boat, and tossed it around like flotsam. We couldn't believe that after our first escape we were back out at sea in the storm. After ten minutes the captain told us that he was turning back. It was hopeless. Although we wanted to go on, we could see that the ferry was in danger of capsizing.

The fishing boat was never found. Kristen and I left Mexico two days later. I had to learn to live with the question of whether the fishermen would have gone out to sea that day if it hadn't been for us. Two fishermen and two tourists had drowned, and a fishing boat was lost. I wondered if we and the other two tourists should have waved a handful of dollars in front of them.

Although when we had been washed up together on the beach and Kristen and I had sworn that we would stay together forever, our marriage rapidly unraveled once we were back in London. It ended where it had started: on board a houseboat. One night we both went around to have dinner with Kevin Ayers and his wife on board *Duende*. Throughout the evening it became clear that Kevin rather fancied Kristen and I rather fancied Kevin's wife. We soon found ourselves chatting on two separate sofas, then kissing, and then Kevin and Kristen went off to his bedroom while his wife and I stayed on the sofa.

Rather like the Roald Dahl story where the two neighbors slip into each other's bedrooms and make love to each other's wives, it was clear that something pretty amazing happened between Kristen and Kevin that night. What had started as a harmless bit of fun with my wife resulted in Kristen leaving me and moving in with Kevin on board *Duende.* I knew that she must be serious if she went back to live on *Duende.* After a few weeks they started traveling around Europe. I tried to persuade her to come back to me, but she refused. I was desperate to make her change her mind. I followed them to Paris and then to Majorca, each time having ghastly, pleading conversations with Kristen, trying to talk her into coming home with me. When I heard that they had moved to Hydra, I couldn't stop myself. I knew that I was going to get hurt, but I had to try one last time. I flew to Athens and then found my way to Hydra. After arriving on the island, where there are no cars, I sent a mule up the hill carrying a basket full of roses with a message that I was in the port. Kristen came down to see me. I looked at her, but her face was set. We had a wretched conversation in a bar by the quayside, where we both cried so much that the barkeeper refused to take payment for the ouzo we drank. Kristen felt hopelessly torn between the two of us, but she finally told me that she couldn't see how we could live together. I watched her walk up the steps away from me and forced myself to accept that I had lost her. Then I turned back into the bar, where the Greek barkeeper poured me another glass of ouzo and put his arms around me. I resolved to leave Kristen alone and get on with my own life.

As well as my marriage breaking up in 1974, Virgin Records was beginning to have some problems. In August 1974 Mike Oldfield's next album, *Hergest Ridge,* went straight to Number 1. Since *Tubular Bells* was still at Number 2, money kept coming in. But Virgin was in danger of being seen as just Mike Oldfield's label. In spite of Mike's refusing to do any promotion himself, his sales were so large that he eclipsed anyone else.

Simon and I were anxious to sign up more acts. In order to balance Oldfield's success, we needed a big breakthrough. Any new band still had to meet Simon's exacting criteria. In January 1975 Simon showed me an article in *Sounds.* The band 10cc was leaving its recording company, and they were on the market for a new contract.

Named after the average amount of sperm in a human ejaculation, 10cc fit Simon's criteria. They were highly commercial but without appealing to the lowest common denominator. They were witty, clever, catchy, and successful. Songs like "Rubber Bullets" had sold over 750,000 copies. We realized that 10cc would want a large up-front payment in order to buy them out of their previous record contract. We called up and spoke to one of their two managers, Harvey Lisberg, in Manchester and took the train to meet him and the band on 18 January 1975.

10cc comprised four players, Eric Stewart, Graham Gouldman, Lol Creme, and Kevin Godley, but Harvey Lisberg did most of the talking. He explained that 10cc was under contract to a small record firm, and they would need, as Simon had already guessed, a large up-front payment. They were sure that their next album, *Original Soundtrack,* would be big enough to cover this risk. Harvey Lisberg also told us that they were negotiating with Phonogram.

Simon and I had a quick chat in one corner, and then offered £100,000 as an up-front payment. We told the band that we would like to have a long-term commitment to them, and we proposed a deal that would take us around six years to fulfill. The band said that they would like to sign with Virgin, although £100,000 was less than Phonogram had offered. As January dragged on, the bidding increased. On the last day of January, Harvey Lisberg asked for £200,000 rather than £100,000 as up-front money. Simon and I agreed to go along with this. Simon was so sure about *Original Soundtrack* that he didn't flinch when the bidding reached £300,000 and then £350,000 for the down payment. We rang around the Virgin licensees in France, Germany, and Holland, and they agreed to support us. We also managed to get Ahmet Ertegun at Atlantic Records to pledge £200,000. This was our first big signing in the marketplace against the major international record companies, and for the first time we were dealing in vast sums of money.

Simon and I got on very well with Lol and Eric, but it was clear that there was a split in the group. The day before the contract was due to be signed, Eric and Lol flew off to Saint Lucia for a holiday. The timing could have been better, but they left a power of attorney with Harvey Lisberg. The day they left, I wrote a letter to all the Virgin shop managers telling them about the signing and telling them each to go out and buy a bottle of champagne on Virgin to celebrate. Then I called Harvey Lisberg to talk about the cutting process on the new album. To my amazement, he was suddenly very frosty.

"We'll look after the cutting," he said. "We haven't signed with you yet. Stop bugging us."

I couldn't understand his attitude, and pointed out that we had a deal completed bar the signature. That evening the deal fell apart. Tom Dixon, 10cc's other manager, rang me and told me not to come to the signing since he had a meeting with Phonogram. 10cc was eventually signed to Phonogram. One of the things this episode taught me was not to count our chickens. Simon was right about *Original Soundtrack:* it went on to sell several million copies.

• • •

During that rather awkward patch between 1974 and 1976 when Mike Oldfield was our only superstar, Virgin also failed to sign the Who and Pink Floyd. It seemed that we were destined to be forever the second choice, and in music, like so many other things, the second choice means nothing. At the end of 1975 I pitched for the Rolling Stones. Word had traveled that we had been prepared to pay £350,000 for 10cc, which astonished our rival record labels like Island. When I called up the Stones' manager, Prince Rupert Loewenstein, he was prepared to listen to me seriously since he had heard about our 10cc offer.

"How much are you asking for?" I asked him.

"You'll never be able to afford it," Prince Rupert told me sympathetically. "It'll be at least three million dollars. And anyway, Virgin is just too small."

I knew that the only way to get his attention was to considerably better that offer.

"I'll offer four million dollars," I said, "as long as there is some back catalog available."

Buying the back catalog would enable Virgin to release a Greatest Hits album and would be a good insurance policy if the new record failed.

"I'll send you around the list of the back catalog which is available," Prince Rupert said. "If you can bring a bank guarantee for four million dollars to my office by Monday, then I'll look at it very seriously. Best of luck."

It was Friday. Prince Rupert assumed that he had set me an impossible task. That weekend I traveled around the chain of Virgin distributors we had set up across Europe in France, Germany, Italy, Holland, Sweden, and Norway. As I traveled I was constantly on the telephone to those in the rest of the world. I was looking to raise about £250,000 from each distributor. By the end of the weekend I had tracked them all down and asked them to send telegrams to Coutts in London confirming that they would provide the money. By Monday morning I was back in London but still short of the $4 million I had promised Prince Rupert. After adding up all the different commitments from the distributors, Coutts promised to make up the difference, and I drove around to Prince Rupert's house in Petersham just before eleven o'clock with a bank guarantee for $4 million.

Prince Rupert was dumbfounded. I had caught him completely off guard. He fingered the $4 million check but then gave it back.

"You'll have a chance to match the highest offer," he promised. "But you've started an auction."

Finally EMI won the auction and signed the Rolling Stones. I couldn't raise any more than the $4 million. Although I was disappointed to have failed, I knew that I had done the Stones a good turn by increasing the asking price from the $3 million Prince Rupert would have been happy to accept to $5 million.

By 1976 the necessity of signing the really big bands was beyond frustration. Virgin had two albums in the Top Ten, Gong's and Mike Oldfield's *Ommadawn*. These were the days of Genesis' *Trick of the Tail* and Bob Dylan's *Desire*. Our trouble was that we had spent most of Mike Oldfield's royalties on signing up new bands and with the exception of Tangerine Dream had had no major breakthroughs. Tangerine Dream's *Phaedra* had become a top-selling album across Europe and had greatly enhanced Virgin's reputation. Our catalog was full of wonderful, credible music, but we did not have enough really big sellers, and more immediately we were running out of cash.

On top of that Mike Oldfield wanted to renegotiate his contract. We were happy to renegotiate, but after we agreed on a second version with an increased royalty to him, he instructed another lawyer, who began to push for an even higher royalty. Simon and I decided that Virgin couldn't go any higher. We pointed out that Virgin Records as a company was making less money than he was personally. When he asked how this was possible, I made the mistake of being completely honest with him. I told him that we needed successful artists like him to pay for our unsuccessful ones. His sympathy evaporated.

"I'm not giving money away for you to blow on a whole load of rubbish," he said. "I'm going back to my lawyer."

Eventually we agreed on another contract, and Mike stayed with us. But it was a close-run thing.

In the summer of 1976 we had a crisis meeting with Simon, Nik, and Ken Berry. Ken had started in the Notting Hill record shop as a clerk. It was his job to check the shop's takings, but soon he took over a whole range of other jobs. We all found that whenever we needed to know anything—the sales of Pink Floyd that week, the staff wages due, the depreciation on the old Saabs we ran—Ken knew all the answers. Soon Ken was indispensable, and he effectively joined the core team consisting of me, Simon, and Nik. He was quiet and unassuming, and as well as dealing with the numbers, his great skill was dealing with people: he was utterly unfazed by negotiating with top rock stars and their lawyers, and soon he became involved in work-ing through the contract negotiations. Simon and I watched him, and as we realized that he would never lose a deal by throwing his ego around and try-ing to score points off the other side, we gave him more and more responsi-bility.

The original trio of me, Nik, and Simon made room for Ken, and in many ways he became the rock that held us all together. At that crisis meeting, we went through the figures of all the shops, which were trading well but not profitably. I knew that Nik was pushing them for all he was worth, and we were loath to criticize anything he was doing. Then we started going through the Virgin roster. One by one we debated whether we could afford to keep bands that cost us money to promote and looked unlikely ever to break into the big time, bands such as Hatfield and the North or Dave Bedford.

"It's clear to me," Ken Berry said, adding up a column of figures. "We have to seriously consider scrapping all our bands apart from Mike Old-field."

We looked at him in amazement.

"All our other bands are losing us money," he went on. "If we sacked at least half our staff, then we could cope very well, but at the moment Mike Oldfield is bankrolling the entire company."

I have always believed that the only way to cope with a cash crisis is not to contract but to try to expand out of it.

"What about if we found ten more Mike Oldfields?" I asked, teasing him. "How would that do?"

Ultimately we had two options: either tuck away a little money and eke out a living without taking any more risks, or use our last few pounds to try to sign up another band that could break us back into the big time. If we chose the first option, we could get by: we would be running a tiny com-pany, but we could survive and make a living without any risks attached. If we chose the second, Virgin could be bust within a few months, but at least we would have one last chance to break out.

Simon and I wanted to have one last go at breaking a new band. Nik and Ken eventually agreed with us, although I could see that they were reluctant to bet the entire company on a breakthrough. From that night, we were on an emergency footing looking for the "next big thing."

In the meantime we cut back on whatever we could: we sold our cars, we closed down the swimming pool at the Manor, we cut down on the stock in the record shops, we didn't pay ourselves, we dropped a few artists from the record label and made nine staff redundant. This was the most difficult of all, and I shied away from the emotional confrontation and let Nik do it.

One of the artists we reluctantly dropped was Dave Bedford, a brilliantly gifted classical composer. Dave reacted well to the bad news. He wrote a long letter to me saying how much he understood the decision—that he appreciated that his records had not sold, that he would have done the same if he had been in my shoes, that he bore Virgin no grudges, and that he wished us all the best for the future. At the same time he wrote a letter to Mike Oldfield in which he described me as a complete shit; an utter bastard; and a vile, tone-deaf, money-grabbing parasite on musical talent. Unfortunately for Dave, he then put the letters in the wrong envelopes.

Chapter 9

"Nobody could possibly doubt a priest, under oath, saying that 'bollocks' really means 'priest' or 'rubbish' and not 'balls.' "

1976

The first major band we went after was called Dire Straits. Arthur Frolows, who helped Simon with spotting new bands, was in the bath one Sunday lunchtime when he heard a new band called Dire Straits singing "Sultans of Swing" on the radio. He was so excited by it that he leaped out of the bath and called the station to find out how to get hold of the band. He discovered that the band had not yet recorded their music in a studio, but that this song was a live recording specially commissioned by Charlie Gillett, the radio show host.

Virgin was not the only record label interested in signing Dire Straits, but since we were there quickly, we had a good chance. Simon and Ken found them rather precious, and they and their lawyers continued to argue over every tiny point.

On the evening before we were due to sign contracts, we took the band out to our favorite Greek restaurant off Westbourne Grove to celebrate. It was an enjoyable meal. Since all the negotiations were out of the way, we could relax and look forward to producing the record. At the end of the meal, the Greek owner came out carrying two saucers, one upturned on top of the other. With a conjurer's flourish he lifted off the top one to reveal ten marijuana joints. I rarely took drugs after my LSD experience, but this seemed a nice way to end the evening, and in order not to offend the restaurant manager, who clearly thought that he was doing us all a great favor, I took one. Everyone smoked a joint and the evening wound down.

The next morning Dire Straits called us up and told us that they were going to sign with PolyGram. No reason was given. Simon and I were horrified. We couldn't believe it.

"What's the matter?" Simon asked. "We've got everything in place. There's nothing more to agree."

"No reason," they said, and cut off all communication with us.

There was nothing Simon and I could do to persuade them to change their minds. It was only ten years later when I read a book about Dire Straits that two little sentences explained it: "The band did not sign with Virgin since they thought that Virgin had plied them with drugs before the signing to befuddle them."

That well-meaning, spontaneous gesture by the Greek manager, which Dire Straits had seemed to enjoy at the time, cost Virgin Records over £500 million. Meanwhile, Dire Straits went on to become one of the world's top bands, with their album *Brothers in Arms* selling eighteen million copies.

By August of 1976 Virgin was in real trouble. We were trying to sign some of the aggressive punk bands that were coming on the scene, but we seemed to keep missing out. For instance, we missed getting the Boomtown Rats because I insisted on including the music-publishing rights, which they wanted to sell elsewhere. We had been unable to find a new band who could lift us out of our rut or dispel our image as a rather hippie label. Among our other worries we were in the middle of a dispute with Gong over some recording rights. Some of their followers came into the Vernon Yard offices to stage a protest. Our offices were invaded by a host of benign, bearded, long-haired, and peaceful activists wearing caftans and sandals and smoking joints. They had the appearance of a wandering band of druids and wizards. After an enjoyable afternoon spent slouched on the sofas listening to Gong, Henry Cow, and Mike Oldfield and trying to talk me into signing some petition, they decided to leave. We stood by the front door and thanked them for coming. As they left we gently relieved them of their pickings—mainly records they had tried to conceal in the flowing folds of their caftans, but one or two of them were trying to make off with posters, tapes, staplers, and even a telephone. They all smiled when they were caught and left on the best of terms.

I followed them out into Portobello Road and watched them wander away through the fruit stalls. One of them stopped to buy some dates. As the stall holder sold him the fruit, a man with his head shaved into a Mohican strip and dyed pink and green walked by. The caftaned followers of Gong looked uncomprehendingly at the punk, picked up their dates, and walked off, munching slowly.

"I'm going to be out for ten minutes," I told Penni.

I went up Portobello Road and found somewhere to have a haircut.

"How much off?" asked the barber.

"I think it's about time I got some value for money," I said. "Take about a foot and a half off and let's see what I look like underneath."

In place of names like Hatfield and the North and Tangerine Dream a string of new bands had taken over the poster sites. They were called names such as the Damned, the Clash, the Stranglers, and, most notorious of all, the Sex Pistols.

In the last week of November I was working in my office when I heard this extraordinary song being played in Simon's office directly below me. I had never heard anything like it. I ran downstairs to see him.

"What was that?" I asked.

"It's the Sex Pistols' new single. It's called 'Anarchy in the UK.' "

"How's it doing?"

"Very well," Simon admitted. "Very well indeed."

"Who's signed them up?"

"EMI. I turned them down a couple of months ago. I could have made a mistake."

There was something so raw and powerful about the song that I was determined to see whether we could win them back. I called up Leslie Hill, the managing director of EMI. He was far too busy and important to take my call, so I left a message with his secretary saying that if he ever wanted to get rid of his "embarrassment," then he should contact me. Half an hour later she called me back to say that EMI were quite happy with the Sex Pistols, thank you.

That very evening, 1 December, at 5:30 P.M., the Sex Pistols caused a national furor. They were being interviewed on *Today,* an afternoon television show hosted by Bill Grundy. Bill Grundy had rolled back from a good lunch at Punch and realized that the four lads in his studio were fairly drunk as well. He started to mock them, talking about other great composers— Mozart, Bach, and Beethoven. It was all a bit silly until Johnny Rotten spilled his drink in one corner and quietly swore: "Shit."

"What did you say?" Grundy asked. "What was that? Didn't I hear you say a rude word?"

"It was nothing," Rotten said.

"Come on, what was it?"

Grundy got what he asked for.

"I said 'shit,' " Rotten told him.

"Really," Grundy said. "Good heavens, you frighten me to death."

Then Grundy turned to Siouxsie Sioux, the other guest, and asked her whether she would meet him afterward. Steve Jones, one of the Sex Pistols, laughed and called him a dirty old sod. Grundy then turned to him and goaded him into saying more swearwords. Jones called him a "dirty fucker" and a "fucking rotter," and that was the end of the show.

The next day the national press were once again outraged by the Sex Pistols' behavior. Nobody criticized Bill Grundy for baiting them into swearing. And as I was having my breakfast, reading the papers about how someone had kicked in their television in disgust at the show, the telephone rang. It was not yet 7 A.M. In a wonderful role reversal, the managing director of EMI was now personally calling me.

"Please come and see me immediately," he said. "I gather that you're interested in signing the Sex Pistols."

I went straight around to EMI's offices. Leslie Hill and I agreed that EMI would transfer the Sex Pistols to Virgin, conditional upon Malcolm McLaren, the group's manager, agreeing. We shook hands. Then Malcolm McLaren was ushered in from the next-door room.

"Virgin have offered to take the Sex Pistols on," Hill said, trying unsuccessfully to keep the relief out of his voice.

"Excellent," McLaren said, offering me his hand. "I'll come to your offices later this afternoon."

I normally make up my mind about whether I can trust somebody within sixty seconds of meeting them. As I watched McLaren with his tight black trousers and pointed boots, I wondered how easy it would be to do business with him. He never showed up at Vernon Yard that afternoon and never returned my phone calls the next day. I stopped ringing him after four attempts. He knew how to get hold of me, but he didn't call.

On 9 March 1977 McLaren signed the Sex Pistols to A&M records. The ceremony was staged outside Buckingham Palace, where the four punks lined up and screamed abuse at the Royal Family. The band were just four regular lads, but they were being whipped up by Malcolm McLaren.

I sat at my desk and wondered about McLaren. I knew that he had a best-seller on his hands, a band that would transform Virgin's image. If Virgin could sign the Sex Pistols, it would at a stroke remove the hippie image that was hanging over us. EMI sneered at Virgin and called us "The Earl's Court Hippies." Never mind that we lived nowhere near Earl's Court, the name stuck and I didn't like it. We were stuck in the image of Gong and Mike Oldfield. The royalty checks were impressive, but I feared that none of the new punk bands would take us seriously if we had only a number of hippie bands. Virgin Music needed to change and to change quickly, and the Sex Pistols could do it for us.

"Every band is a risk," Derek Green, managing director of A&M, airily told the press. "But in my opinion the Sex Pistols are less of a risk than most."

A&M hosted a party to celebrate the signing of the Sex Pistols. Since A&M were "capitalists" making money out of bands by "exploiting" them, the Sex Pistols hated them as they hated all record companies—or at least they pretended to. Sid Vicious, then the band's drummer, excelled himself immediately after the signing by wrecking Green's office and being sick all over his desk. As soon as I heard this I reached for my telephone to try one last shot, hoping that A&M would want to get rid of the Sex Pistols. To my delight Green told me that he was dropping them.

"Can we sign them?" I asked.

"If you can cope with them," he said. "We certainly can't."

The Sex Pistols were given £75,000 by A&M as compensation for the canceled contract. Together with the £50,000 they had been given by EMI, they had earned £125,000 for doing nothing more than a bit of swearing and vomiting, and one single. Once again the Sex Pistols were looking for a record label.

I began to marvel at how McLaren had played his cards so well. The Sex Pistols were now the most shocking band in the country. Among all the punk bands that now rapidly materialized, the Sex Pistols were still the most notorious. They had a single called "God Save the Queen," which I knew they wanted to release in time for the Queen's Silver Jubilee Day in July 1977.

I watched and waited, knowing that McLaren didn't like me. He sneered at me as a hippie who had become a businessman. But as the weeks passed and Jubilee Day came closer, nobody else came forward to sign the Sex Pistols. I knew that Virgin was perhaps the only record label that could do it. We had no shareholders to protest, no parent company or boss to tell me not to. On 12 May 1977 McLaren finally came to see us. The tables had turned. Virgin signed the British rights for the Sex Pistols' first album for £15,000 with a further £50,000 payable for rights for the rest of the world.

"Do you realize what you're getting into?" McLaren asked me.

"I do," I assured him. "The question is, do you?"

From the moment we signed the Sex Pistols, McLaren was looking for ways to alienate us so that we'd be sufficiently embarrassed to want to get rid of them. To McLaren's horror and bemusement, we refused to be outraged. We released "God Save the Queen," which was banned by BBC radio and soared to Number 2 in the charts. It would have been Number 1, but all record shops like Virgin and HMV that would be likely to be selling large quantities of the record were excluded from the sample taken in order to compile the charts.

On Jubilee Day 1977 McLaren rented a Thames pleasure cruiser and steamed upriver toward the House of Commons. The police knew that something was up, and as we set off from Westminster Pier two police launches shadowed us. The band waited until they were right up alongside the House of Commons, and then they picked up their guitars and drumsticks and roared out their own version of the national anthem:

> God Save the Queen,
> A fascist regime.
> Made you a moron,
> A potential H-bomb.
> God save the Queen,
> She ain't no human being.
> There ain't no future in England's dream . . .
> No future! No future!

The police pulled up alongside and insisted that the band stop playing. This was unwarranted since the boat had a license for bands to play. It brought back memories of the last-ever Beatles live performance on the rooftop of the Apple studios when the police pulled the plug on them. If it had been Frank Sinatra on board, there would have been no problem, just as there was no problem with the Beatles' last rooftop concert. The police boarded our boat and steered us back to the pier, where they arrested Malcolm McLaren, mainly because he put up such a spirited fight and started yelling "Fascist pigs!" for closing down the party.

That week we sold over 100,000 copies of "God Save the Queen." It was clearly the Number 1 record, but *Top of the Pops* and the BBC claimed that Rod Stewart was really Number 1. "God Save the Queen" was banned from the television and radio. From our point of view it was good business: the more it was banned, the better it sold.

The Sex Pistols were a turning point for us, the band we had been looking for. They put Virgin back on the map as a record company that could generate a huge amount of publicity and that could cope with punk rock. The Sex Pistols were a national event: every shopper up and down the high street, every farmer, everyone on every bus, every grandmother had heard of the Sex Pistols. And living close to that kind of public outcry was fascinating. As Oscar Wilde pointed out: "The only thing worse than being talked about is not being talked about." The Sex Pistols generated more newspaper cuttings than anything else in 1977 apart from the Silver Jubilee itself. Their notoriety was practically a tangible asset. Most of the press were negative, but so had it been for the Rolling Stones when they had set out fifteen years earlier.

In November 1977 Virgin released *Never Mind the Bollocks, Here's the Sex Pistols*. The lettering on the album sleeve was a brilliant design by Jamie Reid, crudely cut out from newspaper headlines in the same way as kidnappers' notes and hate mail were delivered. Virgin shops put large yellow posters in their windows advertising the record. Not surprisingly there would always be someone who would be offended by this. One day the manager of our Virgin record shop in Nottingham was arrested under the same Indecent Advertisements Act of 1889 for which I had been arrested nearly ten years previously, when the Student Advisory Centre had advertised help for people suffering from venereal disease. I called John Mortimer, who had defended me then.

"I'm afraid I've fallen foul of the Indecent Advertisements Act again," I told him. "The police are saying that we can't use the word 'bollocks.' "

"Bollocks?" he asked. "What on earth's wrong with bollocks? It's one of my favorite words."

"They're making us take down the Sex Pistols posters, 'Never Mind the Bollocks, Here's the Sex Pistols,' and they're threatening to injunct the album."

He told me that we needed a linguistic adviser, a professor of English who could define the exact meaning of bollocks for us. Since the case had been brought in Nottingham, I called up directory inquiries and asked for the number of Nottingham University.

"Please, can I speak to your professor of linguistics?" I asked.

"That would be Professor James Kingsley," said the lady on reception.

I was put through and explained the situation.

"So one of your staff has been arrested for displaying the word 'bollocks'?" said Professor Kingsley. "What a load of bollocks! Actually, the word 'bollocks' is an eighteenth-century nickname for priests. And then because priests generally seemed to speak such a lot of nonsense in their sermons, bollocks gradually transformed to mean rubbish."

"So bollocks actually means either 'priest' or 'rubbish'?" I checked, making sure that I hadn't missed anything.

"That is correct," he said.

"Would you be prepared to be a witness in court?" I asked.

"I'd be delighted," he said.

I enjoyed the court case. The police prosecutor was deteremined to win what was clearly a case of national importance. Our shop manager was cross-examined and admitted that he had prominently displayed the Sex Pistols poster in the shop window. The police officer recited how he had arrested him since he was displaying this offensive poster. The policeman had the smug look of someone who was doing the public a great service and expected to be praised for it.

"No questions," John Mortimer said when he was invited to cross-examine the policeman.

Rather disappointed, the policeman stood down.

"I would like to call my witness," John Mortimer said when he stood up. "Professor John Kingsley, professor of linguistics at Nottingham University."

As Professor John Kingsley explained that "bollocks" had nothing to do with testicles but actually meant "priests" and then—due to priests' sermons being full of it—"rubbish," John Mortimer peered at him myopically and appeared to be struggling to straighten out his thoughts.

"So, Professor Kingsley, are you saying that this expression 'Never mind the bollocks, here's the Sex Pistols,' which is the basis of this prosecution, should more accurately be translated as 'Never mind the priests, here's the Sex Pistols'?" asked John Mortimer.

"I am. Or it could mean 'Never mind the rubbish, here's the Sex Pistols.' "

John Mortimer allowed a silence to develop in the court. " 'Never mind the priests, here's the Sex Pistols,' " he mused. "That is the meaning of this expression. Well, I have nothing further to add. It sounds like a strange title for a record, but I doubt whether the church would mind."

"I doubt they would either," Professor Kingsley agreed.

The prosecutor then pressed Professor Kingsley on this point, asking him how he could be sure that no clergyman would be offended.

Professor Kingsley then played his trump card by folding down his polo neck to reveal a dog collar. Professor Kingsley was also known as Reverend Kingsley.

"That's enough," snapped the magistrate. He straightened his back, squared his shoulders, and, adopting as much magisterial solemnity as he could muster, announced: "The case is dismissed."

Chapter 10

"There was some consolation in that after we had signed
the Sex Pistols, Virgin had become the smart record label
for punk and new wave bands to sign with."

1976–1978

One weekend in early 1976 I met my future wife, Joan Templeman, at the Manor. I make up my mind about someone within thirty seconds of meeting that person, and thus I fell for Joan almost from the moment I saw her. The problem was that she was already married to someone else, a record producer and keyboard player who was producing a Virgin band called Wigwam.

Joan was a down-to-earth Scots lady, and I immediately saw that she did not suffer fools gladly. I knew that I couldn't attract her attention in the same way as I had attracted Kristen. Most of my past relationships with women had been based upon a great public display of showmanship, but for the first time with Joan I felt that there was a woman who didn't want me to get up to my usual antics.

Joan worked in an antiques shop called Dodo on Westbourne Grove close to our offices at Vernon Yard. On Monday morning I hovered uncertainly outside the shop, then screwed up my courage and walked in. The shop sold old signs and advertisements. When I asked the owner of the shop whether Joan was there, she looked at me suspiciously.

"Are you a customer?" she asked, glowering.

"Yes, I'm fascinated by old signs," I said, looking uncertainly around the shop.

Joan came through from the back of the shop.

"I see you've met Liz," she said. "Liz, this is Richard."

"So what would you like to buy?" Liz pressed me.

There was no way out. Over the next few weeks, my visits to Joan amassed me an impressive collection of old hand-painted tin signs that advertised anything from Hovis Bread to Woodbine Cigarettes. One tin sign read Dive in Here for Tea! I also bought a large pig, which played the cymbals and had once stood in a butcher's shop. One of my favorite signs was an old picture advertising Danish bacon and eggs, which showed a pig leaning casually against a wall, listening to a chicken singing. The chicken was celebrating her freshly laid egg and the caption to the scene was "Now, that's what I call music!" I gave this to Simon Draper, since he was always terribly grumpy in the mornings until he had eaten a decent breakfast. He hung it over his desk, where it later inspired us as the title for our annual Greatest Hits compilations *Now That's What I Call Music,* which have reached Number 1 every year since. By the time I had bought all my Christmas presents from Dodo, Liz told Joan that she was the best shop assistant she had ever had.

Joan had been married to her husband, Ronnie Leahy, for almost eight years, but they had no children. Ronnie traveled a good deal, and it seemed to me, perhaps conveniently, that he and Joan had begun to drift apart. Whenever Ronnie was away, I called up Joan's friends and asked whether they were seeing Joan.

"Mind if I tag along?" I asked casually.

They soon called me "Tag-along," which I really didn't mind as long as by tagging along I had the chance to sit somewhere near Joan and talk with her. Our courtship was unlike the other romances I'd had and that I'd been able to control. Joan is an intensely private person, and it was extremely difficult to find out what the state of her marriage was. While I knew what I felt about her, I had very little idea what Joan made of me. I thought that she might be intrigued by my persistence, but beyond that I was in the dark.

Eventually Joan agreed to come with me to the Isle of Wight, and we spent the weekend in a tiny hotel in Bembridge. It was the start of our affair. I was still living in the house in Denbigh Terrace at the time. Since Joan was still married, we both continued living double lives. She could not see me during the week when Ronnie was at home, but early one morning she decided to surprise me by dropping round to my house in Denbigh Terrace. As she let herself in, she saw my cleaning lady, Martha, going up the stairs to my bedroom and carrying a tray with two cups of tea. Joan knew that I was in bed with another woman—which I was—so she stopped Martha and put a flower on the tray.

"Just say to Richard that Joan says hello," she said, and then turned on her heel and went back to the shop.

Mortified, I dashed around to see her at Dodo and persuaded her to have lunch with me.

"So what's all this about undying love?" Joan asked sarcastically.

"Well, I was lonely," I said lamely. "I couldn't wait until the weekend."

"That's a pathetic excuse!" Joan said.

I tried to look ashamed of myself and contrite, but we caught each other's eye and then both burst out laughing.

Our affair continued for almost a year. We were desperate to be with each other, and we would call each other up whenever we had five minutes to spare. Joan would slip away from Dodo and I would leave Vernon Yard and we would meet at Denbigh Terrace, which was right between us. The geography of our affair was tight-knit: Vernon Yard, Westbourne Grove, and Denbigh Terrace all bisect Portobello Road within twenty yards of each other, and so Joan and I lived out our passionate affair within a tiny, intense triangle.

When we stole twenty precious minutes at lunch, or a quarter of an hour before a meeting, or a few moments after Dodo closed, we tried to shut the outside world away. But along with the passion, we were also intensely aware that Joan was married (indeed, on paper I was in the same situation myself) and that we were in danger of causing pain to Ronnie. In some ways Joan and Ronnie had a similar relationship to Kristen's and mine: Ronnie had wanted to experiment with sleeping with other women and had told Joan that she needed to broaden her horizons too. Joan had been at a loss because she wasn't able to cope with a series of one-night stands, and so she gradually began to fall in love with me.

Our love affair was further complicated when Kristen heard that I was in love with Joan and arrived back in London. By this time I had managed to buy *Duende* back from Kevin Ayers, who I think was rather bemused by the whole episode. At more or less the same time, Kristen had left him. She now told me that she wanted to get back together with me—we were, after all, still married. My family has always maintained that you stick through your marriage through thick and thin, and so I felt a great responsibility to agree with Kristen. But I was in love with Joan. It was a nightmarish situation for each of us: Joan felt torn between me and Ronnie, Kristen had been torn between me and Kevin, and now I felt torn between Kristen and Joan. What had started off as a dream affair with Joan in the tiny bedroom in the house at Denbigh Terrace was now beginning to destroy five people's lives.

The matrix of these four relationships finally resolved itself when I was at a party with both Joan and Kristen. Joan's best friend, Linda, cornered me:

"So who are you actually in love with?" she demanded. "This can't go on. You're all killing yourselves, and you need to sort it out."

I saw Joan talking to someone else.

"I'm in love with one woman," I said, looking across at Joan. "But she's not in love with me."

"I'm telling you that she is," said Linda, following my look. We left it at that.

The next night I was alone on *Duende*. It was a dark February night and raining hard. I was on the telephone, so I didn't hear the sound of knocking. Then the door opened and I swung around. It was Joan.

"I'll call you back later," I said to the phone, and moved across to embrace her.

"Well, I thought I'd move in," Joan said.

That spring of 1977 I was approached by a man called Richard Ellis, who claimed to have made a startling invention, which he called a "pterodactyl flying machine." He sent me a photograph that showed a man on a tricycle soaring over the treetops beneath two large wings. Richard Ellis wanted me to try the pterodactyl flying machine and then buy the license to distribute it. I invited him up to the Manor so that I could have a look at it. The flying machine looked like a cross between something invented by Leonardo da Vinci and Heath Robinson. The tricycle had a small outboard engine with rotors suspended above the pilot's head. Ellis told me that if I pedaled like mad along the road or an airstrip, then the engine would cut in and power me along until I took off. The engine would then power the rotors, which would keep me airborne.

I was rather flattered that Richard Ellis had chosen me to be the second person to fly this machine. He had heard about the hot-air balloons I had arranged for the Virgin summer party that year and thought that if I liked this machine, I would be able to promote it. Once again my willingness to try anything once landed me in serious trouble.

"It'll take a couple of weekends to get the hang of it," Ellis said. "So you won't take off this time."

He rigged up some cable to the engine with a rubber switch at the end and gave it to me to put in my mouth.

"When the engine is going well and you are bowling along the runway, bite on this and it will cut the engine."

Joan and a few friends stood at the end of the runway of the local airport to get a good view. I was strapped into the harness and put the rubber bung in my mouth. It all seemed as if it would be a lot of fun.

"Okay! Go!" Ellis shouted.

I started to pedal as fast as I could down the runway. The engine kicked into life, and the bike started to whiz along. I couldn't hear anybody above the noise of the engine, but I could see their faces. I decided that I was going fast enough and that the experiment was over, so I bit hard into the bung. Nothing happened. The engine roared even faster. I bit again. Nothing. I was skimming along at some thirty miles an hour—it felt incredibly fast—when suddenly the tricycle lurched up into the air and the whole contraption took off. I bit again, but the engine just roared on. I looked down and saw the faces turned up to watch me. Only Joan seemed rather uninterested. I rose up in the air in great lolloping movements like the men who take off from Brighton Pier. In a few seconds I had cleared the beech trees in the wood next door to the airport. I had no idea what to do. I was one hundred feet up in the air, and nobody had told me how to fly it.

With my free hand I reached up into the engine and started to pull at any wires I could feel. The engine was boiling hot and I burned my hand, but one after the other I yanked out wires and pulled away anything that would come. I had to stop the engine. I was well over the trees and over the next field when the engine finally cut out. It was quiet. I tried to balance the bike, but the wings above me were very heavy. I spun down, heading toward the ground. At the last moment I caught some kind of wind, which flipped the machine over the other way, and it crashed down sideways. I lay on the ground, paralyzed with shock.

"We thought that you got the hang of it rather well," I heard Joan say.

"I wasn't meant to take off," I said. "That was terrifying."

As I had soared above her head, frantically wrestling with the engine and narrowly escaping death, Joan had been only marginally impressed that I had got the hang of it. The next week Richard Ellis took off in the same flying machine and crashed down to the ground. He died on impact.

"We've had another Nigerian order," Chris Stylianou told me. "They love this guy U-Roy."

Chris Stylianou was Virgin's exports manager and throughout the last few months of 1977 had picked up thousands of pounds worth of business from, of all the bizarre places, Nigeria. The Nigerians loved reggae music. At the time virtually the only British record label that sold reggae was Chris Blackwell's Island Records.

In 1976 I had followed Chris Blackwell's footsteps to Jamaica with a view to signing some reggae acts. After sitting on his veranda for days on end I had finally managed to sign up Peter Tosh, who had sung with Bob Marley, and a performer called U-Roy. *Legalize It,* Peter Tosh's first album with Virgin, had sold well in 1977. But now there was a different sound: the Jamaican DJs and radio jocks used to cut their own records and chant a whole lot of rhyming slang and political slogans to a background beat. It was an early form of rap music. They were called "toasters," and it was U-Roy, a bejeweled hipster, who was doing so well in Nigeria. I knew that there must be more toasters out in Jamaica, and I decided that we should go out there and corner the market.

I always like to get away from London in the middle of winter. I've found that the sunshine and long-distance travel always give me a clearer perspective on London life. And this time I had two extra reasons to get away from the city: I wanted to take with me Johnny Lydon, who was having some difficulties with the Sex Pistols, and Malcolm McLaren; I also hoped to meet up with Joan, who was going to Los Angeles with Ronnie to give their marriage one last chance. Johnny Lydon was delighted to come since he loved reggae, and Joan and I agreed not to speak until she had resolved her marriage one way or another.

At the last minute Simon was unable to come with me, so I went with Ken. And so at the start of 1978 a punk rocker, an accountant, and a reformed Earl's Court hippie flew together to Kingston, Jamaica, to sign up some reggae bands and look for toasters. Knowing that Jamaicans didn't trust written contracts, we flew in with a briefcase containing $30,000 in cash and set up shop in the Kingston Sheraton. Word soon went around that three gringos were in town looking to audition musicians, and a stream of bands starting coming round to the hotel room. Ken sat on the bed with his briefcase; Johnny Lydon and I listened to the bands' tapes and chatted with the bands. Johnny decided which artists we should sign, and then Ken would open up the briefcase and take out the money. American dollars were hard currency in Jamaica, where imports were banned and everything was bought on the black market. Some of the bands were so keen to impress us that they brought their drums and guitars with them, and our room was soon full of tall Rastafarians wearing massive bobble hats in red, yellow, and green stripes. One tall singer towered over us and sang lovingly about his spiritual homeland of Ethiopia.

I watched Johnny Lydon as he sat on the sofa and nodded his head gently to the music. It was difficult to believe that this was the same man, gaunt and thin as a lightning conductor, who had screeched abuse at everyone, spat at pictures of the queen, and galvanized a generation of anger. Thinking about the emperor Haile Selassie, who had inspired the Rastafarians, I wondered whether the British Royal Family hadn't missed a trick.

Over the course of a week we signed almost twenty reggae bands and found a couple more toasters called Prince Far I and Tappa Zukie into the bargain. I tried to persuade Johnny Lydon to stay with the Sex Pistols but to no avail. He told me that the group had fallen out among themselves and with Malcolm McLaren; that Sid Vicious was in a tailspin, taking all kinds of drugs and growing violent with Nancy, his girlfriend. Johnny wanted to go solo, and he had a couple of musicians in mind to form a new band called PiL: Public Image, Ltd. I was sorry since I wanted to build the Sex Pistols as the next classic rock band to follow the Rolling Stones. After all, the Rolling Stones had started off as the most shocking band in the world, with Mick Jagger being arrested for possessing drugs and scandalizing public opinion. By 1978 the Stones had been going for more than fifteen years and had become part of the rock-and-roll Establishment. And they didn't look like stopping.

Coping with success obviously brings its own difficulties for a rock band, but getting your name into people's minds is almost the hardest thing to achieve. The Sex Pistols had certainly entered the world's vocabulary—if only as a byword for all that most people found revolting—and I felt that they were crazy to throw away that advantage. I tried to persuade Johnny that the Sex Pistols could use their name in slightly different ways and perhaps move away from the extreme punk image that they had made their own. I also wanted to push them overseas, since *Never Mind the Bollocks* had sold only 300,000 records overseas, about the same number as it had sold in Britain, and I felt sure that they could do much better with successive albums. After Mike Oldfield's instant success and then his withdrawal from public life, I was determined that the Sex Pistols would not collapse as well. They were Virgin's top band, and they had been the catalyst for both Virgin and a whole new wave of rock music. But Johnny was in no mood to listen.

On our final evening we found a Rasta bar up along the coast from Kingston, which sold fish in strong jerk sauce. We sat outside watching the sea. A flock of pelicans were dive-bombing in formation, and we watched them methodically work their way through shoals of fish, each one peeling off and diving down before tucking its wings in and plunging into the water. We drank Red Stripe beer and listened to Bob Marley, and although I kept turning the conversation back to what the Sex Pistols could do, Johnny was not really listening. There was a world of difference between Mike Oldfield and the Sex Pistols. Yet both Oldfield and the Sex Pistols had found that they could not cope with the pressures of fame. From my point of view as the head of their record company, there was a further difference: Oldfield had made Virgin a tremendous amount of money, which we had spent building up the company and signing new acts. We would not be in business without him. Although the Sex Pistols had been Number 1 with "God Save the Queen" and their album *Never Mind the Bollocks* had also been Number 1, Virgin had not made very much money from the group.

As I sat there with Johnny Lydon on the Jamaican beach, I was forced to accept that Virgin would never make much more money from the Sex Pistols. Malcolm McLaren had arranged for the Sex Pistols to be in a film called *The Great Rock and Roll Swindle,* and I wondered whether there might be a sound track that we could release from that; but otherwise Simon, Ken, and I were going to have to accept that from now on the Sex Pistols were not a going concern.

Although it was highly frustrating to see them falling apart—and in a far worse way than Mike Oldfield, who continued to produce records that sold well—there was some consolation in that after we had signed the Sex Pistols, Virgin had become the smart record label for punk and new wave bands to sign with. The music world had seen the promotion we had put behind the Sex Pistols, and a whole new generation of exciting bands was approaching us. Simon had picked up bands such as the Motors, XTC, the Skids, Magazine, Penetration, and the Members, which were all selling well, and another band called the Human League were building up a following. Virgin Music Publishing had signed a schoolteacher from Newcastle called Gordon Sumner, who used the stage name Sting and sang with a band called Last Exit, who were thought to have some promise.

I returned to the Kingston Sheraton, mulling over Virgin's prospects without the Sex Pistols. There was a message from Joan, asking me to call her.

"Shall we meet in New York?" she asked.

I left Jamaica the next morning.

Chapter 11

"I heard that if you expressed serious interest in buying an island, then the local estate agent would put you up for nothing in a grand villa and fly you all around the Virgin Islands by helicopter."

1979–1980

I met Joan in New York. Her attempt to patch up her marriage to Ronnie had failed. We spent a week in Manhattan and felt like refugees. My divorce from Kristen had yet to come through, and Joan had only days previously separated from Ronnie. We were thinking of escaping from New York to spend some time together alone, out of reach of any telephone, when somebody asked me if I had named Virgin Records after the Virgin Islands. The answer was no—but they sounded like just the romantic haven that Joan and I needed.

On impulse Joan and I decided to fly down to the Virgin Islands. We had nowhere to stay and not very much money, but I heard that if you expressed a serious interest in buying an island, then the local estate agent would put you up for nothing in a grand villa and fly you all around the Virgin Islands by helicopter. This sounded rather fun. I cheekily made a few calls, and sure enough when I introduced myself and mentioned the Sex Pistols and Mike Oldfield and added that Virgin Music was really expanding and we wanted to buy an island where our rock stars could come and get away from it all, and perhaps put a recording studio there, the estate agent began to get very excited.

Joan and I flew down to the Virgin Islands, where we were greeted like royalty and ushered into a sumptuous villa. The next day we were flown by helicopter all over the Virgin Islands as the estate agent showed us three islands that were for sale. We pretended that we quite liked the first two islands we saw, but we asked him whether there were any more.

"There's one more, which is a real little jewel," he said. "It's being sold by a British lord who's never been here. It's called Necker Island, but I don't think it's a wise idea because it's miles from anywhere."

That did it.

"All right," I said. "Please, can we see it?"

As we flew to Necker Island, I looked down from the helicopter window and marveled at the clear pale-blue sea. We landed on a white sandy beach.

"There's no water on the island," said the estate agent. "The last known inhabitants were two journalists who came here on a survival course. They radioed for help before the week was out. It's the most beautiful island in the whole archipelago, but it needs a lot of money spent on it."

There was a hill above the beach. Joan and I set off for the top, to get a view over the whole island. There were no paths, so by the time we reached the top our legs were scratched and bleeding from squeezing through the cacti. But the view from the top was worth it: we saw the reef all around the island and noticed that the beach ran most of the way around the shoreline. The estate agent had told me that leatherback turtles came up to lay their eggs on the beaches of Necker. The water was so clear that we spotted a giant ray flapping its way serenely along the sandy bottom inside the reef. There were thousands of nesting gulls and terns, and a small flock of pelicans fishing in formation. Higher up a frigate bird came gliding past on an air current, its enormous wings spread wide as it carved its way over the thermals. Looking inland, we saw two saltwater lakes and a small tropical forest. A flock of black parrots flew over the forest canopy. Looking across at the other islands, we could only see their green coastlines—there was not a single house in sight. We walked back down the hill to find the estate agent.

"How much does he want for it?" I asked.

"Three million pounds."

Our dream of watching the sunset from the top of the hill faded into the sand.

"Nice thought," Joan said, and we trudged back to the helicopter.

"How much were you thinking of spending?" the estate agent asked, suddenly smelling a rat.

"We could offer £150,000," I said brightly. "Two hundred thousand dollars," I added, trying to make it sound more.

"I see."

We flew back to the villa, but it was clear that we were no longer welcome. Talk of $200,000 wasn't enough to secure us a night at the villa. Our bags were left at the door, and Joan and I hauled them across the village to a local bed-and-breakfast. It was clear that there would be no more helicopter flights over the islands. Yet Joan and I were determined to buy Necker. We felt that it could be our secret hideaway island, somewhere where we could always retreat. So although we were practically driven off the Virgin Islands as if we were cattle rustlers or carpetbaggers, we vowed to return.

Back in London I found out that the owner of Necker Island wanted to sell in a hurry. He wanted to build a building somewhere in Scotland, which would cost him around £200,000. I upped my offer to £175,000 and held on for three months. Finally I got a call.

"If you offer £180,000, it's yours."

There was never a hint that £180,000 was only a fraction of the £3 million asking price. So I agreed on the spot, and Necker Island was ours. Even at such a low price, the snag with Necker Island was that the Virgin Islands' government had decreed that whoever bought Necker Island would have to develop it within five years or its ownership would pass to the government. It would cost a good deal to build the house and pipe the water across from the neighboring island, but I wanted to go back there with Joan. I was determined to make the money to be able to afford it.

Joan and I stayed in Beef Island for the rest of that holiday, and it was there that I set up Virgin Airways. We were trying to catch a flight to Puerto Rico, but the local Puerto Rican scheduled flight was canceled. The airport terminal was full of stranded passengers. I made a few calls to charter companies and agreed to charter a plane to Puerto Rico for $2,000. I divided the price by the number of seats, borrowed a blackboard, and wrote: Virgin Airways, $39 single flight to Puerto Rico. I walked around the airport terminal and soon filled every seat on the charter plane. As we landed at Puerto Rico, a passenger turned to me and said:

"Virgin Airways isn't too bad. Smarten up up the service a little, and you could be in business."

"I might just do that," I laughed.

"Richard, I want to get married and I want you to be my best man," said Mike Oldfield.

"That's wonderful," I said. "Who is she?"

"She's the daughter of my therapy teacher."

Mike Oldfield had been a lifelong introvert. In September 1976 he went on a therapy course that seemed to involve being alternately humiliated and praised in front of a group of people. To me, it sounded rather like a crash course in surviving public school or the army. But Mike emerged with his introversion banished. Within days he was posing for some nude photographs in the music press as Rodin's *The Thinker*, and now he wanted to get married.

"How long have you known her?" I asked.

"Three days."

"Don't you want to wait?"

"I can't wait," he said. "She won't sleep with me until we're married. It's tomorrow at Chelsea Register Office."

Having failed to persuade him out of it, Joan and I went along to the Chelsea Register Office and waited for Mike and his bride. We brought two carved African stools with us as wedding presents, which we put down on the pavement outside and sat on before Mike's arrival. A stream of men and women passed us and emerged as man and wife. As we sat and waited I could feel the whole idea of marriage becoming less and less appealing. Both Joan and I had suffered failed marriages, and the sight of this production line of wedded couples coming out every six and a half minutes from the register office and, in our jaundiced view, heading for the divorce lawyers put us off saying the vows to each other again. They seemed to ring hollow. I knew that I loved Joan, but I felt that we didn't need to say the clichéd words to confirm it.

Mike and Sarah were married, and we gave them the two African stools. We had dinner together that night, which ended early since Mike was so clearly intent on getting Sarah into bed. The next morning the phone rang.

"Richard, I want a divorce." It was Mike.

"What's wrong?"

"We're not compatible," Mike said in a voice that brooked no further questions.

Mike and Sarah went more or less straight from the registry office to the lawyers, and he ended up paying her over £200,000 in alimony. My mind boggles at what went on that night, but whatever happened it must go down as one of the most expensive one-night stands in history.

In 1977 Virgin as a whole made a pretax profit of £400,000; in 1978 the figure increased to £500,000. After the collapse of the Sex Pistols, we were left with a handful of our original artists, the most important being Mike Oldfield, whose albums sold consistently all the way through the advent of punk and new wave, and a couple of new signings, both of whom seemed rather esoteric and played synthesizer music: Orchestral Manoeuvres in the Dark and the Human League. While these two bands had yet to sell well, XTC, the Skids, and Magazine kept their sales going. We also continued to sell well in France and Germany, particularly with Tangerine Dream.

By 1979 an outsider might have looked at Virgin and come to the conclusion that it was a motley collection of different companies. From our tiny mews house in Vernon Yard, we operated the record shops, which Nik ran; the record company, which was run by Simon and Ken; and the music-publishing company, which was run by Carol Wilson. The Manor was going well, and we had expanded our recording studios with the purchase of a London recording studio. The original plan to set up everything that a rock star needed—recording, publishing, distribution, and retailing—was beginning to work. On top of this we had also set up Virgin Book Publishing, which was primarily to publish books about music and biographies and autobiographies of the rock stars.

In lieu of the Sex Pistols' future albums, which would now never be made, we had acquired the rights to the film Malcolm McLaren was producing, *The Great Rock and Roll Swindle*. This guaranteed one last album, the film sound track. In order to pull this film together we set up Virgin Films, which Nik had started to manage.

Another venture that Nik had set up was the Venue, a nightclub where our bands could play and people could eat and socialize while watching them. As the world of rock music grew increasingly sophisticated, it became clear that bands no longer wanted simply to record their songs and then release them. Pop videos were becoming the most effective way of promoting songs, and some cynics observed that pop videos were as important as the music itself. In order to accommodate this, Nik set up a film-editing studio where our bands could make and edit their own videos.

The other service that Virgin had to offer to our artists was the ability to sell their records overseas. Although we were a tiny company based in a mews house in Notting Hill, I knew that if we had no overseas companies, we stood no chance of signing the international bands. One of the beauties of rock music is that at the top end of the market it is a purely international commodity. The best measure of a group's success is how many records they sell overseas. The large multinational companies had a huge advantage over Virgin or Island since during the negotiations to sign a band, they could point to their sales forces in France and Germany to demonstrate the contrast.

One option open to Virgin was not to compete with the multinationals overseas but purely to concentrate on the domestic U.K. market and license our bands overseas in the same way in which we had licensed Mike Oldfield when we first set up. Although this was a tempting option in that it saved overhead costs, I wasn't happy with it. Island and Chrysalis adopted this approach, and I felt that it restricted their growth because they were at the mercy of the overseas licensees. Once you have licensed a band away to another record company, you lose all control of their promotion. As well as wanting to control the prospects of our British bands overseas, we also wanted to be able to attract overseas bands to Virgin. We wanted French, German, and American bands to feel that they could sign with us for worldwide rights rather than with the large international record labels.

With a skeleton staff at Vernon Yard, it was difficult to imagine that we could really take on the multinationals on their own terms. But we decided to give it a go. In 1978 Ken set off to New York to establish the Virgin label in America. In the same way that Virgin had grown in London and now inhabited a number of small houses around Notting Hill, so I imagined that Virgin America would start off with a house in Greenwich Village and move slowly around the country, buying houses in Chicago, Los Angeles, San Francisco, and other regional centers so that we didn't build up one monolithic head office.

In 1979 I went to France to meet with Jacques Kerner, the French head of PolyGram. I did not know anybody in the French music industry, and although I was ostensibly seeing him with the idea of asking PolyGram to distribute the Virgin records, I was really on the lookout for somebody who could set up Virgin in France. Kerner introduced me to an intriguing looking man called Patrick Zelnick, who ran PolyGram's record side. Patrick had a vaguely distracted look about him, rather like Woody Allen, with thick, wiry, unruly hair and heavy black-framed glasses. Patrick not only looked like Woody Allen, he behaved like him: when we first went out for lunch together, we spent four hours afterward trying to find out where he had parked his car. Patrick told me that he had watched Virgin's progress with interest. He had first tried to meet us when we had a stall at the Cannes Music Festival in 1974 but had been able to find only a sign saying Gone Skiing. Patrick had then started to come over to buy records at the Virgin record shop on Oxford Street. He loved Mike Oldfield and Tangerine Dream.

Jacques Kerner was offering me £300,000 to license the entire Virgin catalog in France with a percentage of royalties on top. Since Virgin had little money at the time and since we had just taken on another loan to pay for Necker Island, the easy option would have been to accept it. But instead of dutifully taking down the details in my notebook, I wrote down "Patrick Zelnick: Virgin France," and I surprised Jacques by asking for some time to think it over.

After the meeting I thanked both men and asked them to drop by and see me on the houseboat when they were next in London. The next month Patrick came to London and called me up. We had lunch on *Duende*, and I asked him whether he would leave PolyGram and set up Virgin as an independent subsidiary in France. I would give him complete independence to sign whichever French bands he liked. We worked out some rough figures on a piece of paper, and Patrick agreed to do it. He set up Virgin France with a friend of his, Philippe Constantine, a wild, ragged individual who was on and off heroin and had excellent musical taste. While Patrick did the business, Philippe spent his time with all the bands.

"When you're invited for dinner," Jacques Kerner said in a reproachful phone call to me when Patrick resigned, "you're not meant to walk away with the cutlery."

I apologized for poaching Patrick but told Jacques that Patrick had made his own decision to set up Virgin. It was only after Patrick had left PolyGram that we looked through the figures again and realized that we had miscalculated: we had forgotten to include VAT in our estimations; we had used the wrong retail margin; we had hopelessly overestimated the numbers of records that were sold in Paris. But by then it was too late—Patrick and Philippe were working for Virgin. One of the first bands they signed was Telephone, who became the best-selling band of the year in France. In later years Patrick would shake his head in disbelief that he had left the security of PolyGram and joined a virtually bust English record company.

As the negotiations with Patrick continued, I went back to France to meet the managing director of Arista Records. We were unable to agree on a distribution deal, but I pricked up my ears when he started boasting how Arista was about to sign Julien Clerc, France's biggest pop star. I had no idea who Julien Clerc was, but I excused myself and slipped into the lavatory. I scribbled "Julien Claire" on my wrist and then carefully pulled the sleeve of my sweater down to hide it. After the meeting was over I rushed to a call box and telephoned Patrick.

"Have you heard of a singer called Julien Claire?" I asked.

"Of course I have," Patrick said. "He's the biggest star in France."

"Well, he's free to sign. Let's try to sign him. Can we meet him for lunch tomorrow?"

At the lunch the next day, Patrick and I managed to persuade Julien Clerc to sign with Virgin from under Arista's nose. Within a fortnight I had succeeded in having my name struck off two record companies' lunch lists, but both Patrick and Julien Clerc went on to make fortunes for Virgin France and themselves.

With Ken in New York, Patrick in Paris, Udo in Germany, and our own operation in London, we could properly market Virgin as an international record label. Our trouble was that we had no cash reserves, so any setback could prove fatal. When I visited Coutts Bank in the Strand, I now wore shoes and my hair was in no danger of getting caught in the revolving door, but they still treated me like a schoolboy prodigy rather than a businessman. Even looking at Virgin's sales of £10 million, they would shake their heads and smile.

"It's all good pop music, isn't it?" the Coutts manager would say genially. "My son loves Mike Oldfield. I just wish my other one didn't play all this loud punk stuff. I keep having to yell up at him to turn it down."

I tried to point out that Virgin was growing into a large company. We had very good sales, and were making as good and steady money as any regular business. But the bankers never saw it like that: "You're doing jolly well," the bank manager said. "But of course the quality of your earnings is so poor. We can't see what they're going to be more than a month in advance."

In spite of this cheerless analysis at the end of 1978 we felt quite confident: in the United Kingdom we had enjoyed a good year with a string of Top Ten hits and good sales through the record shops. But in 1979 Margaret Thatcher was elected prime minister, interest rates soared, and we were hit by a severe recession. Record sales in Britain dropped for the first time in twenty years, and our chain of shops lost a lot of money. Ken had had no luck in New York: Virgin's first single there had cost $50,000 to promote and had completely bombed. Reluctantly, we decided to close the office and to call Ken back home.

Everything seemed to be going wrong, even at home. In November 1979 Joan called me to say that the houseboat had sunk. I had left the water pump on, and rather than pumping water out, it had backfired and started siphoning water in. We met at *Duende* and waded around in the water trying to salvage furniture and boxes of files. After we had retrieved all we could, we stood on the towpath chatting to our neighbors about the best way to pull the boat up. One of the neighbors shifted a box, and to our embarrassment a large vibrator fell out. When it hit the ground, it turned itself on and started to vibrate. As we all watched it, it buzzed around and finally fell into the canal, where it zipped through the water like a torpedo before finally vanishing from view.

"Anything to do with you, Richard?" Joan asked caustically.

"No. You?"

"Of course not."

That box had (of course) been on *Duende* for years. The vanishing circle of ripples where the vibrator had sunk seemed a fitting end to the 1970s.

In 1980 I traveled to Los Angeles to try to interest American record companies in English artists. The trip was a disaster. I took a collection of demo tapes, but nobody was interested in anything new. Mike Oldfield was as popular as ever—someone even misspelled his name "Oilfield," which was certainly closer to the truth for Virgin—but the other bands I was trying to license, such as the Skids, the Motors, XTC, Japan, Orchestral Manoeuvres in the Dark ("Hang on, Richard," said the buyer at CBS. "We haven't got all day. Can't we just call them OMD?"), and the Flying Lizards, were listened to with polite interest but few bids.

As I saw that Virgin's income was drying up, I made continual lists of savings we could make. I sold Denbigh Terrace and put the money into Virgin; we sold the two flats in Vernon Yard; we cut back on everything we could think of. I recently came across a list of immediate priorities of that time in my notebook, which brings back all the sense of desperation:

1. Remortgage the Manor;
2. Turn off the swimming pool heater;
3. Sign Japan [the band];
4. Sell the houses in Vernon's Yard;
5. Ask Mike Oldfield if we can hold back his cash;
6. Sell the houseboat;
7. Sell my car;
8. Lease all the recording equipment;
9. Nik could sell his shares to a merchant bank or Warner Bros.;
10. Sell the Venue.

I wrote to the Virgin staff and told them that we had to tighten our belts urgently: "The good news is that Ian Gillan's new record has gone straight in at Number Three in the charts. But the bad news is that it's only sold 70,000 copies, which is just a half of what a Number-Three record would have been last year. Our profits have been reduced by more than half since we have the same overheads."

By Nik's calculations, Virgin was heading for a £1 million loss in 1980.

"I can't sell my shares to a merchant bank," he told me. "Virgin is losing one million pounds this year. The shares are worthless."

"But what about the brand name?" I asked.

"Virgin? It's worth minus one million pounds," he said. "They won't recognize any value in the brand name. What's the worth of British Leyland as a brand name?"

Virgin was suddenly in desperate trouble. The 1980 recession caught us with all the unexpected ferocity of a squall at sea. For the second time we had to make some staff redundant: nine people, who represented a sixth of the worldwide staff of Virgin Music. This was proportionately less than the cuts being made by other record companies at the time, but it was a gut-wrenching blow for us. Nik, Simon, Ken, and I spent hours arguing over what we should do. With no major rock star on the roster to release a hit record, Virgin had no predictable future income. We found ourselves desperately fighting to try to prove Coutts Bank wrong. Once again we went through our catalog of bands and made several cuts. We had to abandon most of the reggae bands we had signed in Jamaica since a military coup in Nigeria had banned all imports and destroyed our sales.

Tension between Nik and Simon rose as they argued over which bands Virgin should keep. Nik argued that Virgin should drop the Human League, a young band from Sheffield who played synthesizers.

"Over my dead body," Simon told him.

"But they're so marginal," Nik argued. "We can't afford to keep supporting them."

"The Human League is exactly why I'm in this business," Simon said, fighting to keep his temper.

"You just spend all the money I save in the shops," Nik said, wagging his finger in Simon's face.

"Look here," Simon snapped, rising to his feet. "Never, ever, wag that fucking finger in my face again. And the Human League are staying."

I watched Simon and Nik fight it out, knowing that something would have to be done. Nik had been my main partner, my closest childhood friend, and we had worked together since *Student* when we were sixteen. But he was obsessed with cutting back and saving money at a time when we were admittedly in deep trouble. And once again I felt that unless we did something dramatic, which meant spending money, we would never get out of trouble.

Nik and Simon reached an angry stalemate and turned to me to arbitrate between them. To Nik's fury, I backed Simon. This marked a turning point in our triangular relationship, which had worked so well up to this point. I felt that Simon's taste in music was the only thing that could pull Virgin out of the hole we were in. Without Simon's new generation of bands, we would be stuck treading water. Nik thought that we were throwing good money after bad, and he went back to the record shops determined to squeeze even more savings out of them.

At another meeting we argued over another recent signing, the drummer from Genesis. In September 1980 Simon wanted to spend £65,000 to sign up Phil Collins as a solo artist. Once again Simon was supremely confident that this was the right move, and he stood up to all the doubts and criticisms Nik threw at him. The reason why we even had the chance to sign Phil Collins was because of our expansion into the recording-studio business. As well as the Manor, we had acquired a studio in West London, which we called the Town House. At the back of the Town House we had built a second studio, which was hired out at a lower rate. Rather than having the normal padded walls to kill all acoustic reverberations, we had built it with stone walls. When Phil Collins wanted to record some solo material he decided that he couldn't afford the top-of-the-range studio, so he booked the Stone Wall studio instead. There he found that he managed to get the most extraordinary recordings of his drumming for "In the Air Tonight." And Phil got on so well with the sound engineers that he soon found himself talking to Simon, and before we knew what had happened, he was ready to sign up with us.

Nik made Simon do all kinds of sales analyses to try to work out how many copies of a solo album by Phil we could sell. Nik was worried that Genesis fans would not buy him, but Simon proved that even if just 10 percent of known Genesis fans bought Phil's debut solo album, we would make money. As we stared with dismay at our overdraft and the wretchedly low sales figures of our other bands, we knew the gamble we were making. To his credit Nik agreed that we should sign Phil Collins, even taking cash from the tills to make up enough for the advance. Phil proved to be an extraordinarily gifted musician and singer. His voice was haunting and his lyrics poignant: he was destined to become more successful than Genesis itself.

In the meantime, the *New Musical Express* mentioned that Virgin Music was in financial trouble. If Coutts read *NME,* which I doubted, they might think twice about extending the loan I wanted. I immediately tried to squash the idea with a letter to the editor: "Since in your last issue you speculate that I am in deep financial trouble you will appreciate my need to sue you in order to acquire some interest free money rather than approach the merchant banks . . ." Although the *New Musical Express* was hardly the *Financial*

Times, I recognized·that if rumors like that are not hit hard on the head they have a horrible habit of becoming self-perpetuating. Worse still, they were true.

A couple of months after the argument over the Human League and Phil Collins, I came across two deals that I thought were irresistible. They both involved nightclubs. The first one was the Roof Garden in Kensington, which was being offered for sale at £400,000. Virgin, of course, had no money, but the brewer who supplied beer to the Roof Garden was prepared to offer us an interest-free loan if we continued to stock their wines, beers, and spirits. The other nightclub was Heaven, a large gay nightclub under Charing Cross Station. The owner was a friend of my sister Vanessa, and he wanted to sell it to someone who would respect it and keep it as a gay club. Through my work at the Student Advisory Centre, he knew that he could trust me to do this. His asking price was £500,000, and once again the brewer was prepared to give us an interest-free loan to cover the entire purchase price in return for stocking their beers. I had no idea why the brewers did not want to acquire these clubs outright, and I jumped at the chance to buy them.

I knew that Nik would oppose these purchases, so I signed the contracts without telling him. He was furious. He thought that I was squandering money. He looked at the £1 million extra liability that the purchase of these clubs represented and thought that I was ruining Virgin.

"It'll sink us," he argued.

"But we don't have to pay any interest," I said. "It's free money. When someone offers you a Rolls-Royce for the price of a Mini, you have to take it."

"There's no such thing as a free lunch, and there's no such thing as free money," Nik told me. "It's still debt. We can't possibly pay it off. We're practically bust as it is."

"This money is free," I said. "And I think there is such a thing as a free lunch. We'll trade out of trouble."

Nik disagreed with me so vehemently that it became clear that we had to go our separate ways. He thought that I was leading Virgin headlong in a reckless dash that would end in bankruptcy. He wanted to protect the remaining value of his 40 percent share of the business before it was too late. For my part, and in spite of our history, I had been unhappy with our professional relationship for two or three years. Nik and I had always been best friends, but as Virgin had grown bigger and moved from being a record retailer to a music label, I felt that he was out of his depth. Nik thought we were all out of our depth, which may well have been true. There was no room for him in the record label, and in any event he wasn't comfortable doing all the socializing with the musicians that Simon, Ken, and I did. I rather suspected that Nik's puritanical outlook made him resent every pound that was thrown away on ordering another bottle of champagne, even if by charming and so winning a band onto Virgin Records, we would reap vast benefits. I felt that Nik was always trying to stop me from doing the things I wanted to do, most of which admittedly involved risking money on new bands. It is probably an interesting litmus test of our relationship that I don't think Nik came on staff skiing holidays after about 1977. I have always wanted the Virgin staff to have a great time, and I'll be the first one to make a fool of myself in any way if I think that it'll help the party go with a swing. Nik found all that side of life difficult to enjoy. In the end we both realized that while we could write pages about each other's good and bad points, it was best to separate while we were still friends and remain friends, rather than waiting until we had grown into implacable enemies.

I raised another loan from another bank and bought out Nik's shareholding in Virgin. As well as this cash, Nik also took with him some of his favorite parts of the Virgin Group: the Scala cinema and the film- and video-editing studios. Nik's real interest lay in the film world, and when he left he set up Palace Pictures with a view to making movies. With his talent he soon started making wonderful films such as *The Company of Wolves, Mona Lisa,* and the Oscar-winning *The Crying Game.*

With our separation settled, Nik and I hugged each other and made up. We had both got what we wanted, and to celebrate our "divorce" we threw a leaving party at the Roof Garden. In many ways we managed to get the best out of both worlds: we remained great friends, we saw a lot of each other, and we both managed to thrive without each other. Although I had acquired Nik's 40 percent of Virgin, I was well aware that there was no difference between owning 100 percent and owning 60 percent of a busted company. Nik was right about Virgin's trading losses for 1980: we lost £900,000.

Chapter 12

"It was impossible to define why Boy George was so popular—parents wanted to mother him, girls wanted to be as beautiful, boys wanted their girlfriends to be as beautiful."

1980–1982

As well as parting from Nik, I came dangerously close to splitting up with Joan in 1980. I was working frantically to keep Virgin afloat, and I knew that Joan was growing increasingly frustrated. No matter how late I got home the telephone rang, and every time we woke up on a Saturday morning it rang again. One night I returned home to the houseboat to find it empty. Joan had left me a note: "I am pregnant. I am afraid to tell you. I have run away from home. If you miss me, call me at Rose's."

As I looked at the note, I realized that my life had changed. I sat down and thought what to do. Ever since Kristen had left me, I had had a number of affairs. I loved the variety and the fact that nobody was dictating to me. Ever since Joan had moved in with me, I fear, I had taken her too much for granted. My marriage to Kristen had made me skeptical about long-term relationships, and at that time I did not have the same commitment as Joan did. I was also under pressure from my parents to get back together with Kristen or, if not, then to marry some kind of university-educated, tennis-playing girl from Surrey—which Joan emphatically was not.

I remember telling my parents that Joan had moved in with me. Dad was fishing on the shore of a lake, and Mum was pointing out a rising trout.

In the ensuing silence Dad flunked his cast, which landed in a tangle.

"That's torn it," he said.

But that night when I sat holding Joan's scribbled note in the houseboat and thought about our unborn baby, I realized that I really loved her. Until that moment I had been guilty of wanting to have my cake and eat it—to enjoy a great relationship without making a commitment to it. I had enjoyed a number of different relationships and had never thought about the consequences. I think lots of men would happily drift through life without having children unless their women forced the issue. I called Rose, Joan's sister, and dashed around to be with Joan.

About six months into Joan's pregnancy I was in France while Joan was on holiday in Scotland. She had an attack of appendicitis in Fort William. While she was in hospital having the emergency operation, I flew to Scotland. In fact she did not have appendicitis but an ovarian cyst that had burst, and the doctors decided to go ahead and remove her appendix as well—a dangerous operation at the best of times but more so on a woman six months pregnant. The operation triggered Joan into labor. She was put on a drip to reduce the contractions, and we immediately set off in an ambulance for a more modern hospital at Inverness. The drive across Scotland in the snow was a nightmare. Every jolt of the road sent Joan into further contractions. By the time we arrived she was in agony as a result of the operation and the pain of the contractions, and she was desperately trying to keep the baby in.

At Inverness Hospital it became clear that Joan would have to give birth. The baby's chance of survival was small, as it was three months premature. A baby girl was born who weighed just four pounds, and we called her Clare after my aunt. Clare could scarcely feed, and the hospital did not have the necessary equipment to keep her alive.

Although Clare opened her eyes to reveal lovely deep milky blue eyes, she died after four days. All I can remember of her now is her tiny size. Neither of us was allowed to hold or touch her. Her brief home was in an incubator. She was so small she would have fitted into the palm of my hand. We pored over her face and marveled at her tiny hands and the determined set to her face as she slept. But now that memory has faded. When I try to remember Clare, my mind is cluttered by the antiseptic smell of the hospital, the metal chairs in our room scraping over the lino, and the haunted look on the nurse's face as she came to tell us that Clare hadn't made it.

Clare inhabited a world of her own and came in and out of our lives, leaving only despair and emptiness and love behind her. She was so small and lived for so little time that she was almost never here at all, but in that powerful and heartbreaking time, she brought Joan and me intensely close together. Until I had seen Clare's tiny, fragile body, dwarfed by the tiniest nappy, and seen how beautiful she was, and known that she was our baby, I had never thought that I would like to have a child.

After Clare's death, Joan and I were determined to have another baby, and to our delight Joan became pregnant again within a year.

Once again Joan went into labor early, this time by six weeks. Both of us were taken by surprise. I was at a party at the Venue and arrived home at three in the morning, roaring drunk. I fell into a deep sleep and only reluctantly awoke when I felt Joan slapping me about the face and shouting that she was having contractions. I fell out of bed and managed to drive her to hospital. The doctors examined Joan and led her to the maternity ward.

"You look fine," they reassured her.

Then they looked at me.

"You look terrible. You'd better take these aspirins and go to bed."

Sometime later that morning, I was woken up to find four doctors peering at me through their masks. I assumed that I had had a terrible accident and was in a casualty ward somewhere.

"Joan is well into labor," they said. "You'd better come with us."

Holly was born, under six pounds in weight. It was the most incredible experience I've ever been through. And by the end of it I believe I was even more exhausted than Joan. I pledged to myself that I'd never miss the birth of one of our children. However, after what had happened to Clare, our immediate concern was keeping Holly alive.

We drove back to the houseboat on a freezing cold November morning in 1981, and Joan wrapped Holly up with her in bed. For the rest of the winter they stayed primarily in the bedroom while I worked in the room next door. Penni used to walk through the bedroom to her desk, which was tucked between the bilge pump and the stairs.

In 1981 Virgin Music finally began to earn some money. We had nine singles in the Top Twenty, including "Gentlemen Take Polaroids," by Japan, which got to number 1. Other Top Twenty hits were OMD's "Enola Gay," XTC's "Generals and Majors," and Ian Gillan's "Trouble." The Professionals, the Skids, and China Crisis were also successes. We still didn't know what Phil Collins would come up with, and—twenty-fourth on my list of things to do that month—I arranged to go up to Scotland to a concert by one of our new bands, Simple Minds. Simple Minds' album, *New Gold Dream,* was a best-seller.

The best news of 1981 was that Simon's prediction about the Human League was proved right. Their first two albums were quite experimental and built up a loyal cult following. When we noticed that their sales kept steadily rising, we knew that we had every chance of breaking through. Their third album, *Dare,* powered into the Top Ten and then went to Number 1. *Dare* sold over 1 million copies in Britain and 3 million around the world. The hit single "Don't You Want Me, Baby?" was played over and over again and became ingrained in everyone's mind.

Almost as quickly as they had run out, Virgin's cash balances were now restored. Whenever Virgin has money, I always renew my search for new opportunities. I am always trying to broaden the group so that we are not dependent upon a narrow source of income, but I suspect that this is due more to inquisitiveness and restlessness than sound financial sense. This time I thought that I saw a perfect opportunity.

Londoners traditionally read a listing magazine called *Time Out* to find out what's going on in the city. In those days *Time Out* was extremely left-wing. The standing joke was that you read a *Time Out* review and then did the opposite of what they recommended since they brought such an extreme political slant to any review. Mick Jagger had once remarked that getting through to the listings section in *Time Out* was like trying to cross a picket line. I had spoken to the owner of *Time Out*, Tony Elliott, a number of times about buying the magazine because it seemed to me that there was room for a pure entertainment guide without the politics.

In the spring of 1981 Tony Elliott had a dispute with his staff that led to a strike. Since Virgin was an entertainment company, I thought that we could seize the opportunity and publish our own magazine.

Joan and I had bought a house in the country, close to the Manor studios, called Mill End. I invited Tony Elliott up for lunch one weekend and suggested that we join forces to produce a new entertainment magazine while his staff were out on strike. Tony decided against the idea. I therefore decided to bring out our own rival magazine, to be called *Event*.

With the staff of *Time Out* on strike there was no listings magazine on the market. I hoped that if we could bring out *Event* quickly, then even when *Time Out* resurfaced we would be able to keep some of our readers. We hired Pearce Marchbank, who had designed *Time Out*, as the designer for *Event*, and he persuaded me that he should be editor as well. This may have been a mistake, but even as we set about pulling *Event* together, we were suddenly outflanked by developments at *Time Out*.

Knowing that *Event* was waiting in the wings, Tony Elliott rapidly gave his staff an ultimatum and broke the strike. His highly political left-wing staff split away from *Time Out* to form their own magazine, *City Limits*, and without them *Time Out* was free to reappear. We realized that we would not be able to beat *Time Out* back onto the streets, but worse than that, we realized that without their forty left-wing staff, *Time Out* could become the pure listings and entertainment magazine that we had intended *Event* to be—but with a well-established brand name.

The new *Time Out* was published on 18 September, and it met our worst fears: it was a very good, all-round entertainment magazine. The following week the first edition of the splinter publication *City Limits* came out together with our magazine, *Event*. With three listings magazines available, the London market was saturated. At the time Virgin did not have the extensive cash resources to support a new venture. When *Event* failed to win a high circulation, I stepped in to help. But it was a lost cause: *Time Out* was winning the circulation war, so I decided to cut our losses and close down the magazine.

After I closed down *Event, City Limits* and *Time Out* fought over the London market. Eventually, *City Limits* lost and went bust to leave *Time Out* supreme.

It is always difficult to admit to a failure, but the one positive element about the *Event* episode was that I realized how important it was to separate the various Virgin companies so that if one failed, it would not threaten the rest of the Virgin Group. *Event* was a disaster, but it was a contained disaster. Every successful businessman has failed at some ventures, and most entrepreneurs who run their own companies have been declared bankrupt at least once. Rather than defaulting on our debts, we paid them up and shut down the magazine.

The money that *Event* magazine lost Virgin was rapidly repaid to us by the Human League, Simple Minds, Phil Collins's enormously successful debut solo album, *Face Value,* and then, most spectacularly, by a young singer who called himself Boy George.

I had first heard of Boy George and Culture Club after Simon went to see them perform at a recording studio in Stoke Newington in 1981. The music-publishing rights had already been signed by Virgin, and Simon was intrigued by the startling appearance of their lead singer, a beautiful young drag queen, and the soft, easygoing white reggae they played. Simon invited the band back to Vernon Yard, where they agreed on a recording contract.

When Simon introduced me to George O'Dowd, I found myself shaking hands with somebody who looked utterly unlike anyone I had ever met before. His long hair was braided like a Rastafarian's; he had a pale white face and huge arched eyebrows; and he wore the ornate robes of a geisha girl.

Although we knew that Culture Club was an extraordinary creation, their first single, "White Boy," was stillborn. Virgin released it on 30 April 1982, but nothing much happened: it sold around 8,000 copies and reached 114 in the charts. We didn't mind. We really felt that as soon as Boy George was properly photographed or if we could get him onto *Top of the Pops*, his records would take off. People just had to see Boy George, and they would want to buy his music. Teenagers would go mad for him. As well as looking astonishing, George had a fabulous voice and was very witty and charming: he was a rebel in a totally different dimension from the Sex Pistols or James Dean, but a rebel nonetheless. Virgin brought out Culture Club's second single, "I'm Afraid of Me," in June, and although it sold better than "White Boy," it still reached only Number 100 in the charts. Culture Club carried on recording their album *Kissing to Be Clever,* which they had largely written before they signed with us.

When we released Culture Club's third single, "Do You Really Want to Hurt Me?" on 3 September 1982, it was our final attempt to launch the band. Funnily enough, Radio 2 played the song before Radio 1, but general reviews of the single were poor: "Watered down fourth-division reggae," wrote *Smash Hits.* "Awful." But with the Radio 2 exposure it crept up the charts, up to Number 85 in its first week and Number 38 in its second week. We plugged Boy George as hard as we could, but the BBC refused to interview him, calling him a "transvestite." Then we heard about a cancellation on *Top of the Pops.* We did everything we could to get Boy George into that slot, and when *Top of the Pops* finally agreed, we suspected that we had a sensation in the making.

With his white face, his swaying robes, his felt hat, and his impossibly arched eyebrows, Boy George beat every other sophisticated romantic band, such as Spandau Ballet, at their own game. He appealed to all teenagers, as well as to children as young as eight and their grandmothers to boot. It was impossible to define why he was so popular—parents wanted to mother him, girls wanted to be as beautiful, boys wanted their girlfriends to be as beautiful—it's impossible to quantify. The next day the telephones rang off the walls and the orders for the single came pouring in. "Do You Really Want to Hurt Me?" rose to Number 3. George then appeared on Noel Edmonds's *Late Late Breakfast Show,* and Noel asked him whether he was a great fan of Liberace. "Not anymore," George smiled, implying that the roles had now been reversed. The single reached Number 1. When George announced that he preferred a cup of tea to sex, he became an international icon.

For Christmas 1982 we released Culture Club's first album, *Kissing to Be Clever,* which sold 4 million copies around the world. And then in January came another amazing breakthrough: their fourth single, "Karma Chameleon," was the top-selling single of 1983, selling over 1.4 million copies in the United Kingdom and reaching Number 1 in every country around the world that had a chart, over thirty countries to our knowledge. Culture Club was a worldwide pop phenomenon, and their second album, *Colour by Numbers,* sold almost 10 million copies.

Virgin's finances were thrown upside down: from the £900,000 loss in 1981, we made a profit of £2 million in 1982 on sales of £50 million. In 1983 our sales shot up to £94 million and our profits soared to £11 million. Once we had started the Boy George fan club, it was impossible to control it, and in 1983, 40 percent of our profits came from Boy George. For the first two years the Culture Club story was the perfect model. The extraordinary thing about the record industry is how success can take off without warning. One minute nobody had heard of Boy George, the next minute every person around the world from Ireland to Korea and Japan to Ghana was humming "Karma Chameleon." Boy George's success was measured literally by the speed of sound. Many people find that such a vertical run is frightening, and they would be right to think that it creates havoc in a company. Happily I have always thrived on havoc and adrenalin, and so I felt perfectly at home as we fanned the flames of Culture Club's success.

Chapter 13

"New Yorkers craned their necks and wondered what the
cryptic message WAIT FOR THE ENGLISH VIRGI meant."

1983–1984

*I*t is always easier to live with the benefit of hindsight. People often point out that Nik sold his 40 percent stake in
Virgin at the wrong time. But when Nik and I split up, he
was as aware of the sales figures and profit forecast as I
was and things were in bad shape. At the time Nik and I were both happy:
Nik was happy to have left a company that looked as if it was heading into
trouble, and I was happy to have virtually full control of my destiny even if
I knew that Virgin was on a knife-edge. Soon after Nik left, two things happened that could not have been foreseen: first, compact discs became wide-
spread, and so we were able to resell our back catalog on CD. Many people
replicated their entire record collection on compact disc, and certainly an
artist like Mike Oldfield sold tremendously well on CD; the Sex Pistols did
less well.

The second change was that Virgin itself became the undisputed leading
independent record label. Simon's taste in music finally triumphed: Virgin
Music started to dominate the Top Ten singles and albums charts. From
being seen as a one-band record label that had made an incongruous leap
from Mike Oldfield to the Sex Pistols, Virgin Music was now the envy of the
record industry. All Simon's signings of the last couple of years took off at
once: we had the Human League as well as their spin-off Heaven 17, Simple
Minds, Boy George, Phil Collins, China Crisis, and Japan. The wonderful
thing about these artists was that we had broken them all ourselves. I was
still determined to sign a classic act of the caliber of Bryan Ferry or the
Rolling Stones, but the beauty of our roster was that it was all homegrown
and they were finally beginning to sell well overseas.

As I watched the money pour into the bank, I began to think of other
ways to use it. Although I was closely involved in signing bands, I felt that I

knew as much as I wanted to know about negotiating record contracts. I needed another challenge. I had the opportunity to use our cash to set up more Virgin companies and widen the basis of the group so that all our eggs would not be in one basket if we were hit by another recession. I also wanted to expand the Virgin name to stand for more than a record label and become more widely involved in all kinds of media. It was only three years since Virgin had almost gone bust and only two years since Nik had left. From having had very little money with which to play over the last two years, I now had cash mounting up in the bank, and I wanted to reinvest it as fast as possible.

When I began looking for other businesses to start up, I thought about expanding our tiny book-publishing business. I knew that the music-publishing side of Virgin Music made a very good living from publishing the music and collecting royalties, and I wondered whether a properly managed book-publishing division would be as successful. At the back of my mind was the thought that if a rock star is famous, there should be all sorts of other activities that they could explore, including books and videos, appearances in films, and sound tracks.

Vanessa, my youngest sister, had been going out with Robert Devereux since he was at Cambridge University. Robert had become part of the family. Although Virgin is not a family company in the traditional sense in that it has not been passed down vertically from generation to generation, it is a family company in a horizontal sense in that I always involve my wider family in whatever I do, and I listen to their opinions as closely as anyone else's. I know that a number of businessmen shut their families off from their work: they scarcely invite their children into their offices, and when they are at home they never discuss what they do at work. The British characteristically do not discuss money over a meal, but when this boils over into never discussing business with family members, then I think this represents a lost opportunity. Business is a way of life. It is small wonder that there are so few business entrepreneurs when business is excluded from the family circle.

While I was contemplating what to do about Virgin Books, Vanessa suggested that I should talk to Robert, who had been working at Macmillan Publishers for three years. Robert came around to *Duende* with his boss, Rob Shreeve, and I asked them whether they would come and work at Virgin Publishing. I had no clear idea what Virgin Books should do apart from somehow exploiting the growing success of the Virgin rock stars. Robert suggested that books and videos could be sold through the same outlets; he had the idea that Virgin Books could form part of a wider Virgin interest in the media, which could involve television, radio, films, and videos as well as books. Undaunted by the reality that he was actually joining a tiny little publisher, Robert left his job and joined us at Virgin. Rob Shreeve decided to stay at Macmillan for the time being.

When Robert arrived at Virgin Books, he immediately put a stop to the line of novels that we were selling. He recast Virgin Books as a nonfiction specialist in books about rock music and sport. A few years later he decided to buy another publishing house, W. H. Allen, which he put together with Virgin Books. With hindsight this was a mistake: we tried to do too much, and in 1989 the publishing business ran into difficulties and had to be radically cut back. As one of our early acquisitions, it gave us firsthand experience of all the pain that has to come with laying off staff in order to turn a company around. It also demonstrated the benefits of growing a company from scratch, where you can employ exactly those people you want as well as establish the desired atmosphere. A year later, Rob Shreeve joined Virgin Books as managing director, with Robert as chairman. Together they relaunched the business as Virgin Publishing, concentrating on our core strengths of music and entertainment. Within a few years the company had become a highly successful publisher of books on entertainment and probably the world's leading publisher of books on popular music.

As Virgin Music grew into one of the leading record companies, Robert began to push for more funds to invest in what we called "Virgin Vision." As the first diversification from publishing books, Robert wanted Virgin Vision to be involved in the British film industry.

Although I was keen to make films, I was particularly attracted by the tax incentives that would enable us to write off the investment against Virgin Music's profits. We produced a number of films such as *Secret Places* and *Loose Connections*, and then Robert made a film called *Electric Dreams*. The latter film cross-pollinated with Virgin Music in that the theme song was sung by a Virgin artist, Phil Oakey of the Human League, and became a Top Ten hit. The next film Virgin produced was George Orwell's *1984*. The original budget for this film was £2 million: Simon Perry and Mike Radford, who had produced and directed *Loose Connections*, were signed up to produce and direct *1984*, and John Hurt and Richard Burton were signed up as the stars. As the film was shot, the budget ran out of control. Robert and I were reluctant to compromise the quality of the film, but by the time the budget had soared to £5.5 million we decided that we had to take some control. The debt we had to take on to fund *1984* almost brought the whole Virgin Group down, and the banks lent us the money only because the record sales of Virgin Music were so successful. Simon and Ken were deeply skeptical about filmmaking, and I had to lean on them heavily to continue backing *1984*.

Rather than sacking Simon Perry and Mike Radford and replacing them with people who could bring the film in at some kind of sensible budget, we let them carry on to the end but decided to change the sound track, which Mike Radford had wanted to commission. Mike's choice was an unknown composer called Dominic Muldownie. We preferred to use the Eurythmics, who would do an excellent job as well as provide us with a hit album to re-coup some of the disastrous overspend.

After *1984* was released Simon Perry had a great row with us over the sound track and publicly accused us of interfering with his artistic integrity. Fortunately, the Eurythmics' sound track enabled us to salvage some of the money. An outstanding film, *1984* won the Best British Film of the Year award, but we made only one more film, *Absolute Beginners,* before the tax incentives for making films in Britain were cut and we decided, for the time being, to leave the risky business of making films to other people.

Most outsiders bracket films and music together as "entertainment," but we quickly learned that there is a vast difference. When we sign a contract with a rock star, the headline figure may appear huge as the press call it a "£5 million signing," but our financial exposure is rolled out slowly. Our initial commitment would cover the advance and the promotional costs of the first single and album, which might be around £300,000. If the first album is successful, then we would go on to the next album and so on. Thus we could always predict the future knowing the sales figures of the previous album before making the next stage of the investment, and we always had the back catalog to support us as we went along. With films our £5 million would be just that: a straight one-off payment that would be spent virtually all at once on making the film and would give us no guarantees for the film's success or for any future films. It was all or nothing. Even to my instinctive way of thinking, this looked like a precarious way of making money.

Rather than making films, Robert changed direction and began to push Virgin into distributing videos and films instead. This aspect of the business was far less risky than making the films themselves. In order to build a large market share Robert started off distributing pop videos for all record companies. He also bought back catalogs of old movies and distributed those as videos. Whenever I bumped into him, Robert was always working on some new deal—he once made a fortune distributing old Hollywood movies, dubbed over in Cantonese, in Hong Kong. Virgin Vision grew into a large distributor of films and videos with sales passing £50 million by the late 1980s.

Eventually Virgin Vision began to absorb too much cash for us to fund it. We had to spend large amounts on buying the rights to distribute films such as *Robocop 2* and then set about earning our profits. Deciding that we couldn't afford this cash drain, we asked Robert to sell the business. Robert sold Virgin Vision to an American company called MCEG. Just as the acquisition of W. H. Allen taught us a lot about buying companies, so the sale of Virgin Vision taught us a lot about selling them: although the headline price was $83 million, we took our payment in MCEG shares, which were listed on the American Stock Exchange. It all looked respectable enough, and our MCEG shares gave us 22 percent of the company. But within six months MCEG had gone bust and our $83 million consideration—22 percent of MCEG—was worthless. We never made that mistake again.

The growth of Virgin Vision had complemented Virgin Music in that it dealt in intellectual property, and it also broadened our base from being an exclusively music-based group. A number of people started suggesting ideas to us that would have increased Virgin's exposure in entertainment, but my imagination was really captured by a proposal that came entirely out of the blue, and could only remotely be defined as "entertainment." In February 1984 an American lawyer called Randolph Fields asked me whether I was interested in operating an airline.

Randolph Fields was looking for investors to finance a new airline that would use the Gatwick–to–New York route, which had become vacant following the collapse of Sir Freddie Laker's airline in 1982. He sent me a proposal, which I took up to read at Mill End, the house outside Oxford that Joan and I had bought as a weekend retreat. It was obvious that he had contacted lots of other investors before me—a record-label owner was hardly going to be his first call—so as I skimmed through the proposal I kept saying to myself *Don't get tempted. Don't even think about it.*

In the same way that I tend to make up my mind about people within thirty seconds of meeting them, I also make up my mind about a business proposal within thirty seconds and whether it excites me. I rely far more on gut instinct than researching huge amounts of statistics. This might be because, perhaps due to my dyslexia, I distrust numbers, which I feel can be twisted to prove anything. The idea of operating a Virgin airline grabbed my imagination, but I had to work out in my own mind what the potential risks were.

Throughout that weekend I mulled over the proposal. Randolph's idea was to offer an all-business-class airline, but this didn't appeal to me. I worried about what would happen on the days when businessmen didn't fly—

Christmas, Easter, bank holidays, the entire Thanksgiving week. I thought that we would have to have holidaymakers to fill the plane in those weeks. If we were going to be different from other airlines with their first, business, and economy classes, perhaps we could offer just two classes: business and economy. I wondered what the implications of that would be. We'd get both businessmen and tourists, but who would we miss? I wrote out a list of questions that I wanted to understand concerning how the aircraft leasing would work. If I could lease the plane for one year and then have the chance to return the plane, we would have a clear escape route if it all failed. It would be embarrassing, but we would limit the amount of money we lost. By the end of the weekend I had made up my mind: if we could limit everything to one year—the employment contracts, the leasing of the aircraft, the exchange exposure, and anything else that starting up a New York route involved—then I wanted to have a shot at it.

The only airline that was offering cheap fares across the Atlantic in 1984 was People Express. I picked up the phone and tried to call them. Their number was engaged. It was impossible to get through on their reservations line all morning. I reasoned that either People Express was very poorly managed, in which case they would be an easy target for new competition, or that they were so much in demand that there was room for new competition. It was that continual engaged tone on my telephone throughout Saturday more than anything else that triggered my belief that we could set up and run an airline.

I called up Simon on Sunday evening.

"What do you think about starting an airline?" I jauntily asked him. "I've got a proposal here . . ."

"For God's sake!" he cut across me. "You're crazy. Come off it."

"I'm serious."

"You're not," he said. "You're mad."

"Okay," I said. "I won't go into it now. But I think we should have lunch."

On Monday morning I called up international directory inquiries and asked for the number for Boeing. Boeing is based in Seattle, and due to the time difference I couldn't speak to them until late that afternoon. They were rather bemused to hear an Englishman asking what kind of deals were available on a jumbo. I spent all afternoon and all evening on the phone to Boeing, and eventually I spoke to someone who told me that Boeing did lease aircraft and that they had a secondhand jumbo that they would seriously consider taking back after a year if things didn't work out. With this extremely basic, not to say sketchy, information I prepared to face Simon and

Ken. Lunch the next day was not a success. After I told them how impossible it had been to get through to People Express but that Boeing had planes to lease, they looked shocked. I think they realized I had done all the market research that I felt I needed to do and had made up my mind. They were right: I had worked myself up into a state about it.

"You're a megalomaniac, Richard," Simon said. "We've been friends since we were teenagers, but if you do this I'm not sure that we can carry on working together. What I'm telling you is that you go ahead with this over my dead body."

Ken was less outspoken, but he too thought that the idea of combining a record company with an airline was anathema.

"I can't see the connection," he said. "And if you're looking for losses to offset against our profits, we could always invest in new bands."

"All right then," I said. "We won't combine it. We'll keep the two companies separate. We can arrange the financing so that Virgin Music is scarcely at risk. I've spoken to Boeing, and they can offer a lease whereby they take the plane back after a year if it doesn't work. The most Virgin would lose would be two million pounds."

Simon and Ken remained resolutely opposed.

"Come on," I plowed on. "Virgin can afford to make this step. The risk is less than a third of this year's profits. Money from Culture Club is pouring in. And it'll be fun."

Simon and Ken both winced when I said "fun," which is a particularly loaded word for me—it's one of my prime business criteria. Since I had made up my mind, I knew that I had to convince them. I carried on, arguing that we would have only one plane, that we could just dip our toe into the water, and that if the water was too hot we could cut our losses. I explained that the beauty of starting from scratch rather than buying an existing airline was that we could easily retreat if it didn't work. In my mind it was that simple. Simon was most worried that I was risking the value of his shareholding in the Virgin group, and I think that Ken thought that I had gone way over the top.

In the same way that the argument over the Human League had been a turning point in Simon's and my relationship with Nik, the argument over that lunch was a turning point in my relationship with Simon. Over the years I had unnerved him several times, but this time he felt that I was prepared to bet the company and all our accumulated wealth on a scheme that he thought was totally harebrained. Simon's interest in and love for life come from the arts, music, books, his collection of paintings, and beautiful cars. My interest in life comes from setting myself huge, apparently unachievable challenges and trying to rise above them. In a purely commercial sense, Simon was absolutely right; but from the perspective of wanting to live life to the full, I felt that I had to attempt it. From that Monday lunch onward a tension sprang up in our relationship, and it has never fully dissolved.

Randolph was proposing to call the airline British Atlantic, but if I was going to be involved, I wanted to bring Virgin into the title. We agreed to differ on that until the airline was a little closer to reality. There was a lot to learn, so I asked Sir Freddie Laker, whom I've always admired, whether he could help me. Sir Freddie came for lunch on *Duende* and explained the mechanics of running an airline. He quickly confirmed my suspicions about the limitations of starting an airline that was exclusively business class.

"And you don't want to be all no-frills economy service either," he pointed out. "That was my mistake. You'll be vulnerable to the simple cost-cutting attack which put me out of business."

We began a discussion of the philosophy of the business-class service at that lunch: to offer a first-class service at business-class fares and build in all kinds of extra services for the cost. Two of the best ideas that came out of our lunch were to offer a limousine pickup as part of the service and to offer a free economy ticket for anyone who flew business.

Freddie also warned me to expect some fierce competition from British Airways:

"Do all you can to stop BA," he said. "Complain as loudly as possible, use the CAA to stop them, and don't hesitate to take them to court. They're utterly ruthless. My mistake was that I never complained loudly enough. They destroyed my financing, and it's too late for me now. I sued them and won millions of dollars, but I lost my airline. If you ever get into trouble, sue them before it's too late.

"Another thing, Richard, is the stress. I'm not kidding, but you should have regular medical checkups. It is very stressful."

Freddie told me that he was just recovering from cancer of the pancreas.

"You need to go to a doctor and ask him to stick his finger up your bum. He'll be able to tell you what's what," Freddie said.

I was inspired to see that despite all his problems, Freddie was still so ebullient. He was unbowed by the experience, and he saw me as his successor, picking up the flag where he had left off. I asked Freddie whether he would object if I called Virgin Atlantic's first aircraft "Spirit of Sir Freddie," but he laughed it off:

"Not the first one," he said. "My name's a liability now, and you'd send out the wrong signals. But I'd be honored when you've got a larger fleet."

As Freddie left *Duende,* he turned around and shouted back at me:

"One last word of advice, Richard. When you're bent over and the doctor's got his finger up your bum, make sure that he hasn't got both his hands on your shoulders!"

Roaring with laughter, he made his way along the towpath.

The first arrangement I made with Randolph was that we would have an equal partnership. I would invest the funds, and he would run the airline. Randolph had already recruited two key people from Laker Airways: Roy Gardner, who had run the engineering side of Laker, and David Tait, who had run the American side of the operation.

"What do you think of the name?" I asked David Tait.

"British Atlantic?" He snorted. "Just what the world needs: another BA!"

Using David's reaction, I managed to get Randolph to agree to change the name to Virgin Atlantic Airways, and we formed a joint partnership.

"What do you think of the new name?" I asked David Tait.

"Virgin Atlantic?" He snorted. "Nobody will ever step foot inside a plane called Virgin. It's ridiculous. Who'd fly an airline that's not prepared to go full distance?"

Within a couple of weeks it became clear that the arrangement between Randolph and me would not work. At our first meeting in front of the Civil Aviation Authority, Randolph arrived to talk about his plans for the new airline. Colin Howes, my lawyer from Harbottle and Lewis, was there. After watching Randolph blustering for a few minutes, Colin slipped out of the hearing to call and advise me to get across to Kingsway:

"It's not going very well," Colin said. "I think that Randolph is digging a hole for himself."

I came into the hearing and saw that Randolph was being fiercely cross-examined by British Caledonian, who were objecting to our license application. Our airline was purely an idea, a paper airline, so it was easy for them to run rings around us, asking what we intended to do about safety drills, how we were going to maintain our plane, how we could guarantee our passengers' safety. Randolph, an impatient man, was growing angry and confused in the face of this sustained questioning. Equally, the CAA appeared rather skeptical about Randolph's ability to get an airline off the ground. When the CAA came onto the question of finances, the British Caledonian lawyer looked across the room at me and said:

"You'll have to have a lot of hits on *Top of the Pops* to keep the airline going."

"Actually," I pointed out tartly, "Virgin made profits of eleven million pounds last year—more than twice those of your client, British Caledonian."

I decided not to mention that we were having to pay out large sums of money to continue making the film *1984*, which was running way over budget. After the CAA specified that the new airline would have to have working capital of £3 million, they gave their permission for us to fly in theory. This permission was the official blessing. Of course, the CAA could withdraw their permission at any time if we failed to meet safety requirements. We would have to have another CAA test once we had leased the aircraft, but for now we had the go-ahead to establish the airline. We rented a warehouse near Gatwick Airport, where we based Roy Gardner and his engineering team and started recruiting pilots and cabin staff; we rented office space in the Air Florida office on Woodstock Street, just off Oxford Street, where we piggybacked on their computer reservations system and created a dummy file for the Virgin Atlantic flights. David Tait moved his family up from Miami back to their home in Toronto and started living at the Virgin Music office in New York. A team of lawyers representing Boeing came over to London to start negotiating over the lease of the aircraft, and soon they were spending most of their days with me on the upper deck of *Duende* while Joan and Holly lived on the floor below.

The houseboat was becoming increasingly crowded with the addition of Holly and the comings and goings to do with the airline. Joan and I decided to look for a home on land for the family and finally settled in a large, comfortable house off Ladbroke Grove.

The first casualty of Virgin Atlantic Airways was my relationship with Randolph Fields. Two things became clear: the first was that since Virgin Group was being asked to guarantee the entire finances of Virgin Atlantic, Coutts Bank would countenance extending credit to us only if we had control of Virgin Atlantic. They would not lend us money if we controlled only half the new airline. Since Randolph was not putting up any money, he saw the sense of this and reluctantly agreed that Virgin should have a controlling share of the airline. A far more difficult problem with Randolph came about in his relations with the new Virgin Atlantic staff. Perhaps if we had had a longer time than the four months we gave ourselves, it would have been different. But we felt that if we were to survive the first year, then we must launch in June in order to take advantage of the heavy summer traffic and build up reserves and cash flow to keep us going through the lean winter months. The timetable was virtually impossible, demanding that we work flat out. One moment we might be choosing the design of the air hostesses' uniform or working out the menu, the next we were arguing over some legal clause in the ninety-six-page document that we were negotiating with Boeing over the lease of the aircraft.

I first got wind of serious trouble from David Tait, whom Randolph had employed in America and who was going to be crucial to our chances of succeeding.

"I've resigned," he told me. "I'm sorry, but Randolph is impossible to work with."

"What's the matter?" I asked. I knew that without David selling tickets in America, Virgin Atlantic would be stillborn.

"I can't tell you everything," David said. "It's just impossible. I'm sorry, but I wish you all the best and hope that it's a great success."

Sensing that David was about to ring off, I begged him to come to London to see me. He had no money to buy a ticket, so I sent him one and he came two days later. When he arrived at *Duende,* he found me holding Holly, who was feverish and screaming. Joan had gone off to buy more Calpol. We smiled at each other above the noise as I cuddled Holly.

"You may think that's loud," David said. "But I can tell you that Randolph can scream louder. I can't work for him."

David's experience comfirmed the growing realization I was having that we had to move Randolph to one side if we were going to get the airline started. David had taken a great gamble in joining Virgin Atlantic. He had moved his young family back to Toronto and was living by himself on the top floor of our Greenwich Village house, which Ken Berry had first bought. All he had was a desk and a telephone and a tiny bedroom, and he had to try to sell tickets to Americans for a start-up airline. Since he was unable to advertise Virgin Atlantic without an American license (which would come only the day before we took off), David had tried to alert New Yorkers by advertising in the sky above Manhattan. On a cloudless spring afternoon a formation of five small planes had planned to squirt out white-and-red smoke and print the letters WAIT FOR THE ENGLISH VIRGIN across the sky. Unfortunately, just as they were finishing, a single cloud blew over and obliterated the final letter, so New Yorkers craned their necks and wondered what the cryptic message WAIT FOR THE ENGLISH VIRGI meant.

David's fallout with Randolph concerned the ticketing system. Randolph had wanted to avoid all travel agents, who charged 10 percent of the fare for their services and instead to sell every ticket through a theater-booking agency called Ticketron. David had looked at Ticketron, which charged only five dollars for issuing a ticket, but he had refused to deal with them. He argued to Randolph that since the 30,000 travel agents across America sell 90 percent of all airline tickets, if Virgin Atlantic tried to cut them out by using a theater ticket company, the agents would retaliate by cutting us out. On top of that, Ticketron had only six New York offices, which was not enough to sell 200 tickets for each flight to the United Kingdom. Back at home the London ticketing system, run by a reservations manager who had been appointed by Randolph, was in chaos. An airline's ticketing system is its life's blood, and in order to try to sort out a workable system, David had single-handedly come to an agreement with an airline ticketing system owned by Ross Perot called EDS, the industry standard. He had done so because if he had gone ahead with Ticketron, he could see that we would be left without a proper reservations system and the airline would fall apart. When Randolph had heard about this, he had been furious and had shouted down the telephone at David. Eventually David decided that he didn't need to be shouted at by a twenty-nine-year-old lawyer who didn't know how the airline industry worked.

The staff from the Woodstock Street ticketing office had also complained about Randolph's behavior. They had told me that he kept bursting into the room and asking everyone to leave it so that he could make telephone calls in private. I realized that Randolph was not the right person to run the new airline. I promised David Tait that if he stayed, he would soon have no more trouble from Randolph.

"He won't be here much longer," I said. "You can deal with me directly."

As we worked through April and May, more and more of the airline staff dealt with me directly. Cut out of the operation, Randolph became increasingly difficult to cope with. Eventually my lawyers advised me to change the locks on the ticketing office to keep him out. As the inaugural flight fixed for June drew nearer, Randolph and I were on a war footing.

I still wonder how we packed everything into those last few days. The newly trained cabin crew came to the Woodstock Street office to man the telephones, which were ringing off the hook; the lease with Boeing was finally wrapped up, including a complete maze of legal conditions but basically allowing us to return the aircraft to them after a year and to be reimbursed for at least the original cost; if the aircraft had risen in value, then we would receive the upside. After two months of negotiation, I think Boeing were rather surprised at our tenacity: "It's easier to sell a fleet of jumbos to an American airline than just one to Virgin," admitted their negotiator after we had finished. The continual negotiation of music-recording contracts had stood me in good stead. As a side agreement to the lease contract, we had a currency agreement to protect us if the pound fell in value against the dollar (our exposure was in dollars).

At one point I took Boy George to meet all the staff in the Woodstock Street office. He was dressed in his usual bizarre collection of robes, with his hair plaited and braided and tied with ribbons and his gloves festooned with huge diamond rings. He stood for a minute watching the complete chaos as everyone answered the phones, made out tickets, told passengers about our timetable, invited celebrities and journalists for the inaugural flight, and worked on dummy copies of the in-flight magazine. Then he said:

"I'm pleased that I've got my feet squarely on the ground."

Chapter 14

"We were now hurtling down the runway, and these two pilots were doing nothing about it. . . . Then just as the plane's nose rose up . . . the West Indian reached behind his ear, pulled out a joint, and offered it to his copilot."

1984

On 19 June 1984, three days before we were due to launch, I went to Gatwick for our final CAA approval, a test flight. *Maiden Voyager* stood by a departure gate, and I marveled again at her size. I also marveled at the enormous size of the Virgin logo on her tail fin—the largest version of what someone once called "the Virgin scrawl" I had ever seen. I remembered back in the early 1970s, when Simon and I had been talking to a graphic designer about a change of logo. Trevor Key had paused for a moment and then scrawled "Virgin" on the back of a napkin. On the way to the loo I had looked over his shoulder and said: "That'll do." We didn't begrudge him his two-hundred-pound bill. Some marketing experts once analyzed the scrawl and wrote about the upbeat way it rose from left to right. This of course might have been going through Trevor's head when he was writing it, but I just think the napkin might have been at an angle. Seeing it up on the tail fin made me realize what we had started. This thing was going to happen: we had a jumbo.

The entire cabin crew came on board for the ride, as did over 100 staff, and I sat at the back with the CAA official. The plane had arrived only the previous day, flown over from Seattle, and until we received our formal CAA license to fly, the engines were uninsured. We took off, and the crew all burst out clapping and cheering. I could hardly stop myself from shedding a tear, I felt so proud of everyone.

Then there was a loud bang from outside, the plane lurched to the left, and a massive flash of flame followed by a long trail of black smoke poured out of one of the engines.

In that horrible stunned silence, the CAA official put his arm around my shoulders.

"Don't worry, Richard," he said. "These things happen."

We had flown into a flock of birds, and one of the engines had sucked in a few of them and exploded. We needed a new engine overnight in order to do the CAA test flight again. Our inaugural flight to New York was due to take off the day after tomorrow with 250 journalists and cameramen on board.

Roy Gardner was with me, and he radioed through to the maintenance team, who were at British Caledonian. When *Maiden Voyager* had arrived the previous day, Roy had rejected two of the engines on financial grounds and asked for two others to be fitted. Now he recalled one of the engines that had been taken to Heathrow and was about to be flown back to Seattle.

When we landed I was standing beside the plane trying to think how to overcome this problem when a press photographer came up to me smiling broadly.

"I'm sorry," I apologized. "I'm not up to it now."

"I'm sorry, too," he said. "I saw the flames and smoke pouring out of your engine. I actually got a great shot of it."

He looked at my dumbstruck face and then said:

"Don't worry, though. I'm from the *Financial Times;* we're not that kind of paper." He opened up his camera, pulled out the film, and gave it to me. I couldn't find words to thank him. If that photograph had appeared in the press, it would have been the end of Virgin Atlantic before we'd even begun.

Unfortunately, because Virgin Atlantic did not have a CAA license, we were uninsured for the engine. The replacement cost was £600,000, and we had to pay for a new one. After several desperate calls, I realized that there was no alternative. With a sinking feeling I called up Coutts to let them know that a payment of £600,000 would have to go through.

"You're very close to your limit," Chris Rashbrook, the manager of our account, said.

Our overdraft limit with Coutts for the entire Virgin Group was set at £3 million.

"It's a terrible freak accident," I said. "One of the engines blew up, and we can't get our insurance until we get our license. Without a new engine, we won't be able to get our license. It's a catch-22 situation."

"Well, I'm just warning you," Rashbrook told me. "You spent a fortune on filming *Electric Dreams,* and we're still waiting for the MGM check."

The MGM check was the £6 million that MGM had agreed to pay for the American distribution rights to *Electric Dreams.*

"Please, can you wait until I get this inaugural flight out of the way?" I asked. "Let's sort it out when I get home. I'm back on Friday. We'll only be £300,000 over our limit. When the MGM check comes through we'll have no overdraft and around three million pounds on deposit."

He said that he'd think about it.

The day before the inaugural flight, *Maiden Voyager* was fitted with another engine and was ready to fly again. The CAA official came on board and we took off. This time there was no explosion and we were given our license. I dashed back to London to sort out another Randolph Fields crisis. We had offered Randolph £1 million, but he thought that wasn't enough. He had gone to a judge in America and applied for an injunction to stop *Maiden Voyager* taking off. All through the night we had a damage limitation meeting with David Tait and Roy Gardner and my lawyers, attempting to work out an arrangement whereby we could prevent Randolph from ruining the airline. The judge eventually threw his request out, but not before we had battled all night to keep on top of what he was up to. By dawn we felt that we would win, and at 6 A.M. I ran a bath and lay in it. I felt exhausted. I tried to wash my face, but my eyes felt sore and itchy as if a fine blast of sand had blown into them. David Tait came in and sat on the lavatory, and we ran through the final list of things we had to do. David then left to catch the Concorde so that he would arrive in New York before us in order to organize the welcoming reception for the flight.

On board for the inaugural I was surrounded by family and friends—the people who had been most important to me and to Virgin over the last ten years. I sat next to Joan, who had Holly on her lap. Behind us was virtually everyone from the Virgin Group. The aircraft was full of journalists and photographers together with a collection of conjurors, entertainers, and Uri Geller. As *Maiden Voyager* taxied down the runway, the screen at the front of the cabin flickered into life and showed the backs of the pilots and the flight engineer as they sat in the flight deck and manned the controls. Over their shoulders we could see the view through the windscreen. An announcement came over the loudspeakers:

"Since this is our first flight, we thought that you might like to share our view from the flight deck and see what really happens when we take off."

The screen showed a picture of the flight deck with the view of the runway stretching out in front. Then we started speeding down the runway, and the tarmac rushing beneath the windscreen gathered pace until the white lines were just a blur. But the pilots seemed rather relaxed: rather than staring intently ahead and flying the plane, they started looking sideways at each other and smiling. One of them had very long hair beneath his cap; the other was a West Indian. We were now hurtling down the runway, and these two pilots were doing nothing about it. They were simply paying no attention. Everyone watching the screen held their breath: this was all some mad suicide flight by that lunatic Branson. . . . There was a deathly hush. Then just as the plane's nose rose up and the runway disappeared from view, the West Indian reached behind his ear, pulled out a joint, and offered it to his copilot. Before anyone was entirely sure that this was a joke, the plane headed upward, and the two pilots took off their caps and turned around to face the camera: they were Ian Botham and Viv Richards, two well-known cricketers. The bearded flight engineer was me. The whole plane rocked with laughter—we had filmed the takeoff the previous day on a flight simulator.

We had loaded seventy cases of champagne on board, which proved to be just about right for what turned into an eight-hour party. People danced in the aisles as we played Madonna's new hit "Like a Virgin" and Culture Club and Phil Collins. For a quiet interval we showed the movie *Airplane,* and the cabin crew started a Virgin tradition by giving out Choc Ices in the middle of the film. At New Jersey's Newark Airport I realized that in all the excitement, I had forgotten my passport, and I was almost refused entrance to the reception party in the terminal. By some mistake, the cabin crew had thrown away all the cutlery, so they had to scrabble around up to their elbows in all the rubbish bins retrieving the cutlery to wash it up and then get it back on board the plane. I embarrassed everyone except the mayor of Newark when I went up to him and chatted, thinking for some bizarre reason that he had organized the catering. I took the return flight to Gatwick and fell into my first long sleep for many weeks. I dreamed about exploding engines, cabin crew offering meals on plates straight from the rubbish bins, and pilots smoking marijuana. When I awoke, I felt sure that nothing else could go wrong. A bad mistake.

A taxi carried me back to London. As we pulled up at my house I saw a rather uncomfortable-looking man sitting on the steps. At first I thought that he was a journalist, but then I realized that it was Christopher Rashbrook, my bank manager at Coutts. I invited him in, and he sat down in the sitting room. I was exhausted and he was fidgety. I was rather slow to understand what he was saying. But then I suddenly heard him say that Coutts were unable to extend Virgin's overdraft as requested and would therefore regrettably bounce any checks that took our overdraft over £3 million. I rarely lose my temper. In fact, I can count the times I have lost my temper on the fingers of one hand, but as I looked across at this man in his blue pin-striped suit with his neat little black leather briefcase I felt my blood boil. He was standing there in his highly polished black Oxford brogues and calmly telling me that he was going to put the whole of Virgin out of business. I thought of the endless times since March when I and the Virgin Atlantic staff had worked through the night to solve a problem; I thought about how proud the new cabin crew were to be flying with a start-up airline; and I thought about the protracted negotiation we had fought with Boeing. If this bank manager bounced our checks, then Virgin would be out of business within days: nobody would supply an airline with anything such as fuel or food or maintenance if word went about that the checks were bouncing, and no passengers would fly with us.

"Excuse me," I said as he was still talking and making excuses. "You are not welcome in my house. Please get out." I took him by the elbow, led him to the front door, and pushed him outside. I shut the door in his bewildered face, walked back into the sitting room, and collapsed on a sofa in tears of exhaustion, frustration, and worry. Then I showered and called Ken:

"We've got to get as much money in from overseas as possible today. And then we've got to find new bankers."

Our overseas record subsidiaries saved us that week. We managed to pull in enough money on Friday to keep us just below the £3 million overdraft limit. We gave Coutts no reason to bounce our checks, and so we stopped them from pushing the various Virgin companies, together with the new airline, into instant insolvency. It was a surreal situation: Virgin Music was set to make £12 million profit that year and forecast to make £20 million the following one. We were already one of Britain's largest private companies, but Coutts were prepared to push us into insolvency—and make 3,000 people lose their jobs—for the sake of going £300,000 over our limit with a check for £6 million due to arrive any day from the States.

The Coutts crisis made me realize that we needed a tough financier to replace Nik. We needed someone who could cope with the finances of both Virgin Atlantic and Virgin Music and act as a bridge between the two. By living off cash flow and debt, the entire Virgin Group was living too dangerously. The mid-1980s were boom years in the City, and every company seemed able to sell its shares to the public and raise millions of pounds to invest. Perhaps, I began to think, that was the way forward for Virgin.

Apart from the four main operations—Virgin Music, the Virgin record shops, Virgin Vision, and the new airline, Virgin Atlantic—there were now a host of new little companies operating under the Virgin umbrella. There was Top Nosh food, which delivered food around industrial estates; Virgin Rags, a line of clothes; Virgin Pubs; and Vanson Property, a property development company, which looked after our growing collection of properties and as a sideline was making a lot of money by buying, developing, and then selling property. This disparate selection of businesses needed someone to put them in order.

Don Cruickshank was recommended to us by David Puttnam, the English filmmaker. He was a qualified chartered accountant, who had worked at the management consultants McKinsey for five years before moving to be general manager of *The Sunday Times* and then on to Pearson, where he had been managing director of the *Financial Times*. Robert Devereux, who by now was married to my sister Vanessa, had come across him when dealing with Goldcrest films, part of Pearson, but Simon knew nothing about him. Don started work in the cramped offices at Ladbroke Grove, and he was the first person at Virgin who had ever worn a suit and tie. Everyone marveled at him. With Don as managing director, Virgin became organized into a company that could attract outside investors.

Soon Don brought in Trevor Abbott as finance director. Trevor had been with MAM, Management Agency and Music, an entertainment company that had managed the careers of Tom Jones and Engelbert Humperdinck and had set up its own record label to launch Gilbert O'Sullivan. MAM had then diversified into music publishing, had a chain of hotels, operated a fleet of corporate jets, had nightclubs, and leased out slot machines and jukeboxes. MAM had a great deal in common with Virgin, but as Trevor left he was already working on the merger between MAM and Chrysalis.

Don and Trevor were soon holding meetings with banks and rearranging both our finances and the internal structure of the group. As a whole, Virgin's turnover in 1984 would exceed £100 million, and each time Don and Trevor saw me they expressed amazement at how things were run. They were aghast at the lack of computers in the group, the lack of stock control, and the apparently rather casual way Simon, Ken, Robert, and I decided how to invest our money. They came to see us on *Duende* and set out how they proposed to reorganize Virgin with a view to inviting in some outside investors.

The first thing they did was to sort out our overdraft facilities. Coutts and their parent company, National Westminster Bank, had been willing to close us down for exceeding a £3 million overdraft. Taking the same balance sheet to a different consortium of banks, Don and Trevor arranged an overdraft facility of £30 million. They then looked at the structure of the Virgin Group and decided to close down a number of our smaller companies, such as Top Nosh food and the pubs. They divided the Virgin Group into Music, Retail, and Vision, and then hived off Virgin Atlantic together with Virgin Holidays, Heaven and the Roof Garden nightclubs, and Necker Island into a separate private company. Simon and I were both thirty-three years old, as were Trevor and Ken. Don was a little older, Robert a little younger. We felt that we could take on anybody, and we now set our minds to take the Virgin Group public. We were going from the rock market to the stock market.

Chapter 15

"Whatever I did in the next ten minutes would lead to my death or survival. I was on my own. We had broken the record, but I was almost certainly going to die."

1984–1986

I am often asked why I go in for record-breaking challenges with either powerboats or hot-air balloons. People point out that, with success, money, and a happy family, I should stop putting myself and them at risk and enjoy what I am so lucky to have. Part of me wholeheartedly agrees with this obvious truth. I love life, I love my family, and I am horrified by the idea of being killed and leaving Joan without a husband and Holly and Sam without a father. But another part of me is driven to try new adventures, and I still find that I want to push myself to my limits.

If I were to think about it more carefully, I would say that I love to experience as much of life as I can. The physical adventures I have been involved with have added a special dimension to my life, which has reinforced the pleasure I take in my business. If I had refused to contemplate skydiving, or hot-air ballooning or crossing the Atlantic in a boat, my life would have been the duller for it. I never think that I am going to die by accident, but if I die then all I can say is that I was wrong, and the hardened realists who kept their feet on the ground were right—but at least I tried.

Apart from the thrill of the actual event, I love the preparation for it. A tremendous sense of camaraderie builds up within the team when we are preparing for a challenge, and if we are going after a record, there is not only the technological challenge but also a great sense of patriotism as the public become involved and cheer us on. There have been numerous British explorers, all in the best amateur tradition of Scott of the Antarctic, and I feel proud to follow in their footsteps.

The first challenge I was involved in was to try to recapture the Blue Riband for Britain. In the Victorian age of steamships, the Blue Riband was awarded to the fastest ship across the Atlantic. In 1893 the Blue Riband was held by the British Cunard line; then it went to three German ships before Cunard won it back again in 1906 with *Lusitania,* later sunk in 1915 by a German U-boat. After the First World War the Germans won it back, and then the Italian ship *Rex* won it in 1933 with an average crossing speed of 29 knots. In order to celebrate this achievement and to celebrate the whole Blue Riband competition, an English shipowner and member of Parliament called Harold Hales commissioned a monumental trophy. From then on the Hales' Trophy was awarded along with the Blue Riband during the last few years of the great age of the ocean liner.

In the small print of the conditions of the award, Hales offered it to the fastest boat that crossed the Atlantic, defining the Atlantic as the stretch of sea between Ambrose Light Tower on the American coast and the Bishop's Rock Lighthouse off the Scilly Isles. Hales made no mention of the size of boat as long as it carried passengers; indeed, nobody in those days ever considered that a small boat would have any chance of competing safely with the big ships.

The next ship to win the Hales' Trophy was *Normandie,* a French liner that crossed the Atlantic on her maiden voyage at an average speed of 30 knots. In the last year before the age of the big passenger ships died, the SS *United States* won the Hales' Trophy in 1952 with a crossing that took 3 days, 10 hours, and 40 minutes. The Hales' Trophy was put away in the American Merchant Marine Museum in Kings Point, New York. Unfortunately, Harold Hales did not witness the SS *United States;* with horrible irony he had drowned in a boating accident on the River Thames. The glorious days of passenger liners faded as people began to use the new transport industry, the airlines, and everyone forgot about the Hales' Trophy.

In 1980 a powerboat builder called Ted Toleman decided to resurrect the Blue Riband competition and attempt to win the Hales' Trophy back for Britain. In order to do so, he would have to build a boat that could cross the Atlantic in less than 3 days, 10 hours, and 40 minutes. The SS *United States* was a truly impressive ship: she weighed 52,000 tons and needed 240,000 horsepower to shift her. The speed record she set was impressive: an average of 35.6 knots (equivalent to 40 miles per hour). In contrast to this huge 52,000-ton liner with its swimming pool and grand piano, Ted planned a lightweight catamaran.

Sailing a small, fast boat across an open ocean is extremely dangerous. For one, you are very vulnerable to waves. In this respect a larger steamer finds heavy seas much easier: it just slices through them. The passengers may use the excuse of a slight roll to lurch into one another's arms on the dance floor, but the boat's speed is unimpaired. With a small boat, an ill-judged steering move at 30 knots can plunge the prow into the side of the wave and cause the whole boat to go under or break apart.

Ted Toleman designed a 65-foot catamaran, which was launched in 1984. Rather than the SS *United States*' 240,000-horsepower engines, which were the size of small cathedrals, Ted used two 2,000-horsepower engines, which could propel his catamaran at almost 50 knots on calm water. Of course it is one thing being able to race along a calm lake at 50 knots, quite another to reach those speeds on the choppy surface of the Atlantic Ocean, where the waves swell to twenty feet or higher. Ted knew that he would be lucky to reach speeds of 35 knots. It would still be a three- to four-day crossing. The challenge was whether it would be three days and nine hours or three days and eleven hours.

During 1984 Ted's boat budget overran, and he approached me to sponsor the cost of the trip in return for being able to name the boat and join him in the challenge. He had already asked Chay Blyth, the round-the-world yachtsman, to help him. Virgin Atlantic had just started flying, and although I was immediately attracted by the idea of winning a trophy back for Britain—Britain doesn't have that many trophies—I also relished the chance to promote our new airline. A successful Atlantic crossing would attract publicity in both New York and London, our sole destinations.

"How fit are you?" Chay asked me.

"Not bad," I ventured.

"That's not good enough," Chay said. "There's no room for passengers. You need to get into shape."

And so I started the most grueling fitness program of my life.

"You're going to be pounded for three solid days," Ted said as we killed ourselves in the gym. "You've got to be able to take it."

We asked Esso to sponsor the trip by providing the fuel, and when they kindly agreed to do so, we all went along to a celebratory lunch with their whole board of directors.

"I want to thank you all very much," I said sincerely. "It's going to be a great trip, and we're really going to advertise BP as much as we can." I thought that I heard a collective intake of breath, but I plowed on regardless. "We're going to plaster BP all over the refueling ships, have your logo on the boat, really put BP on the map. Nobody will ever confuse you with that old rival of yours . . ."

Then, looking at the wall opposite me and noticing the huge Esso logo, I realized my mistake. The Esso top executives looked at me with horror as if I were a ghost. I fell down to the floor and crawled under the table.

"I am sorry," I croaked, and started to spit and polish their shoes.

Remarkably, Esso, as good as their word, went ahead and sponsored the trip.

The boat and the crew were put through their paces for two months until we were finally ready. Joan was nearly eight months pregnant with our second child, and I was desperately hoping to do the crossing so that I could be home in time for the birth. But we were stuck in New York for three weeks, waiting for the stormy weather to clear. In those three weeks I kept returning to London to be with Joan and then flying back to New York until they told me we were about to set sail. By the time I had crossed the Atlantic eight times, I felt as though I knew it as well as I wanted to at 30,000 feet.

The storms cleared and we got the green light. Joan, who still had two weeks before the baby was due, told me that she was feeling fine and that I should go. And so we roared out of Manhattan and headed north.

The other crucial difference between *Virgin Atlantic Challenger* and the great liners was comfort: while the passengers in the 1930s danced to jazz bands and played deck quoits, we were strapped in airline seats and pounded relentlessly up and down. With the deafening noise of the engines and the constant reverberation, it was like being strapped to the blade of a vast pneumatic drill. We could hardly talk, let alone move; we just had to stomach an unending sequence of banging, shaking, and clattering.

Toward the end of the first day I got a radio message.

"Richard." It was Penni, who was at the control center. "Joan's in hospital, and she's just had a baby boy. Rose was with her, and it all went fine."

I'd broken my pledge, but most important, we'd had a healthy child. We all whooped with joy, and Steve Ridgeway rustled up a bottle of champagne to toast Joan and my new son. Without any extra shaking from me, the bottle exploded and fizzed everywhere. It was impossible to drink. The champagne foamed between our teeth, foamed up and down our throats, and, holding on to a lifeline, I staggered to the side and threw the bottle overboard, where it bobbed in the wake. Now I had to power on to see Joan, Holly, and our baby boy.

The first crossing would have comfortably won the record. We endured three hellish days of mental pile driving over 3,000 miles. We had three refueling stops lined up at 800-mile intervals. These were enormous ships, which loomed out over the horizon at us like skyscrapers. Even with a small swell, the approach to them was terrifying: we drew up about thirty yards away, and they fired a harpoon toward us with a buoy on the end of the line. We hauled this on board and then pulled out the great hose from the ship with the fuel. When this was clamped on, we gave the go-ahead and the fuel was pumped on board. The smell of petrol and the rolling swell made us all sick. And as we staggered to the edge and retched, we seemed in danger of smashing into the vast black-and-rusted cliff face of the fuel boat's side, which towered above us.

As we approached Ireland with only a few hundred miles to go, we hit a ferocious storm. We had been battered solidly for three days, but this was the worst yet. The boat smashed up and down. We held on to our seats and could see nothing. As we approached the Scilly Isles with only sixty miles left and the Hales' Trophy nearly in our hands, we hit a massive wave. A second later there was a shout from Pete Downie, our engineer.

"We're going down. The hull's split right open. Get out fast."

"Mayday! Mayday! Mayday!" Chay was on the radio in a flash. "Virgin *Challenger* is sinking. We are abandoning ship. Repeat: We are abandoning ship. Hey, Ted!" Chay swung round. "You're the skipper. You're meant to be the last off!"

Within seconds the boat started to go down. The first life raft we inflated snagged on something and ripped open. We had a backup raft, which we threw overboard and pulled the rip cord to inflate.

"Nobody panic!" Chay shouted. "There's no hurry! Everyone take their time!"

As we edged along the rail to get into the life raft, Chay shouted out:

"Panic! Panic! We're going down. Move it!"

The life raft was like a tiny inflatable coracle with a hooded tent. We huddled together, rocking up and down in the sea like a crazy funfair ride. I was sitting next to the radio, and I picked up the mike. An RAF Nimrod picked up our Mayday. I gave the pilot our position, and he rapidly radioed any ships in the area.

"Okay, there are three vessels in the area, which are heading towards you," the pilot came back to me. "In no particular order there is the *QE2*, which is heading for New York; a RAF helicopter from the Scilly Isles has been mobilized; and a Geest boat heading to Jamaica is also on its way. Please take the first one which arrives."

"Tell him I'm not going in a fucking banana boat to Jamaica," Chay said. "Neither am I going back to New York. I want the bloody helicopter."

"That'll be fine," I said over the radio, deciding not to pass on Chay's comment, since for once I thought that we were in no position to negotiate.

Ted was gutted. He sat there in silence, his dream shattered.

From the tiny hatch door we could see the stern of Virgin *Challenger* sticking headlong above the water. The rest of the boat was underwater. All you could see was the word "Virgin."

"Well, Richard," Chay said, pointing at the logo, "as usual, you got the last word in."

As we waited I started a chorus of "We're all going on a summer holiday . . ." Everyone sang along, even Ted.

Eventually we were picked up by the Geest banana boat on its way to the Caribbean. We were winched up in turn and left the life raft spinning by itself.

"Handy in case anyone else capsizes," Chay said.

It was dinnertime, and the guests were gathering in the captain's quarters. Rather like in the great days of ocean steamers, they were all wearing dinner jackets and evening gowns for dinner. We were a bedraggled lot in our damp nylon survival suits.

"My poor boy," one elderly lady said to me. "And you haven't even seen your newborn son yet, have you?"

"No," I said. "I'm afraid we're heading off to Jamaica, so I won't see him for a while."

"Well, I've got this photograph of him for you."

To my astonishment, she pulled out that day's edition of the London *Evening Standard.* And there on the front page was a picture of our tiny son wrapped up in a shawl. I have to admit to a tear in my eye as I looked at it.

A salvage team then radioed us to ask permission to salvage the boat.

"Of course," I said, looking out of the porthole, where we could still see the white stern sticking up like a tombstone.

"You bloody idiot!" Chay snapped at me. "You never want to see that boat again. Just a lot of waterlogged electronics which will never work again. You'll never get a penny from the insurers."

"On second thought," I said, "perhaps I can call you back?"

"Right you are," they said.

I put the phone down, and Chay and I looked across the sea at the Virgin *Challenger.* As we did so, it silently plunged below the surface.

• • •

It took a month for the ringing in my ears to subside. I was beginning to think I had permanent brain damage. However, winning the Blue Riband and the Hales' Trophy became unfinished business. We were determined to succeed, but Chay and I felt that after what had happened to *Challenger,* we should build a single-hulled boat rather than a catamaran because it would be stronger. Since Ted Toleman specialized in catamarans, he refused to change the design and dropped out. We formed a new team with three key members of Ted Toleman's original team—Chris Witty, Steve Ridgeway, and Chris Moss—who asked me whether they could come to work for Virgin. Chay Blyth also stayed with the project as the presiding sailing expert, and together we designed a new boat.

On 15 May 1986 *Virgin Atlantic Challenger II* was launched by Princess Michael of Kent. The boat was seventy-five feet long, with a single hull. We were confident that she could cope with the heavy seas much better than her predecessor. But as we sailed her around the south coast on her maiden voyage toward Salcombe, we cannoned off a vast wave, which almost spun the boat over. Everyone was hurled across the deck, and one of our crew, Pete Downie, broke his leg. The agony on his face was more to do with the realization that he wouldn't be with us than the pain from his leg. Chay fractured a toe, and Steve was almost swept overboard. We arrived at Salcombe like a hospital boat.

We shipped the boat over to New York and once again waited for good weather. When we left New York Harbor on a bright June morning in 1986 and headed up toward Nova Scotia, we braced ourselves once more for the pounding. It was not as bad as the first time, and the trip up the eastern seaboard of America was much faster than we hoped. We sped along and after eighteen hours we met the first refueling ship off the coast of Newfoundland.

We refueled and headed off into the gathering darkness. The summer night was short, and we were traveling northeast, which made it shorter still, so we had just five hours of darkness to cope with. We relied on the radar, trying to squint ahead through night-vision goggles, but still had no idea what was ahead. Motoring at that speed through the night was like driving blindfolded, and we narrowly missed a surfacing whale.

By the second day the adrenaline rush that had kept us going had worn off. It was now just horrible, relentless banging. Each wave smashed us all up and down, up and down, until we could no longer grin and bear it. We just had to clench our teeth and bear it.

As we approached RV2, the refueling boat, off the coast of Canada, we also had to keep intense lookout for icebergs. Large icebergs show up on the radar and can be avoided; it is the "small" ones—tiny blips above the surface, which actually weigh 100 tons and could smash the hull—that are dangerous. Indeed, even an iceberg the size of a beanbag could seriously damage the hull. The difficulty was that as hour after hour passed and we were deafened by the roar of the engines, it was impossible to keep our concentration going. We still had over two thousand miles to travel. Each minute of every hour was a battering. This was where the strength of the team came through: we all rallied round to help each other get through it.

As we waved good-bye and revved up the engines to speed away from the second refueling boat, our engines coughed, choked, and conked out. Eckie Rastig, our new engineer, went belowdecks to investigate. He came back up horrified: the fuel filters were full of water. This was a disaster. He had taken a dipstick sample and reckoned that for every twelve tons of fuel taken on board we had also taken on about four tons of water. It was a complete mystery as to how the water had got in with the fuel, but we had no time to worry about that. Maybe it was the Esso directors' revenge for my blunder over BP! The diesel and the water had emulsified together, which meant that it was impossible to split the water off from the diesel: we had to drain the entire four fuel tanks and start again. The Esso boat came back alongside and we filled up again, taking another precious three hours.

We restarted the engines, but they conked out again. It was now 11 P.M., and we had spent seven hours bobbing up and down next door to the Shell refueling boat in the middle of the freezing ocean. The race was slipping away, the swell was growing progressively worse, and we were stuck there in the middle of the ocean.

"The storm's catching up with us," Chay said. "This isn't funny."

The storm that was following the wonderful weather we had enjoyed on the first day was not an abrupt, fierce storm but just a big spell of filthy weather, our worst nightmare. Soon the boat was riding waves that had grown to fifty feet. We hardly dared stand on deck because one moment we were well beneath the vast Esso ship so that it looked as if it must topple over on top of us; the next moment we were thrown up way above it, and we couldn't believe that we wouldn't skate down the edge of the wave and crash into it. By now the suffocating petrol fumes made us all sick. Everyone was retching and puking and doubled up in pain. Our survival suits were soaked with sea spray and flecked with vomit, our faces were white and green, our hair was frozen.

"It's not worth going on," Chay shouted in my ear. "We've all spoken and we're all gutted. It's over. I'm sorry, Richard."

I knew that if we failed on this attempt, there would be no third time. We had to go for it. I had to persuade them.

"Let's just try to get the engines going and see how far we can get," I said. "Come on. We've got to make a stab at this."

An engine specialist called Steve Lawes, whom I knew, was on board the Esso boat. I asked him to come aboard and help us. They set up their winch and swung him out over the side. With the two boats swinging up and down on the giant waves, it was astonishingly brave of him to try. With perfect timing they dropped him on our deck and he snapped off the belt before he was swept back into the air as another wave drove us down and the Esso boat up. Steve went down to join Eckie in the engine room. From a tiny space beside the engines, they drained the fuel tanks and took on more fuel. I went down to see them, but there was no room for anyone else.

I didn't have to beg Steve to stay with us.

"I'll stay just for the pleasure of the ride," he grinned, oil stains already covering his face.

I suddenly felt that we had a chance.

"There's still water in the fuel," Eckie said. "But we can filter it out as we go. We're going to have to do it every few hours."

I hauled myself back upstairs and found Chay of all people throwing up over the side. I pulled him by the shoulder.

"Steve's going to stay," I shouted in his ear. "We can go on."

"It's over, Richard," Chay shouted at me. "It's fucking well over. This boat's knackered."

"We've got to go on," I yelled.

For a moment we stood there eyeball-to-eyeball, clutching on to each other like two old drunks. We had flecks of vomit in our beards, our eyes were red and bloodshot from the salt and the fumes, our faces were drained of color, and our hands were raw and bleeding. With another lurch of the sea we staggered against each other, utterly exhausted. We hated this boat, we hated this trip, we hated the sea, we hated the weather, and—right now—we certainly hated each other.

"We've got to go on and do it," I repeated like a madman. "We've just got to do it. It's the only way. What are you suggesting? That we get towed home?"

"God, you're worse than me," Chay said. "All right. We'll give it one last shot."

I hugged him, and we both fell against the railings.

"Right!" Chay yelled to the crew. "We're casting off."

We all summoned up our strength again and went into action. We cast off from the Esso boat, and with fine tuning from Eckie and Steve, the engines roared back into life. But they were coughing and spluttering and liable to cut out. At least they worked and we didn't have to get out the oars. We waved up at the Esso boat and headed off into a gray light. Although we felt better now that we were away from the oil fumes, we were all exhausted. I felt as if my stomach had been punched through and through by a prizefighter. Everyone was now in his own world, fighting to get through each hour. I just kept repeating to myself that we had to get on. As well as fighting the weather and the fuel, we were all immersed in fighting our own will not to collapse.

Every four hours the fuel filters were so clogged up that they needed replacing. We stopped the engines, Steve and Eckie replaced the filters, and on we went. As hour by hour passed, it became clear that we were not going to have enough filters to make the last refueling stop. The filters would run out, the engines would break down, and we would be marooned at sea. I was in touch with a passing Nimrod that had taken us under its wing. These planes spend hour after hour flying over the Atlantic searching for submarines, and we were a welcome diversion. The pilot suggested that another Nimrod could come out and drop a load of filters, but they would need to get clearance from the top. I radioed Tim Powell, who was running the control center from the Oxford Street Megastore.

"Tim, we need help. We need some fuel filters dropped. The Nimrod has offered to do it, but they need to get clearance—right from the top."

Within an hour Tim had spoken to the right people at Downing Street and an RAF Nimrod had picked up the filters from Southampton and was flying to meet us.

We didn't hear the plane coming. It just swooped low overhead, coming straight out of the gray cloud behind us. It was huge, and although there was no sun, the plane seemed to drain all the light and cast us in shadow. The Nimrod roared overhead with a rumble that shook the boat and dropped a small drum attached to a buoy in our path. We all danced and whooped with joy. Chay cut back the engines and aimed for the little red marker. Steve picked it up with a long hook, and we hauled it on board: it was a steel drum packed with filters. On top of the filters were some chocolate bars and a little handwritten note that said: "Good Luck!"

We radioed up to the pilot and thanked him.

"I've got a TV crew on board," he said. "The whole country's on the edge of their seats. Godspeed."

We reached the third Esso ship and with another set of full tanks and some Irish stew, our first hot meal in two days, inside us, we approached the last leg of the crossing with rising determination. We calculated that we had to travel at an average speed of 39 or 40 knots for the final twelve hours if we were to break the record. With our engines in the state they were, it was going to be extremely close. We battled through more heavy weather, unable to go faster than 30 knots for three hours; then the sun came out and the sea calmed. Steve and Eckie replaced the filters for the last time, and we opened the throttles and went flat out across the sea, hurtling over the waves toward the Scilly Isles.

When we passed the point where we had sunk the previous year—just off the Scilly Isles—we all cheered and suddenly knew that we could do it. Five miles out from the Scilly Isles, we were met by a posse of helicopters and then hundreds of boats that welcomed us home. We zoomed past Bishop's Rock Lighthouse at 7:30 P.M. Eckie and Steve staggered up from the engine room. They were the heroes who had endured three days of pounding in a hot, cramped engine room, standing ankle-deep in oil while they fought to keep the engines going. Dag Pike switched off his navigational system, and we all threw our arms around each other. We had done it. Our total journey had lasted 3 days, 8 hours, and 31 minutes: in a voyage of over 3,000 miles, we had beaten the Blue Riband record by a mere 2 hours and 9 minutes.

Chapter 16

"If you thought that crossing the Atlantic by boat was impressive, think again. I am planning to build the world's largest hot-air balloon, and I'm planning to fly it in the jet stream at thirty thousand feet."

1986

"After the Big Bang, how about a little pop?"

By 1986 everyone was heading for the City. Everyone who had bought shares in the formerly government-owned British Telecom had doubled their money. Those who bought into the British Gas privatization had also done well.

I will never forget going into the City to see the lines of people queuing up to buy Virgin shares. We already had over 70,000 postal applicants to buy Virgin shares, but these people had left it until the last day, 13 November 1986. I walked up and down the queue thanking people for their confidence, and a number of their replies stuck in my mind:

"We're not going on holiday this year; we're putting our savings into Virgin."

"Go on, Richard, prove us right."

"We're banking on you, Richard."

At one point I noticed that the press photographers were taking pictures of my feet. I couldn't understand it. Then I looked down and noticed with a shock that in the rush to get dressed, I had put on shoes that didn't match.

The flotation of Virgin attracted more applications from the public than any other stock market debut issue apart from the massive government privatizations. Over 100,000 private individuals applied for our shares, and the post office drafted in twenty extra staff to cope with the mail sacks. That day we heard that the Human League had gone to Number 1 in America. Beneath this euphoria we were worried to hear that only a small number of

City institutions had applied for shares. It was the first sign of the difficulty we were going to have in our dealings with the City.

By 1986 Virgin had become one of Britain's largest private companies with some 4,000 employees. For the year ending July 1986 Virgin had sales of £189 million compared with £119 million for the previous year, an increase of 60 percent. Our pretax profits were £19 million, up from £15 million. Although we were a large company, we had very little flexibility to expand: all we could do was either to use up our own cash we had earned or to ask our bankers for a bigger overdraft. I watched a number of other private companies sell their shares on the stock market: Body Shop, TSB, Sock Shop, Our Price Records, Reuters, Atlantic Computers. There was practically a new company every week, and the stock exchange had to set up a queuing system so that in between the massive privatizations of British Telecom, British Airways, and BP, there was an orderly procession.

In many ways going public was an attractive option: it would enable Virgin to raise money that we could invest in new subsidiaries; it would swell our balance sheet and so enable us to enjoy more freedom from the banks and use our expanded capital base to borrow more if we wished; it would enable me to issue shares as incentives to the Virgin staff, which they could easily trade; it would increase Virgin's profile; and, a thought lurking at the back of my mind, in due course it would enable us to use the Virgin shares as currency to make a bid for Thorn EMI, the largest record label in the country. Don was enthusiastic about the prospect of Virgin going public, and he was very happy with the idea of being the chief executive of a publicly quoted company. Trevor and Ken were not keen, and they warned me that we would all hate it, that the City was a very fickle place, and that we were giving up a great slice of our independence. For Simon it offered a free market in which to sell their shares in Virgin if they ever wanted to. All in all I had pushed away the negative reasons and decided to go for it. As a first step, Trevor had arranged a private placing of convertible preference shares in Virgin the previous year. He had set out to raise £10 million, but as word about Virgin spread, Morgan Grenfell, who were underwriting the issue, finally closed the private offer off at £25 million.

In the public offer for sale, the financial institutions converted their preference shares into some 15 percent of the ordinary shares, and we created new shares to sell to outside investors, which raised £30 million. After the flotation, I held 55 percent of the Virgin Group; Simon held 9 percent; Ken, Don, Trevor, Robert, and some of the other members of staff held 2 percent each; and the outside investors held 34 percent. We had sold each Virgin share at £1.40, and at that share price Virgin Group PLC was valued at £240 million. Of course this was only part of the company—Virgin Atlantic, Virgin Holidays, Virgin Cargo, and the nightclubs were all excluded because the City felt they were too financially risky to be part of the flotation. Virgin PLC was part of the same business that just twelve months ago Coutts had been prepared to push into insolvency for going £300,000 beyond our £3 million overdraft limit. We immediately switched some of the cash raised across to finance Voyager, the holding company for the airline, which we saw as a vehicle to invest in a wide range of other businesses.

Beneath the facade of stability that a public company is meant to engender, my life was as hectic as ever. The mid-1980s and the launch of Virgin Atlantic was the period when I really had to put myself forward to promote Virgin. We did not have the same budgets as British Airways and others had to spend on advertising, but I found that the press enjoyed writing stories about Virgin if they could put a face to the name. In contrast to promoting Virgin Music, where we were actually promoting the bands rather than Virgin as a brand name, for the first time I began to use myself to promote the companies and the brand. And so my name and the Virgin brand name became intertwined.

Apart from never involving my family in the press, I was happy to do anything to increase Virgin's profile: promotion was one of the keys to our growth. If nobody knew about us, nobody would fly us. And if nobody flew us, then we would go out of business. So if dressing up in Biggles goggles and lying in a bubble bath helped the airline, I was happy to do it.

One of my greatest failures with the press was my involvement in the UK 2000 project, which had been dreamed up by the Department of Employment to create jobs. Kenneth Baker, then secretary for the environment, asked me to become the chairman of this project. I agreed to do so only if the government made an unconditional financial commitment so that as far as possible this endeavor could be seen as nonpolitical. Unemployment was heading toward four million, and this project seemed a good way of helping to reduce it.

The idea behind UK 2000 was to match up a large number of unemployed people with jobs that would benefit the environment. These jobs would include various activities ranging from clearing up inner-city sites to building playgrounds; from clearing out canals and re-creating footpaths to clearing out old industrial sites and planting trees. I made contact with a large number of charities such as Friends of the Earth and Groundwork, who agreed to help supervise some of the projects and come up with their own list of things they would like to see done but lacked the money and man-power to do.

Over the weekend while I was down in the Scilly Isles, thanking the people there for their hospitality over the Atlantic crossing, I was mulling over whether to take on the role. A helicopter arrived, which caused some excitement. It turned out to be a journalist from *The Sun*. For some reason he was carrying a broom.

"Here, Richard," he said. "Hold this for me, will you? That's right." He shot off a number of pictures. "Give us a grin."

I thought nothing more about it until the next day when I saw *The Sun's* headline: "Litter King."

From that moment UK 2000 was branded as a campaign to clean up litter. Try as I might to reverse this impression, the image stuck. Whenever any newspaper ran a story about the work we were trying to do, they trivialized it as "cleaning up litter." I sent countless letters to countless editors, pointing out all our environmental projects up and down the country, but these were either ignored or reproduced on the letters page, where they were safely out of sight. As it happened, not one of our projects involved cleaning up litter since that was not what we'd been asked to do. Our brief was to find useful work that would involve some kind of training and lead on to full-time employment. Picking up litter—commendable though that is—did not fit the brief.

I stayed with UK 2000 for three years, but it was a lost cause. Everyone involved in it began to lose morale since whatever they did, they were mocked as little more than people picking up litter. No matter that some of the leading environmentalists of the day, such as Jonathon Porrit, were involved, people still dismissed the idea—a great shame, as the project could have created many more jobs than it did and made Britain a slightly better place in which to live.

Apart from the disappointment of UK 2000, everything else was going swimmingly. When we arrived back from the Atlantic crossing, the entire country seemed to have enjoyed the challenge. Mrs. Thatcher expressed an interest in seeing the boat, and I offered her a ride up the River Thames. We managed to win approval to break the 5-mph speed limit on the River Thames, and the Tower Bridge opened its gates as *Virgin Atlantic Challenger II* came whizzing through. We picked up Mrs. Thatcher, and together with Bob Geldof and Sting, we did a lap of honor up to the Houses of Parliament and back as other boats on the river all blared their horns and the fire brigade pumped up great plumes of water into the air in salute. Mrs.

Thatcher, the Iron Lady, stood up on the deck beside me and faced into the keen wind.

"I must admit," she said as we accelerated up the river, "I do enjoy going fast. I love powerful boats."

I looked across at her. She was indeed enjoying herself. Her profile cut through the wind like a bowsprit, and not a single strand of hair had blown out of place.

So riding on the crest of a wave that included all sorts of strange surveys, which voted me both the best-dressed man in Britain and the worst-dressed man in Britain, and Virgin the most-admired company in Britain, I felt that we could do no wrong. Every day I was being asked to give an interview to a newspaper or to open a shopping mall or to give a speech to a business school. One day I was probably feeling rather self-important with all this floating around in my head when I hailed a taxi and jumped in.

"Where to, guv?" asked the driver.

"Billingsgate, please," I said.

As we set off he looked at me quizzically in the mirror as if he half recognized me and said:

"Give me a clue?"

"You know," I said modestly. "A record company, an airline, Heaven nightclub, record shops."

"No," the taxi driver repeated. "Give me a clue."

"The Atlantic crossing," I went on, "the Sex Pistols, Boy George, Phil Collins . . ."

"Excuse me, sir," the driver said, completely nonplussed. "I don't understand what you're rabbiting on about. Give me a clue as to how to get to Billingsgate."

Another time, after I had been working virtually through the night on a problem with the airline, I had to take a taxi early the next morning to a meeting. As usual I was running just a fraction late as I struggled to say good-bye to the family, pick up my papers, and make a last telephone call all at once. I flopped into the back of the taxi, looking forward to reading the papers and getting ready for the meeting.

"Oi!" said the cab driver. "I know you. You're that Dick Branson. You've got a record label."

"Yes, that's right," I admitted.

"Well, ain't it my lucky day?" the cabbie went on. "Fancy having Mister Branson in my cab. Now I know I'm a cabbie, I mean, that's clear isn't it, but you know what? I'm also a musician. I really am. I'm a drummer in a band."

"Great," I said unenthusiastically, feeling tired and hoping that he would shut up so that I could get on with my papers.

"Now, do you mind if I play you my demo tape? I mean, this could be my lucky day—and it could be yours too. I could make you a fortune . . ."

"That would be lovely," I said.

"No, you look a bit tired," the cabbie said, squinting in the mirror. "You must have this the whole time."

"No, please put the tape on."

"No, you look too tired. But I tell you what: my mum lives just round the corner. Would you mind if I just dropped you round there and we had a cup of tea?"

"Well, I've got to go to a TV studio," I said, my heart sinking.

"She'd love to meet you. It'd make her day," the cabbie said. "Just a quick cup of tea."

"All right, that'd be lovely," I said, resigning myself to being horribly late. The cab turned down a side street.

"You know what," the cabbie said, "I will put on my tape. Just to show you."

As the cab pulled up alongside a small house, the tape started with a familiar drumbeat. Over the speakers came the words: "I can feel it coming in the air tonight . . ."

The cabbie jumped out and opened my door. It was Phil Collins.

I had mentioned in a recent interview that although I was not very good at knowing who rock stars were or remembering their names, I was sure that I would always recognize Phil Collins.

Although we had raised £30 million from the stock market flotation, I soon began to feel that we had made the wrong decision. A few weeks after our flotation in November, our investment banker at Morgan Grenfell, Roger Seelig, was investigated by the Department of Trade and Industry over his role in Guinness's takeover of Distillers, which he had orchestrated in January. Roger resigned from Morgan Grenfell, and although the case against him was eventually abandoned, his career was ruined. Unable to use Roger as a touchstone, I began to lose faith in the City and the onerous obligations they put on us.

First, the City had insisted that Virgin appoint some nonexecutive directors. Sir Phil Harris was recommended as a self-made man, who had made a fortune from selling carpets. We also appointed Cob Stenham, who had been finance director of Unilever and was a well-respected banker. I found it difficult to comply with all the formality they insisted we adopt. I was used to chatting with Simon and Ken about which bands to sign and then letting them get on with it. Virgin board meetings had always been highly informal affairs. We met on *Duende* or at my house in Oxford Gardens or while we were on a weekend together. Our business was not one that could be boxed into a rigid timetable of meetings. We had to make decisions quickly, off-the-cuff: if we had to wait four weeks for the next board meeting before authorizing Simon to sign UB40, then we would probably lose them altogether.

I also had a number of disagreements with Don, notably about dividends. I was extremely reluctant to follow British tradition and pay out a large dividend. I preferred the American or Japanese tradition whereby a company concentrated upon reinvesting its profits to build itself and increase shareholder value. To me a large dividend meant a loss of cash that would be better employed within Virgin than by paying it away. Our outside shareholders had entrusted their money to Virgin in order for us to grow it, not hand 5 percent of it back on a plate—which would be taxed as income and so immediately lose 40 percent of its value to the tax man. This argument may sound petty, but it illustrates the general loss of control I had experienced. Most people think that owning 50 percent of a public company is the key to controlling it. While this is true in theory, to a large extent you lose control just by having to appoint nonexecutive directors and generally give up your time to satisfying the City. Previously, I had always felt confident about any decision we made, but now that Virgin was a publicly quoted company, I began to lose faith in myself. I felt uneasy about making the rapid decisions I had always made and wondered whether every decision should be formally ratified and minuted at a board meeting. In many ways 1987, our year of being a public company, was Virgin's least creative year. We spent at least 50 percent of our time heading off to the City to explain to fund managers, financial advisers, and City PR firms what we were doing rather than just getting on and doing it.

I also felt responsible to the people who had invested in Virgin shares. Phil Collins, Mike Oldfield, and Bryan Ferry had bought shares; Peter and Ceris, my neighbors and close friends in Kidlington, had invested some of their life savings in Virgin; and my family, my cousins, and many people who had come across me in various walks of life had all bought shares. Trevor Abbott had borrowed £250,000 from me to buy Virgin shares, and although he knew the figures even better than I, I still felt responsible if the shares fell in value.

I would not have minded if the City analysts had been correct in their assessment that Virgin was doing badly or that the management was incompetent. What infuriated me was that no matter how often Simon, Ken, or I tried to explain that over 30 percent of our income came from royalties from the back catalog and even if we failed to release another record we would still enjoy a stream of earnings, or that 40 percent of our royalties in France came from French singers rather than Boy George or Phil Collins, who gave us a steady local income, the City continually oversimplified how Virgin worked. The analysts still assumed that Virgin was wholly dependent upon me and Boy George. Simon and Ken started taking recordings to the City analysts' meetings and playing them UB40, the Human League, and Simple Minds, but they remained unimpressed. Virgin shares, which had started trading at 140p, soon slipped down to 120p. The faith that the people in the queue had placed in me as well as the faith that the Virgin artists and staff had placed in me by spending their own money on buying Virgin shares began to overwhelm me.

As 1987 progressed, the Virgin share price recovered to around 140p but never took off. We began to use the money we had raised from the flotation to make two investments: the first was to establish a proper Virgin subsidiary in America; the second was to start stalking Thorn EMI with a view to launching a takeover bid for the company. Virgin Records America was not a cheap investment. We had learned the hard way before, and this time we invested heavily. During 1987 we managed to release four Top Twenty singles and one gold album. Although Virgin America lost us money that year, it was a long-term investment and we felt sure that eventually we would make far more money from having our own record company there than from licensing our best artists to American companies.

The second challenge, stalking Thorn EMI, had to be done with care. We felt that the EMI record label was managed in a rather sleepy way and that their incredible back catalog, which included the Beatles, could be run far more profitably. The Thorn EMI Group as a whole was valued at around £750 million, three times the size of Virgin. Eventually, I thought that the best thing to do was to go around and have a chat with Sir Colin Southgate, the managing director of Thorn EMI, and ask him in a friendly way whether he would like to sell us EMI Music.

"Shall we come along?" Simon and Ken asked.

"It might be a bit overbearing," I said. "I'll slip in and see him face-to-face, and then if he's keen we can all meet him."

I called Sir Colin and arranged a meeting at Manchester Square. I was shown up to the top floor of the office building and ushered into a room, which fell silent. At least twenty unsmiling faces confronted me. They lined one side of the table, their blue pin-striped suits shoulder-to-shoulder forming an unbreachable wall. Sir Colin shook my hand and peered over my shoulder to see whether there was anyone else.

"It's just me," I said. "Where shall I sit?"

One side of the long gleaming mahogany table was empty, lined with ten or fifteen memo pads and sharpened pencils. I sat down and looked across at the sea of faces.

"Well, let me introduce you," Sir Colin began, and as he rattled off their names I realized that these were bankers, lawyers, accountants, and management consultants.

"I'm Richard Branson," I introduced myself with a nervous laugh. "And the reason I'm here is that I just wondered whether you would like to, might like to . . ." I paused. The necks opposite all stretched and craned toward me. "Might like to sell your EMI subsidiary," I said. "It seems to me that Thorn EMI is such a big group and that EMI Music might not be your top priority. You have so much else going on. That's all."

There was a hushed silence.

"We're quite happy with EMI," Sir Colin said. "We are taking all steps to run it as a leading member of the Thorn EMI Group."

"Oh, well," I said. "I thought it was worth a try."

And with that I stood up and left the room.

I went straight round to see Simon and Ken at Vernon Yard.

"They're serious," I said. "They're on an emergency footing. They thought I was going to bid for them. They practically had their bayonets fixed. If Sir Colin's that worried that he brought all his heavies along, then they clearly are vulnerable and I think we should have a crack at them."

Simon and Ken agreed with me. Trevor arranged for us to go and see Samuel Montagu, another investment bank. Samuel Montagu introduced us to Mountleigh, a property group, and suggested that we could make a joint bid. Since Sir Colin would not sell EMI separately to us, we could bid for the whole group with Mountleigh and then split it up: in a nutshell, Mountleigh would take the national chain of television rental shops and we would take EMI Music.

We knew that our first year's profits as a public company were on course to more than double to over £30 million (despite the cost of setting up in the States), and so we planned to release these results in October at the same time as announcing our bid for Thorn EMI.

During the course of the summer, Trevor arranged a £100 million loan with the Bank of Nova Scotia, and we slowly began buying shares in Thorn

EMI, paying about £7 a share as we built up a stake we could use as a launch pad for the bid. As the stock market soared higher through the summer months and some rumors began to circulate that Thorn EMI was vulnerable to a bid, I began to worry that if we left it until October we might be too late. There was not much I could do about it, because I was determined to set off on a challenge that many people thought would be the end of me—a challenge as daunting and as daring as anything in the world of business. Per Lindstrand and I were planning to fly across the Atlantic Ocean in a hot-air balloon. Until I returned safe and sound, nobody was going to take the idea of Virgin bidding for Thorn EMI too seriously.

It all dated from my first day back at the office after the Atlantic *Challenger* crossing, when I had received a telephone call.

"It's someone called Per Lindstrand," Penni said. "He says that he's got an incredible proposal."

I picked up the phone.

"If you thought that crossing the Atlantic by boat was impressive," said a stilted Swedish voice, "think again. I am planning to build the world's largest hot-air balloon, and I'm planning to fly it in the jet stream at thirty thousand feet. I believe that it can cross the Atlantic."

I had vaguely heard of Per Lindstrand. I knew that he was a world expert at ballooning and held several records, including one for reaching the highest altitude. Per explained to me that nobody had flown a hot-air balloon further than 600 miles, and nobody had been able to keep a hot-air balloon up in the air for longer than 27 hours. In order to cross the Atlantic, a balloon would have to fly more than 3,000 miles, five times farther than anyone had ever managed before, and spend three times longer up in the air.

A balloon filled with helium, like the old zeppelins, can stay in the air for several days. A hot-air balloon relies upon the hot air within the envelope rising above the surrounding cold air and taking the balloon with it. But the loss of heat through the balloon's envelope is rapid, and in order to heat the air, balloonists burn propane. Until Per's proposed flight, hot-air balloons had been hampered by the impossible weight of fuel needed to keep them afloat.

Per thought that we could break the flight record by putting three new theories into practice: the first one was to take the balloon up to an altitude of around 30,000 feet and fly along in the fast winds, the jet streams, which move along at speeds of up to 200 miles per hour. This had previously been considered impossible as their power and turbulence would shred any balloon. The second was to use solar power to heat the balloon's air during the day and thus save fuel, which had never been attempted; and since the balloon would be flying at 30,000 feet, the pilots would be in a pressurized capsule rather than the traditional wicker basket.

As I studied Per's proposal, I realized with amazement that this vast balloon, a huge, round, ungainly shape that could swallow the Royal Albert Hall without showing a bulge, was actually intended to cross the Atlantic Ocean in far less time than our *Virgin Atlantic Challenger II* boat with its 4,000-horsepower engine. Per reckoned upon a flying time of under two days: an average speed of 90 knots compared with the boat's average of just under 40 knots. It would be rather like driving along in the fast lane of the motorway only to be overtaken by the Royal Albert Hall traveling twice as fast.

After wrestling with some of the science and the academic calculations about inertia and wind speeds, I asked Per to come and see me. When we met, I put my hand on the pile of theoretical calculations.

"I'll never understand all the science and the theory," I said. "But I'll come with you if you answer me this one question."

"Of course," Per said, stiffening his back in readiness for some incredibly challenging question.

"Do you have any children?"

"Yes, I've got two."

"Right, then." I stood up and shook his hand. "I'll come. But I'd better learn how to fly one of these things first."

It was only later that I learned that seven people had already tried to cross the Atlantic and that five of them had perished. Per took me on a week's crash course in ballooning in Spain. I discovered ballooning to be one of the most exhilarating things I had ever done. The combination of soaring up over the world, the silence when the burners were off, the sensation of floating, and the breathtaking panoramic views all immediately seduced me. After a week of being shouted at by Robin Batchelor, my instructor who looked like my double, I had my balloon license. I was ready.

As the prevailing jet stream flows from west to east, we found a launch site in Maine, close to Boston, about 100 miles inland to avoid the effect of sea breezes. Per reckoned that by the time we crossed the coast we should be up in the jet stream and above the local weather. Our key guiding mentors were Tom Barrow, who headed the engineering team, and Bob Rice, an expert meteorologist. Both men were clearly such authorities that I unreservedly put my trust in them. The jet stream winds parted over the Atlantic with one branch heading up to the Arctic and another branch swerving down to the Azores and back out to the middle of the ocean. Bob Rice told us that getting our route right was like "rolling a ball bearing between two magnets." In the event of running out of fuel or icing up, we would have to ditch the balloon at sea.

"There's flotation collars around the capsule which will keep it buoyant," Tom Barrow said.

"What if they don't work?" I asked.

"You'll get your money back," he said. "Or rather we'll get the money back on your behalf."

At our final briefing with Tom at Sugarloaf Mountain, Maine, the day before the balloon went up, Tom went through the last emergency drills:

"Landing this thing is going to be like freewheeling a Sherman tank without any brakes. It's going to be a crash."

His last warning was the most telling: "Now, even though we're here, I can still abort this project if I think that it is too dangerous or if you develop health problems."

"Does that include mental health problems?" I joked.

"No," Tom said. "That's a prerequisite for doing this flight. If you're not completely nuts and scared to death, then you shouldn't be on board in the first place."

I was certainly scared to death.

Chapter 17

"Without British Caledonian offering competition, British Airways could now turn its attention to mopping up the last tiny competitor—us."

1987–1988

*P*er and I took sleeping pills the evening before the launch. When we were woken up at 2 A.M. it was pitch-dark, but as we were driven to the launch site we saw the vast balloon lit up by floodlights and towering over the trees. It looked astonishing: the sides were silver and the dome was black. It was monumental. The balloon was fully inflated and straining at the anchors. We were worried that a wind might strike up and tip it over, so we climbed into the capsule and the ground crew set about the final checks.

Inside the capsule, we were unaware of the accident that actually catapulted us upward. A cable became caught round two of the propane tanks, and as the balloon strained up and down it pulled them off. Without their weight, the balloon shot up, still trailing a couple of cables carrying sandbags. As we gained height and headed over the Maine forest toward the sea, Per climbed out of the capsule and cut the last two cables. We made rapid progress toward the glowing dawn, soaring along in the jet stream at 85 knots—just under 100 miles an hour. After ten hours we had flown over 900 miles and had easily broken the long-distance record for a hot-air balloon. Over the radio Bob Rice told us to keep at 27,000 feet whatever happened, since that was where the fast winds were.

That first night we hit a storm and descended to calmer weather. But we immediately lost the speed of the jet stream.

"We need to get back up there," Per said. He fired the burners, and we rose again to meet the bad weather. The balloon was buffeted hard by the storm and the capsule was tossed to and fro, but just when we wondered whether we should head back down, we shot out into clear weather and reached a speed of 140 knots—over 160 miles an hour. The next morning the Virgin 747 *Maiden Voyager* arrived and flew in a figure eight round us. My mother's voice came crackling over the radio:

"Faster, Richard, faster! We'll race you."

"I'm doing my best, Mum. Please thank the crew and passengers for going out of their way to greet us," I said.

In fact, we sped along and crossed the coast of Ireland at 2:30 that afternoon, Friday 3 July. It was a dream crossing compared with the boat. We had been in the air for just twenty-nine hours.

The incredible speed of our flight gave us an unexpected problem: we still had three full tanks of fuel attached to the capsule, and they could well explode on landing. We decided to swoop down very low and drop off the fuel tanks in an empty field, and then come down a second time for a controlled landing. Per stopped burning propane and brought the balloon down low so that we could see where we could safely jettison the extra fuel tanks. As we came down, the wind suddenly swirled around us, much harder than we expected. The ground rushed up to meet us. Traveling at a speed of almost 30 knots, 34.5 miles an hour, our ground speed was not so much the problem as our sudden plunge downward. We hit the ground and bounced along a field. All our fuel tanks were torn off by the impact, along with our radio aerials. Without the weight of the tanks, we hurtled back upward. I didn't see it, but we narrowly missed a house and an electricity pylon. We had hit the ground in Limavardy, a tiny Irish village.

With no fuel tanks we were utterly out of control. Unless we could heat the air, once this rise topped out we would fall rapidly, gathering speed like someone in an unopened parachute. We had one small reserve fuel tank inside the capsule with us, and Per quickly connected it to the burners.

"It's tangled," Per said. "The cables are tangled."

The balloon was rising like a rocket. The top of the dome was forced down by the pressure, and the cable that hung down the middle of the balloon snagged on something and started spinning us round in a knot. The whole balloon was twisting itself into a corkscrew, closing the mouth so that there was no chance of heating the hot air inside. As we began to drift downward, I opened the capsule hatch and climbed out on top. I took my knife and hacked away at the twisted cable.

"Quick!" Per shouted up at me. "We're falling fast."

I finally managed to cut the cable, and the balloon whipped round. The dome straightened out, and the hole in the bottom of the envelope was open.

"Get in!" Per yelled.

As I dropped down through the hatch, he fired the burners full blast. We were within 300 feet of the ground, but the burst of heat steadied our descent and we rose again. I tried some switches, but there was no power in the capsule.

"Damn," I said. "No lights, no radio, no fuel gauge. Only the altimeter's working."

"Let's try coming down on the beach," Per said. "We can't risk anywhere inland."

I put on my life jacket and my parachute and attached the life raft to my belt. We saw the coastline approaching, and Per vented hot air from the top of the balloon to reduce our height. But once again the ground wind was considerably stronger than we expected, and it swept us out to sea. We were heading northeast, and without the radio or electricity in the capsule we were more than ever at the mercy of the wind.

"Hold tight," Per said.

He let out more air, alternating this with burning propane to try to reduce the speed of our descent through the thick gray cloud. As we finally came out of the fog, I saw the foaming sea rising up to meet us. We'd missed the beach. We were going far too fast. I realized the truth of Tom Barrow's words: it was like trying to stop a Sherman tank without brakes. With horror, I watched the ocean rushing toward us.

We hit the sea, crashing me into Per. We were tilted at a crazy angle, unable to stand upright. The balloon started to drag us across the surface of the ocean. We were being bounced from wave to wave.

"The bolts!" Per shouted.

He grabbed hold of the chair and hauled himself upward. I tried to help push him to his feet, but the capsule was smashing up and down, and each time I reached up I was knocked back. I watched Per's hand stretch out, grasp the red lever, and pull it down. This was supposed to fire the explosive bolts, which would sever the cables connecting the capsule to the balloon. In theory the balloon would then sail away and crumple into the sea, leaving the capsule to float on the water.

But nothing happened. Per yanked the lever up and down, but the bolts did not fire.

"Jesus Christ!" Per yelled. "The bolts are dead."

The balloon was now bouncing us across the Irish Sea like a monstrous beach ball. I was knocked sideways again and hit the upturned edge of the flight deck.

"Get out!" Per shouted at me. "Richard, we've got to get out."

Per braced himself against the hatch, wrenched down the levers, and pushed it open. The balloon slowed for a moment as the capsule dug into the water, and Per heaved himself up and climbed through the hatch. As I saw Per's backside squeeze through the hatch and disappear from view, I lunged after him and followed him up the rungs. I noticed that Per was still wearing his parachute. We clutched at the steel hawsers and tried to balance on the tilting capsule.

"Where's your life jacket?" I shouted.

Per didn't seem to hear me. The wind and the roar of the sea blew my words straight back into my face. The balloon was lurching at an angle, one side of it plowing through the gray sea. It showed no signs of slowing down. Behind us we left a foaming white wake. Then a gust of wind caught us and the balloon lifted off the surface.

Per threw himself off the top of the capsule into the cold black water. The drop seemed at least one hundred feet. I was sure that he'd killed himself.

I hesitated. Then I realized with horror that I was too late. Without Per's weight, the huge balloon soared up. I almost fell backward over the edge of the capsule as it swung underneath the balloon like a pendulum. I ducked down, grabbed hold of the railing, and watched the gray sea fall away beneath me. I was rising rapidly, and I couldn't see Per. Now that the balloon was sailing with the wind and no longer dragging the capsule through the water, it was much quieter. I watched with mounting dread as I soared upward into thick cloud and lost sight of everything.

I was now by myself, flying in the biggest balloon ever built, and heading toward Scotland. The wind was freezing cold; the sea below me was icy; and I was in thick fog. I had only the tiny emergency fuel tank left.

I climbed back into the capsule. It was now the right way up, and I felt reassured to see the screens and controls the way they had been as we crossed the Atlantic. I ran through the options: I could parachute into the sea, where nobody would be likely to find me and I would drown; or I could sail up into the darkening sky and try a night landing, should I be lucky enough to reach land. I picked up the microphone, but the radio was still dead. I had no contact with the outside world.

The altimeter ticked down, so I instinctively fired the propane. To my delight, the flame surged up inside the balloon and steadied it. I had assumed that the seawater had killed the burners. I gave a good long blast, and the balloon started rising again. I was having difficulty breathing, so I put on an oxygen mask. I checked the altimeter: 12,000 feet. Thick white cloud pressed all around me. I had no sense of where I was. All I knew was that the gray, foaming sea was waiting for me below. Before Per had ditched the balloon, he had told me that it was unlikely we had enough fuel to reach Scotland before dark. The remaining spare fuel tank gave me only about an hour's worth of flying. Sooner or later I would have to face the Irish Sea again.

I wondered about the explosive bolts. Perhaps they had cut through one, two, three, or even four of the five key cables that held the capsule to the balloon. Perhaps even now that last cable was straining and fraying under the weight and might give way. If so, the capsule would plunge straight down into the sea and I would be killed on impact. It was this fear that had prompted Per to jump. The capsule hatch was still open, and I gave the propane one good long burn before climbing out once more onto the top of the capsule to look at the cables. It was now completely quiet. I could not see all the cables without leaning out over the capsule railings. Standing amid the swirling white cloud, I felt an overwhelming sense of loneliness. The cables looked intact, so I squeezed back inside the hatch.

Whatever I did in the next ten minutes would lead to my death or survival. I was on my own. We had broken the record, but I was almost certainly going to die. Per, with no survival suit, was either dead or trying to swim on. I had to get somebody to find him. I had to survive. I cleared my mind and concentrated on the options in front of me. I hadn't slept for over twenty-four hours, and my mind felt fuzzy. I decided to take the balloon up high enough that I could parachute off the capsule. I blasted the burners and then found my notebook and scrawled across the open page, "Joan, Holly, Sam, I love you." I waited until the altimeter showed 8,000 feet and then climbed outside.

I was alone in the cloud. I crouched by the railings and looked down. I was still wheeling through the possibilities. If I jumped, I would have only two minutes to live. If I managed to open my parachute, I would still end up in the sea, where I would probably drown. I felt for the parachute release tag and wondered whether it was the right one. Perhaps due to my dyslexia, I have a mental block about which is right and which is left, especially with parachutes. The last time I had free-fallen I had pulled the wrong release tag and jettisoned my parachute. At the time I had several sky divers around me, so they activated my reserve parachute. But now I was by myself at 8,000 feet. I slapped myself hard across the face to concentrate. There had to be a better way.

"Give yourself more time," I said out loud. "Come on."

As I crouched on top of the capsule, I looked up at the vast balloon above me. The realization dawned that I was standing beneath the world's largest parachute. If I could bring the balloon down, then perhaps I could jump off into the sea at the last moment before we crashed. I now knew I had enough fuel for another thirty minutes. It must be better to live for thirty minutes than jump off with my parachute and perhaps live for only two minutes.

"While I'm alive I can still do something," I said. "Something must turn up."

I climbed back inside and took off my parachute. I made up my mind. I would do anything for those extra minutes. I grabbed some chocolate, zipped it into my jacket pocket, and checked that my torch was still there.

Peering out of the capsule into the fog below me, I tried to work out when I should stop burning, when I should open the vent, and when I should leave the controls and climb out on top of the capsule for my final jump. I knew that I had to judge the last burn exactly so that the balloon would hit the sea as slowly as possible. Despite losing all our fuel tanks, the balloon was still carrying a weight of around three tons.

As I came out through the bottom of the clouds, I saw the gray sea below me. I also saw an RAF helicopter. I gave a last burn on the propane to slow my descent and then left the balloon to come down of its own accord. I grabbed a red rag and climbed out through the hatch. I squatted on the top of the capsule and waved the rag at the helicopter pilot. He waved back rather casually, seemingly oblivious to my panic.

I peered over the edge and saw the sea coming up. I shuffled around the capsule, trying to work out where the wind was coming from. It was difficult to be sure, since it seemed to be gusting from all directions. I finally chose the upwind side and looked down. I was fifty feet away, the height of a house, and the sea was racing up to hit me. I checked my life jacket and held on to the railing. Without my weight, I hoped, the balloon would rise up again rather than crashing on top of me. I waited until I was just above the sea before pulling my life-jacket rip cord and hurling myself away from the capsule.

The sea was icy. I spun deep into it and felt my scalp freeze with the water. Then the life jacket bobbed me straight back up to the surface. It was heaven: I was alive. I turned and watched the balloon. Without my weight, it quietly soared back up through the cloud like a magnificent alien spaceship, vanishing from sight.

The helicopter flew over me and lowered a sling. I sat inside it like a swing, but each time it tried to lift me it dunked me back in the water. I couldn't understand what was wrong, and I was too weak to hold on much longer. Eventually it winched me up and someone reached out and pulled me inside.

"You should have put the sling under your arms," said a Scottish voice.

"Where's Per?" I asked. "Have you picked up Per yet?"

"Isn't he in the balloon?" the RAF man asked.

"Haven't you got him? He's in the water. He's been there ever since I took off again. About forty minutes ago."

The pilot pulled a face. He spoke to someone on the radio, but it was difficult to make out what was said. The helicopter spun on its axis and headed off.

"We're taking you to our boat," the pilot said.

"I want to look for Per," I said. "I'm fine."

If he had survived the fall, Per would still be swimming—or, more likely, drowning—in the Irish Sea. The light was fading and, from the air, only his head would be visible. It was like looking for a football—a gray football in a gray stormy sea. The pilot took no notice of my arguments. Within two minutes we had landed on a ship and I was pulled on board. Without pausing for breath, the pilot took off immediately and headed back over the sea. I was marched across the deck and put into a hot bath. Then I went up to the bridge to see how the search was going. For ten minutes, fifteen minutes, twenty minutes, there was nothing. Then the radio crackled.

"We've spotted him," the pilot said. "And he's still swimming. He's alive."

Per's struggles weren't over. The winch that had pulled me up was now jammed, and so they had to attract a dinghy to rescue him. By the time the dinghy arrived, Per was almost dead. He had been in the water for two hours, swimming as vigorously as possible to keep his circulation going but making no headway against the tide. He had no life vest on, and by the time of his rescue he was completely frozen and exhausted. It was extraordinary that he'd survived, and he later put it down to his experiences as a child, being forced by his father to swim every day in the icy lakes of Sweden.

We met on board the ship and fell into each other's arms. Per had been stripped naked and wore a survival blanket. His face looked like white marble. He was blue with cold, and he couldn't stop his teeth chattering.

For what it was worth, we were the first to cross the Atlantic in a hot-air balloon. More important, we were alive. We could not believe that we had both survived.

During the summer of 1987 British Caledonian had been struggling to stay in business. It took out a series of advertisements that showed businessmen singing "I wish they all could be Caledonian girls" to the tune of the

Beach Boys' "California Girls," and they made a great play about their cabin crews' tartan. But it was no good: British Caledonian was losing money. In August they announced that they had agreed to terms for British Airways to take them over. Although, in my opinion, this takeover breached the strictures of the Monopolies and Mergers Commission in that it was the largest and the second largest U.K. carriers forming one company with a market share across the Atlantic of well over 50 percent, both carriers made great play that British Caledonian would be run independently and that the Caledonian cabin crews would continue to wear their tartan uniforms and retain their independence.

Without British Caledonian offering competition, British Airways could now turn its full attention to mopping up the last tiny British competitor—us—and then concentrate on dominating the Atlantic routes. We complained to the Monopolies and Mergers Commission that this deal, in our opinion, exceeded all definitions of market share since it increased British Airway's share from around 45 percent to 80 percent on several transatlantic routes, but the deal was still given the go-ahead in September.

As the British Airways and British Caledonian deal went ahead, we realized that as well as the threat that a larger British Airways would pose to us, this takeover could also contain a hidden opportunity for us. We had already used the increased value of our first jumbo, which had risen in worth by $10 million, to leverage up and lease a second plane, which we were flying to Miami. And we wanted to expand further. Under the terms of the Bermuda Agreement, which governs international air traffic between America and Britain, there is provision for two British carriers between America and Britain. Our lawyers also discovered that the Japanese intergovernmental agreement contained a provision for two British and two Japanese carriers. With British Caledonian removed from the scene, Virgin Atlantic was now free to push itself forward and apply to fly these routes.

Just as surely as Mike Oldfield and the Sex Pistols had been turning points for Virgin Music, British Airways' takeover of British Caledonian was a turning point for Virgin Atlantic. Prior to their merger we had flown only to Miami and to Newark Airport in New Jersey. Now, as the second British long-haul carrier, Virgin Atlantic was entitled to apply for the routes that British Caledonian had served and were duplicated by the British Airways–British Caledonian alliance. Top of our list was to fly to JFK, the main airport at New York; Los Angeles; and Tokyo. Further down the line we listed two other American destinations that British Caledonian had operated—San Francisco and Boston—and Hong Kong. In 1987 we had just two aircraft. In order to fly to Los Angeles and Tokyo we would have to lease two more aircraft and double the number of our cabin crew.

In the meantime, as well as stalking British Caledonian's routes, we were also continuing to stalk Thorn EMI. In the last week of September, Trevor had finalized our £100 million loan with the Bank of Nova Scotia. Despite the stock market rising all summer, we felt that Thorn EMI was still undervalued. With £100 million at our disposal, we started buying on 25 September 1987. Undaunted by the size of EMI, we started putting in buying orders for 100,000 shares at a time. We decided to buy up to 5 percent of the company before announcing our takeover bid. Even if our bid failed, we knew that in the long run the 5 percent stake would increase in value.

Immediately rumors started going around the market that Thorn EMI was going to be bid for. Some days we bought 250,000 shares, costing us £1.75 million; other days we spent £5 million. Sometimes we sold shares to keep people guessing. We were stirring up the pot and ensuring that a high number of Thorn EMI shares were traded, which kept the bid rumors going. By the second week of October, our shareholdings had cost £30 million.

During the night of Thursday 15 October 1987, there was a hurricane in Britain. I remember walking from Oxford Gardens to *Duende* and looking across the streets—they were carpeted with green leaves. As a result the stock market was closed on Friday with so few people able to get to work. But in America, the selling of shares that had started on Wednesday became a stampede. I watched with amazement through the evening as the Dow Jones fell 95 points, then its largest one-day fall. The full significance of Wall Street's crash did not really hit London and the rest of the world until Monday. The Sunday newspapers were full of optimistic noises, even encouraging their readers to buy as many BP shares as they could. On Monday the Australian market was the first to open, and it fell by a fifth. Tokyo fell 1,500 points. I thought that this was a great opportunity to buy more Thorn EMI shares, so I called up our broker and asked him to buy £5 million worth of Thorn EMI shares first thing. I wanted to get in there before anyone else, and I was worried that someone else might have seized the opportunity. But there had been no need to worry. I don't think anyone could believe their luck that there was a buyer in the market. The broker filled his order within twenty seconds and asked me if I wanted to buy any more.

"There's tons more of it where it came from," he said.

Finally sensing a crisis, I paused. Even as I thought about it, the London stock market fell by 100 points, then another 100 points, then another 50 points—a full day's fall of 250 points. That afternoon the Dow Jones crashed by another 500 points. Within a three-day period, the world stock markets lost around a quarter of their value.

Trevor and I got together. For me the immediate damage was that the price of Virgin had nearly halved in value from 160p to 90p. Someone worked out that I had lost £41 million in value on my shares in Virgin PLC. The actual picture was much worse than this. The share price of Thorn EMI had dropped from £7.30 to £5.80, a drop of over 20 percent, and the value of our shareholding had crashed to £18 million.

The Bank of Nova Scotia were not amused. With the crash in share prices, they asked for an immediate cash payment of £5 million. Oddly enough I was still rather confident about buying Thorn EMI. I felt unaffected by the slump in Virgin's own share price since I was never going to sell my shares anyway, and I was absolutely certain that the share price was grossly undervalued. And since I was focusing more on the profits and cash flow from EMI, I began to see the stock market crash as a golden opportunity to buy the company. But Mountleigh were blown apart by the crash—their share price collapsed by 60 percent and they were unable to borrow any more money to buy shares in Thorn EMI or anyone else for that matter.

That week I had a furious argument with the two nonexecutive directors whom we had brought in to represent the outside shareholders' interests when Virgin went public. Sir Phil Harris and Cob Stenham were utterly opposed to continuing the siege of Thorn EMI and announcing a bid when we released our results later in October.

"But it's a unique buying opportunity," I said. "It simply cannot be true that Thorn is now worth only two-thirds of its value on Friday. We know the cash which we can earn from its back catalog, so in terms of straight cash to us it's a bargain."

"There could be tough times ahead," they warned me. "This crash has changed the whole picture."

"But the people who buy records won't stop," I said. "Most people don't hold any shares anyway. They'll carry on buying Beatles and Phil Collins albums."

But everyone disagreed with me. They all wanted to see where the stock market went next. The Thorn EMI share price continued to fall until it reached £5.30. I was sure that if we could present a united front, then we would be able to raise the money and buy Thorn EMI at a bargain price. I argued that there was no good reason for the crash and that share prices would recover soon. I told them that there would never again be such a wonderful opportunity. But they all disagreed, and since I could not persuade them, I had to let the matter drop. I expected the Virgin share price to jump up when we released our results. And so when we announced that Virgin's profits for the year ended July 1987 had doubled from £14 million to £32 million, we made no reference to Thorn EMI. As it happened, our share price did not move upwards—anything but. It was difficult to understand how Virgin could have floated with a share price of 140p last year and to see our share price halved on the back of doubled profits.

The stock market crash was the final nail in Virgin's coffin as a public company. I knew that Don would be opposed to changing direction, but Trevor and I had a quiet chat about the logistics of going private again, and Trevor set about working out the finances that such a large buyback would entail.

In July 1988 we announced that the management of Virgin would conduct a management buyout of Virgin PLC. We could have probably got away with paying less than the original 140p per share, but we decided that we would offer the same price we had sold the group for on the stock market, a large premium over the 70p at which shares were changing hands just before our announcement. This meant that nobody who had invested in Virgin when it was floated—all those people in the queue outside the bank who had wished me well—would lose money. Our reputation would stay intact.

Trevor renegotiated the entire financial structure of the Virgin Group and set in place the mechanics for going private at the end of November 1988. This colossal task was made no easier when our advisers Samuel Montagu approached their parent bank, Midland Bank, to join the syndicate of lending banks, but were turned down out of hand.

Trevor decided to dispense with Samuel Montagu's services in all but name. Rather than set up a syndicate of banks with one leading bank as the point of contact and prime negotiator, he began to pull together a consortium of banks, each of which he approached directly. This approach meant that he would have to do much more legwork since he was speaking to them all individually, but it also meant that he could play each of them off against the other. In the end he arranged lines of credit with twenty different banks, and we drew up an overdraft of £300 million. We bought in the outside shareholders' shares, refinanced the debt that had been secured upon our Virgin Group PLC shares, and similarly for Virgin Atlantic.

With over £300 million of debt, we were so heavily borrowed that we knew that we would have to move rapidly if we were to survive. We had to give up the idea of buying Thorn EMI, so we sold our shares and concentrated on dealing with our own problems. I had always felt that the City had undervalued Virgin Music, and now we would have to see what its real value was. Don Cruickshank, Sir Phil Harris, and Cob Stenham left Virgin. Don had carried out a superb job in recasting the company as one that could now demonstrate clear lines of management, and Trevor took his place as managing director. Trevor and I set about finding other companies that might wish to invest in any of the Virgin subsidiaries as joint ventures. We wanted to replace the shareholders in the City with one or two key partners in various Virgin subsidiaries. The structure of the Virgin Group was about to become extremely complicated.

Chapter 18

"Virgin has always enjoyed an excellent rapport with the Japanese. I put it down to the success of my first-ever trip to Tokyo.... Nowadays I am booked into huge hotels that are very nice, but nothing compares with that first business trip."

1988-1989

When I had bought back Nik's 40 percent stake, I had been able to repay my £1 million overdraft because Virgin had suddenly released a string of hits starting off with Phil Collins. At the time I knew I was on a knife-edge. Now the sums of money were far more daunting: we had a debt mountain of over £300 million, and we had to reduce it by £200 million within the first year. This pressure meant that everything was now up for sale. There were no sacred cows. If we received a good offer for a part of any Virgin business, then we would take it. Trevor, Ken, and I put out feelers to see what level of interest there was. One of the first areas we examined was Virgin Retail.

Right from the beginning in 1971 Virgin had never made much profit from our record shops. The shops put our name out onto the high street, so they were a big part of the public perception about Virgin. They also helped us keep in touch with the kind of bands people were buying. But after we had paid our staff, paid the rent, and allocated the central-group overheads, the shops had always lost money.

The problem with Virgin Retail was that after Nik had left in 1980 nobody had been able to organize them effectively. HMV and Our Price began to outstrip us. Don Cruickshank instigated a review of the company in 1987, and it became clear that retailing was not making us money and apparently was never likely to.

"Let's sell the lot," I said at a board meeting after we once again went through the expected losses for Virgin Retail. After second thoughts I changed my mind and wondered whether we should sell the smaller record shops and keep the Megastores. I had two reasons for changing my mind: the new HMV store on Oxford Street, the world's largest record store, had opened to great acclaim and had actually increased record sales along Oxford Street; and secondly, Patrick Zelnick had found a building on the Champs-Élysées in Paris that he thought would make a sensational conversion into a Virgin Megastore. In Britain we had 102 Virgin record shops up and down the country, and when W. H. Smith asked us whether they could buy some and rename them Our Price Records, we jumped at the chance. In June 1988 we agreed to sell 67 of the smaller shops for £23 million.

Trevor and I then divided Virgin Retail into three separate divisions: the first comprised the rump of the record shops we had kept back from selling to W. H. Smith, the typical high street shops together with the Oxford Street Megastore; the second comprised Patrick Zelnick's proposed Paris Megastore on the Champs-Élysées, where Patrick set up a separate French subsidiary to invest in the shop; the third comprised the plans we had for the man who had designed and set up the HMV record shop on Oxford Street, and whom we had managed to persuade to join Virgin: Ian Duffell.

I'm still not sure why Ian decided to leave Thorn EMI and come to Virgin. I know that in the short term he forfeited a decent salary with a large, reputable company to come and work for us at a time when Virgin was having great trouble in retailing. But we offered him the chance to set up Virgin Megastores anywhere in the world, and we promised to back his judgment and to let him have a direct share in the Megastores. Ian was one of the best record retailers in the business: he had excellent plans for the record shops, and for the first time since we had opened our first batch of Virgin shops, I felt that we could be back on the map. His interest lay in opening a sequence of overseas Virgin Megastores.

We thought about setting up in America, but the retail rents at the time were astronomical and the competition was high. Instead we chose to open the first one in Sydney, which was a quiet market without much competition, where we could open a Megastore and experiment a little with different formulas without losing a lot of money. Ian went to Sydney, where we said—only half jokingly—that Thorn EMI would never be able to track him down to persuade him to come back again. Ian recruited his old partner from HMV, Mike Inman, to join him, and together they started work on the Sydney Megastore.

In the meantime the Paris Megastore was the first overseas shop to materialize. Patrick had found a grand old bank dating from the late nineteenth century. It had marble floors, soaring high ceilings, and the most spectacular staircase. This old bank grabbed my imagination. We knew that small record shops did not make enough money; they just attracted passersby who were disappointed by the lack of depth of stock. Now that the 1970s were over and the cushions on the floor had been cleared away, the traditional Virgin shops seemed to have lost their identity and customer loyalty. We had to go for something bigger, where we could offer the best range of products in the world.

The rest of the Virgin board hated the idea of the Paris Megastore. I saw it as our final gamble with retailing. If it didn't work, we could sell the whole business off. When Patrick first presented the idea of the Paris Megastore, none of the other directors believed his sales forecasts:

"If we can't make money from Oxford Street," Simon Draper pointed out, "how on earth are we going to make money from the wrong end of the Champs-Élysées?"

I knew that he was particularly angry about the continuing failure of Virgin Retail since the record company, in which Simon had a shareholding of 20 percent, subsidized Virgin Retail's losses. With the whole board against the idea, I would have to do something if Patrick was to get permission to go ahead. The next week I was asked whether I would do a television commercial about doing business in Europe. I immediately agreed and quietly asked whether we could film it in Paris. The next thing the Virgin board saw was the television commercial, where I stood on the Champs-Élysées and announced that it was great doing business in Europe—indeed, the next Virgin Megastore was going to be right here. Simon, Ken, and Trevor were furious with me, but I trusted Patrick and was sure that he was onto a winner. Although I listen carefully to everyone, there are times when I make up my mind and just do it. And at times like those—the more people disagree with me—the more obstinate I become.

Patrick's Paris Megastore was an incredible success. From its opening day it smashed all his sales forecasts and became the most celebrated shop in Paris. Indeed, it became far more than a shop, it became a landmark and a tourist destination. After a few months the Paris Megastore attracted as many visitors as the Louvre. Today it still generates twice as many sales per square foot as that of any other record store in the world. It seems that every teenage Japanese and German tourist makes a pilgrimage there and buys huge numbers of CDs, and even the café at the top has become a smart place for French executives to meet. I was delighted for Patrick, but I still had no idea what to do about the British record shops.

It was the disaster of Valentine's Day 1988 that brought matters to a head. The retail team decided to sell orchids that day and ordered 5,000. Unfortunately, either nobody knew about this stock of orchids or people preferred to buy roses, but by 15 February we had sold only 50 orchids. The retail chain found themselves left with 4,950 flowers, which unlike CDs were wilting and dying and had to be chucked away. I couldn't even have given Joan that many. We decided that it was time to bring some other people in to turn Virgin Retail around. Giving people their notice is always heart-wrenching, and I hate doing it. I hate confrontation and I hate disappointing people; I always try to give people another chance. But it was clear that this team were out of their depth and losing money without any hope of turning the company around. The final straw came when, after the end of the financial year, they admitted to us that the losses of Virgin Retail would be £2 million more than they had anticipated. By leaving it so late we were stuck. We asked some headhunters to draw up a short list of suitable candidates, but I was most intrigued when Simon Burke applied for the job of chief executive. Simon had joined Virgin a couple of years previously as the development manager; his job was to sift through all the business proposals we received and to see whether we wanted to follow up on any of them.

One of the things I am always trying to do with Virgin is to make people reinvent themselves. I firmly believe that anything is possible, and despite Simon having no obvious qualifications to turn a large chain of unsuccessful record shops into a chain of successful ones, I was certain that if anyone could do it, he could. And sure enough, as soon as Simon started work at Virgin Retail in August 1988, things began to change. After the initial sale of the 67 shops to W. H. Smith, we were left with 35 shops. Of these 35 shops, 25 were shops within various Debenham's stores.

Simon's first move was to clean out all the rubbish that had accumulated in the stores. In response to the pressure from the Virgin board to make money, the retail team had done all kinds of deals with all kinds of people to try to bring in more money: they had expanded the range of goods to include everything from metallic badges and boxer shorts to Filofaxes and stationery. Several shops had subtenants selling skateboards or American football gear; others had Athena posters and greeting cards. The worst concession was the Birmingham shop, which had subleased space to Comet, so that the entrance to the shop was occupied by washing machines. Although these deals brought in some immediate cash, in the long run they confused people and stopped them from treating the record shops as proper places to buy records.

In the Oxford Street store there was a mini–CD factory. I have to admit that this was my idea, and it was a disaster. I had dreamed up the idea because I thought that people would be intrigued to see the CDs being made right in front of their eyes. When CDs had first been introduced, we had invested in a CD factory in Wales called Nimbus. We asked Nimbus to set up the production line, and they brought up all the gleaming stainless steel machinery from Wales. I thought that it would become a tourist attraction in its own right. But it was a mistake. For a start it was probably the only factory on the valuable real estate of Oxford Street this century. But it was also a disaster for a number of other reasons: First, a good deal of stock was stolen and sold onto the black market. Second, the staff who operated the machines had to be bused up from Wales and worked four days on, three days off. And although we were happy to press any record company's CD, our minifactory was too small to compete properly on price with the giant CD factories. As a result the long-suffering recipient of the CDs produced by this megastore was of course Virgin Music. Ken and Simon accepted them through gritted teeth only because I twisted their arms halfway up their backs. I was determined that this example of vertical integration would work in the same way as the integration between owning a recording studio, a record label, and record shops had worked.

Simon Burke finally put his foot down and insisted that we immediately dismantle the CD factory and return the space to selling records.

"It's just a gimmick," he told me. "It's got to go."

Simon Draper and Ken both gratefully agreed, and we reverted to our normal way of doing business, which was and is to minimize the amount of cash we have tied up in fixed assets and buy services from the most efficient supplier. I have a weakness for vertical integration, which I admit does not always work: the CD factory was one of my biggest mistakes, but I also once bought the Earl of Lonsdale pub on Portobello Road because so many Virgin staff spent so much time there and I hated seeing all our money disappear over the bar. That didn't work out. On another occasion I almost bought a property maintenance company because we had so many properties that needed repair and I thought it would be better to keep this service in-house. In some instances, I was right—notably, in the signing to the record label of Phil Collins, who had struck up a rapport with us during his time at the Town House—but in many others I had to eat my words and admit that it is better to pay an outside expert.

Simon Burke's strategy began to pay off, and by June 1989 Virgin Retail produced its first-ever profit. It must have been galling for him: in his first presentation to the Virgin board he showed us some slides and asked for £10 million to invest in new shops. He pointed out that the retail side was falling apart, and he showed us some pictures of the shops where tiles were hanging off the roof and the wiring was coming apart. He suggested that if any airline customers saw this, they would worry about the state of the aircraft. Unfortunately for Simon, Patrick Zelnick was also asking for £10 million to develop Virgin Megastores in Bordeaux and Marseilles. Flushed with the recent success of the Paris Megastore, I felt more inclined to divert the funding to France than to the United Kingdom. In the meantime, the Sydney Megastore was ready to open, and Ian and Mike were looking at Japan.

In order to create the investment in the U.K. branch and help pay down the general debt, we set up another joint venture. Ideally we would have liked a financial investor to take a 30 percent stake, but with the high interest rates and the feeling that high street retailing was heading for recession, we had no takers. We began talks with Kingfisher, the owner of Woolworth's. As these talks dragged on, W. H. Smith got wind of them and called me to see whether they could make an offer. And so just as Simon Burke was getting on with the job of sorting out Virgin Retail for Virgin, he suddenly found himself with a new boss: a two-headed creature comprising both Virgin and W. H. Smith. W. H. Smith bought a 50 percent stake in our ten U.K. Megastores, which, unlike the earlier shops we had sold to W. H. Smith, continued to trade under the Virgin name. Their sale raised £12 million, which we immediately used to pay down borrowings in Virgin Atlantic. It was another case of some frantic juggling to keep one step ahead of the bankers.

While the U.K. retail arm spun off into a joint venture with W. H. Smith and the European retail side started to expand from Paris into Bordeaux, Marseilles, and then Germany, several different Virgin companies turned their attention toward Japan.

Many British companies complain about how difficult it is to do business in Japan, but Virgin has always enjoyed an excellent rapport with the Japanese. I put it down to the success of my first-ever trip to Tokyo. I had gone there as a twenty-year-old, before I was married to Kristen, and rather ambitiously arranged a number of meetings with people in the entertainment and media world to see whether we could set up some kind of joint venture distributing records. I think that it was before we started Virgin Music, so I didn't even have Mike Oldfield to sell them. I was young and impoverished and had very little to offer. I went along to a number of meetings where immaculate geisha girls served tea, and I sat in my jeans and sweater and enthused about business to polite groups of kind and patient Japanese businessmen. No business deals were forthcoming, but the great success was at my hotel.

When I had arrived at the airport and taken a coach into Tokyo, I realized that I could not afford to stay at any of the hotels on the list suggested by the tourist board. So I took a taxi and asked for a cheap local hotel. The hotel looked utterly anonymous from the outside, just a plain little concrete building, and my room was very small. But that night, bored and alone, I saw that room service offered a massage. Two beautiful Japanese girls came up to my room, asking me to lie in the bath and giving me the most erotic massage of my life. We all ended up in my bathtub. When I breathlessly called up for a massage the next night to repeat the experience, I was confronted by two huge women in severe aprons. After explaining that the other two girls were having a night off, they proceeded to karate chop and pummel me to within an inch of my life. Nowadays I am booked into huge hotels that are very nice, but nothing compares with that first business trip.

By 1988 Virgin had become quite a well-known brand name in Japan. Several of our artists sold well there, particularly the Human League, Simple Minds, and Phil Collins; Boy George had also been a huge success. After the British Airways takeover of British Caledonian, we successfully applied for the right to fly to Tokyo. When we looked at ways of reducing our overdraft, we realized that we would have to sell shares in both Virgin Atlantic and Virgin Music in order to reduce our mountain of debt.

Our first deal was to sell 10 percent of the airline to Seibu-Saison, a large Japanese travel group. Virgin Atlantic had just announced doubled pretax profits of £10 million, and Seibu-Saison bought the 10 percent stake for £36 million. At the same time as this deal was going through, Robert Devereux was signing up a longer-term contract with Sega for Virgin Communications to distribute Sega games. It was becoming clear that Japanese companies shared much of the same philosophy as Virgin. Like us, they tended to operate on long-term objectives. As well as the constrictions of having to report to nonexecutive directors and shareholders, one of my main frustrations with being a public company quoted on the stock market was the short-term view investors took. We were under pressure to produce instant results, and unless we paid out a large dividend our share price would suffer. Japanese investors do not invest with the dividend payment in mind; they almost exclusively look for capital growth. And given that it can take a long time for investments to pay off, Japanese share prices are very high in comparison with the companies' earnings. Hence Japanese price-earnings ratios are often three times as high as British ones. I once heard of a Japanese company which was working to a 200-year business plan! It reminds me of the Chinese leader Deng Xiaoping's remark in the 1980s: when he was asked what he thought the implications were of the French Revolution in 1789, he replied, "Too early to tell."

The next part of the Virgin Group to embrace a Japanese partner was Virgin Music. This was the key sale. If we were going to make any sense of buying back Virgin PLC, then we had to raise a good price for Virgin Music. Simon, Trevor, and I had spoken to a number of American companies about taking a stake in Virgin Music. One of them offered the most money but was not prepared to take the role of a passive, long-term investor. We all gravitated toward a Japanese media company, Fujisankei. I think my mind was made up at a meeting with Mr. Agichi of Fujisankei in the garden of our house at 11 Holland Park.

"Mr. Branson," came the quiet question, "would you prefer an American wife or a Japanese wife? American wives very difficult—lots of litigation and alimony. Japanese wives very good and quiet."

Chapter 19

"Joan and I were finally getting married, and I didn't want the Cadbury Milk Tray to melt. I prepared to jump."

1989–1990

*B*y selling 25 percent of Virgin Music for $150 million (£100 million) we had vindicated our argument that the City had undervalued Virgin. It was a clear sign that that company alone was worth at least £400 million, and that was without any value at all placed on the various other companies, such as retail, that had made up the public group. This figure was way above the £180 million at which the City had valued us before we offered to buy the company back, and still way above the £240 million price we had eventually paid to go private.

With Japanese partners in our two main businesses, the airline and music, we then turned to our third business and decided to expand the retail side in Japan as well. Ian Duffell and Mike Inman, along with our Japanese adviser, Shu Ueyama, had already begun their research. Mike had started learning Japanese in Sydney because his brother had married a Japanese girl. Ian sent Mike to Tokyo, and he himself then headed to Los Angeles to look for a Megastore site along Sunset Boulevard.

Mike reported that it would be impossible to set up a Megastore in Tokyo by ourselves: Tokyo, a vast city with few distinguishable regions, is extremely difficult for outsiders to identify the key parts of. Retail, residential, and commercial properties are all jumbled together, so unlike London, which has easily definable shopping areas like Oxford Street, Knightsbridge, and Kensington High Street, and where it is relatively easy to get your bearings, Tokyo looks all the same. Property is extremely expensive, and in order to rent a shop you have to put down a huge deposit called "key money." Trevor, Ian, and Shu had met up with a great many potential Japanese partners, eventually choosing to team up with the fashion retailer Marui. Trevor formed a fifty-fifty partnership, which would be the start of Virgin Mega-stores in Japan.

The difficulty with a record shop is that every one is trying to sell the same product as every other record shop. A record is a commodity in the way most other products available on the high street are not. Virgin had nothing that we could call our own or that was available only at Virgin shops. We knew that our competitors were losing a lot of money in Tokyo not only because they had had to pay such high key money deposits on their shops but also because they had not established any customer loyalty and therefore did not get the vital return visits.

In order to avoid these pitfalls, we set up the joint venture with Marui. They were the first retailer really to understand the importance of railway stations. They positioned their stores as closely as possible to the large rail-way stations, thereby securing a vast crowd of passing pedestrians. Marui had also pioneered an in-house credit card, which was popular, and their clothes were aimed at the young, increasingly affluent generation. Marui managed to secure a fabulous site for us in Shinjuku, a prime shopping area in central Tokyo, and we took 10,000 square feet. It was Marui's property, and we agreed to a system whereby we paid Marui a certain percentage of our sales instead of a fixed monthly rent. In this way we avoided paying the ruinous key money deposit, and although 10,000 square feet was small by European standards, it was still larger than any other record shop in Tokyo.

To be different from our competitors and to attract customers, we in-stalled listening facilities and hired a DJ. The DJ was not only an entertainer; by playing great songs he soon covered his costs by triggering sales. The Tokyo Virgin Megastore soon acquired the kind of cult status as the early shops in Oxford Street and Notting Hill. Teenagers from across the city flocked there, and it became famous as *the* place to go. Tokyo is an expensive city, and so teenagers came along to Virgin, where they could spend a cheap afternoon listening to music, chatting, and buying records. It was almost like an extension of our original retail philosophy. The average time spent in our Tokyo Megastores is forty minutes—considerably longer than people spend having a meal in McDonald's. With 10,000 customers a day the Japanese re-sponded way above our expectations. With Ian in Los Angeles, Mike was by himself. In due course he followed his brother's footsteps by falling in love with a Japanese girl. They got married on Necker Island.

Within a space of two years, between 1988 and 1990, each Virgin sub-sidiary had set up a deal with a Japanese company. With Sega, Marui, Seibu-Saison, and Fujisankei, we were uniquely placed to expand in Japan. I was also about to become involved in Japan in an altogether different venture: Per and I were planning to fly across the Pacific Ocean from Japan to America on our second hot-air balloon adventure.

Per told me his worst fear when it was too late. We were on the plane on our way to Japan when he confessed that he had been unable to test the capsule in a pressure chamber to be 100 percent sure that it would survive at 40,000 feet. If a window blew out at that height, we would have between seven and eight seconds to put on our oxygen masks.

"We'll need to keep them handy," Per said in his usual understated way. "And of course, if the other person is asleep, then it'll be necessary to put the mask on and get it going in three seconds and then put on the other person's in three seconds, allowing two seconds for a fumble."

I didn't fancy a fumble with Per, even for two seconds, and I vowed that I wouldn't go to sleep during the flight.

"Will we have any advance warning about this?" I asked.

"If the capsule decompresses, you'll notice that it suddenly becomes misty. The capsule will appear to fill with fog. You will hear a screaming in your ears, and you will experience the sensation of your lungs being sucked out of your chest and through your mouth."

When a journalist asked me about the dangers of the flight, I recounted Per's words.

"So you see it's essential that one of us stays awake during the flight," I added. "So rather than using the comfortable Virgin seats, which we used to cross the Atlantic, we've asked British Airways for two of theirs."

We were attempting the flight in November, when the jet stream across the Pacific is at its strongest, but it is also the time of year when the ocean is extremely stormy. We would take off from Japan and almost immediately be above the sea. We would then have to more than double our Atlantic record of 3,000 miles to reach America.

Per's team had taken the balloon and capsule to the launch site in Miyakonojo, a small town in the south of Japan, which they had calculated lay directly below the jet stream. On my first night there, I was called by Tom Barrow, who had fallen out with Per since the Atlantic crossing. We had replaced Tom with Mike Kendrick, but Tom had been following Per's progress and was extremely worried:

"You're going to end up in the water," he told me. "Your first priority is to be prepared for a safe, survivable ditch in the sea. If against all odds you reach the mainland, you'll have a sixty percent chance that it'll be dark. In November it's dark for fifteen hours of the day in North America, particularly the further north you go. You can't land in the dark, so you may well have to fly for another fifteen hours. Even at thirty miles an hour this'll take you a thousand miles inland and you could well be in trouble then. You should assume that there'll be storm conditions—it's hardly likely to be a still, calm day. Up in the north you get people trapped in cabins waiting for the weather to clear, so for God's sake have your search-and-rescue team in place. Don't be dependent upon calm weather for your landing.

"Check all the systems before you take off. Don't get pressured into taking off. Even if everything's well built and works, then the flight is still terribly dangerous."

I thanked Tom for his advice.

"My last word on the matter," he told me. "The Atlantic crossing was a successful flight that was out of control. We all know that. It was fully out of control at the end, but both of you survived. You both taught yourselves to fly that balloon as you went along. In the Atlantic you can ditch near a boat. In the Pacific you're dead. So you'll either ditch in the sea and die, or you'll hit land in the dark and that'll be a close call."

I put down the telephone. I was sweating. I had hardly finished scribbling down what he'd told me when it rang again. It was Joan. Today was Holly's eighth birthday. She came on the line.

"I'm keeping a diary, Dad," she told me. "We can swap diaries when you come home."

"Yes, darling," I said, swallowing hard.

When I mentioned the survivability of ditching in the sea to Per, he agreed.

"We don't need to bother with health insurance," he said casually. "It's only worthwhile taking out life insurance."

As Per's team assembled all the electrical systems in the capsule, Per and I sat down together and went through all the flight operations. It was hard to believe that we were once again going to be incarcerated in this tiny capsule, surrounded by all these gadgets that were our only way of communicating with the outside world.

"Look," I found myself saying to one reporter who was running through a list of everything that could go wrong. "It'll either be a piece of cake, or it won't."

The jet stream above the Pacific is a different shape from the one above the Atlantic. The Atlantic jet stream is a V-shaped polar jet stream. Flying along inside it is like flying along an inverted Toblerone—as you rise up, the jet stream becomes wider and the wind becomes faster. As you rise, you gradually increase your ground speed. At 10,000 feet the air current might be 50 knots; then at 27,000 feet it will be 100 knots, and so on. A balloon can ease into it without being buffeted. The Pacific jet stream is a different beast altogether. It is a subtropical jet shaped like a single bore cable. At 20,000 feet the air current could be completely still; at 25,000 feet it could be the same; and suddenly at 27,000 feet you hit the jet stream, which is moving anywhere from 100 to 200 knots. Nobody had ever flown a balloon in the Pacific jet stream before, and we knew a danger existed that when the top of our balloon hit the current, it could be sheared off from the capsule suspended below. If that didn't happen, we knew it would be a pretty rough buffeting. With the capsule traveling at 5 knots and the balloon at 200 knots, we knew it would be like being pulled along by 1,000 horses.

If we managed to get into the jet stream, we knew that it had an inner core generally about 4,000 feet in diameter. To keep within this tube meant constantly monitoring the altimeter and watching out for any buffeting that would imply that the balloon and capsule were in different streams.

The atmosphere at Miyakonojo was bordering upon a carnival. A Shinto priest came to bless the site, and my parents arrived. Joan had chosen to stay at home until the balloon went up and then to take a plane to Los Angeles so that she and the children could be on the receiving end of the flight. By Sunday night our weatherman, Bob Rice, was forecasting perfect conditions for Tuesday, but by Monday these conditions had been delayed to Wednesday. Per and I spent another day in the capsule going over and over again everything that could go wrong.

"Keep the fire burning, that's all that matters," I wrote down across the width of my notebook after one three-hour session on all the likely outcomes of our flight. The delay gave me the chance to revisit the banks of dials, gauges, and switches built into the capsule walls. It also gave me time to make sure that I remembered the difference between the switches that released the empty fuel tanks and the ones that separated the balloon from the capsule.

"It's code yellow," Bob Rice announced. "Expect a green light by 2100 hours, November 23."

"Is the Pacific Ocean the largest ocean in the world?" asked Holly down the telephone. "How many miles is it? And how long would it take you to fly all around the world?"

It was time for a sleep. I lay on my hotel bed but couldn't keep my eyes shut.

"Trying to have a couple of hours rest," I wrote in my diary. "Failing miserably. Just looked out of the window to see the end of a beautiful day. The smoke from the volcano looks like thin cloud in the sky. Cars with loudspeakers going through the streets announcing the time of our departure. Civic fireworks planned for 2:30 am for anybody from the town not already awake. Imagine an English City Council doing that! Still not feeling nervous: elated, excited, but not really nervous. Everything seems to have gone so well. Bob feels the crossing and landing conditions as nearly good as we can expect. Still have some nervousness about the inflation. In two hours must go back to site for a live interview for News at One."

When I went back to the site, I sensed trouble. The balloon's envelope was still laid out on the ground—inflation had not started. The operation room was full of Per's team being debriefed: "Too windy, too risky, too much downwind." They decided to leave the envelope laid out on the ground and hope that the wind would fall away the next night. With seventy tons of inertia in the balloon, a gust of wind could rip the fabric. I went back out and asked for our translator. Somebody gave me a microphone, and I apologized to the huge crowd who were huddled on the hillside above the launch site. We promised to try the next day.

The next day was long and listless. The jet stream seemed to be behaving peculiarly, and Bob Rice was struggling to work out whether we would land in California or Yukon.

"Oh, fuck the weather," America's most renowned and sophisticated meteorologist finally said. "Just go!"

I went back to the hotel for a final sleep, and once again I ended up staring out of the window at the volcano. Then I heard the drummers starting in town, and a fax was pushed under my door. In spidery, slanting letters Holly had written: "I hope you don't land in the water and have a bad landing. I hope you have a good landing and land on dry land, and Miss Salavesen said to have a good landing too. I hope you have a nice trip. Love from Holly. P.S. Good luck and I love you too."

I took a sleeping pill and fell onto my bed. A few hours later Per woke me up and we drove to the site. A crowd of around five thousand people had come out to watch in the freezing cold. There were families, old ladies, young babies. I heard massive cheers as the balloon rose from the ground and swung up above the capsule. The burners were roaring now to heat up the air. The wind was still, but we now needed to take off as soon as possible in case any gusts caught us on the ground. In the dim, milky light around the slope, hundreds of coal braziers had been brought out, and their smoke rose straight up into the starry night air—clear proof of how absolutely still it was.

I was just standing with my parents admiring the magnificence of the balloon when a strip of the fabric suddenly peeled off the envelope and hung down.

"What's that?" Dad asked me.

I ran to find Per.

"What's happening?"

"Nothing to worry about," Per said. "Just a little heat loss. The balloon's big enough to cope."

I took Per back into the operation room, and Dad grabbed his arm.

"What's that flapping off halfway up the envelope?" he said.

"It's air coming up the side of the balloon," Per said.

Dad didn't look convinced. Per and I then walked out toward the balloon. We stood underneath it and looked up. It effectively had a hole where the lamination had peeled off. We went back to the control room. I found Dad.

"Dad, don't tell Mum," I said, "but we've got a hole. Per still feels we'll make it to America."

"You can't fly in that thing," Dad said.

A minute later more strips of lamination started falling off.

"Richard, I'm afraid we're going to have to abort the flight," Per said. "If we take off, we'll end up in the Pacific."

I looked out at the crowded hillside. I was going to have to let them all down. With my hands trembling with cold and bitter disappointment, I once again picked up the microphone.

"I'm so sorry," I said, trying to stop my voice from choking. "The lamination of the balloon has torn apart. We think that it was because we left the balloon out all last night and the frost got into it . . ."

As the translator repeated my words, a groan rose from the crowd. But then there was a gasp and I saw three or four huge chunks of fabric crash off the envelope and fall down on top of the burners. Someone pulled them off, but the whole balloon was disintegrating in front of our eyes.

"Shut off the burners!" I yelled. "Stand back from there."

Without the burners, the balloon sagged. It fell to one side, hot air seeping out of its holes.

"We'll come back next year," I promised. "Please have faith in us."

"Well, Richard," said Dad as we all drove back to the hotel, "holidays with you are never dull."

Joan was two hours into her flight to Los Angeles when she heard the news.

"Excellent!" she exclaimed. "Champagne all round, please!"

The pilot pulled back the throttle, and the helicopter rose still higher. The pale-blue sea shimmered and glittered beneath us. I watched as we approached Necker: the white coral reef and then the pale strip of white beach, the leaning palm trees and the pointed roof of the Bali house, the deep green of the forest inland. We circled high overhead, and I saw our family and friends standing on the beach. Most of them wore white with wide-brimmed hats, although there was a splash of color from some tropical shirts. I spotted Vanessa and Robert; Lindi and her husband, Robin; all their children; Peter and Keris, my friends and neighbors from Oxfordshire; Ken and his wife, Nancy; Simon and his wife, Françoise. I waved down at their upturned faces. In the middle of the crowd I saw Joan in her stunning white dress, with Holly and Sam, her sister Rose, her brother John, and her mother beside her. Granny was standing with Mum and Dad, waving up at me merrily.

I tapped the pilot on the shoulder and he brought the helicopter around once more.

I picked up the box of Milk Tray and gripped it in my teeth. Everything was in place. I crouched low and paused at the open door. The wind was hot and fast in my face, the beach and silvery blue sea spinning crazily beneath me as I stared down. We were hovering over the swimming pool. I gripped the side of the door and looked back inside to the pilot.

"All because the lady loves Milk Tray!" he shouted.

I took the box out of my mouth for a moment.

"The kids do too!" I shouted back.

Then I flashed him a thumbs-up, took one last look at the swimming pool directly beneath me, and then climbed out onto the struts and swung off them. Joan and I were finally getting married, and I didn't want the Cadbury Milk Tray to melt. I prepared to jump.

Chapter 20

"Who the hell does Richard Branson think he is? Part of the bloody Foreign Office?"

August–October 1990

I was woken up by a heavy kick in my back. I had been kicked and prodded all night, but since it was now 5:30 A.M. I slipped out of bed and put on my dressing gown. I looked back and watched Sam snuggle onto my warm hollowed-out pillow, which he had been fighting to occupy all night. He and Holly often slept in our bed with us. I turned on CNN and put my head close to the screen to hear the news. I didn't need much sound to understand that it was bad. Iraq had invaded Kuwait the previous week, and the world was in a tailspin. The price of crude oil had soared from $19 a barrel before the invasion to $36 after; the price of aviation fuel had rocketed from 75¢ a gallon to $1.50, an even sharper increase than the rise in crude oil because the allied forces had begun stockpiling aviation fuel in preparation for an airborne attack on Iraq.

Two of the main ingredients of an airline's profitability are the number of passengers and the cost of aviation fuel. All independent airlines were now facing disaster: we were having to operate when the price of fuel, which represents 20 percent of our total overheads, had more than doubled and the number of passengers flying had dried up. In the first week following the invasion, Virgin Atlantic received 3,000 cancellations. We had a £25 million overdraft facility with Lloyds Bank, which we had just broken. I wondered how far we could go before Lloyds asked us to do something about it. I pushed the worry to the back of my mind and hoped that Trevor would be able to cope.

Turning my attention back to the television, I wondered how many more passengers would cancel today. The big state-owned airlines were hit even worse since nobody wanted to risk flying on a flag carrier with the chances of a terrorist attack. Despite being a normal public company, British Airways still proclaimed itself as the British flag carrier, and for the first time this reputation played to our advantage. After the first week of empty flights, I was beginning to feel a glimmer of hope that passengers were cautiously returning; indeed, we had noticed a slight preference toward Virgin Atlantic in place of any American airlines or British Airways. Since Mrs. Thatcher had allowed the American jets to refuel in Britain on their Libyan raid, companies that were closely aligned with the government were seen as vulnerable to terrorist retaliation. The Pan Am bomb over Lockerbie, Scotland, had shown how devastating such retaliation could be.

In the summer of 1990 Virgin Atlantic was still a tiny airline. We flew to just four destinations in two countries. Each day we scanned the bookings for these four routes to see whether there was any sign that we were winning passengers back. The Tokyo route was our worst hit. We were allowed to fly only four times a week excluding Sunday, the most popular day for businessmen to travel, and so the route was losing money even before Iraq invaded Kuwait. Throughout the summer we had been lobbying to be awarded the two extra flights to Tokyo that were about to be released, but as always we were up against British Airways. Our flights to Newark and Los Angeles had been hit in the first week after the invasion, but now we detected a swing toward Virgin in preference to the American carriers. The best news was that our holiday flights to Miami and Orlando seemed to be largely unaffected.

We had celebrated my fortieth birthday the previous month, and although Joan had arranged a wonderful party in Necker, I had found myself feeling uncharacteristically depressed. I felt that Simon had lost interest in Virgin Music, and I sympathized with him. It was extremely tough negotiating every contract, and sometimes going over the same points time and again felt rather repetitive. Although we had built Virgin Music into one of the major independent record labels, all Simon's wealth was tied up in that single company, and I knew he was worried that I might jeopardize it by some new risky venture. Simon wasn't interested in the other projects that I talked about and had seen Virgin Atlantic only as a large liability to the rest of the Virgin Group, a business that could be driven to the wall by British Airways or by something out of the blue—something like a war in the Persian Gulf.

As I turned forty, I also wondered what I was doing with my life. After the great leap into setting up Virgin Atlantic, I found it difficult to develop the airline as quickly as I wanted. Although we had had a wonderful year and had been voted the Best Business Class Airline, Virgin Atlantic was confined to operating from Gatwick Airport. Due to its single short runway and the lack of connecting flights, Gatwick was less profitable for both cargo and passengers than Heathrow. We were struggling to make money, and we had fallen into a bitter maintenance dispute with British Airways.

Given Simon's gradual loss of interest and our endless struggles to make ends meet at Virgin Atlantic, I began to question whether I should do something completely different. I even thought of going to university and studying history since I had never had the time to read anything. When I mentioned this to Joan, she squashed the idea by bluntly pointing out that this was really just an excuse to meet a whole lot of pretty girls away from home. I mulled over the idea of setting up as a full-time political campaigner, studying some of the major issues such as health care and homelessness, understanding what the best solutions were, and then fighting hard for the political change to implement them.

But all these thoughts were pushed out of my mind by Saddam Hussein's invasion of Kuwait. We had a full-blown crisis at the airline, and I found myself caught up in the Gulf War in an extraordinarily personal way.

"Daddy, please, can you help me find my shoes?"

It was Holly.

"Which ones?"

"You know, my new trainers."

As the world on the television continued to disintegrate toward war and as our half-empty 747 *Maiden Voyager* headed across the Atlantic toward a dawn over Gatwick, my family gathered in bed for breakfast. Joan brought up a huge tray with fried eggs, fried bread, bacon, and baked beans. As we ate, some of the Virgin staff let themselves into the front door. I heard Penni start up the photocopier downstairs. Our new press officer, Will Whitehorn, trooped upstairs to his office. A dynamo of perpetually cheerful energy, Will had already proved himself to be a·terrific asset.

Getting Holly and Sam ready for school was always a kind of mad initiative test. Shoes, socks, vests, shirts, blazers, and berets had to be found from wherever they had inexplicably vanished overnight. They could be conjured up only by the most inspired lateral thinking.

"Here they are!" Joan had somehow thought to look for Holly's shoes inside the large doll's house, which hadn't been used by anyone for as long as I could remember.

"What were they doing there?" I asked.

"No idea," Holly said and put them in her school rucksack without further explanation.

"Sam, we're going in *two* minutes," Joan threatened.

Sam had started to reassemble the Scalectrix.

As they finally managed to pick up all their bits and pieces and head for the door, the phone rang. It was Queen Noor of Jordan.

My friendship with Queen Noor was one of the unlikely consequences of Per's and my balloon trip across the Atlantic. Queen Noor was the Grace Kelly of Jordan: she was American and had once worked as an air stewardess. Tall, blond, and wholly glamorous, she now lived in a walled and heavily guarded palace in Amman. Queen Noor had heard about our balloon flight and telephoned me to ask whether I would teach her and her family how to fly a balloon. I went out to Jordan with Tom Barrow and spent a week at King Hussein's palace teaching the Royal Family how to fly a hot-air balloon. In a magical moment we flew over Amman, hovering over the rooftops and looking down on the ancient city with its minarets, whitewashed walls, and faded orange-tiled rooftops. Nobody in Amman had ever seen a hot-air balloon before, and they stared up with amazement as we loomed overhead. When they realized that their king and queen were standing in the wicker basket, they all cheered and ran beneath the balloon, waving up at us. When we fired the gas burner, all the dogs in the city started barking, and together with the cheering and the broadcast calls to prayers from the minarets, the city gave in to total pandemonium. King Hussein, Queen Noor, and the royal princes waved down as the balloon hovered to within three feet of the rooftops. I think that the only people who didn't enjoy the trip were King Hussein's bodyguards, who had successfully shielded him from nine assassination attempts but who could do nothing to protect him as he floated around in a wicker basket.

When Saddam Hussein invaded Kuwait, King Hussein of Jordan was one of the few world leaders who refused to condemn him out of hand. King Hussein pointed out that Kuwait had promised Iraq a number of oil wells as part of its contribution toward the long war against Iran. Yet Kuwait had since continually reneged on that promise as well as cheated on its OPEC quotas.

Amid all the chaos that followed the invasion, a huge number of foreign workers fled from Iraq into Jordan. There were around 150,000 refugees congregating in a makeshift camp with no water and no blankets. It was extremely hot during the day, when they had no shade, and freezing cold at night, when they had no warmth. A blanket can be rigged up as shade or wrapped up in for warmth. As soon as I heard of this problem, I contacted King Hussein and Queen Noor offering to do whatever I could to help.

Queen Noor now telephoned me to say that although the Red Cross were in the process of setting up a water distribution system, the single other priority was trying to find up to 100,000 blankets.

"A few very young children have already died," Queen Noor said. "But it hasn't turned into a full-scale catastrophe yet. I think that we've only got about two or three days' grace before we start to lose hundreds of refugees."

That day I drove down to Crawley and talked to some of the Virgin Atlantic staff about how we would set about finding and then flying 100,000 blankets to Amman. Everyone at Virgin rallied round. During the course of the day we called up the Red Cross, William Waldegrave at the Foreign Office, and Lynda Chalker at the Overseas Development Office, and managed to secure 30,000 blankets with the promise of more to come from UNICEF in Copenhagen. Now that we had offered to provide the plane, the Red Cross put out an appeal on national radio, and from that evening a warehouse at Gatwick started filling up with blankets. On top of that David Sainsbury, who owns a chain of supermarkets, promised me he would supply several tons of rice. Two days later all the seats were removed from one of our 747s and replaced by over 40,000 blankets, several tons of rice, and medical supplies. The 747 then flew to Amman. The blankets were loaded up into a line of trucks waiting at the airport, and we returned with a number of British nationals who had been stranded in Jordan and wanted to come home.

When I returned to Britain, William Waldegrave told me that he had had a call from Lord King, chairman of British Airways, who had been surprised to see the Virgin Atlantic flight to Jordan featured on *News at Ten*.

"We should be doing that," Lord King had told Waldegrave.

William Waldegrave had pointed out to Lord King that I had just offered to help and Virgin Atlantic happened to have an aircraft available to make it possible. The next week British Airways flew some supplies out to Jordan and brought back some more nationals. Christian Aid told us that they were amazed: over many years they had unsuccessfully appealed to British Airways to help them, but ever since the Virgin Atlantic flight to Amman, British Airways had been practically suffocating them with offers of help. Healthy competition benefits even charities sometimes.

Since I had heard that some of our original shipment had not reached the refugee camps, I decided to go to Amman for a few days to watch the procession of the next delivery of supplies until it finally reached the camps. Once again I stayed with King Hussein and Queen Noor at the palace. I had fierce arguments with the minister of interior about the need for strict accountability over these supplies so that the people who had provided them could be confident that they reached the camps. I also had several long talks with King Hussein about the Gulf crisis. King Hussein was sure that war could be averted but was worried that the West wanted diplomacy to fail so that they could defend Kuwait at all costs and protect their oil supply. By the time I returned home it was clear that there would not be a full-blown refugee crisis in Jordan. Over the next fortnight Queen Noor told me that there were no more deaths from dysentery or dehydration, and over time the 150,000 refugees slowly dispersed.

A few days later I was watching the news when I saw the extraordinary footage of Saddam Hussein giving a broadcast while surrounded by the British nationals who had been detained in Baghdad. In one of the most chilling moments I have seen on television, he sat down and motioned a young boy to come and stand by him. He put his hand on this young boy's head and then continued to address the camera while gently patting his shoulder. The boy was about the same age as Sam, and as I watched this public address I knew that I had to do something to help these people. If that boy had been my son, I would have moved heaven and earth to try to bring him back home.

I had no idea how I would set about helping bring these hostages home, but I knew that Virgin Atlantic had an aircraft and that if we could somehow obtain permission to fly into Baghdad, we would be able to pick up any hostages whom Saddam Hussein agreed to release. The reporters were expecting that these hostages would be used as "human shields" and would be incarcerated inside the prime allied targets. The thought struck me that in the same way I had been able to help the crisis in Jordan, I might be able to provide the vehicle for releasing these hostages.

The next day Frank Hessey called me. Frank introduced himself and asked me to help. He had telephoned every department in the Foreign Office, the Iraqi ambassadors in Europe, and even the Iraqi government in Baghdad, but nobody seemed able to do anything: his sister Maureen and his brother-in-law Tony were hostages in Baghdad. Tony had severe lung cancer and needed urgent medical attention.

As well as being in touch with the Foreign Office about flying the blankets to Jordan, I also had my friendship with King Hussein and Queen Noor. King Hussein was effectively one of the few points of contact any government in the West had with Iraq. I had heard that Iraq was short of medical supplies, and I wondered whether there were grounds for a deal whereby if we flew in medical supplies, Iraq could release some foreign detainees. I called Queen Noor and asked her whether she could help me. When I described my proposal, she suggested that I should come out to Amman once again and discuss it with King Hussein.

Spending the next three days in Amman with King Hussein and Queen Noor helped me discern how a businessman could help in moments of crisis. On the face of it, all I had to recommend me to Saddam Hussein was that I had once taken King Hussein and Queen Noor up in a hot-air balloon and that I owned a tiny airline that operated four Boeing 747s. Although nobody else had taken King Hussein hot-air ballooning, many businessmen own large aircraft. These two bizarre qualifications had propelled me into a unique situation: I was one of the only Westerners in whom King Hussein was prepared to confide, and I had therefore virtually direct access to Saddam Hussein.

I drafted a letter to Saddam Hussein and told him that I was staying in Amman, where I was helping out with the repatriation of immigrants and organizing some medical and food supplies. I asked him whether he would consider releasing any foreigners who were caught in Baghdad, particularly women and children and those who were sick. As a gesture of goodwill I offered to fly in some medical supplies that Iraq needed. I mentioned Frank Hessey's brother and his lung cancer. I signed it "Yours respectfully, Richard Branson."

Later King Hussein, Queen Noor, and I met downstairs in his drawing room, where he spoke for an hour about the problems in the Middle East. As I sat there and listened, I looked around at the room, where a signed photograph of Margaret Thatcher stood beside one of Saddam Hussein. King Hussein pointed out to me why he did not automatically support the Kuwaiti position against Iraq:

"The people of Kuwait are divided into three categories," he said. "There are 400,000 Kuwaitis who are either very rich or very, very rich; and there are two million impoverished immigrant workers looking after them."

He pointed out that there were no free press and no free elections in Kuwait, so that it was hardly the "democracy" that the West was defending.

"The Kuwaitis do nothing for the Arab world," he went on. "All their money is in Swiss bank accounts, not in Arabia. I've asked a number of world leaders whether the West would come to Jordan's rescue if Iraq had invaded Jordan, a country with no oil. Each time there was a silence. I doubt it." Then he laughed: "I know that you would though, Richard! Yes, you'd come sailing over the horizon in your balloon with your Virgin planes beside you!

"No, seriously," he said. "This is the chance to resolve the entire Middle

Eastern question. Kuwait promised Saddam Hussein that it would pay its share of the costs of the war against Iran, which Iraq fought on its behalf. It has reneged on that promise. Originally, Saddam only planned to take the disputed oil fields he thought were rightfully his. He only occupied the whole country because he heard that the Kuwaitis were preparing the landing strips to let the Americans come in and defend them. He is certainly not interested in invading Saudi Arabia."

King Hussein's peace plan involved Iraq pulling back to the border but keeping the disputed strip of land he felt that Kuwait owed Iraq; in three years' time there should be elections in Kuwait to see whether these border people wanted to remain part of Kuwait or Iraq. He told me that the West had little idea of the months of negotiation that had gone on between Iraq and Kuwait and how the Kuwaitis had continually failed to honor their promises. On top of that, the Kuwaitis had not waived the debts that Iraq had incurred over the Iran war, and the Kuwaitis continued to cheat all the Arab states by overproducing oil and selling it too cheaply.

At the end of dinner, King Hussein took my letter off to his study, where he translated it into Arabic. He wrote a covering letter to Saddam Hussein and dispatched it by special courier to Baghdad. Before going to bed, he quoted something his brother had said: "Why did the sheep bells of the Falkland Islands ring louder than the church bells of Jerusalem?"

Back in London I began talking to the Foreign Office. I tried to get the medical details of all those people stuck in Baghdad so that we could "prove" they were ill. I then called around other foreign embassies to alert them that there might be a rescue flight going into Baghdad and that they should try to get some of their people on it by showing "proof" that they were ill.

Two nights later we got a response from Saddam Hussein. He promised us that he would release the women and children and the sick hostages, but he wanted someone of stature to be flown in to ask him publicly to do so. I telephoned Edward Heath, the previous Conservative British prime minister, and asked him whether he would do so. He agreed. King Hussein contacted Saddam Hussein and put forward Ted Heath's name. Saddam Hussein agreed too. The next day we flew Edward Heath out to Amman, where King Hussein arranged for him to go to Baghdad.

A day later King Hussein was on the phone to me.

"I have good news for you, sir," he said. He was impeccably polite and always addressed people as sir or madam, as did his children. "You can set off for Baghdad. I have Saddam's word that you will be safe."

We had spent the last few days planning for this call and had found a brave volunteer crew, whom I'd like to name: Les Millgate, Geoff New, Paul Green, Ray Maidment, Peter Johnson, Jane-Ann Riley, Sam Rasheed, Anita Sinclair, Caroline Spencer, Ralph Mutton, Peter Marnick, Paul Keithly, Helen Burn, Nicola Collins, Janine Swift, and Stephen Leitch. We had forewarned passengers that there might be delays on Virgin Atlantic and that we might have to move them onto another airline.

When I told my fellow airline directors that we had permission to fly, they were understandably concerned. They knew that if the plane were delayed for more than a handful of days in Baghdad, we would go bust.

"The government has confirmed that they will stand behind our insurance company if the plane is destroyed," Nigel Primrose, the Virgin Atlantic finance director, confirmed. "But nobody will give us loss-of-business insurance if the plane is hijacked and kept in Baghdad. Remember, BA have already had one 747 wrecked in Kuwait."

There was silence around the table as they digested this.

"There is one upside," David Tait said with a serious face. "They'll hold Richard there too and spare us any more of his harebrained schemes!"

Everyone laughed. Although I knew that I was risking everything on this flight, I also knew by now that there was no backing out.

We took off from Gatwick at 11 A.M. on 23 October 1990 and headed east over Europe. We sat huddled together at the front of the plane, a strange collection of hostage relatives, doctors, nurses, Virgin cabin crew, and one journalist to represent the press. The remaining four hundred seats behind us were empty. It was rather eerie. After a couple of hours we all walked up and down the aisles to get some exercise.

The daylight outside rapidly fell away, and by the time we entered Iraqi airspace it was dark. I looked out onto the desert below us and wondered where the Iraqi army was. I imagined the radars monitoring us as we headed toward Baghdad. We would be a single luminous green blob moving slowly across their dark screens. I half expected to see a couple of fighter planes appear and give us an escort, but it remained unnervingly quiet. The plane hummed and shuddered its way toward Baghdad, the first plane in twelve months to do so. Everyone stopped talking. We were entering the most dangerous airspace in the world, the concentrated target of the allied forces' planned attack. I wondered when the assault would begin.

I let myself into the flight deck and sat behind the captain, Les Millgate, and the two first officers, Geoff New and Paul Green. They were talking to air traffic control over the radio, but that was the only sign that Baghdad was out there. Ahead of us through the windscreen there was nothing. Iraq had a complete blackout. I wondered who lived down there, whether they could hear us flying overhead, and whether they thought that we were the first allied bomber. We seemed to be the only plane in the sky.

"We're getting close to the city," Les Millgate said.

I scanned the screens in front of us and watched the altimeters drop as we descended. Flying a long-haul flight is deceptive: for most of the time up in the air you are above the cloud level in that magical world of the jet stream, hardly aware that you are moving. Then, as the plane starts coming down, you suddenly realize that you are flying a massive piece of metal at over 400 miles an hour that must be brought to a standstill. We descended lower, and the plane hurtled through the darkness. Normally an airport is a blaze of orange-and-silver lights and it is difficult to distinguish the runway lights among them. The runways, ramps, planes themselves, and control tower are all brilliant with fluorescent and halogen lighting. But for the first time, we were flying over a land that was so blacked out we could have been flying over the sea.

Geoff New was talking to the air traffic control at Baghdad who were guiding us in. He opened the wing flaps and let down the undercarriage. I watched as we came lower and lower. Now we were only 600 feet up, now 500 feet, and the disembodied voice in the flight deck started counting out our height. Suddenly two lines of landing lights lit up in the darkness below us. We aimed straight down the middle; the plane touched down and raced along the tarmac. A few more lights appeared to guide us, and we taxied to the loading gates. I could dimly make out men with machine guns standing alongside a flight of steps. Jane-Ann Riley, our in-flight supervisor, signaled the door was safe to open, and I looked out.

It was freezing cold. The steps were being maneuvered toward us. I led the way down to Iraqi tarmac. Two lines of soldiers fanned out around us. A couple of senior government officials wearing brown camel-hair overcoats greeted us and indicated that the relatives should stay aboard. Baghdad airport is bigger than Heathrow, but it was completely deserted—ours was the only aircraft there. I looked back at the incongruous picture of the Virgin cabin crew with their red miniskirts and red stiletto shoes walking past the group of Iraqi soldiers in the vast empty airport. Their heels clacked loudly in the silence. We all smiled. The soldiers were a little timid at first but then grinned back.

We left the plane parked on the runway. Without any other planes alongside, it it looked unnaturally large. We were taken into a bare departure lounge where all the technology such as computer terminals and telephones and even light fittings had been stripped out. This dismantling would have taken some time, which indicated that the Iraqis were fully expecting to be bombed and had already salvaged everything they wanted from the airport. We handed out some presents we'd bought: boxes of chocolates for the officers and lots of Virgin kids' flight packs for the soldiers to send home to their families. Then I heard a movement outside, and Ted Heath came through the glass doors at the head of a large crowd of men, women, and children. They looked pale under the fluorescent lights, but as soon as they saw us they all broke into a cheer and ran forward to embrace us. Ted was smiling and laughing and clasping everybody by the hand.

I soon realized that we weren't going to take all these people back with us. People were crying and laughing and hugging each other, tears streaming down their faces. Outside, the soldiers unloaded the medical supplies we had brought. We opened bottles of champagne and toasted each other and those who were being left behind. I found Frank Hessey's brother and we embraced. A pregnant Filipino woman who was having to leave her husband behind came up to me. She was in tears. Another man came along and handed his three-year-old daughter to his nanny and had to say good-bye to her. I just hugged him. There was nothing else I could do. We both had tears in our eyes. I was a father too.

An hour later the Iraqis told us to get back on the plane. We walked back out across the freezing tarmac, and I shook hands with the soldiers and gave them more children's packs for their kids. We all shook hands and wished each other well. It was disturbing to think that when we flew away, we would leave these frail-looking, scared soldiers, standing in their uncomfortable boots and olive-green trousers, clutching their guns and keeping guard at one of the first targets to be bombed to smithereens. Most of the hostages walked arm in arm across the runway to keep warm and to support each other. They looked like ghosts. The lone 747 dwarfed them. All the lights had once again been turned off apart from a single spotlight illuminating the stepladders. I went up and turned to wave good-bye.

"You're always late!" said a gruff voice. It was Frank Hessey. He had stayed on board to surprise his sister and brother-in-law. They burst into tears and hugged each other.

My last sight of the Iraqi soldiers was of them gathering together and opening the red Virgin packs we had given them. We may well have been the first Westerners they had ever met, but they knew full well that the second lot would soon arrive, roaring overhead and firing missiles. Will Whitehorn had been checking through all the bags the relatives had brought with them. At the last minute he found a bag with a transistor radio that nobody claimed. Just as the plane door was about to be closed he ran toward it and threw the bag down onto the concrete. The soldiers were too startled to do anything. The bag lay there as the doors shut, and the plane rolled back off the blocks.

Inside the plane there was a great cheer as the relatives swarmed down the aisles to hug each other. We put on seat belts for takeoff, but as soon as the plane leveled out the party started. We had got away. We were all standing around with glasses of champagne and swapping stories when the pilot announced that we had left Iraqi airspace. A huge cheer went up. I grabbed the microphone and pulled Ted Heath's leg by announcing: "And I've just had word that Mrs. Thatcher is *absolutely* delighted that Ted has managed to return safely!" Her bête noire was on the way home.

Frank Hessey, his sister Maureen, and his brother-in-law Tony sat together, all holding hands in a state of disbelief: they couldn't believe that they were together and that they had left Baghdad. Others on the plane were crying; they were delighted to be free but in turmoil over those they had left behind. Two months later Tony was to die of lung cancer, and Baghdad airport was reduced to rubble by the heaviest concentration of firepower ever used by a military force. I hope that the Iraqi soldiers with their badly cut uniforms and rifles had managed to escape.

"Who the hell does Richard Branson think he is?" Lord King demanded of William Waldegrave in his second call to him. "Part of the bloody Foreign Office?"

Lord King's indignation was echoed by some newspapers that suggested I was doing it only for personal glory. Stung by this criticism while staying with King Hussein, I wrote in my diary, trying to analyze my motives:

Feel absolutely shattered. Been burning the candle at both ends. During an interview with ITN about the various people I saw, I choked up. Telling the story of the British father who had to hand his 3 year old child to a nanny at Baghdad airport to take her out of the country; and the woman from the Philippines who had that day left the country to have her second baby. I could only get half way through telling it.

What are the motives for doing things? Is there any truth in the jibes?

One month ago I was doing an interview with *Vanity Fair* and was at an all-time low. I'd seemed to have run out of a purpose in my life. I'd proved myself to myself in many areas. I'd just turned 40. I was seeking a new challenge. I was even considering selling up everything except for the airline. Getting smaller. Being able to focus on one business venture that 1 loved. But also to have the time to try to use my business skills to tackle issues that I felt I could help, such as attacking the cigarette companies, cervical cancer, etc.

I felt I'd get better self-satisfaction in this way and would not be wasting the next 40 years of my life just running companies, getting bigger—a repeat of the first 40 years.

Do I need recognition for this? No, I don't think so. The dilemma is that to campaign on many issues you need to use yourself publicly to get people moving. Television is a very powerful medium. By speaking on TV, the tons of medicine, the foodstuffs and blankets and tents that have now reached the refugees have done so. The £2 million money from Mrs Thatcher's government has come through. An emergency meeting has taken place between the 5 main charities. Free advertising is to start on the BBC and ITV. I believe that by moving quickly a major disaster in this case has been averted. But by not speaking out, it would not have been.

The dilemma is how often can one use the Press in this way in one small country like England without losing one's appeal to the public. If there should be a hint that I'm doing it for personal glory, then I won't be able to do it at all.

By flying into Baghdad and rescuing the hostages, Virgin had again usurped British Airways' traditional role. At the time I had no idea that the Virgin flight into Baghdad would annoy Lord King so much. I was trying to help out, I had an airplane at my disposal, and I could act quickly. Although this plane was one of just four planes Virgin Atlantic operated, suddenly we looked a much larger airline. We had successfully negotiated with Saddam Hussein, we had carried in medical supplies, and we had brought back the hostages. I found out only later that Lord King's indignant reaction was the start of an entire campaign by British Airways to try to put Virgin Atlantic out of business.

Chapter 21

"We had to land soon after dawn. If we left it for another two or three hours, the sun would heat up the balloon's envelope, and we would continue to fly past Greenland deeper into the Arctic and out of reach of any rescue team."

November 1990–January 1991

"Duck!" I shouted to Janet and her husband, René, and fired the gas. I always wore a hat in my balloon to stop my head from getting scalded, and I didn't want Janet's hair to go up in flames. We all looked up as the flame surged up inside the envelope. The balloon strained at the rope, and I cast off. Janet peered over the edge of the wicker basket as the ground fell away beneath us. She was wearing an old fur coat we had found in the cloakroom because she hadn't brought anything warm enough in which to fly. She looked tiny. René had borrowed an old flying jacket.

We drifted silently through the autumnal afternoon. The trees had lost most of their leaves, but the remaining few were red and golden. The pale November sun cast long speckled shadows through the branches. Shadows are one of the great pleasures of ballooning: each tree, hedge, even the cows have long, clearly delineated shadows that are hardly noticed from ground level.

While I had been negotiating with Saddam Hussein, I had also started negotiations with Janet Jackson, who had shown an interest in signing with Virgin Music. Rather like Queen Noor, Janet had asked whether she could go up in a balloon, and so I invited her over to Kidlington.

I love ballooning. It is one of the most peaceful things I have ever done and makes me feel completely immersed in nature. Apart from the times when I fire the burner to heat up the propane, which can frighten horses and cows and make them stampede across their fields, when I am gliding along I feel absolutely apart from the rest of the world. Nobody can telephone me, nobody can interfere with my flight or cut across me: I am free. A balloon is one of the most natural forms of transport, and when I see a balloon suspended in the sky I feel that it's just as lovely as the rest of the landscape; it doesn't ruin it in the way a motorboat or a car does. From up in a balloon the magnificent views that surround me are directly beneath my feet and are far better than the views from an airplane. I once flew over a haystack and found two stark-naked lovers curled up on the top, out of sight of everybody except a balloonist. They didn't notice me until I was ten feet above them, and they leaped apart when I fired the propane burner.

With Janet and René on board, we followed the River Cherwell down toward Oxford, and soon we could see the Oxford spires. As we came closer I stopped firing the gas and we slowly descended. The wind was so still that we drifted almost imperceptibly and we could hear all the noises on the streets below.

"Hello down there!" Janet leaned over and waved down at some undergraduates. They stopped on their bikes and waved up at us.

"The last time I flew over Oxford I was with Mike Oldfield," I told Janet. "I ran out of fuel and crash-landed on the roof of the local bread factory and the fire brigade had to be called to get us down. The Oxford paper ran a cartoon asking if I didn't have enough bread already!"

We were still in the sunlight when we saw the ground below us fall into shadow. The sun started a deep red autumnal sunset, and a flock of geese flew in a V-shaped formation across the sky. We could almost have reached out and touched their wings. Eventually we came down to land in Christchurch meadows, and our car picked us up. That night we had supper around the kitchen table and Joan cooked roast chicken. We ended up playing Trivial Pursuit and went to bed exhausted after all the fresh air. Although we hadn't mentioned the record business once, I felt sure that Janet Jackson would want to sign with Virgin.

My next balloon trip was not going to be as lyrical as that autumnal flight over Oxford in the wicker basket. Ever since we had abandoned our attempt the previous December, Per had been building the new envelope for the balloon that would attempt to take us across the Pacific Ocean. By the beginning of December it had been shipped out to Miyakonojo to join the capsule and await a good jet stream overhead.

A Japanese balloonist, Fumio Niwa, was challenging us to be the first to cross the Pacific and was planning to fly a helium balloon. Per and I and our families and the balloon team all arrived in Miyakonojo, and Fumio and I talked and joked over the radio as the preparation went on. He too was grounded by the unseasonably slow jet stream, which our weather-forecasting charts implied would leave us stranded somewhere over the Pacific. We waited and practiced safety drills and watched the mounting tension in the Gulf on CNN. We felt sure that the allied attack would take place just after Christmas. Per and I agreed that if the allied forces declared war on Iraq, then we would have to cancel the trip for a second time and return home.

Just before Christmas there was still no war in the Gulf, but there was also no sign of a sufficiently strong jet stream to take us across the Pacific. Bob Rice gave us at least a week's stand-down before a likely improvement. Per flew back to England for Christmas. Joan and I took our family down to Ishigaki, an island off the south Japanese coast.

The island was very quiet with the classic Japanese landscapes of mountains and sea. I spent time with my mother and father, and we watched the cormorant fishermen in their canoes, who carried out a tradition dating back several thousand years. These fishermen used six or seven cormorants with rings around their necks to prevent them swallowing the fish. The birds lined up along the edge of the boat and one by one went diving for fish. They brought them back to the boat, where they opened their beaks and the fisherman removed the fish.

I would have loved to have spoken to these fishermen. Probably they were as worried and stressed about their money and families as anyone else, but their life seemed so tranquil and rooted in such an ancient tradition that I felt they must have come to terms with time in a way that I never had. I wondered how they would have viewed my constant rushing about, my wish to set up new companies, to challenge myself, and to fly over the Pacific at 30,000 feet in a hot-air balloon.

At the end of our holiday, Joan took the children back to London to start school. Joan does not—understandably—like the idea of my ballooning and likes even less the idea of seeing me take off. I hugged them all farewell at Tokyo's Narita Airport and then braced myself for the trip. As my parents and I passed through the airport to catch an internal flight to Miyakonojo, I saw a television screen. In wildly flickering footage the news showed a helicopter hovering over the sea and winching a body on board. From the respectful tone of the reporter, I immediately knew that it was Fumio and that he was dead. We had all been on such a high, but this put our lives and the risks I was taking with them into perspective: it could have been us. We found somebody who could speak a little English, who explained that Fumio had taken off yesterday morning but had crashed into the sea just off the coast. He had radioed for help from his capsule, but he was dead by the time the rescue helicopter arrived. He had died of exposure.

The sight of Fumio's body being winched out of the freezing ocean killed off much of my enthusiasm for the flight. I already felt a deep sense of forboding, but I now was equally helpless to withdraw. If the weather conditions were right, then we would climb into the capsule and take off. I resigned myself to fate and forced myself to make the best of it. Later we found out what had happened to Fumio: he had taken off the day before we arrived back, hoping to steal a march on us. The strong winds had torn the envelope of his balloon, forcing him to ditch in the Pacific in his capsule, ready to be rescued. But the ocean was so rough that when the seaplane arrived, it was unable to pick him up and had radioed for a helicopter. There was a delay while the rescue services sorted out which helicopter should come, and by the time it arrived Fumio was dead. He'd only been about 10 miles into the 8,000-mile journey. It was a salutary warning.

Per and I planned to launch the balloon on Sunday, 13 January. The allied forces had given Saddam Hussein a deadline of 15 January by which to leave Kuwait, and we felt sure that the attack would take place very soon after that deadline. Unfortunately the weather was too windy for us to inflate the balloon on Sunday, so we postponed it until Monday. The jet stream now picked up speed, and by Monday, 14 January, it looked as if it might be possible. In the evening the weather cleared and we started inflating the balloon.

After taking a sleeping pill that afternoon, Per and I were awoken at 2:30 A.M. to come down to the launch site. We made our way through the thousands of people who had come to watch. We walked behind a police car, which slowly inched along. The Japanese children all held up candles and waved Union Jacks at us. They were muffled up against the cold, and they sang "God Save the Queen" in perfect soft English voices. The balloon towered over everyone, this time large enough to swallow the dome of Saint Paul's Cathedral. Once again people had set up braziers and were barbecuing fish and sweet corn.

"Don't eat anything," I warned Per as he was about to accept some fish. "The last thing I need is you having a bout of food poisoning up there."

In front of us, absorbing all the attention, the balloon was straining at its steel hawsers. It had been heated up to a great temperature and was ready to soar upward as soon as the cables were cut.

We thanked the people of Miyakonojo for their hospitality and released some white doves as a rather futile peace gesture. Just before I climbed up the steps into the capsule, I sent someone to fetch my parents. Everyone was now very edgy, looking up at the straining balloon overhead, which was bursting to rise. My parents made their way through the barriers and police, and we just hugged each other. My mother gave me a letter, which I zipped into a trouser pocket.

"Time to go!" Per yelled. As we turned we saw Alex, our designer and engineer, emerge from the capsule with the biggest adjustable wrench we'd ever seen. "I think it will be OK now," he said.

We climbed up the steps and ducked down into the capsule.

As the ground crew backed away, we started firing the burners. The pressure to lift grew increasingly strong, and then Per fired the bolts that released the steel hawsers and we rocketed upward. After the first few breathless minutes when we just marveled at the silent speed, the balloon rose above the dark edge of the cloud and we saw the silver dawn on the horizon. I got onto the radio and made contact with the ground crew.

"You're up and away!" Will shouted. "The crowd down here are cheering like crazy. It looks amazing. You're heading up fast."

Within five minutes we were over the horizon from Miyakonojo and heading up into the jet stream. Within half an hour we were well over the Pacific Ocean. Then at 23,000 feet we hit the bottom of the jet stream. But it was as if we had hit a glass ceiling. As much as we burned, the balloon refused to go in. The winds were too strong, and the flat dome of the balloon was being pushed down. We kept pushing up against it, and we kept being buffeted back down. We put on our parachutes and clipped ourselves to the life rafts in case the balloon fell to pieces. Then, on our next attempt, the balloon edged through the jet stream. The top of the balloon took off ahead of us, and I saw it streaming in front of us and even below us. We were knocked to one side. From traveling at 20 knots we were suddenly flying at 100 knots. For a moment I thought that we were going to be torn apart, and I remembered my image of a thousand horses pulling us apart, but then the capsule came into the jet alongside the balloon and we were righted. The balloon rose above us again, and we were safely tucked in the jet. Per's relief didn't give me the greatest confidence.

"Nobody's done that before," he said. "We're in uncharted territory."

After seven hours it was time to dump an empty fuel tank. We had six tanks of propane bolted to the capsule. The idea was that we would change the fuel tanks when one was empty, jettison the deadweight, and fly correspondingly faster. We had a video camera beneath the capsule which pointed vertically downward, in effect an extra window for us. We decided to come down out of the jet stream as we dropped the tank in case anything went wrong. The sea below us looked dangerous: it was running to great waves, and although we were 25,000 feet above it, we could clearly see the white tops and the deep shadows of the troughs.

I looked at the video monitor as Per pressed the button to release the empty fuel tank. Before I could see what happened, the whole capsule lurched sideways. I was thrown across the capsule and landed on top of Per.

"What's happened?"

"No bloody idea."

I crawled up the sloping floor of the capsule back to my seat. We were suspended at an angle of about twenty-five degrees. Per checked all the controls to see if he could see what had gone wrong. We had no idea whether we were hanging by just one steel rope or the capsule itself was about to part company with the balloon and plummet down into the sea. I reran the video and watched what happened when the fuel tanks had fallen away. To my horror I saw three tanks falling down to the sea rather than one.

"Per, look at this."

We watched again in silence.

"Bloody hell!" Per said. "All the tanks on one side of the capsule have gone."

The implications of this were horrific: rather than jettisoning one empty tank, we had actually jettisoned three tanks all from the same side of the capsule—the empty one and two full ones. We had flown only around 1,000 miles, and now we had just half the fuel available to us. We had only three full tanks of propane rather than five to fly us across the most dangerous and remote part of the Pacific Ocean.

"Watch out!" Per said. "We're rising."

I looked at the altimeter. Without the extra weight of the two full tanks of fuel, the balloon was soaring upward. We were once again buffeted as we entered the jet stream, but we hit it with such speed that we carried on rising. The altimeter ticked steadily upward from 31,000 feet to 34,000 feet.

"I'm letting air out," Per said. "We've got to come down."

I stared at the altimeter, willing it to slow down: 35,000 ft; 36,000 ft; 37,000 ft; 38,000 ft.

We had no idea how strong the capsule was. We knew that the glass dome was able to withstand pressure only up to approximately 42,000 feet, and even that was something of a guess. If we reached 43,000 feet, the glass dome would explode. We would have about two seconds in which to say our last prayers, long enough to see our lungs being sucked out of our chests and feel our eyeballs pop out of their sockets. We would reconvene as a scattering of debris somewhere in the Pacific.

Per had opened the vent at the top of the balloon, but it was still rising. The huge difference between the weight of the three fuel tanks we had dropped and the amount of hot air needed to support them was the deciding factor. It was a race between time and the altimeter. Thank goodness we had come down out of the jet stream before we had dropped the fuel tanks.

"It's slowing," I said with hopeless optimism. "I'm sure it's slowing."

The altimeter ticked up: 39,000 ft; 39,500 ft; 40,000 ft; 40,500 ft; 41,000 ft.

We were now at the mercy of unknown forces. None of our equipment had been tested at these kind of heights, and anything could go wrong.

At 42,500 feet the altimeter finally stopped rising. I wondered bleakly whether this was because it had broken and simply could not register any greater height. We were way above the heights flown by most passenger jets except Concorde. But then the altimeter clicked down 500 feet. And then some more.

"We don't want to come down too fast," Per said. "We'll only have to burn fuel to bring us back up again."

He shut the vent and the balloon continued to fall down through to 35,000. Then we had to start firing the burners again to stay in the jet stream.

At last we could confront the problem of the lost fuel tanks. The radio contact with the San Jose flight center remained good, and they were clearly as devastated by the loss of the tanks as we were. There were some rapid calculations. If we were to reach land in the time available to us before the fuel ran out, we had to fly at an average speed of 170 miles an hour, twice as fast as any hot-air balloon had ever flown before. The odds against us were overwhelming.

"What about Hawaii?" I asked. "Can we aim to land nearby?"

"It's a needle in a haystack," Per said. "We'll never get anywhere near it."

"I wonder if America is doable?" I asked Per.

"Of course it's doable," he said. "The question is whether we can do it."

Per's a precise logician when he wants to be.

I asked over the radio about the conditions below us. Mike Kendrick, the project manager, came on loud and agitated:

"I've just spoken to a cargo ship which is in the area," he crackled. "They said that there is a strong wind and high seas. 'Atrocious' is the word he used."

Per leaned over and urbanely asked Mike: "What do you mean by atrocious? Over."

"I mean *fucking atrocious*. You're not going to ditch in there. No boat will turn around to pick you up. There are waves over fifty feet high. The nearest boat says that the seas are running so high that their boat would be bust in half if it tried to turn. Do you understand? Over."

"Keep going on your current altitude," Bob Rice came on. "The jet is reasonably strong."

Then, all of a sudden, the radio cut out.

For the next six hours we were out of contact with the outside world. Due to the terrible weather around us we were in a high-frequency blackout spot. We were somewhere over the Pacific, hanging by a few steel hawsers to a vast balloon, the remaining fuel tanks dangling off the side of the capsule like a necklace, and we could not make any contact with anybody. We could barely control where we were going or how fast we were getting there, and we hardly dared move around the capsule. Our main points of reference were the Global Positioning System (GPS), our watches, and the altimeter. Every ten or fifteen minutes we took a reading off the GPS and calculated our ground speed. As we flew on, Per began to show signs of utter exhaustion.

"I'm just going to have a rest," he mumbled, and lay down on the floor.

I was alone. Unlike the Atlantic crossing, where I had been more of a passenger than a pilot, I now really understood what was happening. If we were to make land, our only chance was if we kept the balloon absolutely in the center of the jet stream. The vein of wind there is only a hundred meters wide, four times the width of the balloon itself, but it was our only hope.

The sky was pitch-black all around us. I scarcely looked out of the capsule but concentrated on the instruments. As I sat there with Per lying comatose at the bottom of the capsule, it seemed clear that we were both going to die. With just three fuel tanks we would run out of fuel some thousand miles off the American coast and have to ditch in the sea. It could well be nighttime, the ground weather was, as Mike said, atrocious—fucking atrocious—and nobody would be able to find us. We would have to fly this balloon for another thirty hours if we were to live. I knew that the only chance of us living was for me to fly the balloon right in the core of the jet stream. I put all thoughts of death out of my head and for the next ten hours concentrated intently on the dials.

I do not believe in God, but as I sat there in the damaged capsule, hopelessly vulnerable to the slightest shift in weather or mechanical fault, I could not believe my eyes. It was as if a spirit had entered the capsule and was helping us along. As I watched the instruments and calculated our ground speed, it became clear that we were beginning to fly very fast, close to the necessary 170 miles an hour. Before we had dropped the fuel tanks, we had been flying at about 80 miles an hour, which had been very good progress. Now we needed a miracle.

I slapped myself across the face to make sure that I wasn't hallucinating, but each fifteen minutes the speeds grew faster: 160 mph, 180 mph, 200 mph, and even 240 mph. The increase was astounding. I tried not to imagine the size of the balloon above me but looked instead at the dials and pretended that I was driving some kind of weightless car that I had to keep within a broad ribbon of road. I hunched over the instruments and willed myself to stay awake. Whenever we dropped speed, I assumed that we had dropped out of the inner core of the jet stream and so I burned a little gas—as little as possible—and generally we picked up speed again.

Even at this amazing speed, it still takes an hour to fly 200 miles, and we had 7,000 of them to fly. I tried not to be daunted by the length of the journey ahead but concentrated on each fifteen-minute section. I was desperately trying to keep awake. My head kept dropping forward, and I kept having to pinch myself and slap myself to keep awake. I suddenly saw an eerie light on the glass dome above us. I looked up and marveled at it: it was white and orange, and was flickering. Then I yelled—it was fire. I squinted at it and realized that burning white lumps of propane were tumbling all around the glass dome, just missing it.

"Per!" I yelled. "We're on fire!"

Per lurched awake and looked up. He has incredibly quick reactions, and in spite of his condition it took him only a split second to decide what to do:

"Take her up," he said. "We've got to get up to forty thousand feet, where there's no oxygen. Then the fire'll go out."

I fired the burners and the balloon began to rise. It seemed to rise too slowly, and the lumps of propane continued to drop all around the glass dome. With the outside temperature at minus seventy degrees and the heat of the fireballs, it would take only one hitting the glass to explode it.

We rose through 36,000 feet, 38,000 feet, and we put on our oxygen masks. We both knew that this was scant comfort. If the glass dome cracked or melted, we would die within seconds from loss of air pressure. We were caught in a dilemma: the lack of oxygen at 40,000 feet would snuff out the flames on the glass dome, but it could also snuff out the burners. If the burners went out before the propane fireballs, we'd drift back down to 36,000 feet before we could restart the burners, and the propane fire could continue to eat into the glass. We rose to 43,000 feet before the engines spluttered and the fire was eventually snuffed out. Per opened the vent at the top of the balloon and we headed back down. As well as risking the capsule pressure at 43,000 feet, we had also wasted precious fuel.

We flew on without radio communication for another hour. I kept myself going by talking into the video camera. I imagined that I was talking to Joan and Holly and Sam and kept chatting away, telling them how much I loved them and that we were coming back to land in America. The balloon stayed at 29,000 feet and continued to sweep up northeastward toward the west coast of America. We were in a tiny metal capsule, swinging around in the stratosphere above a dark ocean. I was too frightened to eat anything other than some apples and chocolate, and I wrote in my logbook:

> Flown 17 hours and 4 minutes. Feels like a lifetime. Coming near the dateline. When we cross the dateline we beat our world hot-air ballooning record. However, right now we are about as far away from help as anyone could ever be, sitting in a tilting capsule with half our fuel gone, terrified that if we move the rest will fall off. Not sure whether war has broken out because we have lost all communication with the outside world. Unlikely to reach the coast. But spirits up and the speed we're going is amazing.

As our hours out of contact with San Jose continued, I wrote: "Things look pretty desperate. I'm not certain at this moment that we'll get home."

Then just as abruptly as we had lost contact, we made it. I heard voices on the radio. By this time radio contact had been down for six hours, ten minutes. Mike thought he'd lost us as two of the ships he had steaming toward us had reported sighting wreckage.

"Mike, is that you?"

"Richard! Where are you?"

"Sitting in a tin can over the Pacific."

We nearly wept with relief.

"We thought that you must have ditched. God, we practically mobilized the air force."

"We're okay," I lied. "We've had a fire up on the capsule from propane, but it's gone out."

I gave them our position.

"Any other problems apart from not having enough fuel to get home?" Mike wanted to know.

"No, we're still tilting. We're not going to fire off any more fuel tanks."

"War's broken out in the Gulf," a girl's voice said. It was Penni, who was in the control room with them. "The Americans are bombing Baghdad."

I thought of the soldiers I had met at Baghdad airport. The outbreak of the Gulf War meant that if we did have to ditch, quite rightly we would be the last priority for anyone.

"Thank God we've got hold of you," Bob Rice said. "I've worked out your route. You need to come down immediately. Your current jet stream will soon start bending back towards Japan. You'll be marooned over the Pacific. If you come down from thirty thousand feet to eighteen thousand feet, you might get the jet that's heading north. It's sweeping up towards the Arctic, but at least it's land."

"Christ!" Mike swore. "Another half an hour and you'd have been swinging back away from us."

We cut off the burners and began to descend. After five hours Bob told us to rise up again. We went back up to 30,000 feet and sure enough found ourselves heading northeast. We now flew steadily hour after hour. We stayed in the jet stream, pushing northward, and kept the fuel that we burned to a minimum. We were still over the Pacific flying at 200 mph in a lopsided capsule, and we were exhausted, but now that we had radio contact I felt that anything was possible. And the miracle continued. Our speeds were extraordinary: 210 mph, 220 mph, 200 mph. We were just beating the average 180 mph we needed. Someone was being very kind to us.

The good news was that we were now heading steadily toward the Canadian coastline. The fuel was lasting well, our speed kept up, and Per and I began to believe that we might even make land. I was still too frightened to doze off since the only few seconds I had fallen asleep I had had terrifying nightmares of skulls and death. We were both exhausted and dehydrated and fighting to keep our concentration.

"You're heading way north," Mike Kendrick told us. "The rescue team is chasing you to try to get to where you're going to land. They're in a Learjet. Will's there, and so are your parents."

After thirty-six hours of flying, we finally crossed the coast over northern Canada. It was pitch-black, but we felt safer. Even though we were now heading for the Rockies, one of the most inhospitable mountain ranges you could find, at least it was land. We hugged each other and shared a chocolate bar. It was an incredible feeling. As we headed over the Rockies, we made radio contact with the local ground control, Watson Lake Flight Service.

"Put your rescue beacon on," they advised. "You're heading into a blizzard. There's zero visibility and a wind of 35 knots. The Learjet has turned back to shelter at Yellowknife."

Our exhilaration turned again to despair. We had missed Los Angeles by 3,000 miles, and whereas we had been expecting to land in California with an escort of helicopters, we were heading into an Arctic blizzard. From then on every five seconds was punctuated by an ear-splitting beep from the rescue beacon. We knew we could land safely and then die, just as easily as Fumio had done. Hot-air balloons are fragile things; they are not designed to be flown in blizzards. A bad blizzard could tear up the balloon, and we could drop out of the sky. We were flying at 1,000 feet in the dark just before dawn in the Arctic Circle, and we could see nothing below us.

We had to land soon after dawn. If we left it for another two or three hours, the sun would heat up the balloon's envelope, and we would continue to fly past Greenland deeper into the Arctic and out of reach of any rescue team.

One of my allotted jobs was to prepare the balloon for landing. When we were at 750 feet, I opened the hatch. Cold air and snow rushed into the hatch. We were in the middle of a snowstorm, whirling along at around 80 miles an hour. I climbed out on to the top of the capsule. It was difficult to keep my balance as the capsule was still hanging at an angle and the top of the metal capsule was frozen. I held on to the steel hawsers and leaned across to remove the safety pins that prevent the bolts from firing if we hit a lightning storm. I pulled them out and threw them away. I crouched there for a minute and watched the snowstorm around me. The only light was the huge orange flame above me, licking into the balloon. Snowflakes were spinning around me and falling into the flame, where they vanished. One of the most magical things about ballooning is that the wind is inaudible because the balloon is traveling at the same speed as the wind. Flying at 150 miles an hour, one can put a tissue paper on the capsule which, in theory, shouldn't blow off. And so although we were in the middle of a snowstorm, it was very quiet. I was mesmerized by the sight of the snowflakes vanishing into the flames. Then I peered around at the horizons and began to see the ground below us. I realized that one of the reasons why it was so dark was that we were flying over a thick pine forest. I shouted down to Per:

"Don't get too low. It's all forest. We'll never get out of there."

I stayed on the top of the capsule and shouted down what I could see.

"There's a space ahead. Can you see it?"

"Prepare for landing," Per said and shut off the burner.

I climbed back into the capsule and we headed down. Our ground speed was around 40 miles an hour when we crashed to earth with a hell of a bang. We were skidding across the ground before Per fired the explosive bolts. Mercifully this time they worked, and the capsule ground to a halt as the envelope ballooned off without us. We were strapped in but in a trice were struggling to get out.

"Get out!" we both shouted.

We wrenched open the hatch and clambered outside. Both of us thought the capsule might blow up with the last of the propane fuel. We hugged each other and danced a little jig outside in the snow. The wind was shredding the silver balloon envelope, which had draped itself across the pine trees. Then we realized two things: the capsule wasn't going to blow up, and it was minus sixty degrees outside. Unless we got back inside, we'd get frostbite. We crawled back inside the capsule, and I made radio contact with Watson Lake Flight Service.

"We've done it. We've arrived. We're all in one piece."

"Where are you?"

"We've landed on a lake surrounded by trees."

"It's a frozen lake," came the laconic Canadian voice. "It's quite safe. The only trouble is that there are about eight hundred thousand lakes in your vicinity and they've all got plenty of trees."

We had to wait in our capsule for another eight hours, by which time it was nearly dark again. Per had frostbite in one of his feet, and I had frostbite in one finger. We huddled together, half asleep, eating our supplies and desperate for warmth in our tin capsule as the snow and wind howled around us. We had landed over 300 miles from the nearest habitation, 150 miles from the nearest road in an area of wilderness about 200 times the size of Britain.

"We've flown for 6,761 miles," Per said with weary triumph. "We flew for forty-six hours and six minutes. That makes our average speed 127 knots, 147 miles per hour. These are all significant records. We've flown further than any other balloon has ever flown."

"I'm dying for a hot drink," was all I could say, "and a log fire. And a sunny beach. Why aren't we in California!"

"Next time it's the ultimate flight," Per started fantasizing. "It's around the world."

When I peered out of the capsule, I thought I saw something move. For a moment I thought that it was a dog, and I had the surreal image of somebody taking their dog for a walk along the frozen lake. As I watched the creature it came up to the capsule and sniffed at it. It was an otter. It sniffed around at us, then turned up its nose as if to say "Big deal, a capsule," and slunk off. It was the only creature to have witnessed that we were the first to cross the Pacific—and it didn't even have a camera.

Every five seconds for those next eight hours the emergency bleeper went off, piercing our eardrums. As we huddled together, I relived the flight and wondered why I had trusted Per with my life. We had landed over two thousand miles away from our destination, we had lost three fuel tanks, we had caught fire, and we had flown across the Pacific in the dark with no radio contact. I remembered the previous flights—the first attempt from Japan had seen the balloon disintegrate and catch fire, and the Atlantic crossing had nearly killed us.

As Per talked about us flying around the world, I wondered whether I was mad to consider ever going with him again. I knew that he had pushed the technological boundaries of balloon flying further forward than anyone else, but it was sad that we hadn't developed a stronger bond with each other. I get close to most of the people with whom I spend a long time. But Per is not a team player. He's a loner. He's often difficult to read. He's quick to criticize. I'd always been brought up to look for the best in people. Per somehow always seemed to find the worst. Yet we somehow managed to get on together as two opposites respecting each other's strengths and weaknesses. And when it came to ballooning I had plenty of weaknesses for him to respect. He also had to put up with the branding of every project we did as a "Branson" or "Virgin" challenge, and he coped with that very well. Certainly, we have been through more together than most people experience in a lifetime.

As I tried to imagine us setting off around the world in a high-altitude balloon, I realized that for all our horrendous moments together, our balloon flights had been some of the greatest adventures of my life. During all other moments of my life, I am—to a greater or lesser extent—in control of my destiny. Up in a balloon we were at the mercy of the elements, the technology, and the teams of engineers who had built it, and we were 30,000 feet up. The odds were not the best, but I have always been unable to resist taking on formidable odds and then proving them wrong. And once again fortune had been kind to us.

At last we heard the thudding sound of a helicopter's blades. They came louder and louder, circled overhead, and eventually landed beside us. We had the bags of videos and our logbooks all ready, and we staggered over to the helicopter, Per limping with frostbite.

It was another four hours' flight back to Yellowknife, and when we landed at a tiny airfield, the yellow fluorescent lights made blurred circles in the driving snow. We crunched across the snow to the hangar.

Gusts of snow blew across us as we opened the door and stepped inside. There were Will, Mum, Dad, Per's wife Helen, and some people from Yellowknife. I almost didn't recognize anyone since they were all wearing strange bulky clothing, bright-red padded jackets and thermal trousers. They roared with delight when we came in.

"Have a cold beer!" Will shouted. "It's all there is!"

Per and I ripped off the pull rings and sprayed everyone there.

"You've made it!" said Mum.

"Never again!" said Dad.

"What do you mean?" Per joked. "We're going around the world next time. If those fuel tanks had stayed on, we'd be over England now!"

"Have you got that letter I gave you?" Mum asked me.

It was still in my trouser pocket.

"It was written by some Japanese schoolchildren. You have to give it to a local child closest to where you land."

One of the ground crew at Yellowknife had brought his six-year-old son along to see these two balloonists who had arrived from Japan, so I knelt down and gave him the letter.

"It's from some children who live in Miyakonojo in Japan," I told him. "You'd better go there one day. But perhaps not by balloon!"

Yellowknife is so cold in January that diesel fuel freezes solid. To stop a car from freezing, one must keep the engine heated either by running it outside or by plugging it into special electrical equipment, which looks like a parking meter. We had a meal in the town's largest steak house, and half the people living in Yellowknife turned up. When we came out of the restaurant, we could hardly breathe for exhaust fumes. Most of the shops are in underground shopping malls, which are easier to heat without the windchill to worry about. During the meal a fax arrived from the new prime minister, John Major, congratulating us on the flight, surely one of the most remote places the 10 Downing Street letterhead has ever found itself.

The next day we said good-bye to the gold miners and fur trappers who had looked after us so well at such short notice. It's not often they have guests ballooning down on them from Japan, and they invited us to come again. We flew down to Seattle and then on to the warmth of Los Angeles. That night we caught the plane back to London, and I had a chance to read the newspapers and understand what was going on. The stock market had soared on the back of the invasion, and looking at the amount of firepower that the allied forces were using, it seemed hard to imagine that Iraq would survive for long. I spent some time talking to the crew and the pilots and heard how empty the flights were. One of the pilots warned me that the Gulf War was actually hiding a recession that was going to last a very long time.

"After all the bombing is over and Saddam Hussein is dead," he said, "the world will suddenly realize that it wasn't the 'Mother of All Wars' which was the issue, but the 'Mother of All Recessions.' "

Chapter 22

"In the same way that British Airways was trying to steamroller Virgin Atlantic out of sight, it struck me that Lord King was pretending I didn't exist."

January–February 1991

Friday, 25 January, was the end of a bad week for Sidney Shaw, our account director from Lloyds Bank. He sat on the edge of my sofa and fidgeted with his pen and papers, refused to have a cup of coffee, and then changed his mind. Trevor and I began to worry. He expressed no interest in last week's Pacific crossing and was reluctant to meet my eye. He was behaving ominously like my old Coutts bank manager.

"I saw Air Europe on Monday and Dan Air on Wednesday," Sidney began, "and I suspect that you're in much the same trouble. I'm afraid that we're pulling our loans out of both those airlines, and I don't see why we should support you anymore. We can't see how you can possibly keep Virgin Atlantic going."

It was clear where he was heading. He had come to see us in perhaps the worst week in what would become the worst year in aviation history. Virgin's group overdraft facility with Lloyds Bank was formally set at £20 million, but we had now hit £50 million. After a visit by Lloyds Bank on Monday and the subsequent withdrawal of their loans, Air Europe, the largest independent short-haul airline in Europe, run by Harry Goodman, had been declared bust on Wednesday with four thousand redundancies. Like Laker, like British Caledonian, like Dan Air, and of course like Virgin Atlantic, Air Europe had been confined to Gatwick by British Airways.

As the Gulf War continued, the price of aviation fuel was still over $1.20 a gallon, and passengers were still not flying—and certainly not flying the flag carriers. To an outsider, the airline industry looked like a disaster. Yet for the rest of the Virgin Group, the picture was pretty good: Virgin Communications would reach sales of over £150 million this year on the sales of Sega equipment alone. Simon and Ken were having no problems in selling records; indeed, Virgin singers Paula Abdul and Steve Winwood were top of the charts in America and Bryan Ferry was there in Britain. The Gulf War and the gathering recession were not affecting record sales. The Virgin Megastores weren't making much money but weren't losing anything either.

Virgin Atlantic was our biggest liability in that we had high overheads that we couldn't cut down. But even here the underlying picture was encouraging. Virgin holidaymakers were still all taking their holidays, and Ron Sims, the managing director of Virgin Holidays, forecast that we would increase this number from 83,000 the previous year to around 100,000 in 1991, a jump of nearly 20 percent. Ron had built up Virgin Holidays into one of the most profitable parts of Virgin Travel, and since I've never known him to make a forecast he couldn't comfortably beat by several thousand, I took his forecast as a concrete figure. Given that the average value of a Virgin holiday was £730, this meant that we would receive sales of over £73 million from these customers alone, and they would be taking seats that would otherwise be empty. The cargo side appeared equally promising: the rates for cargo to Japan had actually increased. Alan Chambers, who had built up our cargo division successfully, pointed out that so many airlines had suspended services to the Far East, he was now able to charge a premium to transport cargo to Japan.

"What are we shipping out there?" I asked him.

"You'd never guess," he said. "Scottish smoked salmon and whisky are the bulk of it. Then we're bringing back computer games. It's a roaring business."

It sometimes seems to me that I have spent all my life trying to persuade bankers to extend their loans. Given that Virgin's policy has always been to reinvest our surplus cash back into the business, our profit-and-loss statements always understate the underlying value of the businesses. This policy has worked over the long term, but whenever there is a crisis it disguises the real picture and means that the banks worry about our short-term profits and ability to pay our immediate interest. Trevor explained to Sidney Shaw that our balance sheet had included no value either for the Virgin brand name itself or for the contracts with the Virgin artists.

"Look," I told Sidney Shaw. "In a nutshell we have very sound businesses. The record company alone will make a thirty-million-pound profit this year, and that's in spite of the cost of making a massive investment in America. It's forecast to make seventy-five million pounds next year. Virgin

Communications and Virgin Retail are profitable. The airline, the holiday company, and the freight company will also make profits by the end of the year. They're just having a bad patch. With the Gulf War and the winter, we've got a cash flow shortage of ten to twenty million pounds. This is a tiny percentage of the total value of the Virgin Group, and it'll be ironed out by the end of the year.

"Anyway," I pointed out, "we could easily sell some or all of Virgin Music. The latest Citibank valuation shows it to be valued at nine hundred million dollars. Now, are you going to withdraw your loan because of a temporary blip due to a war?"

"No, no, no," Sidney backed down. "But you must see it from our point of view."

I could see it all too clearly from his point of view: Virgin Atlantic had a small cash flow deficit, which, despite the great value in the rest of the group, put us at the mercy of Lloyds Bank. Under the British banking system, banks make their money from charging high interest rates rather than taking any kind of equity stake as they often do in Japan and Germany. British banks therefore have a greater incentive to cut and run from a company rather than seeing it through bad times. It is in desperate times like the middle of a war that perfectly good profitable businesses go bust. The frightening thing about an airline is that it can go bust faster than almost any other business: all it takes is for the telephones to go quiet and for passengers to stop booking flights. Even a large airline can unravel in a matter of days.

By the time Sidney Shaw walked away from Holland Park, he seemed to have had most of his worries put to rest, and he wrote me a letter admitting that his worst fears had been unfounded; he even apologized for "overreacting." For the time being Lloyds Bank was back on our side. The only trouble was that the idea of us selling part or all of Virgin Music was now firmly on their agenda.

Trevor had made a number of forecasts for 1991, even the worst of which showed that over the year Virgin Atlantic would make a profit of £7 million. So we ourselves felt quite confident. As soon as I arrived back in London, however, I realized that beyond the immediate concerns of Lloyds Bank, there were some wider rumors going around the City that Virgin was going the way of Air Europe and Dan Air and that I was destined to become another Freddie Laker.

Rather than spending time searching for the right partner to invest in Virgin Music, I had to switch my attention to stamping out a bizarre variety of rumors about Virgin Atlantic. I am closely in touch with journalists, and so when I started receiving a series of calls from them asking me in one breath whether there was a drug problem at Heaven nightclub, and in another breath about the finances of Virgin Atlantic, I was rather baffled. Up until then journalists had typically asked me about our new services on board the planes, or the latest record signing and what was Janet Jackson really like? And so when "serious" newspapers began firing questions about the drug scene at Heaven, and in the same conversation about the impact of currency movements on our profit-and-loss statement, I felt that something rather strange was happening. I was bewildered. By the time almost every newspaper had inquired about Heaven, I felt that there must be some kind of campaign against us. It was most odd.

The news coming from the airline was also disturbing. The number of passengers who booked seats and then didn't turn up, the "no-shows," had increased way beyond the levels any of us remembered since we had set up.

One day Will came into my office looking worried.

"I've just had a call from Rothschilds," he said. "Apparently Lord King was there for lunch yesterday, and he was bad-mouthing Virgin."

An accusation of financial weakness can rapidly become a self-fulfilling prophecy, particularly when it comes from such a lofty and authoritative source as Lord King of Wartnaby, whom nobody would assume would ever feel threatened by a tiny airline like Virgin Atlantic. Lord King's accusation of Virgin Atlantic's financial weakness had a number of key audiences: for a start there was the press, which would not be slow to run a story about another successful entrepreneur who—like Alan Bond, Ralph Halpern, George Davis, Gerald Ronson, the Reichmanns, and many others—was now overstretched and running into trouble. But more significantly for us, the bankers in the City whom we were considering approaching to place some shares in Virgin Atlantic would also be listening to Lord King. We had had some preliminary talks with the American bankers Salomon Brothers, who were preparing a selling document to raise around £20 million. Rumors of our impending bankruptcy would pull the carpet from under our feet when trying to negotiate. The third audience whose antennae would pick up this rumor were the aircraft manufacturers and leasing companies: despite the recession we were looking to expand our fleet, but nobody would do business with a crippled airline. The last key audience was in many ways the most important to us in those first months of 1991: the Civil Aviation Authority, which has a duty to ensure that all airline companies are trading viably.

I am no stranger to healthy competition where you work hard and play hard, but there was no love lost between Virgin and British Airways. Over the last two years we had become embroiled in an increasingly acrimonious dispute over some maintenance that British Airways had carried out on one of our planes.

When we first set up Virgin Atlantic, our maintenance was carried out by British Caledonian. When British Airways took over British Caledonian, they promised the Department of Transport and the CAA that they would honor all existing maintenance contracts. When we acquired our third and fourth 747s in September 1988, however, British Airways quoted an outrageous cost for servicing them: their average charge for labor flipped from £16 to £61 per hour. At first we thought that this must be a simple typing mistake, but to our horror it wasn't. Since British Airways were the only company that had wide-bodied hangar space large enough to service 747s, they thought that they had us over a barrel: even tripling our costs, they believed, we would have no alternative but to use them. Although it was expensive and very inconvenient, we had to start flying our planes to Ireland to be serviced by Aer Lingus instead.

The other aspect of our maintenance dispute dated from the summer of 1988, when British Airways were servicing one of our 747s. British Airways engineers had failed to spot a crack in the pylon, the link between the engine and the wing. A new pylon was ordered, and the plane was out of service. They refused to let us have one of their spare aircraft to replace our 747. Roy Gardner therefore chartered a 747 to replace our 747 for two days. The situation became worse. The spare part wasn't available, which caused another delay. Next the plane lost its space at the hangar. Then the engineers weren't available, and so the saga went on. By the time the British Airways engineers welded the struts to the pylon upside down, we thought that the whole sorry episode had been jinxed. All in all, our 747 was grounded for sixteen days in August, the busiest time of the year.

In desperation I called Sir Colin Marshall, chief executive of British Airways.

"Your engineering was so bad that it could have brought an aircraft down," I told him.

"That's one of the perils of being in the aviation business," he told me coldly. "If you'd stuck to popular music, you wouldn't have had this problem. No, we won't lend you a plane."

The upshot of the entire fiasco was that instead of making good money in the summer and living off it through the winter's lean months, Virgin Atlantic not only had a terrible summer but also had alienated passengers. Since we had paid out to lease the replacement aircraft, our cash flow was severely hit. When we tried to agree compensation, British Airways dragged its heels. They owed us several million pounds of compensation but, by delaying payment, precipitated a cash crisis at the airline, which Virgin Music had to bail out. Just before I set off to Japan for the balloon flight, we had sued British Airways.

Alongside the maintenance dispute, our major battle with British Airways was our application for the two extra flights a week to Japan, which were being negotiated with the Japanese government. Flight timetables and slots may have no appeal outside the world of aviation, but they are our lifeblood. Without permission to fly somewhere, we literally can't take off. The battle over the slots and routes to Tokyo was vital for Virgin to win if we were to expand.

After the British Caledonian takeover, their four flights to Tokyo were transferred to Virgin, but it still wasn't enough. For the route to be viable we needed to be able to fly daily from Heathrow. Surely that had to be a priority before British Airways were allowed to fly twice a day during the week. Two frequencies—i.e., four slots—were then offered by the Japanese government, which naturally enough British Airways presumed to be theirs. After consultations with our lawyers and even though we knew that British Airways had already lined up for the slots, we quickly made an application. Our future depended on it: we needed the slots, and, more crucially, we needed access to Heathrow. At last here was our chance to gain the keys to the fortress. If we were successful, Virgin would win not just the routes but, crucially, the slots that BA had arranged for them at Narita Airport, Tokyo.

When news of our application leaked out, British Airways went berserk. This kind of thing had never happened before: small airlines were meant to let British Airways walk all over them and to be grateful for any slots at all. But to ask for slots that were "rightfully" theirs! They went into action. Lord King and his team lobbied good and hard that these slots were British Airways' rightful inheritance and that it was illegal to transfer them to Virgin Atlantic. Their argument backfired:

"They're not 'your' slots," Malcolm Rifkind, then secretary for transport, said curtly to British Airways. "They actually belong to the government and we issue them to you. BA does not own them."

When British Airways realized that they had lost that argument, they turned to more damaging allegations and pointed out that Virgin Atlantic was not financially strong enough to take on these slots; in fact, they muttered, word was in the trade that Virgin Atlantic was about to go bust. Hence Lord King's comments at the Rothschilds lunch. They also wrote "confidential" letters to the Department of Transport casting doubt on our finances. This hit the CAA on their Achilles' heel. They could not award the frequencies to Virgin Atlantic only to see us suddenly go bust.

We had to battle to persuade the CAA that Virgin Atlantic was a viable airline. Throughout January, as the CAA deliberated whether to award these two Tokyo frequencies to us, I heard an increasing number of rumors about both Virgin and me, all of which implied that we were in trouble.

Finally, in the last week of January, the CAA made two historic decisions in our favor: it awarded the two extra frequencies to Virgin Atlantic, ordering British Airways to hand over to us the four slots it had organized at Narita Airport; and it announced that it would recommend to the Department of Transport that Virgin Atlantic should be allowed to operate from Heathrow. Lord King was furious. As a major donor to the Tory party's finances, he announced that he had been betrayed and appealed against the Narita decision.

On 29 January, Thames Television broadcast the first television documentary about the rivalry between Virgin Atlantic and British Airways. This program described the battle we were having over the Tokyo frequencies and open access to Heathrow, and also highlighted some of the other complaints Virgin Atlantic had about BA, including our long-standing maintenance dispute. The day after the Thames Television program, British Airways issued a press release that claimed Virgin Atlantic was abusing them; it referred to our attack on them as an "onslaught." After hearing of another tirade of abuse from Lord King about me and recognizing that it could indirectly drive Virgin Atlantic bust, I wanted to have the rumors stopped. I didn't mind competition from British Airways or anyone else as long as it was fair competition, but I continued to hear a growing collection of damaging rumors.

On 31 January, I wrote my first letter to Lord King. I hoped that by bringing matters out into the open, I would be able to stop it. I have always believed that personal relationships are vital in business and that people should be directly accountable for their actions. If I alerted Lord King to what he had set in motion, I hoped that he would then call me back and we would have a quick chat about it and bury the hatchet. I wrote:

> I am writing to put on record to you that I resent the level of personal abuse your people at British Airways have recently resorted to. As Chairman of a small independent airline I have behaved no differently than you would have done in my place. I have argued our case with the CAA over Tokyo slots. They have decided in our favour. That decision is now

under review. We have argued our case for access to Heathrow. The CAA
have decided in our favour and we are waiting on the Secretary of State's
final decision.

In none of these issues have we behaved improperly. We have sought
remedies through the CAA, the Department of Transport, the EEC and
the High Court when appropriate. We have not at any stage made offensive personal remarks about you or Sir Colin Marshall. I would expect
the same courtesy from your company.

My letter was wishful thinking.

The next week Will was called by a man who introduced himself as
Frank Dobson, private detective. He wanted to have an urgent meeting with
Will. He suggested a pub underneath Waterloo Station. Will went along with
Gerrard Tyrrell, our lawyer from Harbottle and Lewis. Frank Dobson told
them that a detective agency called Kroll Associates were investigating me
and the whole Virgin group. Frank Dobson asked Will whether he could
work for Virgin to counteract whatever Kroll was up to. Will thanked him
for his information but turned down the offer of his help since we never use
private detectives.

I received Lord King's reply on 5 February. He merely quoted what he
had said to the *Sunday Telegraph:* "I run my airline, Richard Branson runs his.
Best of luck to him." He added that he intended to say nothing more on the
subject.

The letter's brevity was matched only by its arrogance. It was clear that
Lord King treated me with mockery and contempt that would rub off on
how everyone at British Airways felt they could treat Virgin Atlantic.

Lord King's letter contained two short sentences. Lord King did not mean
me to have the "best of luck." Indeed if he could have anything to do with it,
luck would not enter into it. And Lord King would go on to say a great deal
about "the subject" to a number of people.

The other peculiar thing about Lord King's letter was that it did not address me personally but only quoted a response he had made to a newspaper. It was as if he could not bring himself to address me as a person or
even acknowledge me. I knew that he had coined the contemptuous expression "the grinning pullover" to describe me. In the same way that British Airways was trying to steamroller Virgin Atlantic out of sight, it struck me that
Lord King was pretending I didn't exist.

Chapter 23

"I decided to offer Janet Jackson the largest amount of money ever offered to any singer."

February–April 1991

*I*n the aftermath of the television program, more alarming proof emerged of some kind of campaign against me and Virgin.

"I've had a call from an ex–British Airways man," Chris Moss, our marketing manager at Virgin Atlantic, told me. "Peter Fleming saw the Thames Television program and says that he can confirm all sorts of things BA have been up to."

"Will he write it down?" I asked. "Is it hard evidence?"

"He says that Virgin is BA's number one enemy and that after the Baghdad flight they set up a special team to undermine you."

"Can you get it in writing?"

"I'll try."

Throughout February and March we discussed the question of Tokyo frequencies and access to Heathrow with Malcolm Rifkind, the secretary for transport. He was a down-to-earth Scot who gave us a very fair hearing. I really felt that he was on our wavelength when he pointed out how vastly improved the Heathrow–Glasgow shuttle had become:

"I now get a decent meal with proper cutlery," he said. "It used to be a damp little white sandwich."

"That's British Midland bringing in some competition," I pointed out. "And they've got the slots to do it from Heathrow."

I thought our lunch meeting had gone well, but right at the end he floored me:

"Richard," he said, "you must admit that BA does do an excellent job."

"Yes, they're much improved," I agreed. "But they have been given everything on a plate. For instance, they were given Concorde for nothing with all the debts written off, and they were given the exclusive use of Heathrow."

"They were," Rifkind admitted. "But it's all in the national interest."

A silence fell between us. To my mind he had just undermined the entire lunch.

"There's no national interest at stake here," I argued. "British Airways is just a large airline which is owned by its shareholders. It happens to have a monopoly because that's what it was given while it was nationalized. But it's no longer like Aeroflot. Think of your old white sandwiches on the Glasgow shuttle. And unlike other privatized monopolies, which have their market dominance reduced by regulators, BA has no regulator and has actually been allowed to increase its dominance since it was privatized."

I thought that I might have gone too far because Malcolm Rifkind nodded rather awkwardly and made his way to the black Rover outside. I knew that he'd never flown Virgin because all members of Parliament, all civil servants, and all soldiers were still encouraged to fly British Airways as if it were somehow still the "national carrier." As I watched his car head off back to Westminster, I wondered whether he really believed that British Airways operated in the national interest or whether he had just been playing devil's advocate.

"Good news, Richard," said Malcolm Rifkind. "I am pleased to say that the government is going to allow Virgin Atlantic to operate from Heathrow. And on top of this, we are also going to nominate you as the British carrier to operate the two extra flights to Tokyo."

It was the crucial turning point we had been waiting for. It was 15 March 1991.

"Fantastic news!" I shouted. "Penni, let's have some champagne! Call down Will, call down everyone!"

As everyone gathered in my office to celebrate I dialed Hugh Welburn's number. Hugh had written the paper that pointed out the critical importance for an airline to operate from Heathrow. The paper's conclusion was that due to the single short runway at Gatwick and the lack of connecting flights, an identical route from Heathrow would be 15 percent more profitable than from Gatwick. Hugh's paper and the revelation that Virgin would be able to fly more cargo from the longer Heathrow runways and thus earn more taxable revenue had made a powerful impression on Malcolm Rifkind.

"We've won," I told Hugh. "Well done. We've finally managed to get into Heathrow."

Hugh was delighted and amazed. He had been a consultant in the aviation industry for a long time, and he had seen the demise of British Caledonian and several other smaller airlines that had failed to make ends meet from Gatwick.

"This is your breakthrough," he said. "But watch out. British Airways won't like it at all—they'll go berserk."

As we drank champagne, the telephone started ringing with journalists who had picked up the story. They were also ringing up Lord King, and the following day and over the weekend I read his reaction with interest:

"Government transport policy?" Lord King snorted in *The Observer*, of which his son-in-law Melvin Marckus was the business editor. "What transport policy?"

I didn't know whether to laugh at the interview or to be annoyed. I read on with growing amazement:

"It seems that every time we build up a profitable route," Lord King went on to say, "someone comes along and says: 'I'll have some of that' and the Government obliges."

Lord King estimated that Malcolm Rifkind's decision to allow Virgin Atlantic to fly the extra two flights to Tokyo would lose British Airways around £250 million a year in lost revenue: "That is £250 million of revenue lost to our public shareholders which has gone straight into Richard Branson's back pocket," he fulminated.

If only revenue did go straight into my back pocket. Perhaps in his rage Lord King had forgotten that there are costs that unfortunately crop up between revenue and profit.

On the same day the *Sunday Telegraph* commented: "This week Lord King was breathing fire over the decision finally to allow Virgin into Heathrow. Its long confinement at Gatwick has been a boon to BA and now I can see why. British Airways' approach to its services is hidebound by the managerial thinking of a national airline while Virgin has all the cheek, determination and original thinking of the whippersnapper entrepreneur snapping at the heels of the giant conglomerate. In terms of food and service, Upper Class Virgin is like First Class."

In *The Observer* Lord King argued that each time the government tried to foster a strong second airline it had ended in disaster. No doubt with a straight face he gave the examples of Laker Airlines, British Caledonian, and Air Europe. This assertion was stunning hypocrisy. British Airways had helped push Freddie Laker out of business, and at one stage a grand jury was empaneled to look into the issue, but ultimately no charges were brought after the intervention of the UK and U.S. governments. All three airlines had been confined to Gatwick. British Airways championed the benefits of competition, as long as the competition stayed out of sight at Gatwick. My parents had always drilled into me that the best motto to follow is Nothing ventured, nothing gained. By fighting tooth and claw for access to Heathrow, we had finally won. Virgin Atlantic was still tiny in comparison with British Airways, but we were now a serious threat to their long-term future in a way that British Caledonian had never been.

The demise of Pan Am and TWA was to play a role in the question of our access to Heathrow. American Airlines and United Airlines, the two giant American carriers, moved in to buy the rights to the routes into Heathrow that Pan Am and TWA had operated. In order for these routes to be activated, these two airlines asked for the Heathrow slots to be transferred over to them. Under the strict letter of the Traffic Distribution Rules these slots could not be transferred but should revert to the Heathrow Slot Committee. We immediately argued that if this should happen, then Virgin Atlantic should be allowed to apply for them alongside all other carriers who were interested in flying from Heathrow. Although Malcolm Rifkind had opened up Heathrow in principle, we still had a battle on our hands over how we would actually get the slots to fly from there.

The letter I had asked Chris Moss to try to extract from the British Airways employee Peter Fleming came through on Monday morning and added to my sense of unease. Dated 18 March, Peter Fleming's letter said: "There is no doubt that BA's UK sales management had Virgin as public enemy Number One. The real crisis was precipitated by the high profile Richard Branson achieved during his campaign to return hostages from the Gulf. During this period I was debriefed from a UK sales management meeting and told that a management team had been set up to undermine the 'Branson image.'

"The development of actions in the European Court [Virgin had put in a formal complaint] has however precipitated a thorough 'cover-up' of activities. In the last few months at BA I was told on three separate occasions to destroy 'any reference to Virgin in my files.' Staff in sensitive areas have been briefed on 'anti-trust' laws and how to respond to a sensitive situation involving Virgin. Actually, the current situation is verging on paranoia!"

Peter Fleming had been a senior marketing executive based at BA's Victoria office. This letter was the first real intimation I had that British Airways had actually set up a special internal unit to discredit me and had ordered the shredding of documents relating to Virgin. Why were those documents so incriminating that they needed to be shredded? I decided to put Peter Fleming's letter on file while we watched to see how British Airways' campaign, which became known as their "dirty tricks" campaign, developed.

• • •

In the meantime, we had plenty to do. If Virgin Atlantic was going to operate from Heathrow, we had to set up check-in desks, baggage handlers, and an engineering team, and of course we had to have a working timetable that we could offer our passengers—all of which meant being allocated slots. Only when we had the slots in place could Virgin Atlantic set up a timetable and then sell tickets. If we were going to benefit from the busy summer traffic, we had to have these in place by April at the latest. Every single item was a battle.

First of all, we were told there were no check-in desks available. When I walked around Terminal 3, I saw a whole line of empty check-in desks.

"Whose are those?" I asked.

"British Airways'," was the answer.

British Airways refused to subrent them to us when they weren't using them. Since we were being blocked on both slots and check-in desks, I appealed to the British Airports Authority, BAA, which had been privatized in the burst of privatization in the 1980s and ran all the airports in Britain. Its chief executive was Sir John Egan, who used to run Jaguar. I thought that Sir John might show me some sympathy since he was an entrepreneur who had built up Jaguar into a thriving company. When I explained to him that Virgin Atlantic was being continually blocked with our slot applications and even the small detail of where to have our check-in desks and that I was seriously considering having to file a lawsuit at the European Court, he promised to try to help.

We spoke again over the telephone, and I told him that I just wanted the chance to compete with British Airways and that I wasn't going to let them walk all over me.

Eventually the BAA found some check-in desks that could be allocated to Virgin Atlantic, but we weren't allowed to use our own baggage handlers. Faced with a choice of British Midland or British Airways, we chose British Midland.

The most difficult question remained the slot allocation. The system of slot allocation at a congested airport gives "historical precedence" to airlines already established there. In 1993 the European Commission modified it a little to give "new entrants" priority, but there is still an overwhelming degree of priority given to established airlines.

We applied for sixty-four slots so that we could operate our flights to Los Angeles, Tokyo, and New York from Heathrow. Despite all the press comment welcoming Virgin to Heathrow and the high expectations of the passengers, the Heathrow slot coordinator (Peter Morrisroe, then a secondee from British Airways) offered us just twenty-three rather than sixty-four slots. These twenty-three slots were mostly at absurd times of day, and some of them enabled us to depart but not to return.

"You know these don't work," I told him. "They're ridiculous. Nobody in their right mind would fly out of Heathrow at two A.M. to arrive in New York at four in the morning!"

"You didn't have to come to Heathrow," he said. "You could have stayed at Gatwick."

This refrain that I should have stayed out of the airline business began to annoy me.

The deadlock with the slot coordinator continued throughout March and into April. Winning access to Heathrow was a phony victory unless we could take off and land. I talked to Colin Howes at Harbottle and Lewis about the legal basis for slot allocation. We reached two conclusions. First was that the entire system was a voluntary code: any one airline, by refusing to accept the cartel system, which fixed slot allocations, could blow the voluntary system apart and force the government to intervene. And second, that the system was in breach of EU competition law because it effectively kept new competing airlines from coming into an airport as congested as Heathrow.

I decided that we had a strong enough hand to take on Heathrow's established players and their slot allocation system.

Before playing either of our trump cards, we argued that the slot coordinator had not complied with the procedures the airport had appointed him to apply: he had simply handed over Pan Am's and TWA's slots to American and United instead of putting them back into the pot for everyone to share.

At government level, Malcolm Rifkind had given American and United, together with Virgin Atlantic, access to Heathrow. He had made it clear to them that all three airlines would have to take their chances of securing scarce slots, thus balancing the British and American carriers' opportunities to some extent.

He had created the possibility for this to happen by abolishing part of an obscure but incredibly anticompetitive piece of legislation called the Traffic Distribution Rules. One of the rules said baldly that only the airlines that operated scheduled services from Heathrow to airports outside the United Kingdom when the rules were made (in the 1970s) could operate new overseas scheduled services from Heathrow. Not surprisingly, the government had been unable to find any argument to justify a piece of law that made new competition illegal, and it had abolished the rule. It was that which had created Virgin's opportunity.

But we could hardly expect monopolists who had been protected from new competition for more than a decade to welcome us with open arms. The coordinator, with the backing of other airlines already operating from Heathrow, tipped the balance by handing the slots that Pan Am and TWA had used to the two American carriers while offering Virgin Atlantic unworkable ones. Despite the government's permission to operate from Heathrow, Virgin Atlantic was being prevented from doing so.

I decided that I was ready either to go to the European Commission or to refuse to join the consensus that allowed a voluntary system to operate. As the deadlock with the slot coordinator continued and time ticked on, it looked as if we would miss the busy summer months. My back was against the wall, and I was prepared to lash out.

At the last possible moment before it would be too late and we would be unable to publish a summer timetable, Peter Morrisroe agreed to come and have lunch with me at Mill End. I was encouraged that he told me he wanted to bring his lawyer, Diana Guy. Colin Howes had told me that she was a competition law specialist; it looked as if one of our trump cards had been spotted. Over Sunday lunch the four of us discussed the future of Heathrow's slot allocation system.

I again told Peter that I thought that what he had done was wrong: he should not have simply handed over all the TWA and Pan Am slots but should have put them into a pool where all airlines could apply for them. We had a fierce debate about that. I also suggested that we ask the European Commission to review the slot allocation system or force an unwilling British government to take over Heathrow slot allocations. Just when it seemed that we were never going to agree, I offered to compromise: I told him that I would not force the government to intervene if we could work out a feasible timetable for a workable set of slots to be created. Morrisroe said that, given a few more days, he could juggle and adjust slots in a way that could create some new spaces for us. I decided that it was better to compromise than to create chaos by forcing government intervention. I also knew that by the time the European Commission could deal with any complaint we could make, the airline would be out of business.

After we had both climbed down, Morrisroe and I buried the hatchet over that Sunday lunch around our kitchen table, and Virgin Atlantic was finally able to operate from Heathrow.

• • •

At the same time as I was locked in my debate with the Heathrow slot co-ordinator, Jordan Harris and Jeff Ayeroff, who ran our American record label, called me to say that Janet Jackson had told them she would like to sign up with Virgin Music. This sensational breakthrough for Virgin Music equaled Virgin Atlantic's success in winning access to Heathrow. Janet Jackson was the world's top female singer, and I recognized that she had the single-minded determination to stay at the top. She wanted to become even more successful than her brother Michael. Alongside talent, one of the deciding factors in a singer's success is his or her mental strength. (And Janet had plenty of that.)

Janet Jackson had built up her success over a number of records, and I knew that she had the talent and stamina to stay at the top. In many ways it is better for a band if they take a long time to build their success since they can then learn to live with it, and they have a broader, more loyal fan base. When Janet had come to Necker Island, I had seen some of that determination; for instance, she insisted that she didn't go out into the sun since it would spoil her complexion. Avoiding the sun in the Virgin Islands is almost impossible, but Janet put her mind to it. Without being stopped from having as much fun as everyone else, she managed to avoid all direct sunlight—even if she did look a little out of place sitting on the beach in a shroud.

Although Janet told me that she would like to sign with Virgin, there was still to be an auction for her, and Virgin would have to match the highest offer before her preference for us would swing it. It was going to cost far more money than we had at our immediate disposal, but I instinctively knew that we had to have her: signing Janet Jackson would confirm Virgin's position as the world's sexiest record company, and I was damned if I was going to let the caution of our bankers stop us.

Throughout my business life I have always tried to keep on top of costs and to protect the downside risk as much as possible. The Virgin Group has survived only because we have always kept tight control of our cash. But I also know that sometimes it is essential to break these rules and spend lavishly. The chance of signing Janet Jackson was one of these moments; she could not be missed. After talking with Simon and Ken, I decided to offer Janet Jackson the largest amount of money ever offered to any singer. On top of this, I decided to break all the rules of the record industry: rather than tying her down for a number of future albums, Virgin would offer her a contract for just one album—a virtually unprecedented offer. I wanted to blow away the rest of the competition. I felt confident that once Janet started working with Virgin, she wouldn't want to go anywhere else.

As well as cementing Virgin Music's position as the best record label, signing Janet Jackson would send out the right message to all the people in the City and the CAA who might believe British Airways' rumors that the Virgin Group was suffering a cash crisis.

The only trouble was that we were indeed suffering a cash crisis. I knew that we would receive no help from Lloyds Bank if I asked for an extension of the overdraft to sign her, so Trevor and I looked for ways to juggle our assets and try to find more finance so that we could make the down payment. After a rapid number of meetings with banks, Trevor finally won the approval of the Bank of Nova Scotia, who told us that they would fund the Janet Jackson contract.

We offered Janet Jackson $15 million, with a payment on signature of $5 million. However, the auction soon topped that, and we had to jump up to $20 million and finally $25 million, just for the one album. It was millions more dollars than any record company had ever paid for a single album. We pointed out to the bank that Janet was the world's top female singer and had had more Top Five singles from her last album than any other singer had ever had, including her brother Michael. The Bank of Nova Scotia assured us that they would stretch to the $25 million.

As good as her word, when the bidding leveled out at $25 million, Janet chose Virgin. The contract was ours for the signing, and we had to find $11 million to pay her upon signature.

Feeling totally exhilarated, I left Trevor in London to finalize the negotiations with the Bank of Nova Scotia and Ken in Los Angeles with Janet's lawyers, and I took the family and Peter Gabriel on an Easter skiing holiday to Zermatt. We arrived on Thursday night and skied on Friday morning. Peter, one of my closest friends, had been the original singer with Genesis and was now signed to Virgin as a solo artist. We came back to the hotel for an early lunch, and Holly and Sam decided they wanted to have a swim in the hotel pool. Peter and I agreed to play a game of tennis. As I passed by the reception Alex, the owner, called after me:

"Richard, there's a telephone call for you."

There were no telephones in our bedrooms, so I took the call in the little kiosk just by the foyer. It was Trevor.

"Bad news, I'm afraid. We can't get the money together to sign Janet Jackson. As you know, we're due to sign today, but Nova Scotia have pulled out. We need eleven million dollars by close of business in Los Angeles. Ken thinks that we'd better tell her that we can't raise it and call it a day."

Before I'd left on Thursday, the Bank of Nova Scotia had promised to come up with the $11 million down payment we needed on signature of the contract. As I listened to Trevor, I watched the snow melt off my boots and form a small puddle on the tiled floor around me. I wondered which other assets we could juggle to raise the money. I had no intention of either delaying until next week or backing down. It would allow our rival bidders the opportunity to steal in and sign her.

Peter Gabriel came back with his tennis things. I knew that we were due to pay him a royalty check of nearly £2 million the following week.

"Hold the line, Trevor," I put my hand over the mouthpiece. "Peter, I'm sorry, but this is going to take quite a long time."

"Don't worry," he said cheerfully. "I'll join the kids in the pool."

Chapter 24

"What the hell. Janet Jackson's a terrific lady. Let's go
ahead and do the deal. But I wouldn't do this for Madonna!"

April–July 1991

I waited for Peter to disappear out of sight before asking Trevor about the royalty checks.

"We've got about five million pounds going out next week, including the big one to Peter Gabriel."

"Well, we could do something there. I'm sure that Peter wouldn't mind." I said. Then trying to convince myself, I added, "I'm sure he wouldn't—I'll buy him a drink. But what else is there?"

By now it was midmorning in London, almost lunchtime in Switzerland, and we had to have the $11 million by close of business in Los Angeles. It looked impossible. The only thing in our favor was that nobody in Los Angeles was awake yet, and we had fifteen hours' extra time to raise the money.

We rapidly ran over the list of options: we could ask Fujisankei to make a further investment in Virgin Music, we could ask Seibu-Saison to invest more in Virgin Atlantic, we could see what cash we could strip out of Virgin Communications.

"How's Robert doing with the sale of the Sega license?" I asked.

"It's not to be agreed for some weeks yet," said Trevor.

I added a few other ideas: selling Necker Island, selling my house in London, sublicensing some of our artists. The trouble was that all this would take time, and I knew that neither Fujisankei nor Seibu-Saison would be able to commit even $1 million at the drop of a hat, let alone $11 million. Indeed, Seibu-Saison had invested heavily in hotels and was suffering a large loss in the aftermath of the Gulf War.

It seemed to me that we'd never raise the money from a cold start, so we'd have to go back to the Bank of Nova Scotia.

"Were you dealing with the bankers in London?"

"Yes," Trevor said.

"Well, I wonder whether we shouldn't go over their heads?" I suggested. "If you went to see the chairman in Toronto, then perhaps he could overrule the London branch."

"I could go and see Bruce Birmingham, the vice chairman," Trevor said. "I know him pretty well. I'll just find out the flights."

I heard Trevor call out to Shirley in his office.

"When's the flight?" I asked.

"There's a one o'clock flight from Heathrow."

As Trevor set off to fly with the clock to Toronto, I found Peter with Holly and Sam in the pool and decided that I couldn't bring myself to ask him whether we could delay our royalty check to him. Bruce Birmingham at the Bank of Nova Scotia was our only hope. I called Ken in Los Angeles. It was the middle of the night there, but Ken had clearly not slept.

"Trevor's heading towards Toronto," I told him. "We're trying to get Nova Scotia back on track."

"We've got until this evening to close the deal," Ken said gloomily, having worked enormously hard to negotiate the contract and have it ready for signature.

"Whereabouts is the Los Angeles branch of the Bank of Nova Scotia?" I asked.

"I'll find out," Ken said. "We'll have a courier waiting outside."

It was an eight-hour flight to Toronto. I spent most of the rest of that afternoon trying to see whether we could raise any funds in London. It became clear that there was no chance.

By teatime in Zermatt, Ken was up and had started his final meeting with Janet Jackson's lawyers in Beverly Hills. They started through the contract one last time. Peter, Joan, the children, and I all had a late supper together. Trevor arrived in Toronto at 3 P.M. Toronto time, and he arrived at the Bank of Nova Scotia just before their close of business.

By 3 A.M. the hotel lobby in Zermatt was quiet. The children and Peter had long since given up on me, and even the night porter had disappeared into the back office. I sat on a plastic sofa by the pay phone and fretted, imagining Trevor in Toronto, locked in conversation with Bruce Birmingham. After a while my pay phone rang: it was Trevor and Bruce calling me from the Bank of Nova Scotia's dining room. They connected me to the speakerphone on the table, and we went through the problem.

I blindly promised that Virgin would sell as many copies of Janet Jackson's next album as her brother Michael Jackson's *Thriller.* I felt that Bruce

Birmingham understood the value of the album to Virgin, but he was reluctant to overrule the decision of his London office to pull out. The easy option for him would be to sit on the fence over the weekend, by which time the decision would be unnecessary.

"We need a decision now," I said. "I'm sitting in this hotel foyer and it's nearly four in the morning. Thank goodness Ken's negotiating in L.A. because if he was trying to sign this in Hong Kong we'd have lost it by now. If we're to sign Janet Jackson, we have to have a banker's draft in Los Angeles by close of business L.A. time."

"It's a matter of trust," Trevor said. "Virgin has never let you down on any of our loan repayments. This will be no different."

"Trev," Bruce said, "can I trust you? Otherwise I'm dead."

"Yes, you can."

There was a long pause.

"I guess they'll be mad at me in London," Bruce finally said. "But what the hell. Janet Jackson's a terrific lady. Let's go ahead and do the deal. But I wouldn't do this for Madonna!"

It took another agonizing two hours to release the banker's draft from the Los Angeles branch of the Bank of Nova Scotia. Then at 5 P.M. Los Angeles time, while Trevor and Bruce were celebrating with a dinner in Toronto and I was trying to get some sleep, a banker's draft for $11 million arrived at the meeting in Beverly Hills and was handed over to Janet Jackson's lawyers. Janet Jackson was blithely unaware that there had been any kind of problem, and she and Ken Berry signed the contract.

"Damn!" one of her lawyers said, holding up the banker's draft. "We should have asked for this earlier. We can't cash it until Monday."

We still had the balance of the contract to pay when Janet delivered her album, so we didn't stop our search to realize assets. In the aftermath of the Janet Jackson signing, which caused alarm bells to ring at Lloyds Bank as they saw us take another load of debt on board, Trevor and Robert managed to sell the European license to distribute Sega computer games back to the parent company, Sega, in Japan. It was a perfectly timed sale since we needed the cash and we needed to show the outside world some of the hidden value within the Virgin Group. None of the bankers had put much value on the license, which we sold for £33 million. The sale was also perfectly timed—a year later the bottom had fallen out of the computer-games market, and the value of the yen had soared and sliced the value of the license to practically nothing.

Virgin had acquired the European license to distribute Sega games when we bought a company called Mastertronic in 1988. At the time we had little idea of the potential of the computer-games business. All I knew was that Holly, Sam, and their friends were suddenly spending a lot of time playing computer games on the television. While Trevor had been at MAM, he had spent time with Sega as he leased out their arcade amusement machines. He felt sure that Sega would be able to draw upon their software expertise to rival Nintendo and that their new portfolio of small machines to play at home would sell well. It seemed a good business to get into.

Mastertronic was only five years old. Frank Hermann had set it up in 1983 and acquired the rights to a number of computer games. At that time he distributed these games, which were on cassettes and played through consoles, through newsagents. Frank noticed that a new game series manufactured by Nintendo was selling well in America.

Frank tried to sign up the license to distribute Nintendo in Britain, but Nintendo had already signed it to Mattel, an American toy manufacturer. Nintendo had a 95 percent share of the computer-games market in America, so Frank went to see its only other competitor, Sega. He signed up to become Sega's British distributor in 1986, and in the first year his company, Mastertronic, managed to sell 20,000 Sega consoles. The next year, 1987, Mastertronic's sales of Sega were soaring; but given that Sega were charging £55 for each console, which he needed to buy in, Frank needed a partner because he was finding it difficult to finance the sales. Although he could sell the consoles for £99, he needed a large amount of working capital to finance the gap between the £55 outlay to Sega for supplying the console, which was cash in advance, and receiving the £99 from selling it.

In June 1987 Roger Seelig called and asked me to meet a friend of his, Frank Hermann, who had stumbled into this rather amazing business. Trevor and Simon Burke negotiated to buy a 45 percent stake in Mastertronic, and we put it in with Virgin Communications. Frank and Robert started working together, and they bought the license to distribute Sega in Spain, France, and Germany for five years. The challenge was to build the Sega name from scratch in Europe. Virgin marketed Sega as the cool game to play, and initially we sold it on the basis that while your younger brother may be happy with Nintendo games such as Super Mario and Gameboy, the smarter games for smarter kids were Sega with Sonic the Hedgehog. Then, as the market developed rapidly, we found that younger and younger boys were buying Sonic: they all wanted to be like their older brothers. Our trick was to position Sega above Nintendo and to force them further and further down market. And it worked: in Europe, where Virgin was selling it, Sega overtook Nintendo with a 45 percent market share, compared with a tiny market share back home in Japan.

By 1991 the sales of Sega in Europe had soared to £150 million, up from £2 million in 1988. By then we were beginning to be rather terrified that the bubble might burst. In order to maintain our position we were having to spend £70 million marketing Sega before the cost of financing the sales. There was always the danger that because these games were primarily sold to an extremely narrow section of teenage boys, if another craze came along out of the blue, then Sega's sales would collapse. Peer pressure ensures that nobody wants to be left behind for a moment.

At home I noticed that Sam and Holly began to grow bored with their computer games. They spent less time tapping away at their consoles and Gameboys. Sam began to listen to music more, and Holly began to do other things. Just as they had turned us on to the idea of buying into this business, so Holly and Sam gave us the first warning signs that the market was topping out. Sales had rocketed from £2 million to £150 million, and if we stayed in the business we would have to commit to another huge budget promoting Sega. It was time to sell.

The sale of the Sega license surprised both the outside world and our bankers: £33 million in cash had been conjured up for a business on which they had placed no value. This was over ten times our original purchase price.

Before starting discussions to sell the Sega license, Robert had hived off the small team of researchers who wrote the software programs into a separate company called Virgin Interactive. In 1990 the next wave of technology would be games played on compact disc, and Robert commissioned a number of software writers to write some programs for compact discs. Without Sega and Sonic the Hedgehog to worry about, the tiny team of software programmers that Robert had assembled in America began to devise a new game for CD-ROM technology. They named it "The 7th Guest," and I noticed that people were growing increasingly excited about it. This game involved battling your way through a haunted house where all kinds of attacks were launched at you without warning.

"I've no idea what happens in this game since I'm always killed by the kick boxer with the boleros in the first room," Robert told me. "All I know is that these guys tell me that 'The 7th Guest' is going to be big. They say it's way ahead of anything else on the market."

As the world of virtual reality and CD-ROMs expanded into new dimensions and kids fought their way out of haunted houses on their computer screens, I found myself in an equally weird world in which I had to fight off a growing number of attacks that arrived from every side without warning.

"Perhaps it was just a bad day but one of Virgin's passengers was clearly not impressed with the service in Upper Class last week. An entry in the visitors' book read: 'No wonder your boss travels around the world in a balloon.' "

This small piece entitled "Verdict on Virgin" was among the sheaf of press cuttings I looked through one Monday morning in June. The journalist was Frank Kane, who wrote extensively about aviation and in particular British Airways; the newspaper was the *Sunday Telegraph,* of which Lord King was a nonexecutive director. I picked up the phone to Syd Pennington, the managing director at Virgin Atlantic:

"Did you see that piece in the *Sunday Telegraph*? Please can you send me the pages of the visitors' book for the last fortnight?"

It sounded all wrong to me. We had so few passenger complaints that I felt sure that the crew would have alerted me to this one. I found the entry in the visitors' book. It read exactly as Frank Kane had quoted it, but he'd missed out the punch line: "But seriously, I had a great time."

All the other quotes in the book of that flight were highly complimentary. I don't mind bad press as long as it is accurate, but this clearly was not. I traced the passenger, Cathy Holland, and phoned her up to check that she'd had a good flight. She assured me that she'd had a wonderful flight and that—as she'd made clear—it was just a joke. Then I wrote to the *Sunday Telegraph* and pointed out that Frank Kane had failed to quote her comment in its entirety. I knew that many elderly *Sunday Telegraph* readers would be skeptical about flying Virgin anyway, but this snippet would put them off even more. What was a casual mean joke to a journalist meant many thousands of lost pounds to Virgin Atlantic—and to my bankers. Worse still, Margaret Thatcher's daughter, Carol, then read the piece out on the David Frost show on television. I wrote to her pointing out that the journalist had misled her, but the damage was done. Six million viewers did not know that this comment was taken out of context.

I called up Frank Kane to complain, and he was apologetic.

"Oops, I'm sorry about that misquote," he said. "I looked over a neighbor's shoulder, and that's all I could see."

"That's all right," I said.

"There was another comment in the book," Kane went on. "It said: 'I couldn't get a seat on the BA flight because they were giving tickets away today. I'm glad. I shall fly Virgin from now on.' "

A couple of days later he was on the phone again.

"Do you still own Heaven nightclub?" he asked.

I was astonished. Frank Kane was a financial journalist working for the *Sunday Telegraph*. Heaven, the largest gay nightclub in Europe, was always good for a "sleaze attack" from the tabloids, but I couldn't see how a responsible journalist working on the business section of the *Sunday Telegraph* could possibly be interested.

"Yes, I do."

"Is it very salacious?"

"No, it's just a gay nightclub."

"Aren't you having problems with licensing? I've heard that there have been some complaints."

"No, I don't think so."

"I've just been looking at your accounts for last year, and I think they're misleading," Kane said, changing the subject. "The foreign exchange transactions look misleading."

I tried my best to explain how the accounting worked, and before he rang off he said:

"Don't worry, I'm not trying to do a hatchet job."

It was extraordinary that a City journalist should be remotely interested in Heaven nightclub. His comments also echoed the other string of questions I'd received about Heaven nightclub and our accounting policies. I couldn't understand what the connection was: I was obviously missing something, but I couldn't see what it was. It was very mysterious. To be fair to Frank, he was only doing his job, but the question going round in my mind was who was the source of all this nonsense.

I put the phone down and wrote a letter to Trevor Grove, the *Sunday Telegraph* editor, setting out my concern that the newspaper was indeed trying to do a hatchet job. Trevor Grove called me back to say that the battle between British Airways and Virgin had been fully reported and that the point of the question about Heaven nightclub was purely to establish which subsidiary it was in. He accepted that the quote from the visitors' book had been misleading, and we left it at that.

I crouched inside the van waiting for the signal. It was 4 A.M. on 7 July 1991, just before dawn, and we were parked on the roundabout outside

Heathrow. We had hired a crane that was slowly lowering a red flag with the Virgin logo over the tail of the Concorde parked on the Heathrow roundabout. Boards proclaiming Virgin Territory were put up against the British Airways boards. The flag was ready, and I sprinted across the roundabout. From the van parked beside us the press and film crews came out loaded with their equipment.

To celebrate the occasion I was wearing a brocaded frock coat with a stuffed parrot wobbling on one shoulder. I had a patch over one eye and a sword hanging off a sash. As the rush hour traffic built up, the passing cars all paused to hoot their horns and the drivers cheered. After our passionate lobbying, we'd finally been let into Heathrow, and we wanted the world to know. Soon the police came to see us.

"Everyone's having a good laugh, I see," the policeman said. "But British Airways has asked us to arrest you."

"Are you arresting me then?" I asked.

"Of course not," the policeman laughed. "I told BA that nothing would play into your hands more!"

I had dressed up as a pirate because Lord King had called me one. He felt that I was "robbing" him of air routes and revenue, which somehow rightfully belonged to British Airways. I had decided to take him at his word and "hijack" Concorde by putting the Virgin logo over Concorde's tail.

One of the reasons I dress up is to give press photographers a good picture that will make it into the papers and so promote the Virgin brand name. Today was no exception, with the picture running on the front page of papers worldwide. A pleasant by-product is that it makes people smile.

On 7 July Virgin started flying in and out of Heathrow. As Hugh Welburn had predicted, our sales on the three routes we offered—JFK, Tokyo, and Los Angeles—rapidly increased by 15 percent. On 14 July British Airways' internal magazine, *BA News*, published an article entitled "Virgin Out to Snatch More Slots" and once again reiterated how unfair it was that a lower-priced competitor should be allowed to compete with them.

Then on 16 July Lord King stood up at the British Airways annual general meeting and announced that British Airways would stop making its annual donations to the Conservative Party. Lord King had failed to spot that this gave away how they clearly thought that donating money to the Conservatives in the past had helped them secure various privileges. If an airline in Nigeria gave money and free air tickets to the ruling party in return for being granted a monopoly, it would be scorned in the West as being blatantly corrupt. "It's impossible to do business in Africa!" people would retort. "Look at the Nigerians: they're so damned corrupt!" The round of applause that British Airways won at its annual general meeting on 16 July on hearing this announcement struck me as ironic. Some critics point out that these same donations, which had totaled £180,000 since British Airways had been privatized in 1987, had helped secure a sympathetic hearing whenever British Airways needed to speak to the Department of Transport.

Indeed, British Airways' influence went further than merely giving money to the Conservative Party. During the summer I had given a presentation to a group of MPs about the lack of competition in British aviation. After the presentation I was having a drink with the MPs, and I found myself chatting to two of them about their holiday plans.

"Have you seen your travel agent yet?" one asked.

"No, I'm just going to give them a call to get my free ticket."

"Who's this travel agent?" I asked.

"British Airways, of course!" they chorused.

When Lord King stopped British Airways' donations to the Conservatives, I hoped that this would put British Airways as firmly out of favor as the previous donations had clearly kept him in favor. I hoped that the government would start encouraging more competition. The day after British Airways' annual general meeting, Sir Michael Bishop, the chairman of British Midland, and I released a press statement that congratulated the British government on freeing up Heathrow and supported it against British Airways' criticism.

Despite the excitement of starting our Heathrow operation in July 1991, it was clear that Virgin Atlantic would be unable to expand any further for a while. In any event we couldn't offer a new route for another three years until we started flying to Hong Kong in 1994. This was due to one of the fiercest, most focused, and most vicious attacks ever launched by an airline against a smaller competitor.

Chapter 25

"I've said it before, and unless you do it soon, I'll say it
again: Sue the bastards!"

September–October 1991

My grandfather on Dad's side was a cousin of Scott of the Antarctic. As a child I remember being taken to visit Bertie Scott, an elderly and distant relative who lived in Hampshire. I used to sit on the sofa beside him eating digestive biscuits while he told all kinds of stories about Scott and his fatal race to the South Pole. I was mesmerized by Scott's battle against the elements and determined to do something similar, although I had no idea what it could be. Scott of the Antarctic was my childhood hero, and in later life I also met and greatly admired his son, Sir Peter Scott.

Sir Peter Scott was an extraordinarily talented man, a true Renaissance man. Rather like his father, Sir Peter proved that if you put your mind to something, you can attempt anything. He fought in the war and became an expert at sailing small boats. He was picked for the British Olympic team and won a bronze medal at the Olympic Games for sailing. He then took up gliding and promptly won the world record for the longest flight. In later life he set up the World Wildlife Fund. Sir Peter Scott also set up the Wildfowl and Wetlands Trust at his home in Slimbridge near the mudflats of the estuary of the River Severn. He was one of the great amateurs of our lifetime. I met him in his sitting room at Slimbridge, which overlooked the lake. The muddy water came right up to the window, where he stood and painted ducks, teal, and Berwick swans coming in to land on the lake he had created. Slimbridge is a huge sanctuary for these migrating birds, and as well as inspiring me by the wide variety of different causes he followed, Sir Peter also inspired me to build my own lake as a wildfowl reserve in our fields at Kidlington.

The land is quite flat around our house. The River Cherwell meanders between the fields and along the edge of our lawn and disappears beneath the old Mill House, which belongs to Peter and Ceris. We live next door in two cottages knocked together to form one house, Mill End. I drew up a plan for a lake in one of the fields that had been dug out in the 1980s. It soon began to attract a wealth of wildfowl, and like Sir Peter Scott I also kept a selection of resident exotic birds whose wings were clipped. These birds mingle with the wild ones and help attract more of them. The most dramatic of these exotic birds are the huge black swans with red beaks from Australia.

After the lake was full of water I noticed that the numbers of birds were far fewer than those at Slimbridge, so I asked Sir Peter to come up and take a look at it. He advised me to build lots of small islands so that the birds would have dozens of different places to nest and, more important, dozens of different escape routes when they were threatened by predators or other birds trying to invade their nesting sites. Now from some sides the lake looks almost like a marsh. There are large tracts of water, which we keep clear of algae by placing special bales of barley near the edge, and dozens of small islands and inlets and reed beds. The lake teems with birds. Every year I am thrilled to see the first Berwick swans arrive on the lake after their epic flight down from Siberia.

Whenever we are at Kidlington, I take a walk around the lake before I start work, another one after lunch, and a last one in the evening. I not only find the walk both inspiring and relaxing but also enjoy the brief solitude. When I was a child my parents would always insist that all the children had to come out for walks after Sunday lunch with them, whatever the weather. We had no prospect of lounging around in the sitting room. Today I do the opposite: I never insist that anyone come with me, and I'm quite happy to set off and leave the family watching television or doing whatever they want to. (Actually, I don't think I have a choice!)

We were up at Mill End one weekend in September 1991 when it really looked as if my world was falling apart. From the high point of signing Janet Jackson and getting into Heathrow earlier in the year, everything was now going wrong. With the burden of funding the Janet Jackson deal, even Virgin Music was having difficulties. And the airline was stretched almost to the breaking point by trying to operate out of both Gatwick and Heathrow. On top of that, the rumors about Virgin's financial troubles were mounting. It was rather like being engulfed in a bush fire: although I kept stamping out outbursts, I was aware that more people than ever were talking about my impending bankruptcy. High-flying businessmen all over the country were going out of business. Robert Maxwell, Rupert Murdoch, Alan Bond, and Tiny Rowland were all rumored to be in trouble. I had taken so many telephone calls from so many journalists demanding to know whether our checks were bouncing that I could barely think straight. I needed some fresh air and some privacy, so I walked around the lake several times to work out what to do. I felt overwhelmed by the problems I faced.

Although we had signed Janet, I was growing increasingly worried about Simon's commitment to Virgin Music. He had stopped visiting clubs to search for new talent, and as a result Virgin had failed to break any significant new bands for a couple of years. In many ways, breaking a new band is the acid test of how dynamic a record company is. I knew that Simon was worried that the value of his shares in Virgin Music was at risk if something went wrong with Virgin Atlantic. But equally I was worried that his lack of commitment to Virgin Music would damage the value of my shareholding. His heart wasn't in the business anymore; he seemed more interested in his own personal projects.

On the other side of the Virgin Group, Virgin Atlantic was having an extremely hard time competing with British Airways. Our engineering teams were now driving three or four times a day between Heathrow and Gatwick to service each flight, and if a flight was delayed at one airport, it had a knock-on effect at the other. Will had heard that Lord King was going around announcing proudly that the "battle of Fortress Heathrow has been won—Virgin's about to collapse."

On top of all this, British Airways were now blatantly poaching our passengers. We had two reports that British Airways had called up a Virgin Atlantic passenger at home and tried to persuade them to change their flight from Virgin to British Airways; and our staff had also seen British Airways staff approaching Virgin Atlantic passengers at the terminals and trying to persuade them to switch to British Airways.

I was caught in the middle between Virgin Atlantic and Virgin Music, and I was alone in being the only person with a foot in each camp. The only other thing that bound them together was Lloyds Bank in that the loans that Lloyds had made to Virgin Atlantic were guaranteed by Virgin Music. This arrangement was the nub of Simon's worry, but the airline would not have been able to function any other way.

Our troubles at Virgin Atlantic brought the question of the future of Virgin Music to a head. Throughout the summer Simon, Trevor, Ken, Robert, and I had tried to work out what to do. I had effectively put the idea of the possible sale of the record company to the back of my mind, but with the rumors about Virgin Atlantic piling up into a great wave I realized that something had to give.

When I had decided to set up the airline in 1984, I had done so against Simon's wishes. Our friendship never fully recovered. He thought that I was mad to risk everything we had built up on a new venture, and I think that he must have resented how I rode over him. Now, when Virgin Atlantic was again under attack and in need of more investment, Simon was implacably opposed to swapping money from Virgin Music into Virgin Atlantic. He had in some ways done all he wanted to do with Virgin Music and was now looking to crystallize his wealth. He certainly didn't want to see it gambled away on Virgin Atlantic, whose value, he rightly felt, could all be destroyed by a winter price war.

We asked John Thornton, an investment banker at Goldman Sachs, to look at the various possibilities open to us in order to realize some of the value within Virgin Music. I would have preferred to have sold part of the company to raise some funds for Virgin Atlantic, but continuing discussions clarified that Simon was not really interested in a partial deal. He wanted to sell the whole company and make a clean break. Ken told me that he didn't mind what happened to Virgin Music since he would stay with the company. In some ways the idea of selling Virgin Music to another company was easier to contemplate if Ken would remain there to look after everyone, both the staff and the artists. John Thornton drew up a list of possible purchasers, and through the summer he quietly explored the prices they would pay. John was also the adviser to Sir Colin Southgate, chairman of Thorn EMI, and it soon became clear that Thorn EMI were very interested in buying Virgin Music.

I was caught in a horrible dilemma. As I walked around the lake that September weekend, I simply couldn't decide what to do about Virgin Music. If we agreed to sell it, I would be able to invest sufficient cash in Virgin Atlantic to survive the winter and see off what I was beginning to suspect was a concerted British Airways attack. But if we sold it, we would be selling the one thing that we had spent the best part of our lives building up. Everyone who had worked at Virgin Music had become close friends, and many of them had been there for over ten years.

I would have been happy to sit on the fence until the last possible moment in the hope that something would turn up. But our banking consortium, led by Lloyds Bank, were continually pushing us to sell. John Hobley had replaced Sidney Shaw as our account director, and as the recession worsened and an increasing number of high-profile businesses went bust, he became increasingly determined to rein in our overdraft from £40 million to £20 million. The trouble with Lloyds Bank was that they were our clearing bank, so rather than having a fixed line of credit as we did with the other members of the consortium, our overdraft with Lloyds fluctuated on a daily basis, soaring up when we paid our salaries, coming down when we received block bookings. Although we had never defaulted on any interest payment, they were becoming increasingly concerned.

On that Saturday evening I played a game of chess with Peter Emerson. Peter and Ceris, whom we saw almost every weekend, had become two of our closest friends. Peter is almost a generation older than I, in his midsixties, yet he still plays a fighting game of tennis and has one of the most incisive minds I've ever come across. After retiring as dean of Westminster Medical School Peter had become a consultant to Chelsea and Westminster Hospital. I couldn't really concentrate on the chess, and during the game John Hobley, the Lloyds Bank director, called. I suppose that he called on a Saturday night to impress upon me how urgent our financial crisis was, and once again he wanted to go over the figures.

"I'm sorry," he said. "I've got a mental block over the security you're offering for this extended loan."

Trevor and I had proposed that we put up Virgin's share of Virgin Retail as additional security for the overdraft.

"What don't you understand about it?" I asked.

"I don't understand whether we'll be able to easily retrieve any value out of the joint venture if we need to call in the loan."

I felt rather exasperated by this and wished that he had thought of it earlier instead of ruining my weekend by calling on a Saturday night.

"Also, the penny's just dropped that you're simply going to use this loan from us to pay off other banks' debt," he added. "We don't like lending money on that basis."

I felt a wave of indignation. Trevor and I had spent all Friday explaining to Lloyds that the Virgin Group was going to make a £35 million pretax profit, which was easily enough to service our debt. I had also explained that Goldman Sachs had valued Virgin Music at more than £500 million, which would give us plenty of funds in hand should Lloyds ever need their loan back. I looked over at Peter, who was sunk in thought over the chessboard, and decided to take a more aggressive line than I previously had. I was beginning to lose my patience, and one way or another I wanted to resolve the situation and bring matters to a head rather than carry on as we were with Lloyds always winding up the pressure on us.

"Well, there's not a lot I can do to help you, I'm afraid," I said with studied carelessness. "Why don't you speak to Trevor about it on Monday?"

When I sat back down at the chess table, Peter looked up at me.

"Was that wise?" he asked.

"I want to test him," I said. "I've realized that I've had enough of being pushed around by banks. Coutts almost put me out of business in 1984, and I know that the company is worth a hell of a lot more than he's giving me credit for."

"It's still not exactly sensible," Peter said.

"But if we sold Virgin Music then we'd be one of the most cash-rich companies in the country."

"That's still an *if*," Peter said. "And anyway, what's stopping that sale?"

"To be honest, I don't want to sell. Therefore I suppose I'm waiting for a knockout price. Thorn EMI are very interested."

"But why are you holding out for so much money from Thorn?" Peter asked. "What's the difference between £500 million and £600 million? I know you're going to say £100 million is a lot of money; of course it is, but it's not a done deal. Why don't you sell for £500 million, which is a hell of a fortune, and be done with it? Then you'll never have these problems again."

I thought about what he said for a while as we sat staring at the game in front of us. I could barely see my way through the game of chess, let alone my bank troubles.

"It's hard to explain," I said finally. "I feel as if I want to test the British banks. I've had enough of being pushed around by them and always having to give in. I want *them* to sweat it out for a change. We've got this massive value in the Virgin Group, which they are refusing to recognize. It seems that in order to prove the value of Virgin Music, we're going to have to sell it. That seems madness. It's like having to kill something to prove that it was alive."

"But you need cash for the airline, don't you?" Peter insisted.

"Yes, we do," I admitted. "The airline has debts of £45 million, and the rest of our borrowings are fully secured. Thorn have already offered us more than £400 million for just Virgin Music. I don't see what the bank is worried about."

Peter shrugged his shoulders and disagreed with me.

"If Lloyds are worried about you, then you have to be worried about them," he said. "You have to deal with them."

I felt better because at least I'd been able to explain to someone why I was pushing the banks so hard. Peter then trounced me at chess.

The next day it was raining, but I took an early-morning walk around the lake anyway. As it began to rain harder, I was joined by Harry Butler, the local butcher, who was out with his dog.

"My father died when I was nine years old," Harry said. "I missed him enormously. I see you playing with your son, and you obviously love having each other around."

I agreed with him, and we plodded on in silence for a while.

"You've proved everything you need to prove," Harry went on. "Don't be selfish. You owe it to your son not to go and kill yourself. So stop this high-altitude ballooning-around-the-world idea."

I was surprised that Harry had heard about it and, sobered by his advice, I went back to the house feeling utterly chastened. I realized that it was one thing to put my business at risk, but another to put my family in jeopardy. Normally when I'm under pressure from the business, I take refuge in my family. But Harry's comments had made me feel that I was taking them for granted and being selfish. The telephone rang again. It was John Hobley. I wondered whether my apparent insouciance the previous evening had alienated him.

"Just thought I'd touch base," he said. "I've had an extremely helpful conversation with Trevor, and I'll follow his line. We're going to drive ahead down the retail route. We'll come back to you with an answer midday Monday."

The Sunday papers were full of Alan Bond's arrest in Australia. He was described as a "troubled entrepreneur." He had to pay $200 million back to the banks within twenty-eight days or face bankruptcy. The papers compared his days when he had won the America's Cup for Australia with his financial collapse and talked of the difficulties all entrepreneurs were currently facing. I looked for any mention of Richard Branson, contrasting his feats of winning the Blue Riband or his ballooning trips with his current predicament, but luckily there was none . . . at least not yet.

"Have you seen this?" Will brought in the new issue of *Fortune* on Monday morning. It had a photograph of me lounging back on the floating deck chair in Necker Island and holding a book entitled *Mavericks in Paradise*. The caption underneath read: "Richard Branson, founder of the Virgin Group, savours the billionaire's life . . . in the British Virgin Islands naturally!"

I read with interest that I was worth $1.5 billion.

"I hope Lloyds read this."

"They may read it," Will said. "But will they believe it?"

"It's in the papers," I laughed. "It must be true!"

• • •

"Will Richard Branson's balloon burst?" was the headline on Wednesday, 2 October. The entire page of *The Guardian's* business section was devoted to discussing my debts. "Behind the Man with the Midas touch there is a picture of a highly-indebted and not-very-profitable conglomerate." The subheadline read: "The melody lingers but won't meet investment needs." This article had come out of the blue. Normally when journalists do a profile, even for a hatchet job, they contact me to go over some of the ground. But this *Guardian* journalist had never made contact.

I started reading: "The latest available accounts for the Virgin companies show an alarming picture of faltering cash flows failing to meet the companies' investment requirements." I looked through the article with a horrible feeling that this could inspire a host of other newspaper stories along similar lines. If it looked to informed financial journalists that Virgin was in such trouble, then the bankers would head straight back to their vaults, taking their money with them.

"Virgin therefore remains highly exposed," the article concluded. "It remains tiny by comparison with its key competitors. Its main businesses are in highly volatile industries. The legacy of the buy-back together with the ballooning growth of the empire keep debts at stubbornly high levels. The Branson balloon appears to be pursuing a dangerous path to the stratosphere. It is an exciting journey, undertaken with no shortage of panache, but Mr. Branson's balloon journeys are unfortunate models for any business to follow."

This article had caught us at our most vulnerable. All the accounts were shown in the worst possible light. To the world at large, or at any rate to *The Guardian's* readers, it looked as if I was in the same boat as Alan Bond: Richard Branson was sinking fast.

The phone started ringing with other journalists asking for my reaction, and I went through the response that Will and I had drafted. We tried to emphasize how factually inaccurate the figures were, how the article ignored the intangible value of Virgin Music's contracts, and how it put no value on Virgin Atlantic's aircraft. I was due to fly to Japan that day, and with the flight leaving at 5 P.M., I didn't have much time to respond to *The Guardian*. I began scribbling a letter to the newspaper's editor. I tried to shrug the article off: "There are many inaccuracies that could have been avoided in your article 'Will Richard Branson's balloon burst?' if your journalist had had the courtesy of speaking with me before writing it. Since I'm off to Japan in a few minutes (amusingly in the context of this letter to be made a Doctor of Economics!) I'll spare your readers a long list of them. However to give you but one inaccuracy our profits didn't 'plunge' as a public company—they doubled!" I went on to argue that the net worth of all my companies after repayment of all debt was around £1 billion. Will came down to discuss the letter.

"It's got to be more than a letter on this one," Will said. "You've been attacked with a whole-page article. What I want to do is get them to give you a whole page to defend yourself."

"They'll never do that."

"They might. It'll cause a commotion, and that's good for *The Guardian*. It's better than a letter tucked away on page 27, which nobody will read."

Together we wrote out a whole article rebutting *The Guardian's* piece, but before I could finish it I had to leave for Tokyo. The moment I arrived there Will was back on the phone.

"OK, we've got half a page," he said. "It's better than nothing. I'm faxing you the draft. *The Guardian* thought we might sue them, so I think they were relieved when we asked for the right to reply."

I called up Trevor and asked what Lloyds thought of the piece.

"Funnily enough, they're quite relaxed about it," he told me.

When I telephoned Lloyds, I found out why.

"Yes, I did see the piece," John Hobley said. "But I don't think many other people did. In any event, nobody I know takes *The Guardian* very seriously. If that piece had been in the *Daily Telegraph* or the *FT,* it'd have been a different matter."

"Now what's your decision on the loan?" I tried to sound casual, as if I really didn't mind one way or another.

"The board have passed it," Hobley said. "We've got a mechanism which will give us precedence over your assets in the retail operation."

I put the phone down, lay back on my hotel bed, and shut my eyes. If that article had appeared almost anywhere else, the City's reaction would have been very different. It is a frightening truth, but perception is everything with some of these bankers. Normally we have been able to use the perception of Virgin to our advantage. But for the first time the boot was on the other foot, and we were fighting to restore confidence. If such an article had appeared in the *Financial Times,* the banks could well have pulled out their loans and brought the Virgin Group crashing down.

At one point I received an honorary doctorate in Japan. The university asked me to fly out to meet the students and suggested that I do a question-

and-answer session rather than a formal speech. As I sat in front of a thousand students, the professor asked for questions. There was a deathly hush that lasted for nearly three minutes. To break the ice I said that the first person to ask me a question would get two first-class tickets to London. Fifty hands shot up. For the next three hours I was kept very busy.

I was also looking at a possible site for a Virgin Megastore in Kyoto. Mike Inman and I took the train from Tokyo to Kyoto. This train, called the Shinkansau, was popularly known as the Bullet Train. It was rather like being on board a plane: there were videos to watch, onboard service, and even vending machines.

"Why can't trains be like this in the U.K.?" I wondered. I jotted down some notes about trains in Britain and trains in Japan and then turned my attention to the Megastore site.

Back in London the next week, Will's telephone rang on Friday evening. It was Toby Helm, the transport correspondent on *The Sunday Times*. He asked Will whether Virgin would be interested in operating trains if the government privatized British Rail. Will came down to ask me.

"Well, are we?" I asked back.

"It's quite an interesting idea," Will said. "I love trains. And they could be run in a completely different way. We could give free meals, free newspapers, all the Virgin onboard services. We could compete directly with British Airways on the London-to-Manchester and London-to-Glasgow routes. Maybe it would free up slots at Heathrow."

The more we talked, the more sense it made. Railways had to be one of the answers to all the traffic problems. Every new motorway was immediately clogged up; driving from London to Manchester was a nightmare.

"Tell him that we are," I suggested. "It can't do any harm."

The headline of *The Sunday Times* read "Virgin to Go into Trains" and explained that Virgin wanted to operate the East Coast franchise and do a joint venture with British Rail. It became the story of the week—a useful distraction from our cash problems and an excellent counter to all the negative publicity we had suffered. It showed us thinking about expanding rather than worrying about our finances. It was a crucial release of pressure for us, and for a while journalists stopped going on about our finances and imminent collapse, and started taking an interest in our bold plans for the future.

All kinds of people called us up on Monday, including Siemens and GEC, and among them someone who introduced himself as Jim Steer from Steer Davies Gleave, Transport Consultants. Will immediately recognized that Jim knew what he was talking about.

"You've got to follow this through," Jim told Will. "I suggest that you should get together with InterCity and offer a joint service on the 125s."

We registered three possible rail trading names, "Virgin Rail," "Virgin Express," and "Virgin Flyer," and asked Jim to commission an artist's impression of a Virgin train. We warned him that our budget was zero, but he went ahead anyway and then put us in touch with a venture capital firm called Electra who, he said, might put up some seed money to investigate the idea. Will and I went along to Electra, where we met someone called Rowan Gormley, who agreed to put up £20,000 to commission a feasibility study.

Armed with a small business plan and a mock-up of a Virgin train, Trevor, Will, and I together with Jim Steer and Rowan Gormley met Chris Green, the director of British Rail's InterCity service, Roger Freeman from the ministry of transport, and John Welsby, the chief executive of British Rail. We talked about the possibility of Virgin running some railway services, but British Rail weren't keen. John Welsby was against any kind of privatization, and he saw our proposal as the thin end of the wedge. As he walked out of the meeting he turned to one of his companions and made a comment which was picked up on the intercom and broadcast all over the office. He said:

"I'll be in my grave before that fucker gets his logo on my trains."

Throughout the week of 21 October, I stood in for Angela Rippon on her early-morning LBC London radio show. This job was not my ideal since it entailed getting up at 5 A.M. and heading off through the dark to the LBC station near Euston. I was in the studio from 6 A.M. to 8 A.M. and then went home for breakfast.

The radio show producer called up Lord King to invite him onto the radio show to debate with me the problems that British Airways and Virgin were having and the sort of tactics that British Airways were employing against us.

"Tell him we're not prepared to lower our standards that much," Lord King snapped at her. "And you can quote me."

It was the first time I had approached Lord King since our exchange of letters in January, but his reply had lost none of its sting. My invitation to Lord King to debate what was going on was only half tongue in cheek. The previous week I had been called by Joseph Campbell, who runs our fleet of company cars.

"Richard," he said, "I'm sorry to bother you, but I thought that you should know something rather sinister has happened. One of the ladies who works for us has a daughter who works for a company of private investigators. And she told her mother that the company has just started spying on you. They followed you to Claridge's last week and sat at the next-door table."

I flicked back my diary: I had indeed had lunch at Claridge's. I thanked Joseph and wondered what to do. Should I call the police? I put the telephone down and looked at it. All my life the telephone had been my lifeline. But now I wondered whether anyone was listening in to my calls. Equally I wondered whether these private detectives were following my children to school. Or sifting through my dustbins. I wandered over to the window and looked up Holland Park. Perhaps the British Telecom van that was parked outside was a fraud and was actually packed with listening devices. Perhaps I had been reading too many spy novels.

Then I pushed the thought out of my mind. I couldn't change the way I lived, and I had nothing to hide. If I tried to second-guess these detectives and whoever was employing them, which ultimately I was sure had to be British Airways, then I would drive myself mad. I couldn't live like that. If I started thinking that I was being continually followed, I'd rapidly become paranoid. I decided that I would carry on my life as normal. I wouldn't even stoop to their level to have my telephone checked for bugs.

All week I was up at 5 A.M., and by Friday I was feeling rather exhausted. In the middle of the afternoon I came back to my office to find a note on my desk from Penni: "Chris Hutchins from *Today* called about a potential gossip story. Wanted you to call him back."

Chris Hutchins was a gossip columnist with *Today* newspaper with a known drinking problem.

I called him back.

"Richard, first of all I want you to know that I've done Alcoholics Anonymous," Chris said. "I'm clean, so you can take what I say seriously."

I began to listen and picked up my notebook.

"I've spoken to Brian Basham."

"Who's he?"

"BA's PR man. He is to Lord King what Tim Bell is to Lord Hanson. I know Basham's wife, Eileen, quite well because she used to work for me here. She called me to say that Brian might have a good story about Branson and drugs."

"Great," I said sarcastically.

"I called Basham up, and he told me that he'd been doing a detailed study for BA on Virgin's operations, its strengths and weaknesses. He also mentioned an unsubstantiated story about Heaven and suggested that I check out the drug position there for myself. He said he didn't particularly want to put you out of business; in fact, the last thing BA wanted was to be seen to have your blood on its hands."

The mention of Heaven struck a chord. I tried to remember which other journalists had been asking about Heaven, and suddenly it came to me: among them was Frank Kane, the financial journalist on the City pages of the *Sunday Telegraph*.

"He then told me that I should also look at the recent piece in *The Guardian* about your cash position. Well, finance isn't my thing and I wasn't that interested."

"Well, perhaps you should turn the tables on BA and investigate them," I suggested.

"I could consider that," Chris said. "But it's not really my style. I just write a gossip column. Anyway, I'm having lunch with Brian Basham on Monday at the Savoy."

"Will you come and see me over the weekend?" I asked. "I'd love to chat this through with you."

"Sure," Chris said.

I buzzed the intercom up to Will.

"Chris Hutchins called me."

"He was the one in 1989 who caused all that fuss by claiming you were in for a knighthood. 'Arise, Sir Richard.' Remember?" Will said.

"He sounds like he's cleaned himself up. He called me with a story about BA and their interest in us." I read from my notes. "Have you heard of Brian Bingham?"

"No," Will said, nonplussed.

"Well, he is to Lord King what Tim Bell is to Lord Hanson."

"Never heard of him," Will said.

"Basham," I corrected. "Brian Basham, and he's talking about drugs at Heaven . . ."

"Brian Basham! Christ! I'm coming down."

Will always looks flustered, as if he's itching to get on and make the next telephone call, but when he stormed into my room he looked in a flat panic.

"Brian Basham is bad news," he said. "He's one of the most influential PR men in the business. If he's against us we're in deep, deep shit. He's got closer ties in Fleet Street than anyone."

"He's spoken to Chris Hutchins about Heaven."

"Yes, but would Chris Hutchins be the first journalist you'd call?"

I saw Will's point. If Brian Basham had told the story to Chris Hutchins, a gossip columnist on *Today*, then who else knew about it?

The phone rang again. Will picked it up.

"Harvey Elliott from *The Times*."

"I gather that Virgin is going to have to make a great many redundancies," Elliott started off. "I've heard that you've sent a letter to your staff explaining these cutbacks."

"I send a letter to my staff every month," I said. "But I haven't written that there are going to be any cutbacks."

"I can get hold of the letter, you know," Elliott said.

"My letter to the staff is private," I told him. "But even if you do get hold of it and read it you will find that there are no redundancies."

The *Sunday Telegraph* was the next on the line. The journalist had a long list of allegations that he rattled off. His method of checking a story was apparently to recite a number of allegations, which he claimed he would print, and then leave it to you to prove them wrong. Every denial sounded exasperated against such a long list:

"I've got a letter you wrote to your staff," the journalist said. "You admit that there are going to be massive redundancies."

"How did you get that letter?" I asked.

"It came to me in a brown envelope."

"Well, if you actually read it, and it is a private letter, you'll see that there are not going to be any redundancies. I have it in front of me now, and it says: 'The Gulf War . . . when the Japanese stopped flying for months . . . subsequent spiraling fuel prices . . . the recession . . . the added competition,' and so on. 'The losses for the industry as a whole have been astronomical.' "

"It's not that bit," the journalist said.

"Then I go on to say: 'Our loads have been good but our yields have slipped considerably. The initial forecast for the next twelve months has given us cause for concern and, therefore, we have taken some immediate measures to counterbalance it.' "

"There you are," the journalist said, jubilant. "Redundancies."

"No," I said, "Virgin isn't making any redundancies. We're making savings elsewhere."

"Like what?"

"I can't tell you. They're just savings within the airline."

"Well, I know from a source inside Virgin that you're planning wage freezes, recruitment freezes, overtime bans, and combining flights."

"No," I said. "None of that's true."

"I've heard that if you keep your eight jumbos going through the winter you'll lose £50 million."

"Look," I finally said. "I don't know why I bother talking to you. You're just a BA puppet."

"Don't accuse me of being a BA puppet," he snapped back at me.

"Then tell me where you got all this information from."

"You know I can't reveal my sources."

"Well, whatever I say will make no difference to whatever you write, so just go and write it up," I said and rang off. As I put the telephone down I realized that I was a clearly defined target. It was a strange and frightening sensation.

I was due to go to a live television interview with talk-show host Clive Anderson. Before we left another call came through. It was Sir Freddie Laker from Miami.

"Hi, Richard." He sounded in high spirits. "Just a quick call to remind you that it was exactly ten years ago to the day when British Airways put me out of business."

"Are you celebrating?" I couldn't keep the exhaustion out of my voice.

"Well, soon enough. The bastards stopped my refinancing package with McDonnell Douglas on 25 October. That was the beginning of the end. I was bust by the next week."

"I'll mention that on the radio," I said, making a note. "I'm doing an early-morning radio show at the moment, so we can do a piece about you."

"I've heard about your problems with BA," Freddie said. "I just want to say that you've got to cry 'Foul!' before it's too late. Don't leave it too long."

"I won't, Freddie." I tried to muster up some energy. "I'll try my best."

"I've said it before, and unless you do it soon, I'll say it again: *Sue the bastards!*"

With this shout ringing in my ears, Will and I went off to the television studio. As I sat waiting to go on all I could think of were the events of the last few hours.

I walked onto the set, but I could hardly hear what Clive Anderson was saying. He sat in front of me, jabbering away about Virgin Atlantic as if it was fair play to take the piss out of it and pull it to pieces. *It's so easy to pull something to pieces,* I thought. *It's so much more difficult to build it up.*

"Now, what about these balloon flights?" Clive Anderson was saying. "Is there nothing you won't do for publicity?"

While I tried to answer him, he flipped to another subject:

"Now, what about your project to clean up litter—whatever came of that?"

I began to answer him, but I could tell he wasn't interested. I stared at him with mounting indignation and fury. I looked at his balding head, which had been carefully powdered so that it wouldn't shine through his remaining hair. *No,* I thought, *I didn't do a litter project, I was trying to create something worthwhile. You can take as much piss out of me as you like, but I've worked flat out for twenty years to build up one of the biggest private companies in the country and the Virgin brand name, and now I've got British Airways trying to put me out of business and chuck all my staff out onto the street. Unless I can do something pretty extraordinary in the very near future, I'm going to go bust like Sir Freddie Laker. And now I'm sitting here in front of a witty journalist who feels that he can ridicule me for trying to run a good airline.*

I scarcely heard the rest of Clive Anderson's comments. I smiled at him with gritted teeth, stood up, picked up my glass of water, and poured it over his head. I then walked out of the studio, brushed through the gang of sound engineers, and tried to find my way out onto the street to get some fresh air.

"Oh well," Clive Anderson said, mopping at his hair and jacket. "I've only got one thing to say to that: Fly British Airways."

Chapter 26

"Looking at it from my client's interest. the last thing they want is to be seen to have Richard Branson's blood on their hands!"

October–November 1991

"I had dinner with Harry Goodman last night," Chris Hutchins told me.

"How's he doing?"

"He's fine. But he told me that he'll never get Air Europe off the ground again."

Harry Goodman had set up Air Europe, which at one point had won almost 20 percent of the European market flying out of Gatwick. The Gulf War had stopped some of his passengers flying, but I still couldn't see how it had stopped so many as to destroy his business. He had gone bust at the beginning of the year, the same week when Sidney Shaw, my bank manager from Lloyds, had almost stopped our credit. Just before he had gone under, there had been a wave of rumors about the difficulty Air Europe was in—the fact that they were having to pay cash for their fuel and that their planes were unsafe.

Chris Hutchins had come to Holland Park to see me on Sunday evening, 27 October 1991, and I sensed that he was caught in a dilemma. The following day he was due to have lunch at the Savoy with Brian Basham. I wanted him to take a hidden microphone and record whatever Brian Basham had to say. This tape would prove whether he was spreading rumors. I also wanted Chris to give me a transcript of the telephone conversation he'd had with Brian Basham on Thursday. He was reluctant on both counts.

"Look at what BA are doing," I said to him. "When Air Europe went down thousands of staff lost their jobs. I need somebody to help me, or Virgin Atlantic will also go bust and thousands more people will be out of work. I need proof so that I can stop them. Why did you originally call me up about Brian Basham if you now say you can't help me?"

"I called you up because I thought that what BA was doing was wrong," Chris said.

"And you were right. And if I'm going to stop BA, then I need proof. We need either a transcript of the conversation or a recording of what is being said."

"But now I'm not so sure I can carry it out. I don't think I could secretly record him."

We sat in silence. I let it build up and decided not to break it. I just looked across at Chris as he sat wrestling with his conscience.

"All right," he finally agreed. "I won't get any more BA upgrades, but what the hell? I'll have done some good to other people."

"What about the tape recorder?" I asked.

"Believe it or not, the *News of the World* are the only paper to have got that all sorted," Chris said. "There'll be nobody there now, and tomorrow's going to be too late."

"All right, we'll buy you one."

I went through a list of questions I wanted Chris to ask. That night Chris called me again. I thought he was going to duck out of the whole thing, but he said: "Basham's just called me. He suggested that I come to his house for coffee at Primrose Hill instead of lunch at the Savoy."

"What time?" I asked

"Eleven o'clock."

"I'll get the tape recorder round to you first thing."

Will bought a tiny tape recorder on Tottenham Court Road on Monday morning and took it around to Chris Hutchins's house. He showed him how to work it and told him to tape the microphone to the inside of his shirt. I had spoken to Martin Dunn, the editor of *Today,* the previous evening and let him know what I had put Chris up to. Martin confirmed that he was happy for Chris to go in with a hidden tape recorder. Things were building up to a head.

I was due to see Tiny Rowland, who was chairman of Lonrho and *The Observer* and had extensive interests in Africa, at the same time as Chris's meeting with Basham. If I hadn't been so preoccupied with how the entire fortunes of my businesses were riding on the shoulders of a reformed alcoholic, I'd have taken Tiny Rowland much more seriously: it was to be the only time I met him. All I could think about was whether Chris Hutchins had managed to operate the tape recorder, whether the microphone was working, and what Brian Basham was saying. This little chat over coffee in a Primrose Hill house was critical for the future of Virgin Atlantic. We would again never have such a good chance to catch British Airways out. As I fretted over the recording and tried to guess the probability of it being successful, I also had to chat away to Tiny Rowland. Tiny had several ideas about working together in some way, and he offered to fix everything so that Virgin Atlantic could fly to South Africa.

"Come and meet Pik Botha on Sunday," Tiny offered me. "I'm sure that we could do lots of business together."

He amused me with one comment: "You're a young man and British Airways is very stuffy. Why don't we bid together for them? Their market capitalization is very low at the moment."

He was absolutely right, of course, and it would have been one way to stop the dirty tricks.

As he walked me back to the lift, he put his arm around my shoulders. "If you have any trouble with anything in *The Observer*," he said. "Just let me know and I'll sort it out for you."

I didn't know what to say. It seemed sad if such a great independent newspaper as *The Observer* could be influenced in this way.

I called up Will and then Penni, but Chris Hutchins hadn't called in.

"Whenever he calls, put him straight through to me," I said.

I was eventually put out of my misery when Chris finally called Penni, who then told me what Chris had said: "I can't say much because I'm at the office and there are lots of people around. Please tell Richard I'll come around tomorrow morning."

When he came around, I could see that Chris was horribly embarrassed. He didn't want to give me either the tape or the investigation into Virgin that Basham had handed over to him. I assumed complete nonchalance and pottered around making us a cup of tea. As I handed over the tea and smiled encouragingly at him, I knew that there was no way he was walking out of my house with either the tape or the report.

"So how was it?"

"Well, I brought you a couple of things, but I don't think that I can hand them over."

"What did you bring?" I asked pleasantly in my most genial manner.

"I brought the printout of my first conversation with Basham and also the tape and Basham's report."

"Let's have a look at the conversation first."

Chris opened his briefcase, and I saw the tape recorder and its mess of wires fleetingly as he pushed over a piece of paper. It was entitled "Chris Hutchins' conversation with Brian Basham in a telephone call which started at 1.40 pm Thursday 24th October." It had been written at 2 P.M., Thursday, 24 October, and read as follows:

"Basham said: 'And you've been talking to my good lady wife about the Heaven story. [Eileen Basham had initially contacted Chris to offer him the story as a favor.] Well, the fact of the matter is that you can apparently buy anything down there in the way of drugs. Personally I'm not interested in what goes on at Heaven, what I'm interested in is how Branson runs his operation. Needless to say my client British Airways are very interested in that. He won the two Japan slots—I take it all this is just between the two of us. Good—and I'm taking a really good look at his cash position. He's always run very tight with money to the point of getting into trouble, then he refinances. For example he sold some stores to WH Smith. Now he's getting Japanese investors. It's a dangerous way to operate but alright as long as your reputation is intact. He'd be in real danger if a story came out exposing what goes on at Heaven, it would certainly inhibit his reputation.'

" 'Then why don't you investigate it yourself?' Hutchins asked.

" 'I have no intention of . . . I don't want to put Branson out of business. In fact looking at it from my client's interest, the last thing they want is to be seen to have Richard Branson's blood on their hands.

" 'There was a huge heap of rubbish outside the British Aerospace office in the Strand which backs onto Heaven and when Admiral Sir Ray Lygo wanted it cleared his office manager called Westminster Council and they said their people wouldn't touch it because of all the needles. It's not there now.

" 'Eileen knows that I've got a major interest in Mr Branson. There was a huge piece in *The Guardian* on Branson analysing his finances and the roller coaster way he operates. He refinances periodically; he must be bleeding at the moment with all these fare cuts. I'd be interested to hear how you get on with your inquiries.' "

"There's worse," he said. "In our chat today he was talking about how a plane of yours would fall out of the sky. He kept calling Virgin a 'dicky business.' I don't know if the tape came out or not, but here's his report."

"Well, let's hear it anyway," I suggested.

Without meeting his eye so that I didn't give away either my mounting fear that he would snatch it back or my growing excitement over what we were about to hear, I took the tape and slotted it into the tape deck. Then I slid Basham's report toward me. I had them both. *This is the turning point,* I thought to myself. *If I ever come out on top against British Airways, it will be because of this moment.*

But the tape was just a maddening combination of whistles and hisses. I heard a whole buzz of raucous scratching as if Chris had just sat there rummaging through his clothes, banging the microphone, and had picked up a jammed radio station. Then quite clearly I heard Basham's voice say: "dicky business . . . ," and then there was another comment, "I'll have to get this place swept for bugs . . . ," which was nicely ironic. After several more agonizing minutes of hiss and crackle I heard Chris asking where the loo was and being directed to one near the front door. The clearest part of the recording was when Chris unzipped his flies and had a long and substantial pee into the loo. Then it cut off. This was hardly the tape to break British Airways.

"I tell you what," I said. "I'll get the tape over to our sound engineers in the studio and see if they can cut some of that background noise out. They might be able to use Dolby or something."

Chris agreed, relieved that I had given him an excuse for handing over the tape. Then I turned to Basham's report. It was headed Private and Confidential and simply dated October 1991. Basham had made a number of key points in the first section of the report:

"Popular *misconceptions* about Virgin include:

" 'Virgin is small': The four private Virgin groups of companies have a combined estimated market value of £860 million;

" 'Virgin's management is of low quality': The Virgin style is informal but the management team has demonstrated itself to be resourceful and fast-reacting to changing situations. Core businesses are managed by professional managers with relevant industry experience;

" 'Virgin is financially weak': Virgin businesses require large amounts of cash to finance investment and organic growth. However, finance has been raised through the use of such devices as joint ventures. Finance could be a source of weakness in future."

As well as identifying our strengths, the report also contained a section pointing out our weaknesses. Basham made a list of the transactions that we had done since going private, culminating in the sale of Sega and our Megastore joint venture with W. H. Smith. I turned the page and was surprised to read:

"Personal Profile: Branson has cultivated an independent, almost 'anti-establishment' image. He has great appeal to young people and also to the Japanese (where there is something akin to 'heroworship')." I skipped to another paragraph where Basham wrote: "With unsuccessful ventures Branson displays what can be characterised as a Houdini-like ability to escape from tight corners" and another revelation: "Branson displays obsessive tendencies in revisiting business areas after previous failures—most notably he appears to want to be in communications."

I turned over another page and saw:

"Weaknesses:

"Branson's strategy has been highly experimental. In the past he has always been able to extricate himself well in advance from unsuccessful ventures, he may not always be successful in the future.

"Branson has been able to finance the organic growth of the business to date from the joint venture and financing deals with the Japanese. Joint venture links with the Japanese investors are likely to lead eventually to constraints on the direction of those businesses, and are limited by the extent to which Branson would wish to dilute his own control. Continued growth of the businesses may lead to unsustainable demands for cash.

"Japanese loss of confidence for any reason could and probably would cut off his cash lifeline and could lead to disaster.

"Branson thrives on publicity. He appears to get bored very quickly when a business becomes routine and dull. He likes to break down barriers. However, he is sensitive to criticism.

"He owns Heaven nightclub which seems to be high risk in terms of his all important image."

There was a further reference to Heaven that comprised the germ of Basham's original call to Chris Hutchins:

"There have been suggestions that Westminster Council would not remove rubbish bags from the club on the grounds that they contained infected sharp objects."

I tossed the report back on the table and looked across at Chris.

"Where do we go from here?" Chris asked.

"I'll have to mull it all over," I said. "But will *Today* expose what BA is up to?"

"I'll have to talk to our editor, Martin Dunn."

Chris didn't seem that enthused. I wondered whether he was unhappy about blowing Brian Basham out of the water by handing this material over to me.

We left it that we'd speak later on the phone once he'd had a chance to talk to Martin Dunn and I'd had a chance to see whether we could salvage anything meaningful from the cassette. I supposed that Chris would look pretty foolish in front of his editor once he'd admitted that he'd passed over the tape to me, but I felt that this scandal was one that *Today* would be pleased to publish.

An hour later Will and I were in the recording studios. Two engineers had been fiddling with all kinds of mixing controls when suddenly Basham's voice came out over the large black speakers loud and clear. We sat in silence and listened to what sounded like a slick and well-rehearsed briefing. To be fair to Basham, he was concentrating on Virgin's corporate profile, and he was later to claim, with some justification, that his role in the whole dirty-tricks affair had been distorted by BA, who were only too happy to blame others for their activities.

Basham was saying "The pattern with Branson is that he has lots of schemes going on, some of them big capital eaters. His whole world is based on *Tubular Bells*—I mean, you know more about the music business than I do, so you know that. He got the cash and he immediately borrowed. Business is not about profit—it's about cash, cash availability. It's about whether you've got enough cash to pay your overheads, and at the end of the day whether you've got enough cash left over. Profit doesn't matter.

"What Branson does, he runs his cash flow close to the wire all the time, and just before he runs out of cash he refinances. He'll sell some record shops in Japan, he'll sell some shops to W. H. Smith, and if you look at the weekend press, Frank Kane in the *Sunday Telegraph* says he's trying to raise twenty million pounds.

"Branson has two things which could really drag him down," Basham went on. "One of them is his physical courage, if you like, in ballooning, which is a very, very dangerous occupation. Even with safeguards and everything, if you're up at whatever it is, thirty thousand feet, right up in the fringes of the atmosphere in a balloon, it's dangerous. Lots of things could go wrong. And if he got into trouble, I believe the business would collapse because it's his charm and his magic that pulls the cash into the business.

"There's also what I call 'moral danger,' which really focuses on Heaven. And if he's got Heaven, I can't believe that there aren't other things."

"What's wrong with Heaven?" Chris asked, the first time he got a word in sideways.

"Nothing," Basham said quickly. "Nothing wrong with Heaven at all. It's a gay nightclub. For Lord King to own Heaven would be bizarre, right? For Branson to own Heaven, if he wants to become a serious businessman, is bizarre and leads him into danger. It not only leads him into danger, it leads the business into danger. Can you imagine a hypothetical case. Salomons get a prospectus together, and they are just in the middle of a float and Heaven is raided? Charges are pressed against the ownership, right? Not inconceivable."

From the way Basham dwelt on "in-con-ceiv-able," it sounded as though he had conceived the ideas very clearly.

"Especially if there are lots of drugs involved," Basham went on. "And that is where I think he is bound to run amiss. I think he has got some problems, and he does run his business very riskily."

Basham then broke off to call his office. The copy of the report he was going to hand over to Hutchins was missing a one-page report on Heaven:

"Hello there, sorry to bother you. I'm just in the middle of a meeting. Thank you very much for getting the document together. It's very useful . . . there's one thing missing from it which is quite crucial, which is the original report that our friend did on Heaven. I want it because it talks about the war between the bouncers. Could you fax it to my home? Thanks very much."

Chris Hutchins asked him about the government's decision to allow Virgin to fly to Tokyo. Brian Basham's voice became warmly persuasive:

"I try to look at my clients' business through their eyes. So when I see Branson getting routes from British Airways, I think it's scandalous for two reasons: first of all I think he runs a dicky business, just dicky. Bits of it are good, but I think it's dicky. I wouldn't care to invest in that business with my money.

"What King understands," Basham said, "is that anybody who runs a business like Branson is taking a big risk on going bust. This is Freddie Laker all over again."

"I think that for the government to give these routes, which are really big assets, to a businessman is bad news, scandalous. To take those routes away from a business which has been privatized, where you've got lots and lots of shareholders, and take it away from all those private shareholders and to give it to somebody who's got a privately run business is, I think, doubly scandalous."

Impervious to my mounting fury, Brian Basham's voice smoothly changed tack to discuss the Virgin management and the extraordinary behavior of Mike Batt, who had left British Airways to work for Virgin and had then returned to British Airways after two days:

"Mike Batt was taken into Virgin to take over from Richard Branson."

"Roy and Trevor will enjoy this!" I said.

"Anyway," Basham went on, overriding me, "he worked for one week and resigned. I took him out for dinner and asked what happened. He said well, actually, the business is appallingly run. He said one day, without doubt, an aircraft is going to fall out of the sky—because aircraft always fall out of the sky, you know. Must happen. If an inquiry takes place, someone is going to swing, because the procedures and the way the business is run are appalling."

"Sue the bastard!" I said, echoing Freddie Laker. "This is incredible."

At least Basham then went on to point out that since that time we'd brought in good people to improve things. On the tape Basham and Hutchins were preparing to leave. The crackling rose as Hutchins stood up and smoothed down his clothes.

"I have a couple of concerns," Basham told him. "First of all, I don't want to be involved in this at all. Secondly, I mustn't have BA involved in this at all. I mean, all the good I might have done by saying 'Here is Virgin, good and bad' would be entirely wiped out if it looked as though BA were in any way running some sort of campaign against Virgin—which they're not. All right? . . ."

"It's not going to get you into trouble with Lord King, is it, if we rubbish Branson?" Chris asked.

"No," Basham said. "If you blow Branson out, it doesn't make any difference to me as long as neither BA nor I are associated with it."

"But it's not going to meet with their disapproval, right?"

"No, not at all. I mean, they don't care if you wipe out United Airlines—they wouldn't mind."

Then there was more crackle and hiss and Basham said:

"I really must get this place swept for bugs."

A few moments later Chris was asking to use the loo.

He unzipped his trousers and had a long, refreshing pee, which we heard in magnificant quadrophonic sound until the tape cut out. Will and I stared at each other.

"Play those last comments of Basham's again," I said.

"No," Basham said. "If you blow Branson out, it doesn't make any difference to me as long as neither BA nor I are associated with it."

"Well, I'm afraid that both you and BA are going to be very associated with it," I said, wondering what we should do with the tape. I felt as though I had just witnessed a crime, and it was doubly strange knowing I was the victim. I asked the engineers to copy it, and we immediately biked a copy around to Gerrard Tyrrell, our lawyer at Harbottle and Lewis. Then I put the original tape back in my pocket together with two more copies and went back to Holland Park.

• • •

Things moved very quickly that week. Chris Hutchins called to say that his editor, Martin Dunn, had put Bob Graham, an investigative journalist, onto the story over his head and that they were about to lead with a front-cover exclusive. I was expecting *Today* to run the story any day, but they began dithering about how to check the British Airways side of the story. I couldn't believe that they weren't rushing it through. In the meantime the phone continued to ring. The first call I received on Tuesday was from Syd Pennington, who had been reading the Virgin upper-class visitors' book.

"There's an entry here which reads: 'You obviously have BA worried! I received a call asking why I booked on a Virgin Atlantic flight today rather than BA. Good job! Good luck!'"

"Who wrote that?"

"Marcia Borne from Procter & Gamble, New York."

"Do you have her contact number?"

"I thought you'd ask," Syd said, and carefully read it out.

I could hardly wait for lunchtime, when I could call Marcia Borne in New York without waking her up. She told me that she normally flew British Airways on her quarterly flights to the United Kingdom, but this time she decided to come back with Virgin to try it out. British Airways had called her to ask why she had changed her return flight to Virgin.

"The guy from BA said: 'If you change your mind, let us know and we can change your ticket.' It didn't bother me at the time, but then I started wondering how my itinerary was such public knowledge. The more I thought about it, the more it bothered me. I didn't know that there was a big computer in the sky which told everybody else where I was going to be. I was a bit upset."

I thanked her for her help and for flying Virgin.

"By the way," Marcia said, "it was a great flight and I can see why BA are so worried. I'm converted."

British Airways was obviously gaining access to various computer information that should have been off bounds. It was confirmed by the next day's post: out of the blue Peter Fleming from British Airways wrote a second letter in which he detailed a number of things that British Airways had done. Dated 29 October 1991, it covered a wider range than his first letter earlier in the year. He started off by repeating how a management task force had been set up to discredit the "Branson image." "This, I felt," he wrote, "would have originated as a strategy at a very senior level within BA. I was shocked that the company could be so open about this and state it in such an un-compromising way."

He went on to say: "However not long after when Virgin took some concerns to the European Courts there was a noticeable backlash which swept the whole company. At this time I was told to destroy all documents that had any references to Virgin, not once but four or five times by different people from managers to managers' secretaries. Again I was reasonably shocked that BA's senior management could be so concerned about its activities that it felt that all references to an airline should be destroyed in this way. I did not destroy anything myself, as I did not feel that my files had anything of a damaging nature, but I know that other people in my department did destroy material because of this directive."

Peter Fleming had already described these two aspects of British Airways' campaign, but I was still surprised to see them set out in black and white. More interesting were the further details he highlighted:

"The following points are the issues that I was aware of in respect of BA trying to squeeze Virgin out of the picture. They do not necessarily constitute anti-competitive behaviour but this is something for you to decide."

The list included British Airways deliberately applying for slots to Japan and Australia, which it didn't need, for the sole purpose of stopping Virgin from getting them; a special sales force getting business in the Gatwick area and offering low fares from Gatwick to squeeze yields for all airlines there (while continuing to operate a high-fare monopoly from Heathrow); refusing to process bookings of passengers from Japan who flew Virgin into Gatwick and then wanted to switch to British Airways, thereby forcing passengers to fly British Airways all the way; and accessing our load factors at Gatwick by delving into the computer reservations system.

"In my opinion," Fleming wrote, "BA lacks integrity and this stems right from the top of the organisation with Lord King and unfortunately permeates the whole structure."

With Peter Fleming's evidence I now knew some of what British Airways were doing behind the scenes; with Chris Hutchins's tape of Brian Basham I also knew what they were doing in the press. Although I was caught in this two-pronged attack, at least I knew exactly which tactics British Airways were using. It was sinister, but I could begin to think about how to retaliate.

While the journalists at *Today* were still wondering what to do with the Brian Basham tape recording, we received a call from *The Sunday Times*. Now that I knew that Basham had prompted some press inquiries, I was always on my guard. And given that a good journalist will phone up to check the allegations, Basham's words were coming straight through to me.

Nick Rufford worked on *The Sunday Times'* Insight team. He was planning an analysis of the Virgin empire, and he had set up a meeting with Brian Basham in the Savoy the previous Friday to hear British Airways' perspective on Virgin. Basham told him some of the same things he had told Chris Hutchins, but because Rufford was a financial journalist he mentioned a rumor within British Airways that Virgin was having to pay for its fuel in cash because of our low credit rating.

After that lunch, Rufford called up Basham again to check some of the details he had mentioned and, unknown to Basham, took the precaution of taping the call. Basham gave Rufford a long list of other airlines that had gone bust:

"The list is extraordinary," Basham told him. "Channel Airways, World Wide Aviation, British Eagle, Scottish European, Air Safari, Southern Airways, Laker Airways, Air Europe, British Caledonian, Highland Express, Donaldson, Scimitar, Senator, Victor, Westwood Aviation, Scillonian, Air Charter, Air Link, Lloyd International, Paramount, and Novair . . . these are all companies that come off the top of the head.

"The question of cash for fuel is something we can't verify . . . but it's something which a number of people I've spoken to have heard and they think it's Shell. We think he's having to pay up front for fuel." Basham told Rufford to call Shell to check the information.

Nick Rufford called up Will to get a response to the story.

"I'm going to say that Virgin Atlantic is having to pay cash for its fuel," he said. "Do you have any comments on that?"

"Yes, I bloody well do," Will said, furious, "That's complete bollocks. I hope you're not going to print that because if that sort of thing gets into print about a small airline it can be fatal—belly-up in days. We'll have to sue you."

Rufford then began to recite the list of airlines that Basham had given him.

"Hang on, this is a put-up job," Will said. "I'll get Richard for you."

Will came into my office and explained the situation. I spoke to Rufford and told him that it was rubbish. I did not have to pay cash for my fuel. Indeed, not only was it rubbish, it was exactly the sort of rumor that would cause the most damage to Virgin and probably lead to Shell demanding cash for fuel, and that in turn would put us out of business in its own momentum. Fuel represented over 20 percent of our costs, and without the cash flow credit that comes from passengers paying for their tickets up front and us paying for the fuel a month later, we'd have to take out a further loan, which no bank would countenance

"Why don't you turn the tables on British Airways," I suggested, "and write about their dirty tricks? That's the real story."

"I could try that," Rufford said. "What other evidence do you have?"

"I don't know where to begin," I said, thinking of the Basham tape, which *Today* was sitting on.

By the time I finished with Rufford I sensed that he might see it from our point of view. He told me that one of British Airways' executives had told him that he'd seen a file on Richard Branson sitting on Colin Marshall's desk.

"I think you'll find that it's a report written by Brian Basham," I said. "I'm not surprised Colin Marshall has got a copy. I only hope he didn't have to pay too much for it."

Nick Rufford promised to check the story with Shell and then call Basham. A few hours later he called me back:

"I checked with Shell, and they told me that Virgin has normal credit terms. So I called up Basham and told him that I was turning the story on its head. We're now running a story about British Airways' campaign to smear Virgin, and mentioning him."

"Was he pleased?"

"He was on a car phone," Rufford said diplomatically. "I think he must have gone through a tunnel."

At this moment I had the gut feeling that the tide was turning in our favor. Over the last few months Will and I had seemed to be the only people who believed that British Airways was up to no good. Other people within Virgin Atlantic told me that they wished that I would take a lower profile since they just wanted to get on and run the airline, and their jobs were becoming increasingly difficult as we were on a virtual war footing with our competitor. I felt that at last I was making some sense.

I had just taken another call from the *Daily Express*, informing me they had heard that *Today* was about to run an exclusive story regarding the drug problem at Heaven and asking what I wanted to say about it, when Penni pushed a note under my nose:

"John Thornton holding for you."

I told the *Daily Express* reporter that there were no drug problems at Heaven and that he should go there one night. Then I pushed line 1 to pick up John.

"Haven't heard from you for a while," John said. "I've been reading a lot about you, though."

"It's building up," I agreed. "The trouble is, so many stories are just plain wrong."

"Journalists and bankers," John said affably. "Never trust them."

"What's the news from Thorn?"

I had put Lloyds Bank and Thorn halfway out of my mind, but I knew that the next call from Lloyds wouldn't be far away. They had extended the overdraft at the beginning of the month, the day of the *Guardian* article, but we had not been able to show them any positive cash flow since then. The pressure to sell Virgin Music was still there.

"Thorn says that it would be emotionally great to do the deal with you," John said.

"What on earth does that mean?" I asked.

"Their accountants are still going through the kinds of figures I don't want to bore you with, but we're looking at the numbers beginning to add up to your price by the end of the year."

"Call me if I can do anything," I said, wondering how we could find some cash to prevent the sale taking place. We were running out of options. We had recently instructed the American investment bank Salomon Brothers to raise some equity in Virgin Atlantic, but they weren't exactly being overwhelmed with calls from investors.

Just before the weekend I had another call from *The Sunday Times,* Andrew Davidson from the business section. He asked me to confirm that Virgin was having difficulty paying for its fuel and had to pay in cash. Since I had been living with this story all week, I found it difficult to treat it as the amazing scoop that Andrew Davidson thought he had. I didn't refer him to his *Sunday Times* colleague Nick Rufford since I reckoned that the Insight team liked to surprise even their own colleagues, and I didn't want his business editor to get hold of the story that Nick Rufford was planning to run on Sunday as he might do his best to kill it.

"Branson Attacks BA 'Tricks' " was the headline in *The Sunday Times,* 3 November 1991. This wasn't exactly what I had in mind, but it was true nonetheless. I'd been hoping that *The Sunday Times* would stick their neck on the line and say how scandalous they thought British Airways' tactics were rather than just repeating my claims, but it was a start. For the first time in the campaign, Brian Basham was publicly linked with British Airways, which blew his cover. Insight reported how Basham had given his confidential report to a number of journalists. I was quoted as saying that I had a list of one hundred complaints that I would take to the European Commission unless BA stopped their dirty tricks. And Nick Rufford made no mention of the cash-for-fuel story which had started his investigation.

But a footnote to the Insight article drew me to a piece in the business section by Andrew Davidson entitled "Branson's Pickle." It was much less positive about Virgin.

Inspired by *The Sunday Times, Today* finally screwed up their courage and faxed me a copy of the front-page splash they were going to publish the next day.

"We're going to call Brian Basham to check his quotes," Bob Graham told me.

An hour later he called back: "The shit's hit the fan," he said. "Basham has gone mad. Burnside from BA has been on the line to Martin Dunn. It's got very nasty."

In the event *Today* decide not to run the story, bowing to the pressure exerted by BA.

I expected a whole lot of journalists to call me in the aftermath of *The Sunday Times'* Insight piece, but the phone was strangely quiet. I didn't know what was going on. Given what the article said, I was surprised that no one was offering to investigate the story.

Now that *Today* had capitulated, I wondered where else I could try to hit back at British Airways. They had to this point escaped lightly. Andrew Davidson's article counteracted the Insight article, and *The Sunday Times* had probably caused me more harm than good. Most of the follow-up stories had quotes from Lord King saying that I was orchestrating a campaign against British Airways, or that I was just seeking publicity, or that British Airways was too busy fighting off the megacarriers to be bothered about Virgin, or that I was just plain "scurrilous."

"Ricky must learn to take the rough with the smooth," said Jeannie Davis, a friend of my parents, to my mother when they next bumped into each other. Jeannie's opinion could be seen as the general opinion of the country. To the outsider it looked as if I was complaining about some tough competition, and they might well believe that I shouldn't be flying my planes if I couldn't stand a bit of competition. But Jean Davis should have known better: she was married to Michael Davis, a nonexecutive director of British Airways.

Chapter 27

"Daddy, who are the Rolling Stones? Are they some kind of pop group?"

November 1991–March 1992

*P*enni put her head around the door: "Prince Rupert for you?"

I almost leaped at the telephone. I had not heard that the Rolling Stones were available, but a call from their manager out of the blue could mean only one thing. Sure enough, Prince Rupert confirmed that the Stones were on the market and told me that he wanted me to be the first to know, so that Virgin Music could put together a package to bid for them. After I put down the phone, I started jotting down numbers. The most important thing was to offer a high enough price that Prince Rupert would deal with us exclusively. I called up Ken, and he started to look at their sales figures. Most of their back catalog was available, and Ken and I thought that we should push for a three-album deal. The recession had hit the music industry as well, so the figures were going to be lower than in previous years. After Ken had run through the future sales figures and looked at possible sales of their back catalog, his hunch was that we would need to make a down payment of around £6 million to secure the Stones. Although it was less than for Janet Jackson, our consortium of banks were in no frame of mind to provide it.

I put the troubles with British Airways and the impending sale of Virgin Music out of my mind for the moment and concentrated on winning the Rolling Stones. A great many people in the record industry were writing off the Stones. Some articles had appeared questioning how much longer a bunch of grandparents could continue playing rock music; and once again everyone thought that the Stones were about to pack it in. But when Simon, Ken, and I sat down and listened to the studio tapes of some of the songs from their next album, *Voodoo Lounge*, we agreed that the Stones sounded better than ever. If we could get them onto Virgin, we'd be able to reinvent them and push them up onto a different level. The best thing about the negative press comment was that it had frightened away some of the other record labels. If we were quick and came up with the right offer, we might have a clear run at them.

Since we had our backs to the wall, we had to be extremely careful. We couldn't let word get out that we were trying to sign the Stones and then fail to raise the finance. Trevor approached a number of the lending banks and finally managed to scrape together the £6 million loan to sign the Stones from Citibank. This loan was repayable the next April. We were living so much from hand to mouth that we didn't care about next April: we felt sure that something would turn up and we'd be able to renegotiate the loan then. The vital thing was to sign the Stones now.

We had a signing ceremony at the private room above Mossiman's restaurant on 20 November, Holly's birthday. As Holly waved Joan and me off, she looked serious for a moment and said:

"Daddy, who are the Rolling Stones? Are they some kind of pop group?"

For a moment I wondered whether I hadn't made a ghastly mistake.

As Joan and I drove there, I remembered that it was almost twenty-five years ago when I had first gone along to interview Mick Jagger in his house on Cheyne Walk. Then I had been a nervous schoolboy and he had been a demigod. A few years later I had ambitiously offered to sign the Rolling Stones and scuttled around Europe trying to raise $4 million. The wheel had now come full circle: Prince Rupert saw Virgin as the best record label for the Stones.

Throughout the dinner I felt rather dazed. Looking around the table at Mick Jagger and Jerry Hall, Keith Richards and Bill Wyman, Charlie Watts and their wives and girlfriends, I tried to enjoy myself but was constantly preoccupied by the impending sale of Virgin Music. I hoped that something would turn up, but without it I would lose control of Virgin Music—or lose it altogether and never have the chance to enjoy releasing the Rolling Stones.

After I had first failed to sign the Stones back in 1975, I had come across them again when they came to record at the Manor. They were there for a week, and I was there one weekend when they were lounging around the sitting room after an all-night session. Keith Richards was still in bed with his girlfriend, a Jamaican girl. There was a crunch of gravel outside and a frenzied knocking at the door. The Stones were all lying around drinking coffee and waking up, so I got up and opened the door.

A tall Jamaican in a purple jacket blocked my way.

"Where is she?" he demanded, giving the name of the girl who was in bed with Keith.

I had assumed that the woman was Keith's girlfriend. It was quickly clear that I was wrong. As I hesitated, he pulled out a gun and pointed it in my face.

"Where is she? You tell me now."

As I looked at the pistol and opened my mouth, out of the corner of my eye I noticed two naked figures tiptoe out of a side door. It was Keith and his girlfriend. They took a quick look at the Jamaican and broke into a spring across the lawn behind him. I admired their speed: Keith's hair flapped up and down his white back as he tore along and hurdled the wooden rail in a great leap. His girlfriend kept up with him, running as if her life depended upon it—which perhaps it did. They both cleared the railings, landed in the field, and sped toward the river.

The Jamaican, realizing that my attention had wavered from his gun, spun around to follow my gaze. He saw the two bare bottoms, one black, the other white, then gave an inarticulate roar of rage and ran to his car. By the time he reached it, Keith and the woman had vanished. He revved up and tore off back down the drive, trying to cut them off. I lost sight of them. Now that I remembered the episode, I wondered how they had escaped.

"Keith?" I leaned across the table at Mossiman's. "How did you and that Jamaican girlfriend of yours escape at the Manor? Do you remember the tall guy with the gun?"

"Yeah," Keith said. "That was her partner. She saw the car coming up the drive and told me to run. He always carried a gun; he was a Yardie or something. She said we just had to get out, we had no time to dress. We ran along the river for miles and finally hid by the riverside and waited for someone to come along.

"The next thing was a punt full of students all wearing these crazy blazers and white floaty dresses. We came out of the bushes and flagged them down. They lent us enough clothes, and we punted down to Oxford in style."

As the meal ended, Mick Jagger and I grinned at each other.

"Look at you two," Bill Wyman said. "I wouldn't fancy being an apple between those two sets of gnashers!"

On the way home, Joan tried to persuade me not to sell Virgin Music. She felt sure that with their next tour the Stones were set to smash all records and argued that we would make more money from having the Stones on the label than we would make on the airline. The dilemma was beginning to tear me apart. With the Rolling Stones and Janet Jackson alongside Phil Collins and Bryan Ferry and all the others, Virgin Music was set to become the world's most exciting record company. If the Stones' next album took off, it would take us with it and we could double our money from the back catalog. I tried to forget the bankers closing in on me and put my mind against selling. I decided to brave it out for as long as possible.

"Richard, you're not gonna believe this about BA," Ronnie Thomas told me.

"Try me," I said. "At this particular moment I'm prepared to believe almost anything."

Ronnie Thomas runs his own limousine company in New York. Twenty years ago he started out as a regular cab driver in Manhattan and slowly saved enough money to trade in his clapped-out yellow cab for a smart limousine, which he offered as a chauffeur-driven service specializing in collecting and dropping off passengers at New York's two airports. By the time I met him in 1986, he had a successful limousine service with over two hundred cars. He had called me as soon as he read that Virgin Atlantic was going to offer a limousine service to all upper-class passengers and pitched for the entire account. He won it, and over the years Ronnie had never let us down. In the last few days he and his drivers were finding that when they dropped passengers off at the curbside, British Airways staff were meeting them and offering them "incentives" to fly British Airways instead of Virgin. Ronnie had had a flaming argument with them and later got a call from British Airways banning him from British Airways' own terminal at JFK.

"Have you ever come across anything like this before?" I asked Ronnie.

"No, man," he said. "I thought that American carriers weren't exactly gentlemen, but this is another ball game altogether."

I had no idea whether this was illegal or not, but it was certainly the most blatant attempt yet to poach our passengers.

After *The Sunday Times* had exposed some of British Airways' tactics, the next paper to follow was *The Guardian* with a front-page headline: "BA Under Fire for Virgin Campaign." *The Guardian* had a full-page analysis of British Airways' tactics entitled "Virgin's Complaint to EC Casts More Doubt on BA's Practices."

As it became clear that British Airways were intent upon seeing the back of us, I knew that I had to fight back even harder. No matter how many accurate press stories were published, British Airways had always been immune to criticism. To the world at large, they shrugged off my allegations as the hysterical overreaction of a man who couldn't take competition. In spite of the articles, the dirty tricks carried on. Their arrogance was overwhelming. In mounting desperation I began to look for any legal action that we could take against British Airways.

"It would amount to an antitrust case in America," Gerrard Tyrrell concluded when we'd finished going through what British Airways was up to. "But there's no equivalent legislation here."

There is a surprising lack of legislation governing competition in the British aviation industry. The Monopolies and Mergers Commission and the Office of Fair Trading had no jurisdiction over British Airways in this instance since they could investigate only an airline merger, and the CAA had little jurisdiction beyond the safety angles involved in servicing the aircraft and supervising the prices of air tickets. Although British Airways was a privatized monopoly like British Telecom, there was no government watchdog like OFTEL to supervise it. We had lodged a complaint with the European Court, but although there were some grounds for this court to rule against British Airways under Article 85 of the Treaty of Rome, which deals with the principles of fair competition, in practice it lacked the teeth to enforce any request it might make for a company to change its business tactics. In effect our list of complaints to the European Court was useful only as a publicity exercise.

I didn't want to take British Airways to court. I knew that it would be expensive and risky, and that they would employ a topflight team of lawyers to try to overwhelm us and the jury with all the weight of statistics that a vast airline can muster. I simply wanted the dirty tricks to stop, and as I cast about for other ways in which to persuade British Airways to call off their campaign, I thought of the nonexecutive directors. Since I had already written to Lord King without success, I thought that the nonexecutive directors of British Airways would be more impartial. If I asked them to investigate what was going on in their company, then in principle they would have to take that request seriously. Nonexecutive company directors have the same legal responsibilities as an executive director, but they typically look after the shareholders' interests if there is a conflict between the directors and the shareholders. As British Airways was now being accused of such behavior, and accused by the press as well as by Virgin Atlantic, the shareholders deserved an explanation of what their company directors were doing.

The British Airways nonexecutive directors comprised Sir Michael Angus (a director of Thorn EMI and formerly chairman of Unilever), Lord White (who ran Hanson Trust with Lord Hanson), the Honorable Charles Price, Sir Francis Kennedy, and Michael Davis. Their names read like a Debrett's of business. The letter took me over a week to compose and set out everything we knew about what British Airways was up to. I eventually signed and sent off an eleven-page document on 11 December 1991 that outlined the facts and concluded:

I have found it hard to believe that a major public company like BA could be behind the sort of conduct identified in this letter whose primary purpose can only be the discrediting of a competitor and the damaging of its business. I am writing to you because I doubt whether you would want a company of which you are a director to conduct itself in such a way and in the hope that the directors of BA would wish to be absolutely and unequivocally disassociated from any such activities because they would agree that it was not the proper way to run a business.

I would like you to investigate the matters raised in this letter, provide detailed responses and give me your assurance that you will ensure that the conduct revealed to you on investigation or any similar conduct is stopped and never again repeated.

I would have thought that British Airways' experience of trying to eliminate the competitive threat posed by Laker Airways was sufficient deterrent against trying to do the same to others. I am sure you remember the impact upon BA of its actions towards Laker Airways. BA's privatisation plans were disrupted, the directors in the United States were threatened with criminal prosecution, there was a huge waste of management time, BA attracted considerable adverse publicity, millions of dollars were spent in legal expenses and BA made the biggest single contribution to the massive legal settlement fund.

I attached an eight-page appendix that covered all details I knew and divided the dirty tricks into six sections: the press campaign; spoiling tactics; engineering matters; sales and marketing; dirty tricks; and private investigators? I put a question mark on the final category because I still found it impossible to believe and wrote: "Bizarre incidents have been taking place recently more suitable for an episode of Dick Tracy than the airline industry." I related the snippets I'd picked up and asked: "Can you shed any light on any of these incidents? I cannot believe that a major public company like British Airways is behind this sort of conduct."

As the letter was sent, I had no idea what reaction to expect. I did not wish to sue British Airways. There was enough to do without having to spend eighteen hours a day fighting British Airways. I was acutely aware that I was having to ignore all the other businesses within the Virgin Group as we fought this battle.

I wondered whether the nonexecutive directors would assume that I couldn't compete with Freddie Laker's court case, which had produced over a million legal documents. Sir Freddie had sued British Airways only after he had gone bust, and he had had time to devote all his energy to the lawsuit.

But by then, of course, British Airways had accomplished their task. The court case may have delayed their privatization and forced them to pay £10 million compensation, but this was nothing compared with the profits they made on the transatlantic route by hiking prices as soon as Laker's planes were grounded. I was trying to stop British Airways while simultaneously running the airline, and BA might not back off until Virgin was grounded too.

Whatever their reaction, I felt sure that the nonexecutive directors could not ignore the eight-page attachment, which detailed their company's dirty tricks. Since they were also responsible to their shareholders, we released copies of this letter to the press to ensure that their shareholders would have the chance to read it too.

To my amazement I received a reply from both Sir Colin Marshall and Sir Michael Angus the very next day. Sir Michael Angus wrote a disclaimer saying that it would be "wholly inappropriate for the non-executive directors of a public company to report to a third party in the manner that you request" and concluded that "the proper course of action is for any such allegation to be directed to the Board as a whole."

Sir Colin Marshall's answer was equally patronizing. He flatly denied that British Airways was attempting to compete "other than through normal marketing and promotional efforts" or was involved in a deliberate attempt to damage Virgin. He suggested that our reason for asking questions about British Airways' activities was simply to gain publicity and that it would be better "to devote [my] undoubted energies to more constructive purposes."

Given the time these two directors had taken to respond to my letter, by definition they could not have begun to investigate any of its contents.

I replied to Sir Colin Marshall on 16 December 1991 and urged him to reconsider his dismissive attitude to my allegations. I did not accuse him of masterminding the dirty tricks or even condoning them but merely asked him to look at the facts without judging his role. I wanted to give him every chance to put a stop to them. "I had always hoped that you personally had no knowledge of the worst that had been going on at British Airways," I wrote. "However having read your response to my letter I'm no longer sure, for your letter continues the lies that we at Virgin have had to contend with. The allegations are certainly not 'unjustified.' In fact many of them are not our allegations but matters that first came to our attention from reports in *The Sunday Times* and *The Guardian.* I notice that you have written to neither paper refuting them. They also came to our attention from Virgin passengers who were shocked that BA could get their home phone numbers and offer them incentives to cancel their firm Virgin tickets and switch to BA. . . . How can you dismiss them out of hand without any enquiry? I ask *you* to take the matters raised seriously and respond to my letter point by point. We can then get on to competing in a fair manner."

But Sir Colin Marshall wrote straight back as if he had barely bothered to read my letter: "I see nothing to be gained from further correspondence."

For a time afterwards it looked as if British Airways' version of events was gaining ground. Sir Colin Marshall was quoted everywhere as saying that my allegations were "utterly without foundation" and although he never said that Marcia Borne or Ronnie Thomas was a figment of my imagination, people outside Virgin could have been forgiven for assuming that there was an element of truth in British Airways' denial.

My allegations against British Airways passed the point of no return. Unless British Airways apologized and put an end to their dirty tricks, I would have to follow up my open letter to the nonexecutive directors with some kind of legal action. The difficulty was finding the appropriate grounds upon which to sue.

The row between us had one immediate casualty that I should have foreseen: Virgin Atlantic was completely unable to raise any money. Salomon, our American investment bank, were trying to raise £20 million of capital by privately offering some of the equity for sale. But in exactly the same way as it had been impossible to sell equity in British Airways while the Laker court case dragged on, so nobody would touch Virgin Atlantic while it looked as if we would go to court aginst British Airways. And we were still losing money. While we had been frantically busy trying to piece together what British Airways were up to, our consortium of lending banks had continued to watch the cash flow. And in the depths of winter the numbers looked much worse.

I suddenly realized that to this extent I'd played straight into British Airways' hands. One of their objectives was to stop me from expanding Virgin Atlantic and the only way I could do so was by refinancing the airline. The louder I complained about their dirty tricks, the less any other airline or venture capital house or investor wanted to invest in Virgin Atlantic. Outsiders probably thought there was no smoke without fire. We lost both ways: nobody wanted to invest in a small airline if it was being squeezed out by a vast organization like British Airways, and nobody wanted to invest in an airline that might embark on lengthy and expensive litigation against one of the world's largest airlines.

Without funds forthcoming from the City, Virgin Atlantic continued to be starved of capital. By Christmas 1991 Virgin Atlantic was plowing through the difficult winter months and losing money. Our six main lending banks continued to write to Trevor, reminding us that our loans were due to be repaid next April, and Lloyds Bank, who were our clearing bank and so saw wide fluctuations as money came in and went out, grew increasingly anxious. Perhaps British Airways gambled that even if we did announce a legal action, they could spin it out long enough that we would go bust in the meantime. Even after my letter of 11 December British Airways were brazen and laughed off my allegations.

For once I did not know what to do. I retreated a little into myself and became very quiet. Will went the opposite way and spent all day in a fury about British Airways, shouting and ranting in his frustration at not being able to land a proper punch on them.

On 21 December 1991 a letter arrived from Lloyds Bank that heightened the sense that we were under siege. It reminded us that we had recently exceeded our £55 million overdraft facility and spelled out that the bank had allowed the excess only because the money had been needed to pay salaries and because IATA had confirmed that £7.5 million was due into the account the following day.

We were told that the bank "might not respond favorably to another request to break the £55 million limit." It finished by wishing us a happy Christmas and a less stressful New Year!

Everyone talks about the importance of cash flow, but if that £7.5 million had been delayed by a week, Lloyds might well have bounced our salary checks. If Virgin Atlantic went bust, I couldn't even be sure that Virgin Music would remain intact. I doubted that Janet Jackson or Phil Collins would be impressed by the airline's collapse.

As we talked about where we could find sufficient funding to replace some of the bank debt, it became increasingly clear that we had to find some radical solution rather than always arguing with banks over small amounts of increased debt. Virgin Music was our only seriously profitable business, and it was our only chance to save the airline. With the weight of bad publicity caused by British Airways hanging over us, we couldn't sell Virgin Atlantic as a going concern, but we could sell Virgin Music as one. Selling Virgin Music would save the airline and leave two strong companies. Closing down Virgin Atlantic would leave one strong company and one bust company with 2,500 redundancies and the Virgin Group's reputation as a company and a brand name in tatters.

I called up John Thornton, who was still talking to several companies that were interested in acquiring Virgin Music. I had continued to watch his progress with a growing sense of foreboding, unable either to feel any enthusiasm for it or to be able to stop it. John told me that Thorn EMI was now offering £425 million up front with an earn-out starting from the second year. This offer was still below the level for which David Geffen had sold his record label to MCA. In March 1990 he had sold his record company for $520 million, which then represented 2.6 times annual sales. On a similar multiple, Virgin Music was worth 2.6 times our sales of £330 million—over £850 million.

Throughout Janaury Lloyds increased their pressure for us to reduce our overdraft. John Hobley from Lloyds toughened his stance considerably. Since we had mentioned the possible sale of Virgin Music a year ago, that was all he wanted to hear about: why wasn't there more progress? Could they talk to Goldman Sachs themselves? From their point of view, if the sale didn't happen, then Virgin Music would remain a collection of music contracts—intangible assets. They couldn't understand why there was such a long delay. Was there something wrong with Virgin Music? Had the bidders walked away? Was the company really worth the $1 billion we had airily mentioned? Their patience was running thin, and they wanted to see their loans to Virgin returned to their vaults as real cash. One of our problems was that a large amount of our debts was due to be repaid in April, and Trevor and I felt doubtful that we could persuade the bank to roll these loans over to a later date.

The bank's correspondence reminded me of some of the letters I had received from Coutts when they were losing their nerve about their client with shoulder-length hair who had padded barefoot into their offices to discuss a loan to buy a manor in Oxfordshire. My hair was now shorter and Virgin was bigger, but the bank remained uneasy. Although we had never failed to make a payment, they had other clients collapsing on them and they were concerned.

The investment atmosphere of early January is summed up by this stock-brokerage report:

> Attention is now focusing on Lonrho's debt mountain and the attitude of its principal lenders Lloyds, Standard Chartered, Barclays and Nat West. Lonrho's director Paul Spicer insists Lonrho's relationships with its bankers are "in good order" and the group "is under no pressure from them." But after the debt debacles at Polly Peck, Brent Walker and Maxwell, there is hardly a banker in London who lives comfortably these

days with large lines of credit to entrepreneurial companies driven by a powerful individual. Rightly or not, Rowland is being squeezed by "the tycoon factor"; and his position is made worse by the recession, which had slashed the value of Lonrho's assets at a time when the company must sell businesses to raise cash. The old maestro has escaped from tight corners before, and nobody can say that he will not do so again. This time however the pressure is really on.

The ingredients of the story looked ominously similar to ours.

As Lloyd's saw their money at risk to an entrepreneurial company, John Hobley made one more effort to control our overdraft. In a letter dated 3 January John pointed out that our overdraft had continued to rise. He reminded us that Lloyds expected the overdraft to be paid off in full by the end of the month and that in the meantime they would not allow us to exceed our limit again. Lloyds were surprised, John said, that we had even considered the idea of holding on to Virgin Music in the hope of getting a better deal than the offer that Thorn EMI had put on the table.

This situation was as bad as the Coutts crisis in 1984. Even then we had had time, and we had been able to see some other banks to form a syndicate. But January 1992 was as bad a month for bankers and airlines as January 1991, when Air Europe and Dan Air had gone under, had been. All the bankers were in a tailspin, and it was difficult to remain calm.

We owed £55 million to Lloyds. As we headed into January, February, and March, the airline would need cash funding of a further £30 million. The winter months are the most expensive, since we have to pay for all the major aircraft maintenance in the same months as the number of passengers drop off. So much for the unsecured debt.

Looking at the cash coming in, we knew that Virgin Music had sales of £330 million this year, making operating profits of £38 million; next year we were forecasting sales of £400 million with operating profits of £75 million. But Lloyds were not willing to wait. I could see that something had to give.

A second Thames Television program about the battle between British Airways and Virgin Atlantic was scheduled for broadcast at the end of February. Will and I had first met the producer, Martyn Gregory, at the beginning of January, when he had come to see us about the documentary. We had told him as much as we could about British Airways and then left him to carry out his own independent research. Martyn had spoken to Peter Fleming, along with various other ex–British Airways staff whom we had not come across, and had managed to verify all my accusations of British Airways' dirty tricks. British Airways refused to participate in the program, and their legal director, Mervyn Walker, wrote to Martyn Gregory and accused him of falling "into the trap of being used as a vehicle for Richard Branson's propaganda." Nothing could have been guaranteed to infuriate an independent television producer more.

I was in two minds about the program. I could see that by showing people all the dirty tricks we were up against, they might have two responses: they would be able to see our vulnerability and thus might back away from Virgin Atlantic as a likely loser. Just the very words "A plane will fall out of the sky," even spoken by Brian Basham, who was working for British Airways, might remain in people's minds and worry them about flying Virgin Atlantic. But equally the public also might rally around and support us as the underdog. This was my main hope. Gerrard Tyrrell also pointed out that since the television audience is so wide, it might jolt some people's memories and prompt them to telephone Virgin Atlantic and tell other stories that would help us as we compiled all our evidence against British Airways. I organized thirty salespeople to sit at the switchboard at our sales office in Crawley on Thursday, 27 February, in case anyone telephoned us.

The *This Week* film "Violating Virgin?" opened with a bird's-eye view of mothballed planes lined up in the Mojave Desert, the equivalent of an airplane morgue where the planes are parked in the dry air, which will not rust them. They are drained of their oil, stripped of some of their parts, and then their engines and valves are sealed with silver foil. Over this haunting picture came the narrator's voice:

"Virgin Airways is crying 'Rape!' and Richard Branson claims that British Airways is putting him out of business."

"There's fair competition and unfair competition," I said to the interviewer. "And I can't believe that British Airways is resorting to these dirty tricks."

The documentary interviewed Peter Fleming with his identity completely concealed and with his voice distorted as he described the special unit British Airways had set up to discredit me and the mass document shredding that had taken place. A second similarly concealed American witness described how British Airways had shredded documents relating to Virgin in the United States. In New York, Ronnie Thomas told the story of British Airways buttonholing Virgin passengers as they were dropped off by his limousines, and a Los Angeles travel agent described how passengers were switching to British Airways since they had heard that Virgin was about to go bust. Then, with subtitles to spell out what he was saying, we heard Brian Basham telling Chris Hutchins that Virgin was a "dicky business—just dicky." There was Nick Rufford's telephone recording of Brian Basham telling him that Virgin was having to pay cash for its fuel. Sir Freddie Laker repeated his advice to sue the bastards.

Thames TV interviewed me standing next to one of the Tristars in the Mojave Desert. I was dwarfed by a line of over twenty Pan Am planes spanning almost a mile. I stood underneath one of seven marooned British Airways planes. It was odd to think that my entire fleet was only eight aircraft.

"I know a lot of these stories come from Brian Basham, who's employed by British Airways, and Brian Basham reports to a man called David Burnside, who is the head PR person at British Airways who then reports to Lord King," I said. "I've never sued anyone in court for anything. We've probably got a good case to say that someone's tried to damage our business, but you know it takes hours of management time. I think our best bet is to get it out into the open, and hopefully there'll be people at BA who'll realize it's counterproductive and that they should not carry on in the future behaving in this kind of way."

British Airways staff were doorstepped by *This Week*. Dick Eberhart, one of British Airways' vice presidents, was confronted in New York, and David Burnside was confronted outside his home in Chelsea. Both men refused to answer any questions. The final shots of the documentary were aerial views of the dead airplanes stretching across the desert, gleaming impotently in the California sunshine, just where British Airways would like to see the Virgin fleet.

"Perhaps it's time for Richard Branson to put up or shut up," said the final voice-over. "Or Virgin Atlantic's planes could end up like Laker's: in the desert sand."

"Violating Virgin?" was seen by over seven million viewers, and that evening the Virgin switchboard received over four hundred calls. Most of the callers just wished us well and said that they would never fly British Airways again, but among all the well-wishers many people said that they too had stories to tell of being approached by British Airways at the airport as they tried to check in to Virgin. And then we hit the jackpot.

A couple of weeks before she watched "Violating Virgin?" Yvonne Parsons had decided never to fly Virgin again. On 6 February she was at home when someone from Virgin's reservations department called her to say that her flight was overbooked. Since she hadn't been issued a ticket, would she mind changing to a British Airways flight? This was the last straw. Yvonne Parsons had flown to and from the States four times in the last eight months, and each time there had been a "booking error" with Virgin. The previous October Parsons had been called in her New York office by a Virgin representative, who gave her name as "Mary Ann" and told her that her Virgin flight on the sixteenth was overbooked, and to compensate for the inconvenience she could fly—at no extra cost—the following day on Concorde. Parsons refused. She flew to and from New York and London regularly, and she preferred Virgin—once she got onto the plane. She was a valuable customer, and she was rather surprised that Virgin was being so casual about her. She asked to be wait-listed for her flight and asked Mary Ann to call her the next day to let her know whether she was on or not.

As with "Bonnie" from Virgin in August, who had told her that the flight was delayed, and "Larry" from Virgin in September, who had said that all nonsmoking seats were full, Mary Ann failed to call Yvonne Parsons back. So Parsons called up Virgin reservations and asked to speak to Mary Ann.

"There's no Mary Ann here," she was told.

"Then who called me yesterday and said that I was bounced off the 16 October flight?" Parsons asked. ·

"The 16 October? No, you're confirmed on that flight, nonsmoking."

Yvonne Parsons was baffled. She was also furious with Virgin and switched to American Airlines and United for her flights for the rest of the year. When she decided to give Virgin one last try in February, she couldn't believe it when another Virgin reservations staff called her to tell her that the flight was overbooked and would she mind flying British Airways?

Then she watched "Violating Virgin?" The next day she called up Virgin and was put through to our lawyers, where she told her story to Gerrard.

"As I watched the program," she told him, "it suddenly dawned on me that I must have been the victim of an elaborate and disgraceful deception by British Airways. I'd always been offered flights on British Airways, never on other airlines. I wondered whether these people were British Airways staff impersonating Virgin."

"We've got an amazing statement," Gerrard told me after taking down this story. "We could build a court case around her alone."

To drive the point home, I wrote to Sir Colin Marshall on 28 February 1992, the day after "Violating Virgin?" and asked him to reconsider my letter to the nonexecutive directors of 11 December 1991. I pointed out that "given the haste of your reply, I take it that you did not have sufficient time within which to investigate the matter. There have been numerous further independent reports in the media on this subject which have all supported the complaints that Virgin have made culminating in the broadcast on ITV last night of the *This Week* television documentary. *This Week* have independently uncovered many more facts which go to prove that our allegations are totally correct. The content of the programme speaks for itself and in fact confirmed that the problem is even more serious and deep rooted than we originally thought. The least your shareholders can now expect is a full and proper explanation as to what exactly has been going on within British Airways and of the activities of Mr Brian Basham and those to whom he reports at British Airways."

I asked him directly whether he would now intervene:

"I should now like from you in your role as Deputy Chairman and Chief Executive of British Airways a clear assurance that you will make certain that the activities that have been highlighted will immediately cease and that you will give a clear apology."

Well, I thought, *it wasn't too late—just. But he'd better make sure that his apology was a good one.*

I was up in Kidlington on Friday when the call came through.

"Richard," Will said, "I'm in a call box. I've just landed at Gatwick, and I've picked up a copy of *BA News*. The front-page headline says: 'Branson "Dirty Tricks" Claim Unfounded.' They're calling you a liar."

Will had been on a skiing holiday when the program was broadcast. The dates of both the program and his skiing holiday had been changed several times so that they wouldn't coincide, but as luck would have it they still did. Since so many people were calling us, I had asked Will to come back to manage the PR storm that was brewing. In response he had just landed at Gatwick. The *BA News* article went on to say: "Thames TV's current affairs programme 'This Week' last night devoted its programme to Richard Branson's allegations of 'dirty tricks' by British Airways against Virgin. British Airways was invited to take part but declined after careful consideration for reasons explained to Thames' producer Martyn Gregory in full in a letter from Mervyn Walker, Legal Director."

The rest of the article reproduced the letter from Mervyn Walker, which accused Thames TV of falling into my trap of publicity and said that British Airways would not be "provoked into playing Mr Branson's futile game and must therefore decline to take part."

"What a load of bollocks!" we said together. "They're calling me a liar, and this is libel."

It was the last straw. Will faxed me the article from Holland Park. We tracked down Gerrard, who immediately agreed that they had libeled me. Suing British Airways for libel would be a far easier case to bring to court and make clear to a jury than a highly complicated case about British Airways abusing its monopolistic position at Heathrow. It would also push everything out into the open.

On Monday morning I discovered that Lord King had written personal letters to viewers who had written in to question him about British Airways' dirty tricks and assured them that there was no truth whatsoever in my allegations. In effect it was the same libel repeated and, once again, to members of the public. I decided that I should sue Lord King as well.

That morning I also received a letter from Sir Colin Marshall. He called my accusations "unjustified," said he had nothing to add to his previous letters to me, and asserted that the idea of a "dirty tricks" campaign was "wholly without foundation."

I stared with amazement at the letter. Perhaps Sir Colin Marshall had been unable to watch "Violating Virgin?" Perhaps he had been stuck in a traffic jam or on board a delayed flight. Perhaps he remained blithely unaware of what was going on in his company. It seemed very odd: by reputation Sir Colin Marshall was a workaholic, a man who was obsessed with detail, who knew every single thing that went on in any of the companies where he worked.

The next week the sale of Virgin Music finally overtook me.

Chapter 28

"Freddie . . . I've decided to take your advice: I'm suing the
bastards."

March 1992–January 1993

On the table was £560 million—$1 billion—but I
didn't want it.

"They need to know by two this afternoon,"
John Thornton told me. I rang off and looked across
at Simon and Ken. We had spent the last twenty years building up the company, but nothing had prepared us for selling it.

In many ways the signing of the Rolling Stones was the culmination of
everything I had ever wanted to do at Virgin Music. We had been fighting to
sign them for twenty years, and now at last we had the greatest rock-and-roll
band in the world on our label. From being a start-up label back in 1973,
which had relied upon the genius of Mike Oldfield, we had now come of age
where we were the label of choice for many of the world's biggest bands.
Artists had seen how we had launched Phil Collins' solo career, how we had
promoted UB40 and Simple Minds, what we had been able to do with Culture Club and Peter Gabriel, and they wanted to sign with us. But just as we
reached this height, it was over.

"Ken?" I asked.

"It's your call," he said.

"Simon?"

"Take the cash. You've got no option."

Whenever anyone tells me that I've got no option, I try to prove them
wrong. Over the last few days Thorn EMI's offer had changed from an all-
share offer—which would have left me as the largest shareholder in Thorn
EMI with 14 percent—or a lower cash alternative, to a higher cash offer.
Even though Thorn had now switched tactics and was offering more cash
than shares, I was more attracted to the share exchange since it would mean

that I would have kept a stake in Thorn EMI that I might use in the future as the basis to bid for the company. The difficulty was that everyone told me that it would be too risky to use this stake as security to borrow any more money to support Virgin Atlantic. Shares in Thorn EMI were not seen as a cast-iron security. Although I had already drafted a letter to the staff explaining that I was going to take up Thorn EMI shares and so keep an interest in the company, I reluctantly had to change my mind and go for the cash offer.

Before finally agreeing, I called up Peter Gabriel and broke the news to him. I wanted his advice, and I was also aware that the sale would affect his career.

"Don't do it, Richard," he said. "You'll wake up one night in a cold sweat and wish that you'd never done it. You'll never get it back again."

I knew that he was right. It was exactly what Joan had been saying. But the pressure from British Airways was too much. By now I felt so sure that Lloyds was going to foreclose on us that I had no alternative. I was also aware that Simon wanted to sell and that he wanted to take cash rather than prolong his involvement with the group by taking shares. If taking shares in Thorn EMI would prolong the agony at Virgin Atlantic, then it would defeat the whole point of the exercise. My overriding objective was to save Virgin Atlantic from going under. And, cruelly, the only reason why I was selling Virgin Music was because it was so successful. If I sold Virgin Music, the Virgin name would be saved. Rather than having one struggling airline and a record company, there would be a secure airline and a secure record company, albeit owned by Thorn EMI. And although I knew that Simon would leave it, I could stay on as president of the company and—most important— Ken was going to remain in charge of Virgin within Thorn, and he would safeguard the Virgin reputation.

I called up Trevor, who confirmed the banks' line:

"Cash is the only choice," he told me. "It means that we can pay back all the debt and start afresh. It'll give you complete freedom. And when thinking about Thorn shares, remember what happened in the stock market crash."

That made up my mind. If I took Thorn shares and they fell dramatically in value, I could be powerless to stop the bank moving in. Sir Freddie Laker had reminded me how it happens so fast that it takes your breath away. Rather like Virgin, his airline had fought a long battle against British Airways, and just when he needed their support the banks pulled in their loans. Invited in to see the banks, he was expecting them to agree to a small increase in his overdraft on the back of an expected boom the following year, but when he arrived he was shown into a side room. Nobody came to see him for thirty minutes. Finally he managed to get hold of the bank director, who then invited him up to another room. One look at their faces as he walked in made him realize that something terrible had happened.

"We've put Laker Airways into receivership," they told him.

It was all over. There was nothing Sir Freddie could do to prevent the receivers from sacking all the staff, changing the locks on the buildings, confiscating all company property, leaving passengers stranded, and handing the planes back. The Laker check-in desks at Gatwick vanished overnight, and the sales desk stopped taking bookings. The telephones were unplugged, and a lifetime's work disappeared in six hours. It was Sir Freddie's experience that more than anything else made me hold back from pushing the banks too far. Once I let them take control, Virgin Atlantic would be finished. To know that $1 billion had once been on the table would be scant consolation.

Obstinate as I am, I recognized that there is a time to back down. "Live for the present"—I heard my parents' advice in the back of my head—"and the future will look after itself." And my instinct for continued involvement with Virgin and the upside by taking Thorn EMI shares was tempered by the need for financial security. John Thornton, who was advocating that I should take the shares, did not know the whole picture; nor did Peter Gabriel, who was arguing that I shouldn't do it at all. And so, pushing Virgin Music into the past tense, I picked up the phone and called John Thornton at Goldman Sachs.

"I'll take the cash," I heard myself say. "I'll leave the rest to you."

"Fine," he said. "The lawyers are on their last round now. I'll call you when it's time to come over."

Although I had saved the airline, I felt that I had killed something inside me. Looking at Simon and Ken, I was saddened that we would each go in separate directions. In some ways I was happiest for Ken: he was going to stay with Virgin within EMI and would soon be releasing Janet Jackson and the Rolling Stones. I had no idea what Simon would do, but I suspected that he would enjoy a quieter life. I knew that as soon as Virgin Music had gone, I would have to come out of the corner and slug it out with British Airways. I'd already lost count of the rounds we had fought and was beginning to feel punch-drunk and exhausted.

We had to wait until the middle of the night to sign contracts since Fujisankei, our 25 percent holder, had a preemptive clause that allowed them to match any offer for Virgin Music. We also had to decide whether to accept Thorn EMI's offer of £510 million in cash and taking on debts fixed at £50 million; or £500 million in cash and whatever debts were in the company at the date of completion in four weeks' time. Although we had to continue to run Virgin Music in the normal manner, Ken felt sure that by completion the debt would be smaller.

"There's some good sales going on at the moment," he said. "Let's take all the money now."

And so we opted for £510 million and £50 million of debt in Virgin Music. In the event Ken was right (as always!) and we earned an extra £10 million by choosing this option. In the meantime we had to wait until 3 A.M. before Fujisankei finally threw in their lot with us and opted for Thorn EMI's cash. We signed contracts as dawn was breaking. The next morning Thorn EMI announced the purchase of Virgin Music for exactly $1 billion—or £560 million.

Simon, Ken, and I went to see the staff at our Harrow Road offices.

"It's like the death of a parent," Simon said to me as we went inside. "You think that you've prepared for it, but when it happens you realize that you're totally unable to cope."

I felt that it was more like the death of a child. Simon, Ken, and I had started Virgin from scratch, kept it going through all the times when it looked as if it was coming to an end, and reinvented it with every generation of music so that it continued to be the most exciting record label in the business. While other record labels such as Apple still symbolized the Beatles and Abbey Road, Virgin had leapfrogged from Mike Oldfield and Gong to the Sex Pistols, then Boy George, then Bryan Ferry, then Janet Jackson and the Rolling Stones. Throughout each era—hippie, punk, new wave—Simon's taste had prevailed and Ken had kept everything together

Ken now stood up and told everyone that they would become part of Thorn EMI and that he would be staying with EMI to ensure Virgin's independence. Simon started to speak but instead burst into tears. Everyone looked at me. I stood up, on the edge of tears myself, but it was no good. I was in an impossible situation. I couldn't tell them the real reason why their company had been sold. If I told them the truth about the banks' attitude to Virgin Atlantic, then the airline and the rest of the Virgin companies would be damaged by lack of confidence. Airlines are all built upon confidence, and an admission of weakness would scare away passengers. And so, hating myself for appearing to just have cashed in, I stood there and offered anyone a job at Virgin Atlantic if they were unhappy with EMI and assured everyone that Ken would look after them. When Jon Webster proposed a vote of thanks to me, Simon, and Ken for "the best years of our lives," I could bear it no longer. I took two steps out of the room and set off at a sprint up Ladbroke Grove, tears streaming down my face.

Oblivious to the stares of passersby, I must have run for almost a mile. When I passed the newspaper stand, I saw an *Evening Standard* poster that should have dried the tears of most grown men: "Branson Sells for £560 Million Cash." I ran past it, tears still streaming down my face, and somehow made my way home. Joan was out, and so I went into the kitchen and put on the kettle. It was a cold March morning, but the cherry trees at the end of the garden and in Holland Park were just beginning to blossom. As I stared outside, a fox broke cover from the hedge and trotted across to the back door, where Joan left out scraps for it. It picked up a chicken carcass and then turned on its heel and vanished into the undergrowth. The last photograph I had seen of Lord King had shown him on horseback, resplendent in full hunting gear.

"Feeling thoroughly depressed," I wrote in my notebook about my decision to go for cash rather than shares. "Decided to go for the conservative route for the first time in my life. All my advisers (bar John Thornton) were advocating it."

As well as picking up an extra £10 million by choosing the fixed debt option, Trevor also gained us another £9 million profit over the currency transfer to Fujisankei. Thorn EMI paid us the £510 million in cash, of which we had to pay £127.5 million to Fujisankei. Fujisankei wanted their money in yen, so we had to change it. We had a month's grace between taking the money and passing it on at completion on 1 June. We had to choose when to switch into yen. Simon and Ken wanted to do it immediately so that we all knew where we stood. Trevor and I were a little more relaxed and inclined to gamble with it. We kept it in sterling, and as luck would have it, sterling appreciated against the yen. We let it run and changed it at the last moment, earning ourselves a further £9 million profit. Nothing like a bit of luck!

And so the present crisis was resolved. From the original cash purchase price of £510 million, Fujisankei received £127.5 million and we received more than £390 million. Simon and Ken took their share of the proceeds and went their separate ways. I used my proceeds to repay the bank, and I invested the remaining cash in Virgin Atlantic. Rumors about Virgin Atlantic having to pay for fuel in cash were now well and truly scotched. We had more disposable cash than British Airways.

The banks immediately started calling me with renewed impatience—no longer to demand their money back since we had returned their debt to them but to offer to put my funds in high-interest deposit accounts or offshore accounts; to invest it; to invite me for lunch; to do some kind of business with me; and, of course without seeing the irony, offering to lend me as much money as I wanted to finance any future deals.

It took a while for me to understand the implications of the sale. For the first time in my life, I had enough money to fulfill my wildest dreams. In the immediate future I had no time to dwell on this, because that very week the British Airways story took a turn that occupied all my attention. In some ways I was pleased that I didn't have time to think about the sale of Virgin Music. I hate living in the past. I particularly didn't want to think about all the lost friendships. But the weight had been lifted from my shoulders, and at the back of my mind I was aware that the Virgin Group was now free to develop in whichever direction we chose. Virgin Music may have gone, Ken and Simon and I had split up, but the best was yet to come.

Friday, 13 March 1992

"Richard, I've just received a rather extraordinary tape," Chris Moss, Virgin Atlantic's marketing director, said. "I got it yesterday, just a tape in a brown envelope. I thought it was some crank sending in a music demo, so I didn't get around to playing it until now."

"What is it?"

"It's of two men talking, and I think one of them's Colin Marshall."

"What are they saying?"

"They're talking about the "Violating Virgin?" program, and they mention Chris Hutchins and the Basham tape. And one of them says that there's a clear case for defamation, and he's very close to instituting proceedings against the program."

I asked Chris to send the tape to me. It was already late on Friday evening, and we were due to go to the country. In the morning we were planning to attend a lunch party with Tony Smith, manager of Genesis. I wondered who on earth could have sent the tape to us. Somebody was apparently bugging British Airways' phones and then sending the tape to Virgin. At first I was lulled into thinking that somebody was being helpful. As we drove up to Kidlington, I realized that it was like being sent stolen goods: it could well be a trap of some kind. I decided to send it straight back to British Airways for the personal attention of Sir Colin Marshall.

Saturday, 14 March 1992

We were just leaving for the lunch party on Saturday morning when the phone rang.

"Hurry up," Joan said to Holly and Sam. "We're getting into the car right now. Richard, it's Frank Kane for you. Don't be too long."

"I gather that you've employed private detectives to investigate British Airways," Frank Kane opened the conversation. "I've also got proof that you're phone tapping, and my sources, who are inside Virgin, have told me that Tiny Rowland is egging you on and that he is also employing Freddie Laker."

"Don't be ridiculous, Frank," I said. "That's complete bollocks."

"I've been told that the detective agency you're using is the American operation IGI and that Goldman Sachs have also been involved."

"Frank, I've never issued a writ against a newspaper, but if you really think that you can publish that, then I'll have to sue you."

I rarely lose my temper with journalists, but I felt utterly helpless with Frank Kane. I knew that he was in danger of publishing some mad story that would damage our reputation. If he wrote that we were employing private detectives, then everyone would assume that Virgin was as bad as British Airways. I had been about to tell him of the extraordinary anonymous tape that had been sent to Virgin, but something stopped me. If I even admitted possession of it to Frank Kane, he would be able to run an untrue story that would be impossible to refute. He could describe Sir Colin Marshall as the victim of a phone-tapping operation, and nobody would believe that anyone other than a phone tapper working for Virgin would supply me with a tape. Who else would? An indignant Sir Colin Marshall could comment about how alarmed he was that Richard Branson had got hold of this tape; he would ask the police to interview me, and all the inferences would be against me.

"I can't talk to you now," I said, seeing Joan waving me off the phone. "I'll call you later."

We drove to Tony Smith's, but I could hardly concentrate on the road ahead. I pictured the tape waiting for me at Holland Park, sitting in its envelope like a time bomb. Whoever had sent it had then alerted the *Sunday Telegraph*. It was deeply sinister and very clever. I was just relieved that I had not received it myself.

Tony lived in a lovely Georgian house with a large front lawn, which ran down to a lake. Mike Rutherford and Phil and Jill Collins were there with their children, and as we got out of the car the children all ran to play by the lake. Everyone wanted to congratulate me on the sale of Virgin Music, and Tony, Phil, and Mike were actually very sympathetic. They understood better than anyone else how torn I had been. I was touched by their concern for me.

"I'm sorry," I said after a while. "I have to make a couple of phone calls. There's some journalist about to accuse Virgin of using a detective agency against BA."

Tony lent me a mobile phone. Taking it to the car, I called up the *Sunday Telegraph* and was put through to Trevor Grove, the editor.

"This is a mad story," I said. "You can't possibly publish it."

I knew that Frank Kane was in the office with him because there was a pause before he answered.

"Frank tells me that he's got impeccable sources for this story," Grove told me.

"Well, as I told Frank Kane, if you publish it, I'll have no choice but to sue you for defamation."

"I'll ask Frank to go back and check the sources," Grove told me.

I called up Jonathan Thornton, whom Frank Kane had mentioned.

"I'm pleased you called," John said. "I've just had a journalist from the *Sunday Telegraph* called Maggie Pagano call me. She wanted to know if it was true that you'd employed private detectives on BA."

"What did you say?"

"I said that it didn't sound like your style. I said that I'd been speaking to you every day for three months over the sale of Virgin Music and that I also knew Terry Lenzer, the head of IGI very well, and that it was very unlikely that neither of you would have mentioned it to me. She then said that BA had told her that you were up to it. I said that in that case they'd better produce the evidence."

I looked through the car windscreen and saw Tony and Phil Collins go off for a game of tennis. They had obviously wanted me to make up a foursome with Mike but recognized that now was not the time to interrupt. My reputation and case against British Airways were about to be blown out of the water. For me, this became the defining moment of the entire British Airways campaign against us.

I called up Gerrard Tyrrell and wondered whether we should take out an injunction on the *Sunday Telegraph*.

"Do you have a tape?" he asked.

"It's either at Holland Park or we have already sent it to Sir Colin Marshall, although I haven't heard it myself."

"Well, they could ascertain that in court," Gerrard said. "I think the best thing is to threaten to sue and see how they stack up the story. We'll have a better idea later this afternoon. We're skating on very thin ice here. This is very, very dangerous."

The entire lunch party was ruined for me. For the first time in the British Airways campaign, I had been caught wrong-footed. I should have insisted to Chris Moss that he send the tape straight back to British Airways without even transcribing it. But my curiosity had got the better of me, and I had fallen into a trap. I had the tape in my possession and was guilty by implication. I should have known better. Whoever had sent the tape in had known that it would be human instinct to want to listen to it.

As the afternoon wore on and I constantly fretted, I received the first signs that the *Sunday Telegraph* was backing down. I could not quite be sure if they knew for certain that I had the tape. The *Sunday Telegraph* never told me what proof they had that I was using detectives to bug British Airway's phones, but the story seemed to totter a little bit. Had I volunteered the information that I had the tape—and it had been on the tip of my tongue—I would have been crucified, even if it was "the other side" who had set the whole thing up. As I repeatedly asked Trevor Grove what proof he had and Gerrard Tyrrell sent in faxes promising that we would sue if the story was published without proper evidence, I sensed that we were grinding Trevor Grove down. Hopefully a sense of fair play and honorable behavior would stop them running the story.

We left the lunch party, and I gave Tony Smith a hug. Although everyone seemed to have enjoyed themselves, I felt that I'd been about as entertaining as Banquo's ghost. They'd been expecting to celebrate with me and also to chat about their next albums and how Virgin under Thorn EMI would produce them, but I'd been stuck to the phone all afternoon.

Sunday, 15 March 1992

"Too Old to Rock 'n' Roll, Too Young to Fly" was the opening line of the *Sunday Telegraph* business editorial. I absorbed the entire piece in one panicked look. There was no mention of detectives or phone tapping. I reread the article, feeling almost light-headed.

"But is Branson for real?" they wrote. "If he was willing to settle his action with an apology and a Basham firing he must be 'too young to fly.' A settlement on those terms would imply BA *had* misbehaved and it would leave it wide open to future anti-trust attack. If Branson did believe BA had been anti-competitive he should not have settled for an apology. It's like allowing me to mug his mother-in-law then offering not to report the matter if I say sorry."

I noticed another nice line in the article:

"Kane spoke to Brian Basham, the BA publicity consultant Branson wanted fired as part of a settlement with BA. Basham provided Kane with information but stressed the strengths as well as the weaknesses of Virgin. There was not a whiff of dirty tricks, just standard commercial lobbying. It happens all the time, particularly in bid."

Monday, 16 March 1992

On Monday morning I immediately wrote to Colin Marshall, enclosing the tape recording:

"Last Thursday, even while talks were taking place, a tape was sent anonymously to Virgin Atlantic. It contains a recording of a private conversation between yourself and Robert Ayling about Virgin Atlantic and other matters."

I told him how the *Sunday Telegraph* had called me up with a view to publishing a story about Virgin employing private detectives.

"I don't know who within British Airways is continuing to supply misinformation about us, but please can we have this stopped once and for all. Someone seems to be playing some mighty dangerous games."

Later that afternoon Joan Thirkettle from ITN called me: "I tried to get Lord King onto television to debate the dirty tricks with you," she said.

"Did he agree?" I asked.

"No, he said that he didn't debate with losers."

I'd had enough.

Tuesday, 17 March 1992

I wrote to Lord King and told him that his assertion in his letters back to viewers of "Violating Virgin?" was totally untrue. I pointed out that it was seriously damaging and deeply insulting to both Virgin Atlantic Airways and myself. I also set a deadline: "By this letter I am asking that, no later than close of business on Wednesday 18th March, both you and British Airways formally withdraw the assertion that I have said things which are untrue for the purpose of obtaining publicity and apologise to Virgin Atlantic Airways and myself for having made such an assertion."

Wednesday, 18 March 1992

I hardly bothered to wait for an answer on Wednesday. I knew that Lord King would never apologize. Indeed, even if he lost a libel action I didn't expect an apology. I sat at home in a mounting fog of panic and despair. I was going to have to put my reputation in the hands of the law. We were certain to win, I felt sure, but the law courts are rarely reliable but usually funny places. If I lost, then Virgin Atlantic would probably lose so much credibility that it would have to fold. No matter what "Violating Virgin?" had concluded, no matter what evidence Ronnie Thomas or Peter Fleming or Yvonne Parsons gave, if I lost the court case my reputation would be in shreds and everyone would turn against Virgin Atlantic. British Airways would be able to make a mockery of us, and the press would be along to finish us off. And down the drain with the airline, I would flush away my chances of anything else I wanted to do. Although I felt supremely confident that we would win, the stakes were high enough to give us a sense of vertigo.

By six o'clock on Wednesday I had not heard anything from British Airways. I checked the fax machine one last time. I even stooped down and ran my hand underneath the desk in case a fax had come in and been blown underneath, but there was nothing there.

"Penni," I said, "please, can you give me Freddie Laker's number in Miami?"

I dialed the number.

"Freddie," I said, "it's Richard here. I've decided to take your advice: I'm suing the bastards."

"Go for it!" said Freddie.

As we embarked up the court case, the single thing I had to keep reminding myself was that this was a libel case, not an argument over business practices. I had to clear my name.

Marshaling the evidence happened in three stages: we had all our own evidence that we already knew; we received a vast collection of documents from British Airways under the rules of legal disclosure; and a great deal of evidence began to materialize from disillusioned British Airways staff. This last evidence was the most powerful.

Out of the blue Gerrard received a call from an ex–British Airways employee called Sadig Khalifa, who had worked in the airline industry since 1974, when he had been employed by British Caledonian in Tripoli. When

British Airways took over British Caledonian in 1988, Khalifa joined a division within British Airways called Special Services, which dealt with any special passenger problems. In 1989 he started work as a check-in agent at Gatwick Airport and then joined the helpline section, which was ostensibly there to meet British Airways passengers, to help them transfer between flights, and to look after elderly people. Another more clandestine activity was to try to poach other airlines' passengers. There was an equivalent team at Heathrow nicknamed the "Hunters."

In April 1990 the helpline team was taken over by sales and reservations, and the new boss, Jeff Day, came into the helpline office and announced to Khalifa and his team of fifteen staff that "money doesn't come from helping old ladies to the gate. What you have to do is get out and get more passengers from other airlines." Khalifa told Gerrard about a second meeting in August that Jeff Day specified had to be a "closed meeting" that no other British Airways staff could attend or were to hear about. At this meeting, Jeff Day told Khalifa and his colleagues that the helpline had a new task: to accumulate as much information about Virgin Atlantic as possible. This included flight information, the numbers of passengers booked on flights, the actual number of passengers who went on board the aircraft, the mix between upper class and economy, and the time of departure. At the end of each shift the helpliners had to fill out a form on each flight and personally give it to a Mrs. Sutton, who gave it to Day. And how were they to get the information? Jeff Day told the helpliners that they could get it by tapping into their computer terminals in the helpline office and using the Virgin flight numbers to gain direct access to the British Airways Booking System, known in the trade as BABS, which they had assured Virgin that they wouldn't do. The locks on their room were changed, and they were to keep the nature of their activities secret. One woman working alongside Khalifa refused to join in these activities since she thought that they were immoral, and the rest of the team covered for her.

Gerrard took down a statement from Khalifa, and we sent it across to British Airways. It was set to become one of the main planks of the court case.

Immediately after Khalifa's affidavit arrived at British Airways' lawyers, I received a call from Michael Davis, a British Airways nonexecutive director who was a long-standing friend of my parents. He asked me whether we could meet for breakfast.

At our meeting, Michael began talking about "egg on face." This was the first hint of apology. He had obviously been singled out as the one nonexecutive who could talk to me. Lord King and Sir Colin Marshall were still clearly unwilling to bring themselves down to my level and acknowledge that there was any truth in my accusations, but Michael Davis—as a family friend—had been designated the person who could best finesse the difficult idea that British Airways might have made some mistakes.

"I think the three of us should have a little chat," Michael said. "A little chat. The three of us—you, me, and Sir Colin."

"Sir Colin?"

"Yes, he's going to be around for the next ten years, you see. You see, the king is dead, long live the marshal. I think it would be a sensible thing to do to meet up, the three of us, and see if anything sensible can come out of it."

I watched Michael Davis grope for the appropriate words. Reading between the lines, he was telling me that Lord King's days at British Airways were over.

"You see, certain people at British Airways recognize that there's been a certain amount of egg on face," he confessed. "There has been an acceptance of that egg, but if we're going to have a sensible relationship in the future I think you, me, and Sir Colin should sit down together."

As I listened to his tortured syntax and his attempt to offer me a deal, I realized that I was listening to somebody talking about somebody else's money and somebody else's livelihood. Michael Davis, Sir Colin Marshall, Robert Ayling, and Lord King would receive their salaries no matter what they had initiated at British Airways. The British Airways shareholders would stump up money to pay for Brian Basham, to pay for the detectives, and to pay for their lawyers when I sued them. Perhaps it was a good investment: if they had managed to put Virgin Atlantic out of business, it would have been money very well spent. But Virgin Atlantic was primarily my own company. It was a private company, and if British Airways poached an upper-class passenger to New York, that was £3,000 that Virgin would lose: £3,000 that we couldn't reinvest in the business. And unlike British Airways I had no vast corporate reserves that I could draw upon to fund salaries. So for all his talk of "egg on face" Michael Davis was missing the point: British Airways had tried very hard to put me out of business and my staff out of their jobs. They had also forced me to sell Virgin Music, which had affected a whole group of other people who had nothing to do with the airline. It made me furious. I was not going to sit back over a gentleman's breakfast and agree that it was all just a certain amount of "egg on face."

Throughout the entire dirty-tricks episode I had always been accused of being "naive"—naive to believe that British Airways could behave in such a manner, naive to think that British Airways would ever stop behaving in such a manner, naive to believe that I would ever be able to bring British Airways to court, and naive to believe that I could ever win a court case. The word "naive" had echoed around and around in my head and at times had almost undermined my resolve to go on. Sir Michael Angus told Sir Colin Southgate that I was naive to take on British Airways "as if it was a *Boy's Own* story." Jeannie Davis told my parents that "Ricky should learn to take the rough with the smooth," and even people like Sir John Egan told me "not to shake the money tree." Perhaps I was naive in fighting for the justice I wanted, perhaps it was idealism, or perhaps I was just plain stubborn. But I knew that British Airways' activities were unlawful, and I wanted compensation. And I was determined to make all those people who had dismissed my stance as naive eat their words.

I was adamant that British Airways was not going to do the same to me. I called Gerrard Tyrrell after the breakfast and told him how sympathetic and persuasive Michael Davis had been.

"Rubbish," he retorted. "BA had the chance to settle at the beginning, but they didn't. It's only because their lawyers are now looking into a black hole of guilt that they're been forced to consider settling."

I had never heard Gerrard sound so angry.

"You'll never have a better opportunity than now to nail them," he went on. "Don't cave in now."

"Just testing you," I said. "Of course I won't cave in."

The next week we met George Carman, our formidable queen's counsel, who was preparing our case. With his white hair and impeccable manners, George looked like everyone's favorite uncle outside the courts. Inside he had the subtlety, tenacity, and killer instinct of a praying mantis. People went to extraordinary lengths to avoid him.

"What do you think of my opening line of address?" George asked us: "The World's Favorite Airline has a favorite pastime. It's called 'shredding documents which are liable to be misconstrued.' "

I called Michael Davis and told him that I couldn't agree to let my accusations slip under the carpet. The court case was set to start in January, and the British Airways directors would be cross-examined by George Carman. I didn't even need to hint at how much George Carman would relish this. Sobered by this prospect, Michael Davis put down the phone.

By now I felt really confident that we could beat BA. Not only had we discovered so much about their dirty tricks, we had also found out details of an extraordinary BA undercover operation.

Someone contacted my office to say that he had some information about an undercover operation set up by BA involving various private detectives. He said that he had a computer disk containing a diary of everything the private detectives had done. He insisted that I meet him personally before he handed over the disk.

I felt rather strange as I climbed into the car with one of my assistants, Julia Madonna. This was partly due to the fact that I was wearing a microphone hidden in my crotch area so that I could tape my conversation with the contact. I knew how vital the tape of Brian Basham's meeting with Chris Hutchins had been, and I wasn't going to leave anything to chance with this meeting. When I set up Virgin Atlantic I had no idea that I would have to resort to James Bond–style activities in order to run it!

I scribbled in my notebook as our contact talked:

> Trying to find out what we were up to [but] didn't want to give that impression. Not at Lord King's level . . . Being careful not to be seen to do any investigation only putting up defences.

Most important, our contact gave us the computer disk. When I had it printed out it was a revelation. The private detectives had kept an extremely detailed log of what they had been up to and who they had been reporting to at British Airways. The log revealed that the operation had been code-named "Covent Garden." The first entry, dated 30 November 1991, stated, "First sight of Project Barbara report seen in S1's office in Enserch House [BA's central London headquarters]." "S1" turned out to be the code name for David Burnside, and "Project Barbara" was the report on Virgin that Basham had given to Chris Hutchins.

Most of British Airways' top management had been named, but they had been given alphanumeric references so that their real names never appeared in print. I found it relatively easy to establish who was who: Lord King was "LK" or "C1"; Colin Marshall was "C2"; and Basham was "S2." There were others, R1 and R2, who were unknown to us. They turned out to be the private detectives, Nick Del Rosso and Tom Crowley, who were leading the team under the guise of trying to find the mole inside British Airways who was leaking information to us. Operation Covent Garden was run by Ian Johnson Associates, "international security management consultants." The log detailed how Johnson and Del Rosso briefed British Airways' director of security, David Hyde, and the legal director, Mervyn Walker, on the progress of operation Covent Garden. It also recorded meetings with Robert Ayling and Colin Marshall.

The log contained astonishing details of how the team of detectives had convinced some of British Airways' senior management that we were running an undercover operation against British Airways. The amount of money they estimated we were spending on our nonexistent operation was £400,000. We later found out that British Airways was spending £15,000 a week on Covent Garden.

The sheer absurdity of the operation was revealed by details of how the detectives had staked out the Tickled Trout Hotel in Lancashire with secret cameras and sound-recording equipment. The idea was to secretly record a meeting between Burnside and an "agent" that the Covent Garden team had convinced themselves was working for Virgin. The log recorded how their plans came unstuck when Burnside failed to turn on his bugging device! I could have spared British Airways the trouble: I never have and never will employ private detectives. That is not how I or Virgin operate.

When I had finished reading the Covent Garden log, I felt as if I had returned from a parallel universe—one created in the imaginations of British Airways' hired conspiracists and senior management at the cost of thousands of pounds. I really began to look forward to the libel case, which was being heralded as the "mother of all libel trials."

7 December 1992

"BA have collapsed," George Carman told me. "They have today paid just under half a million pounds, £485,000 to be precise, into court. They've effectively admitted that they're entirely guilty as charged."

We later discovered that just before the court case was due to start, British Airways' lawyers had told them that they had no hope of winning. If they wanted to avoid the humiliation of having to stand in the witness box and be cross-examined by George Carman, and seeing all their activities written up in the press, then their only option was to make a payment into the court and start negotiating an out-of-court settlement.

At first I was in two minds over whether to accept the money. I was innocent, and we could put all the British Airways directors in the witness box and destroy them. But then as we talked about it, I realized that although this was tempting, such a move could be seen as vindictive and highly risky.

"You've got to remember why you brought this case," George Carman advised me. "You wanted the dirty tricks to stop, and you wanted to clear your name. BA have admitted that you are totally right. You've cleared your name.

"If you persist with the case, then two things may go wrong. The jury might award you damages, but they might think that you were such a rich man that you didn't need £500,000 and just award you £250,000. That would be seen as a failure for you and a triumph for British Airways. If the jury award you less than British Airways have paid into court, then you will have to pay both sets of costs. So you may win the case but lose a lot of money, and people will be confused as to why Virgin Atlantic has to pay £3 million of costs."

This last part of George's advice was very telling. Although in some ways my decision to settle out of court could be something of an anticlimax in that we wouldn't have the satisfaction of watching George Carman cross-examining the directors, by deciding to accept British Airways' offer we would have won a clear-cut victory with no risks attached and would immediately be free to get on and run the business.

"What do we have to do now, then?" I asked.

"We have twenty-one days in which to take the money out of court if we're going to accept it."

"So we'll do that?"

"Good Lord, no," George said, looking shocked. "I'm not going to accept it. I'm going to get them to give us at least £600,000. If they've given £485,000, they can go up to £600,000. Every £100,000 makes an inch bigger headline."

George spent a week negotiating over the payment. On 11 December 1992 we agreed the terms of the highest uncontested libel payment ever made in British legal history: £500,000 to me personally to compensate for the personal libel and £110,000 to Virgin Atlantic to compensate for the corporate libel.

11 January 1993

"Virgin Screws BA" was the The Sun's headline. There wasn't much room for anything else on the front page.

"I'd have preferred it the other way round," Kelvin MacKenzie, The Sun's editor, told me. "It'd have made a better headline."

I was in George Carman's chambers with Gerrard Tyrrell and my father, whom I was delighted to share the triumph with. We walked around to the High Court in the Strand and jostled our way through the mass of photographers outside. The corridor outside Court 11 where the hearing would take place was teeming. Inside the court it was very quiet. British Airways were noticeable by their absence: Lord King, Sir Colin Marshall, and Robert Ayling, the three top protagonists, were absent. David Burnside was absent. Brian Basham had gone abroad, but his lawyers were there making a last-ditch attempt to have his name removed from the statement of apology. The judge listened to the plea and then asked British Airways' counsel for their opinion. They agreed with Virgin that Brian Basham's name should be included in the apology. The judge ruled that the apology should stand as prepared.

George Carman stood up and read the agreed statement. When he came toward the end, there was complete silence in court:

" 'British Airways and Lord King now accept unreservedly that the allegations which they made against the good faith and integrity of Richard Branson and Virgin Atlantic are wholly untrue. They further accept that Richard Branson and Virgin had reasonable grounds for serious concerns about the activities of a number of British Airways employees, and of Mr. Basham and their potential effect on the business interests and reputation of Virgin Atlantic and Richard Branson. In these circumstances, British Airways and Lord King are here now by leading counsel to apologize and to make very substantial payments to the Plaintiffs by way of compensation for the damages and distress caused by their false allegations. They also seek to withdraw their counterclaim against Virgin Atlantic and Richard Branson.

" 'In addition British Airways and Lord King have agreed to pay Richard Branson and Virgin Atlantic's legal costs in respect of the claim and the counterclaim and have undertaken not to repeat the defamatory allegations which are the substance of this action.' "

George Carman paused and took a breath. The court held its breath.

" 'British Airways and Lord King are to pay Richard Branson £500,000 damages and are to pay Virgin Atlantic £110,000 damages.' "

George had to raise his voice to make himself heard above the sudden noise in the court:

" 'In the light of the unqualified nature of the apology and the payment of a very substantial sum by way of damages, Richard Branson and Virgin Atlantic consider that their reputation is publicly vindicated by agreeing to settle the action on those terms.' "

I saw tears running down my father's cheeks as he listened to the settlement. He had a large silk handkerchief in his breast pocket that he took out and wiped his eyes with. I clenched my fists together under the old oak table to stop myself from jumping to my feet.

The single jarring note was in the British Airways apology, where, although they apologized unreservedly, they then went on to absolve themselves of any blame: "The investigation which British Airways carried out during the course of this litigation revealed a number of incidents involving their employees which British Airways accept were regrettable and gave Richard Branson and Virgin Atlantic reasonable grounds for concern. I should however like to emphasize," the counsel said, "that the directors of British Airways were not party to any concerted campaign against Richard Branson and Virgin Atlantic."

A number of people in the court snorted with derision. It had been the one phrase that British Airways had refused to take out of the apology.

"Let them leave it in," George Carman had finally advised me. "People will see exactly what it really means. We haven't heard the last of that word 'concerted.' "

Then, with the judge's permission, Basham's counsel stood up to point out that his client did not accept that the references to him in the foregoing statement were an accurate summary of his actions on behalf of British Airways.

Outside in the mad hustle of journalists and photographers I held up both hands and shook my fists in triumph.

"I accept this award not only for Virgin," I said, "but also for all the other airlines: for Laker, for Dan Air, Air Europe, and B-Cal. They went under and we survived British Airways, but only just."

Back at Holland Park the party started. I decided to share the £500,000 damages that had been awarded to me among all the Virgin Atlantic staff, since they had all had to suffer from the pressure that British Airways had put us under in the form of reduced salaries and cuts in their bonuses. The television was on in the corner, and every news program covered the Virgin success as the main story of the day. ITN went further and interviewed Sadig Khalifa and Yvonne Parsons. Momentarily the party stopped to cheer them, and then went on. Much later I was talking to someone when a wave of exhaustion hit me. I realized that we had won. All the stress cleared out of my shoulders, and I smiled a wide happy contented smile, toppled sideways, and fell deeply asleep.

Feeling on top of the world, I went off to our hotel in Majorca, La Residencia, with Joan and Holly and Sam to celebrate. The press had been photographing me all week, and I felt that we were on the crest of a wave that would transform Virgin over the forthcoming years. We could take on the world.

I was lying by the side of the pool one morning, reading all the press cuttings about Virgin that had been faxed over to me and trying not to let everything go to my head, when a young couple came up to me. They coughed nervously to attract my attention.

"Excuse me," they said, proffering a camera. "Would you mind? We'd love a photograph."

I smiled at them.

"Of course not," I beamed, standing up and grinning. I preened myself and brushed back my hair. "Where do you want to take it?"

"Just here would be nice," they said.

I stood with my back to the swimming pool and puffed out my chest.

"About here?" I asked them.

To my surprise they were looking confused. They whispered together. Instead of pointing the camera at me, I realized that they were holding it out toward me.

"Sorry," the husband said. "We were hoping that you could take our photograph. I'm Edward and this is my wife, Araminta. What's your name?"

Chapter 29

Towards the Millennium

The year 1993 was a watershed for Virgin. From that moment onwards, and for the first time, we had the luxury of money and, in Virgin, we had a strong brand name that could be lent to a wide variety of businesses. We faced uncharted territory, but at last we could afford to follow our instincts rather than spending time persuading others to do so. Once we made the lateral and surprising jump from Virgin Records to Virgin Atlantic, we could try our hand at anything. It was a long way from when we first copied out an old record contract on the houseboat and signed Mike Oldfield—but times had changed and now we had $500 million in the bank.

At this point I could have retired and concentrated my energies on learning how to paint watercolors or how to beat my mum at golf. It wasn't in my nature to do so. People asked me, "Why don't you have some fun now?" but they were missing the point. As far as I was concerned, this was fun. Fun is at the core of how I like to do business, and it has informed everything I've done from the outset. More than any other element, fun is the secret of Virgin's success. I am aware that the idea of business being fun and creative goes right against the grain of convention, and it's certainly not how they teach it at some of those business schools where business means hard grind and lots of discounted cash flows and net present values.

Even though I'm often asked to define my "business philosophy," I generally won't do so because I don't believe that it can be taught as if it's a recipe. There aren't ingredients and techniques that will guarantee success. Parameters exist that, if followed, will ensure that a business can continue, but it's not as if you can clearly define *our* business success and then bottle it as if it's a perfume. It's not that simple: to be successful, you have to be out there, you have to hit the ground running, and if you have a good team around you and more than a fair share of luck, you might make something happen. But you certainly can't guarantee it just by following someone else's formula.

You just need to look at where Virgin is now to see that business is a fluid, changing substance. As far as I'm concerned, the company will never stand still. It has always been a mutating, indefinable entity, and the past few years have demonstrated that. When I began writing this book a couple of years ago, Virgin was not involved in many of the businesses that now take up so much of my time. In writing the book, however, I discovered how far I still want to go. As a result, rather than endlessly trying to make this book keep pace with the explosive growth of Virgin in the five years since 1993, I wanted to publish what I have managed, in business terms, to finish so far. That's how I see it, a comprehensive account of the first forty-something years of my life—the struggling years—but also a work and a life in progress. Much has happened since 1993 that reflects my own outlook on life and on business, but the detail of it is for another book. Since 1993, Virgin has expanded perhaps more quickly than any other European company and has developed radically in the process. Our way of doing business may remain the same, but the context has changed dramatically. For now, I would like to give an impression of where Virgin is and outline some of the elements that are as important now in the closing years of the century as they have ever been for the company for the past twenty-five years, rather than attempt an endless and terminally complex analysis of business strategy. This book was never intended to be as dry as a balance sheet but will, I hope, give an idea of what has been important to my life and to the people around me thus far.

After the sale of Virgin Music and our victory over British Airways in January 1993, I realized that for the first time in my business career I had climbed the wall and could at least peer into the promised land. It hadn't always been possible. For anyone who starts without financial backing a very thin line exists between success and failure. Survival is the key priority. No matter how many successes Virgin had, there was always the danger that the cash would run out. Virgin has made money, but I have always invested it in new projects to keep the company growing. As a result we rarely had the luxury of spare cash to use as a cushion. Over the years we had clung on through three recessions, we had suffered losses, we had closed down some businesses, and in one instance we had had to make some staff redundant; but after 1993 no bank would ever again be able to dictate to us how to run our business. We had financial freedom. We were one of a rare breed: most entrepreneurs don't manage to survive that far or for that long.

In the process of gaining that freedom, we had to overcome all kinds of obstacles thrown without warning into our path. When we were established as a mail-order record company and thus dependent upon the post, out of the blue came a six-month postal strike. If we hadn't reinvented ourselves, we would have gone bust. There was no choice. Within days of the strike, we had opened our first Virgin record shop. It may have been up a dark, narrow flight of stairs above a shoe shop and consisted of some shelves, a shabby sofa, and a till, but in its own small way it taught us all we now know about retailing. I can draw a straight line between that tiny shop and the Virgin Megastores in Paris and New York. It's just a matter of scale—but first you have to believe you can make it happen.

Equally, as the record label gathered momentum throughout those early years, every deal was make-or-break. We may have failed to sign 10cc, but we were still willing to put the company on the line when we tried again with the next band. We launched the airline on a wing and a prayer, and when the engine blew up on our test flight, it could have been over before it had begun. We were lucky: each time something went wrong, we were the smallest jump ahead of the banks.

However tight things are, you still need to have the big picture at the forefront of your mind. The most vivid proof of this came during the depths of the recession in 1992. At the time, I was trying to raise money to install individual seat-back video terminals in all our aircraft—I have always believed that Virgin should offer the best in-flight entertainment. We needed $10 million to install the equipment. Nobody at Virgin Atlantic could raise the necessary funding, and we were all in despair down at Crawley one day and on the point of giving up when I thought I would try one last gamble.

Nervously I picked up the telephone, called Boeing, and asked to speak to the CEO, Phil Conduit. I asked him whether he would throw in the individual seat-back videos in economy if we bought ten new Boeing 747-400s. Amazed that anyone was thinking of buying planes during that recession, Phil readily agreed. I then called Jean Pierson at Airbus and asked him the same question about the new Airbus. Jean, who was in similar financial straits, also agreed. After further inquiries, we discovered that it was easier to get $4 billion credit to buy eighteen new aircraft than it was to get $10 million credit for the seat-back video sets. As a result, Virgin Atlantic suddenly had a brand-new fleet of planes, the youngest and most modern fleet in the industry, at the cheapest price for which we've ever been able to acquire planes either before or since.

Many people ask me what the limits to Virgin are and whether we haven't stretched the brand name beyond its natural tolerance. With monotonous regularity, they point out that there is no other company in the world that puts its name to such a wide variety of companies and products. They are absolutely right, and it's something of which I am proud.

It doesn't stop me thinking about the question nonetheless, and the answer is not easily explicable. I have always lived my life by thriving on opportunism and adventure. Some of the best ideas come out of the blue, and you have to keep an open mind to see their virtue. Just as an American lawyer called me to suggest setting up an airline in 1984, a Swedish ballooning fanatic asked me to fly across the Atlantic with him in 1987. The proposals come in thick and fast, and I have no idea what the next one will be. I do know, however, that if I listen carefully enough, then the good ideas somehow all fit into the framework Virgin has become. By nature I am curious about life, and this extends to my business. That curiosity has led me down many unexpected paths and introduced me to many extraordinary people. Virgin is a collection of such people, and its success rests upon them.

Virgin has always had a life of its own, and I always try to think ahead with it. When I tried to sell *Student* to IPC Magazines, they shied away from me because I started talking about all the other business opportunities I wanted to explore: a Student travel company, which would offer cheaper travel than the existing airlines; a Student bank, because I thought that students were being ripped off when they had no income to protect them. I even wanted to hire trains from British Rail because their tickets were so expensive and their trains always late. Even then I was attempting, with limited resources, to explore what was possible by wanting to take on some of these businesses and turn them upside down. At the time, though, it was all theoretical and beyond my capacity, but some interesting ideas emerged from the process. I may be a businessman in that I set up and run companies for profit, but when I try to plan ahead and dream up new products and new companies, I'm an idealist.

My grandiose plans didn't work for *Student*. But at the start of 1993, I was once again ready to push the barriers. This time it was rather different: not just a few pounds in the *Student* biscuit tin, which we spent on take-away curries, but a treasure chest of hundreds of millions of pounds. In an intoxicating moment, everything seemed possible. We had the finance, and even more important we had the name, Virgin, which already had a track record for reinventing itself. There was nothing to stop us from becoming something else. The land ahead was all Virgin territory.

I could give free rein to my own instincts. First and foremost, any business proposal I like must sound fun. If a market is served by only two giant corporations, it appears to me that there's room for some healthy competition. Second, I love stirring the pot. I love giving big companies a run for their money—especially if they're offering expensive, poor-quality products. In 1993 my notebook already contained notes about the possibility of launching a range of Virgin soft drinks, led by Virgin Cola, which could take on the might of Coca-Cola, one of the world's ten largest companies. The Cott Corporation specializes in bottling own-label colas, and they were looking for a brand with global appeal.

"You've got the X factor, the Y factor—you've got every factor there is," Gerry Pencer, the chief executive of Cott Corporation, said to me. "People like Virgin; they trust the name; they'll buy a product because it's a Virgin product. So how about it? We've got the recipe; you've got the name. What do you say to Virgin Cola?"

The strong points about Coca-Cola and Pepsi are all too obvious: Coca-Cola is the world's best-known brand name. It is also the most profitable company in the world, and yet it has only one competitor. Coke has 40 percent of the American market, Pepsi around 30 percent. Outside the United States, Coke completely dominates. Both companies spend billions of dollars a year advertising their products, and some of their best advertisements remain in the public consciousness even now.

When I studied the cola business closely, I could see some chinks in their armor. The most simple analysis will tell you that Coke is only a fizzy drink with a massive marketing budget, and that simplicity makes the market vulnerable. Having some serious uncertainties over what the "real thing" is, Coca-Cola pulled the original Coca-Cola out of circulation and launched New Coke, a recipe that they said tasted better. The reaction from American consumers forced Coca-Cola to reissue their original recipe under the name Classic Coke. But the seeds of doubt were sown. If Coca-Cola admitted that Classic Coke was not as good as New Coke, then by definition another cola recipe might be even better. To my mind the spell had been broken.

On the other side of the duopoly, Pepsi looked the weaker partner. Significantly, when we launched Virgin Cola, Pepsi was the first to respond: they changed the color of the cans from predominantly red to predominantly blue. It seemed that we had hit a raw nerve. Even so, there was still some re-sistance to the whole enterprise within Virgin. Understandably, people were quite rightly protective of our brand name, but it was only the first of many objections as to its usage.

As usual, when people warn me against doing something once my mind is made up, I grow increasingly determined to try it. In this case we all rec-ognized that it would be an inch-by-inch fight along the shelves of the su-permarkets, but once we established that there was minimal financial risk if we failed, we decided to proceed. We knew that the product was as good as either Coke or Pepsi, and the first blind tasting we had at the local school, which was followed by many across the country, established that most peo-ple preferred Virgin Cola to the others. And so we went into Virgin Cola. Within a few months we were selling £50 million worth of Virgin Cola across the country. We've launched in France, Belgium, and South Africa, and we're now taking on Coke in their homeland: we've even got a Virgin Cola ma-chine right underneath the Coke sign in Times Square, New York.

Looking ahead to the future, I have no idea whether Virgin Cola will be-come a global leader in soft drinks or not. As with all of our businesses, I keep an open mind. But I do know that Virgin Cola is indicative of the Vir-gin philosophy, and beneath all the apparent fun and razzmatazz of selling it there is a sound business plan. The decision to launch Virgin Cola was prompted by three main issues: finding the right people, the use of the Vir-gin brand name, and protection of the downside.

The business plan for Virgin Cola is clear: we will never lose much money selling Virgin Cola. It is so cheap to produce that, unlike most other products, the manufacturing cost is negligible. We can therefore balance the advertising and distribution costs directly against the sales. One look at Coca-Cola's balance sheets reveals what a profitable business it is, and with those kinds of margins there must be plenty of room for someone else to come in with a decent cola to sell alongside Coke and Pepsi.

Once I was convinced that we had protected the downside—always my first concern—the other significant question to resolve was whether the move into Virgin Cola really enhanced the Virgin brand name. Despite ob-jections from colleagues, I firmly believed that cola had a number of attrib-utes people associated with Virgin: fizz, fun, and freedom. Not only that, but ours was a better, cheaper cola than the others. We thrive on the fact that we are small and a newcomer up against the two giants.

"All right," people admit when they hear this explanation, "I can see that cola is fun. It's fizzy and profitable and fits the Virgin image. But surely not life insurance? What on earth are you doing selling life insurance, mortgages, and investments?"

I have to admit that some healthy discussions about life insurance took place before we decided to launch Virgin Direct.

"Life insurance?" everyone snorted when they heard the idea. "People *hate* life insurance. All the salesmen seem so corrupt, barging into your homes and taking secret commissions. It's a terrible industry. It's definitely not a Virgin kind of business."

"Exactly," I said. "It's got potential."

It is no secret that I love playing devil's advocate. I could see all the bad points about the financial services industry. The idea of setting up Virgin Life Insurance and a Virgin Bank would have horrified our original staff at Albion Street or our customers who spread out on the beanbags at the record shop. And yet whenever I see people getting a bad deal, I want to step in and do something about it. Of course this is not pure altruism—there's a profit to be made too. But the difference is that I'm prepared to share more of the profit with the customer so that we're both better off. The maverick in me was also quietly amused that the guy who brought you the Sex Pistols could also sort out your pension. Another part of me was equally amused by the idea that we were going to set up our own bank to give those very banks that nearly foreclosed on us a run for their money.

I was first alerted to the financial services industry by Rowan Gormley, a venture capitalist I had asked to work for Virgin to identify new business opportunities. One of the first things he did was to review the Virgin pension policy, which he said made no sense. When he asked six different pension advisers to give quotes on the best way to restructure it, he was the bemused recipient of six different answers.

"I don't understand it," he told me. "I've three degrees in finance, but none of what they're saying makes sense."

Instinctively I felt that the world of financial services was shrouded in mystery and rip-offs and that there must be room for Virgin to offer a jargon-free alternative with no hidden catches.

As with our other ventures, we needed a partner who both knew the industry and could put up the money to go alongside the Virgin name. Despite some of our difficulties, I still believe that a fifty-fifty partnership is the best solution to financing. When something goes wrong, as it invariably will at some point, both partners have an equal incentive to put it right. Such is not always the case. At worst, such as with Randolph Fields, Virgin will buy out the partner entirely. At its best, as with Marui, our partner in the Megastores in Japan, it stays at fifty-fifty and both sides remain content. In between these poles there can be many variations, and we have tried out most combinations. Ultimately you never know what to expect when dealing with other people, and although you might both appear to go into a project with the same enthusiasm, situations can change. Knowing when and how to renegotiate a contract is all part of the challenge of business.

Virgin Direct, our financial services company, started off with Norwich Union as a fifty-fifty partner. After Virgin entered the financial services industry, I can immodestly say it was never to be the same again. We cut out all commissions, we offered good-value products, and we were practically trampled by investors in their rush to buy. We set up a new office in Norwich rather than renting a gleaming tower block in the City of London. We never employed fund managers, some of the world's most highly paid people, since we discovered their best-kept secret—they could never consistently beat the stock market index.

We launched aggressively and the initial signs were good, but in spite of our success, we realized that we were going faster and further than was comfortable for the Norwich Union. It looked as if we would be three times the size we had predicted. After a short time we arranged for them to sell their shareholding to a partner who shared our ambitions, Australian Mutual Provident (AMP). Together with our great team and AMP we have now cut a broad swath through the financial services jungle. From a standing start in 1995, it is staggering to think that Virgin Direct has become the country's most popular personal equity plan, and 250,000 people have trusted us with more than £1.5 billion.

The success of Rowan Gormley and his vision for Virgin Direct illustrates one of the great strengths of the Virgin Group: we thrive on mavericks. The quality I recognized in Rowan when I first asked him to work for Virgin was that he would make things happen. When he started work perched at a desk on a half landing at 11 Holland Park, neither of us had any idea that a few months later he would start up a financial services company. But when, unsurprisingly with hindsight, he alighted upon financial services, we arranged a company structure that gave him and his team a shareholding in the business and let him get on with it. Like all the managers of Virgin companies, Rowan is highly motivated to succeed because he can clearly see the wealth that success will bring him and his team.

Virgin Direct may appear to be an incongruous departure for Virgin, the rock-and-roll company, but it was only a lateral leap in the same way as was the leap from records to the airline. In all ventures, Virgin is ultimately about service, value for money, and simple products. The vision I have for Virgin does not run along the orthodox lines of building up a company with a vast head office and a pyramid of command from a central board of directors. I am not saying that such a structure is wrong—far from it. It makes for formidable companies from Coca-Cola to GEC to British Airways. It is just that my mind doesn't work like that. I am too informal, too restless, and I like to move on.

The more diffuse the company becomes, the more frequently I am asked about my vision for Virgin. I tend either to avoid this question or to answer it at great length, safe in the knowledge that I will give a different version the next time I'm asked. My vision for Virgin has never been rigid and changes constantly, like the company itself. I have always lived my life by making lists—lists of people to call, lists of ideas, lists of companies to set up, lists of people who can make things happen. Each day I work through these lists, and that sequence of calls propels me forward. Back in the early 1970s I spent my time juggling different banks and suppliers and creditors, playing one off against the other to stay solvent. I'm still living the same way, but I'm now juggling bigger deals instead of banks. Once again, it is only a matter of scale.

As anyone in my office knows when I've lost it, my most essential possession is a standard-sized school notebook, which can be bought at any stationery shop on any high street across the country. I carry this everywhere and write down comments made to me by Virgin staff and anyone else I meet. I make notes of all telephone conversations and all meetings, and I draft out letters to send and lists of telephone calls to make. Over the years I have worked my way through a bookcase of them, and the discipline of writing everything down ensures that I have to listen to people carefully. Flicking back through these notebooks now, I see some ideas that escaped me: I was asked to invest in a board game called Trivial Pursuit and a wind-up radio. But when I was asked to become an underwriting name at Lloyds Insurance, my guardian angel must have been looking after me.

Whenever I'm on a flight or a train or in a record store, I walk around and ask the people I meet for their ideas on how to improve the service. I write them down, and when I get home, I look through all the comments. If there's a good idea, I pick up the phone and implement it. My staff are maddened to hear that I met a man on the airport bus who suggested that we offer onboard massages and, please, can they organize it. They tease me and call it "Richard's Straw Poll of One," but time and again the extra services that Virgin offers have been suggested to us by customers. I don't mind where the ideas come from as long as they make a difference.

I also insist that we continually ask our staff for their suggestions, and I try my hand at their jobs. When I tried pushing a trolley down the aisle of a jumbo, I crashed into everyone. When I talked to the crew about this, they suggested that we introduce a more waitress-style service and keep the trolleys to a minimum.

My vision for Virgin was ultimately summed up by Peter Gabriel, who once said to me on a ski lift: "It's outrageous! Virgin is becoming everything. You wake up in the morning to Virgin Radio; you put on your Virgin jeans; you go to the Virgin Megastore; you drink Virgin Cola; you fly to America on Virgin Atlantic. Soon you'll be offering Virgin births, Virgin marriages, Virgin funerals. I think you should rename Virgin the 'In and Out Company.' Virgin will be there at the beginning and there at the end."

As ever, Peter, an astute businessman as well as a gifted musician, was close to the truth. He had no idea at the time that we had two hundred people down in Eastbourne working on a range of Virgin cosmetics, another designing a range of Virgin clothes, or that we were just about to bid for two British Rail franchises, which would make us the largest train operator in Britain. I doubt that we'll ever go into Virgin Funerals, but Virgin Births has a certain ring to it. If there's a good business plan that offers good value, limited downside, good people, a good product, we'll go for it.

In some ways it all boils down to convention. As you might have noticed, I do not set much store by such so-called wisdom. Conventionally you concentrate upon what you are doing and never stray beyond fairly narrow boundaries when running a company. Not only do I find that restrictive, but also I think that it's dangerous. If you only run record shops and refuse to embrace change, when something new like the Internet is launched, you will lose your sales to the person who makes use of the new medium. Setting up your own Internet operation to which your record shops lose business is far better than losing it to somebody else's.

This partly explains the jigsaw of companies we have. As well as protecting each other, they have symbiotic relationships. When Virgin Atlantic opens a flight to South Africa, I find that we can launch Virgin Radio and Virgin Cola there. We can use our experience in the airline industry to make buying train tickets easier and cheaper. We can draw on our experience of entertaining people on planes to entertain people on trains; we can use our enormous stock of entertainment at the Virgin Megastores to make trips to

Virgin Cinemas more fun. We can use the cinemas to have people sample our Virgin Cola. A trip to the cinema used to involve queuing up in the rain to buy your ticket from a man behind thick plate glass, watching the movie with one cup of popcorn, and then blundering out through a fire escape into some back street piled high with litter. Not anymore it doesn't—and that's because we have put all the Virgin experience together across retailing, entertainment, food, music, and travel to make it an easy-to-organize and enjoyable night.

Despite employing over twenty thousand people, Virgin is not a big company—it's a big brand made up of lots of small companies. Our priorities are the opposite of our large competitors'. Convention dictates that a company look after its shareholders first, its customers next, and last of all worry about its employees. Virgin does the opposite. For us, our employees matter most. It just seems common sense to me that if you start off with a happy, well-motivated workforce, you're far more likely to have happy customers. And in due course the resulting profits will make your shareholders happy.

Convention also dictates that "big is beautiful," but every time one of our ventures gets too big, we divide it up into smaller units. I go to the deputy managing director, the deputy sales director, and the deputy marketing director and say, "Congratulations, you're now MD, sales director, and marketing director—of a new company." Each time we've done this, the people involved haven't had much more work to do, but necessarily they have had a greater incentive to perform and a greater zest for their work. The results for us have been terrific. By the time we sold Virgin Music, we had as many as fifty different subsidiary record companies, and not one of them had more than sixty employees.

But there is little point in looking back, except to note that since then Ken Berry has consolidated and made Virgin Records the most profitable jewel in EMI's crown. For us, we are now free to start again with V2 Records, using the same techniques and skills. Our first signing may not be quite as successful as Mike Oldfield, but the Stereophonics were still named Best Newcomers in the Brit Awards this year and their future is bright.

The Virgin way has been to develop many different ventures and grow organically. For most of our companies, we have started from scratch rather than merely bought them ready-made. We want each of the Virgin subsidiaries to be an efficient, manageable size. As a result, Virgin is housed in lots of different offices around Notting Hill Gate in London, Crawley in West

Sussex, and Norwich, keeping the focus tight and maintaining the great sense of team spirit.

When it comes to setting up new companies, one of my advantages is that I don't have a highly complicated view of business. When I think about which services I want to offer on Virgin Atlantic, I try to imagine whether my family and I would like to buy them for ourselves. Quite often it's as simple as that.

Of course life becomes more complicated when you move away from organic growth. In recent years Virgin has bought companies to add to the ones that we have set up. The purchase of MGM Cinemas was the first big acquisition we made, but we also bought two substantial British Rail train franchises. While we were able to fix the cinema chain relatively quickly, the trains will be a much longer-term prospect. In some ways we became a victim of our own success in that the train passengers expected that as soon as Virgin had taken over the running of the trains, miraculous change would take place. Unfortunately, the logistics of the task were against us: our two train companies have thirty-five hundred employees, and we needed to build a complete new fleet of trains and negotiate with Railtrack over how they could upgrade the tracks and signaling. Despite a difficult start, we're confident that Virgin Rail will eventually succeed and offer a cheap, efficient train service. Each time I get caught in traffic leaving London or trying to get around the M25 or Birmingham, my confidence in the long-term prospects of the railways is refueled. I am still convinced that by 2002 rail will be seen as one of the best things Virgin ever did with its brand. Our new 140-mph trains will reduce journey times all over the country, and their comfort and safety will make them the best trains in Europe if not the world.

Once you have a great product, it is essential to protect its reputation with vigilance. It's not just a question of getting it into the marketplace. As a result, every day I receive a bundle of press cuttings—everything that mentions Virgin. These cuttings—and staff letters—are what I read first in the morning. When I launched the airline, I realized that I would have to use myself to raise the profile of Virgin Atlantic and to build the value of the brand. Most companies don't acknowledge the press and have a tiny press office tucked away out of sight. If an inaccurate story appears in the press and is allowed to run for more than one issue of the paper, it becomes fact. Then every time your product is mentioned, this same story will be repeated.

My reputation has been threatened on two major occasions—first by British Airways and second by Guy Snowden and his company GTECH, the driving force behind the creation of Camelot, which won the franchise to run the British National Lottery. For both companies I was a spanner in the works, costing them millions of pounds of lost earnings.

The GTECH incident was particularly crucial in terms of my reputation. I met Guy Snowden at a time when the British government had finally agreed to go ahead with the National Lottery. Various commercial consortiums were beginning to form, but I felt strongly that the lottery should be run by a company that would donate all the profits to charity. I felt this because it would be a monopoly with no risk involved at all. I had asked John Jackson, with whom I had worked on the Healthcare Foundation when he was chief executive of Body Shop and with whom I had launched Mates condoms, to pull together our charitable bid. GTECH was one of the leading suppliers of lottery equipment, so we thought that we should meet them to see whether they would be interested in supplying us if their consortium failed to win the contract.

John Jackson and I met with Guy Snowden for lunch on 24 September 1993. The conversation we had has since become the stuff of legal legend. After we reached a stalemate because Guy Snowden didn't want to quote for supplying equipment to us and I didn't want to join his consortium, there was a pause. Snowden then pointed out to us that if we went ahead with our bid, it would cost the GTECH consortium millions of pounds since they would have to reduce the percentage they were going to charge as the operators from the 15 percent of turnover mentioned in the government guidelines to 13 percent and possibly lower. Assuming that the annual sales of lottery tickets reached £4 billion (which they did), each percentage reduction of the operators' slice was worth £40 million a year. A great deal of money was at stake.

We were sitting in the conservatory in the garden at 11 Holland Park, and I noticed that he had begun to sweat. He shifted in his seat and looked at me.

"I do not quite know how to phrase this, Richard."

I looked across at him, wondering what he was going to say.

"There's always a bottom line. I will get to the point. In what way can we help you, Richard?"

I didn't know what to say. Snowden clarified his intentions:

"I mean, how can we help you personally?"

My mind reeled at the question. I was being offered a bribe.

"What on earth do you mean?" I said, astonished and angry and trying to give him the chance to stop. But he didn't.

"Everybody needs something in life," Snowden said.

"Thank you," I answered. "I'm quite successful. I only need one breakfast, lunch, and dinner a day. The only way you could have helped is by providing services for our bid."

And with that I stood up and left the conservatory. I wanted no further part in this man's world. While John and I were trying to pull together a bid for the National Lottery, which was intended to give many millions of pounds to charity, this man was trying to bribe me to stand aside and enable his bid to go through, which as well as giving less money to charity would simultaneously enrich him and his company. I bounded down the staircase and into the loo. There I scribbled some of the words he had used onto a piece of paper. I had never been offered a bribe before. Then I went back upstairs, and John and I ushered Snowden out of the house.

"I wasn't mistaken, was I?" I asked John. "That was a bribe, wasn't it?"

"It most certainly was," John told me.

Later, John recited how he nearly fell off his chair when Guy Snowden said those words. To cut a long story short, in the court case that ensued, the jury found in my favor against Guy Snowden and GTECH. My reputation was restored. In his summing up, George Carman pointed out in the court that above any commercial success one might enjoy, one's reputation for honesty is the most important thing. As he said, Guy Snowden "picked the wrong man, said the wrong thing in the wrong place at the wrong time."

The litigation with British Airways continues. In late 1993 Virgin launched an antitrust action against British Airways in the United States. Evidence for this litigation had emerged out of the libel case. Some of this evidence concerned British Airways' sales and marketing programs with travel agents and corporate customers. Virgin alleged that these sales programs used British Airways' monopolistic position in the UK to artificially tie these travel agents and corporate clients to BA. British Airways has denied the allegations and the case is pending.

Virgin also objected to the European Commission about these activities. In January 1997, the European Commission issued a Statement of Objections alleging that British Airways' activities were illegal under European competition law. British Airways filed a response denying that its actions were unlawful, and the issue is pending before the commission.

Ultimately, though, while I have enjoyed much success for a variety of reasons in my business career, my family is the most significant element in my life. They are a guiding light to me, and we never seek to put barriers around each other. Just as I have always felt that I could say anything to my parents, so Joan and I have always kept an open relationship with Holly and Sam. Perversely, it is the strength of my family that has given me the courage to attempt my balloon flights and kept me battling away with my business ventures.

I spend much time traveling and treasure the moments the family is together. In many ways we are closest when we are all on Necker. It has developed from being the jewel that symbolized the feelings Joan and I have for each other into being a place where the whole family feels at home and at peace. We try to go for Easter, summer, and Christmas holidays. With my parents, sisters, their families, our closest friends, and quite a few people from all the different Virgin companies, it is like a melting pot where we all take stock of what is happening and get away from everything apart from the fax machine. I've taught the children to play tennis there, and to swim and snorkel and sail. When we're there we're there for each other. It's a time to relax and to reflect on what we're all doing because we know that when we're back in London it's back to work.

My favorite time of day there is the early evening. By then it's midnight in London and virtually impossible to speak to anyone in Europe. The fax and telephone are silent, and the sun sets quickly. In an hour or so the daylight changes from brilliant, almost white sunshine to dusk, with a deep orange blaze across the horizon. Sitting on the veranda, I can watch the last small flock of pelicans dive for fish and flap creakily away to roost. Within minutes the sky turns a velvet midnight blue, and the first handful of stars are out. The sea in front of me becomes inky black, and everything falls quiet.

We generally have supper on the terrace. Everyone is sunburned and happy. It's great to be together, and I wonder what the future holds for all the kids here. I look over at Holly and Sam, and realize that I don't want to plan their lives for them. At the moment Holly wants to be a doctor and Sam wants to climb trees and rescue cats. I just want them to be happy. I know that other businessmen like Rupert Murdoch and Robert Maxwell had their children reading annual reports and financial accounts before breakfast, but I want none of that. At moments like these I am happy to forget about my notebook with its constant burning list of things to do and people to call, and relax into being among people I love and care about.

Even so, as we sit there I know that *Maiden Voyager,* our original jumbo, is heading from Heathrow to JFK, flight VS009. She's been flying from London to New York since 1984, and it's been the backbone of our airline, the linchpin of our success. *Scarlet Lady* is now humming through the night to Johannesburg, our latest destination, and *Lady in Red,* our first Airbus, which was christened by Princess Diana, is heading overnight toward Hong Kong. Virgin Atlantic's offices at Crawley will be deserted save for the cleaners, and the night shift will be drinking their second or third cup of coffee at Heathrow and Gatwick. The audiences will have long since filed out of the Virgin Cinemas, but there will be queues outside Heaven nightclub, and I wonder who is performing tonight and what the future holds for them. The Japanese and Paris Megastores will be shut, but evening crowds will be leafing through the racks of CDs at the New York Megastore before buying a can of Virgin Cola from a nearby vending machine.

At the outset, each of those individual ventures was a step into the unknown for the company that I felt personally, like a loss of one's virginity, but unlike the real thing, in whatever world you make for yourself, you can keep embracing the new and the different over and over again. That's what I have always wanted for Virgin, and whether it's achieved by judgment or luck, I wouldn't have it any other way.

Epilogue

Diversity and Adversity

An enormous amount has happened in the last decade. Somehow, I've been so busy I just haven't had the time to sit down and write a second volume. However, I have kept my trusty black notebooks, which I still fill in every day. Eventually I will find the time to write it all down properly, but in the meantime I thought I'd give you just a taste of what's gone on in the last few years.

This book opens with my first attempt to fly around the world in a balloon, a trip that ended up in the deserts of Algeria. So it seems appropriate to bring the story up to date by telling you about my last trip, which finally knocked some sense into me. Although it had been a magnificent trip, I realized that it was perhaps time to put to better use everything I'd learned during my personal adventures.

When we were about to set off, someone suggested to me that I keep a diary, and I've dusted that off to use here. Rather than edit it, I'm going to let you see it as I wrote it, so that you can get a sense of what it's like to be adrift, thousands of feet above the surface of the Earth, with just the wind to power you.

Day 1, 18 December 1998

The delightful Moroccans welcomed us like brothers. Holly and Joan arrived at the airport. The balloon looked like a magnificent mosque and the sun was rising up over the Atlas Mountains.

Strangely, I wasn't enormously nervous on this occasion: We'd had such a good team planning this. We'd been through so much heartache in the past that I really felt that this time we had a good chance. The only serious problem was that last night the Americans and British had started bombing Iraq. And we are due to fly along the Iraqi border in thirty hours' time—some fifty miles from it.

We have Bob Rice, the best weatherman (meteorologist) in the world. He believes he can help us find the winds to carry us right along the border without crossing into it. I've promised him that we will stuff him instead of the turkey this Xmas if he gets it wrong. That is, if we are not already stuffed ourselves.

Almost all of my closest friends and family, except Sam, who had to be at school, had flown in to see us off. They had just traveled with us all the way to the Caribbean the day before to go on holiday. The moment we arrived there, I was told to go the entire way back because we had found the perfect weather. Weather so perfect that, if nothing goes too wrong, we could be back on my grandfather's birthday—Boxing Day, the day after Xmas.

Alex Ritchie's children, Alistair and Duncan, my daughter, Holly, and Per's daughter, Jenny, were together to press the button to launch us into the air. We put on our parachutes. We said our good-byes—to my mum and dad, my brother-in-law, my daughter, and my friends. Tears were in their eyes.

Countdown—10, 9, 8, 7, 6, 5, 4, 3, 2, 1—then lift-off!

We gently climbed 2,000 feet. The door was still open. Everyone was clapping and cheering. Then suddenly we started to sink: We had hit a weather inversion. We burned hard to warm the helium. We burst through the inversion. Then I realized we had overburned.

We were shooting up and the bottom of the balloon was smoldering—1,700 feet a minute, 1,800 feet, 1,900 feet—until at last we were slowing, but the liquid burners had burned holes in the bottom of the hot-air balloon. Fortunately for us they were right at the bottom. It was the helium balloon that was the critical one. We could fly on: ugly holes, but nothing to stop us.

It's wonderful. We are flying up with the birds and we are on our way. Everything seems to be working: We are up to flight altitude, the capsule has pressurized, and the balloon has not burst. We are on our way at the beginning of a magnificent adventure; there below us are the beautiful Atlas Mountains covered in snow.

Day 2, 19 December 1998

*F*or hours we had a magnificent flight watching the massive range of the Atlas Mountains that stretches across the whole of the north of Africa, from Morocco across Algeria, Libya, and almost, I believe, to Egypt. We bade farewell to the Moroccans after about seven hours of flying and then headed out over Algeria.

Algeria has become a very sad country due to a terrible civil war that is going on. We were plunged into that two years ago when our balloon failed at night and we had to land. But tonight we're flying along the Atlas Mountains, over the rugged desert where Alex and I once had to throw everything we had out of our balloon to stop a rapid descent—we even threw out an envelope full of dollars! Alex saved our lives on that occasion by climbing out on the roof and releasing fuel tanks just before we hit the deck.

This time everything seemed to be going well. Almost too well! When it began to get dark and the helium above us cooled, we turned on the burners. Instead of plunging, as we had on our last attempt around the world, the heat stopped any descent and the flames lit up the skies around us. We had to be careful not to fly higher than we had during the day or the heat would vent the helium and shorten the time we had in the sky. So to keep alert we took turns flying during the night.

Then, a message from Libya came through saying they had withdrawn our right to fly over their country. It was nighttime, pitch-black, and we could never land before crossing their border. Steve, Per, and I debated what we could do about it. If we had gone very low we might have been able to crawl around the south of Libya, but that would mean abandoning our dreams. In the end we decided to slow up the balloon by dropping lower to give us time to try to persuade Libya's ruler, Colonel Qaddafi, that ours is a sporting mission undertaken in the interest of peace. The King of Jordan had been a great help to us previously, and I also had the honor of knowing Nelson Mandela—and I knew he knew Colonel Qaddafi quite well. So my wonderful secretary Sue opened up my office in the early hours of the morning and got hold of their telephone numbers.

Our next concern was the realization that they would all be asleep. The King of Jordan was unwell with cancer [and has since passed away], and Nelson Mandela is not a young man, so instead I decided to write one of the most important letters in my life to Colonel Qaddafi.

Excellency,

I am making this personal and direct appeal to you from the ICO Global Challenger Balloon in which the general post and telecommunications company of Libya has a significant investment.

A mutual friend of ours, his Royal Highness King Hussein of Jordan, spoke to you about my plans to try to circumnavigate the globe in a balloon. You graciously granted us permission to cross your country.

Early today we took off from Morocco in the certain knowledge that we had permission to overfly your country. We would not have done so had we not had the permission and goodwill of both Algeria and Libya. We are currently over Algeria and we will cross your border in the early hours of this morning.

Libyan overflight clearance permit OVG11@01001 was graciously extended on 20 July 1998 to us for this flight. Your Air Traffic Control personnel have just informed us that this permission has been rescinded. We obviously understand that they have every right to do this, but I'm afraid that it is impossible to land a balloon at night due to the icing that forms on the helium valve. We are unable to vent the helium to descend. Because of this emergency condition, we simply do not know how to avoid crossing your airspace. We hope that you will grant us emergency permission under these circumstances via your air-traffic control services.

Thank you for your understanding of this problem.

I am, Sir, your most obedient servant,
Richard Branson

By that point we were all extremely tired and purposefully flying much slower than the balloon was capable of, to give us time. Then the onboard phone rang and we were told that, even though it was 1 o'clock in the morning, Colonel Qaddafi had granted us permission to go on. Although our route to go around the world had been made more difficult by the slower path, the bigger, immediate problem was that by slowing down we had changed direction and were heading toward a storm over Istanbul in Turkey. Hopefully we could ride above it. Whether through the pressure of all of this, or some bug, I was beginning to lose my voice. We decided I should go on a course of penicillin just in case.

Per remains as calm as I have ever seen him. His dream, which started so many years ago, is finally coming true. And Steve is a pleasure to have on board. He is the only one of us who ventures into the "kitchen," producing an excellent "Steve's Soup."

Morning has now broken and we have crossed the Libyan border. Miles and miles of desert and a warm welcome from air-traffic control in Tripoli. No military planes. Thank you, thank you, Colonel Qaddafi, from all of us in the ICO Global Balloon team.

Day 3, 20 December 1998

I haven't slept since I last wrote in my diary 24 hours ago. With good reason. Let me share these 24 hours with you. I only wish right now that you could be up here with us. However, there were some moments in the day I would not wish on you.

Let me first explain the challenge that faces all balloonists who want to go around the world. It is not just the elements or the technological challenge. Sadly, it also involves people and politics. As always in life, it is not the ordinary people who get in the way. It's a handful of politicians at the top who selfishly make their country and this world a sadder place to live. After all, this is a sporting challenge and a mission flown in peace.

Let me begin by suggesting that you pull out a map; imagine you are a balloonist in Switzerland, in America, or in Morocco as we were. Then cross out some of the countries whose politicians say you cannot cross: Russia, Iran, and Iraq (remember, two balloonists who did cross the Russian border three years ago were cruelly shot down and killed).

Imagine you're in a race to be the first around the world, and there are seven other balloonists waiting to take off. All of them will likely go well south of Russia and Iraq. You know that they will not experience the same holdups that you have, so every second counts and taking a risk becomes a necessity. So, when your weatherman says he believes he can squeeze you between Iran and Russia, instead of saying no, you take that risk. Even though it means flying down a 24-mile-wide piece of land that is 2,600 miles from where you are taking off, and is owned by Turkey and flanked by two countries in which you are not welcome.

Remember, a balloon has no propulsion except the wind. The only way of steering is to change height as you go along to try to find winds going in a different direction. So it helps to have the best weatherman in the world.

That weatherman tells you he thinks it can be done. You and your team decide to go for it. Then the night before you launch you are told that the British and the Americans are bombing Iraq, and you are British and Steve Fossett is American. And this particular path is within 60 miles of Iraq.

You would probably be certifiably mad to continue, and until an hour ago I did think we were mad. But we knew our weatherman—we had worked with Bob Rice before over the Atlantic and Pacific. We knew that if anyone could help get us through this narrow crack between two countries in which we did not have permission to fly, it would be him. And the very minute I am writing this diary, we are coming out the other end of the crack, with Iraq and Iran on one side of us and Russia on the other. We, with the help of our magnificent team back at base, have miraculously crept through.

Twenty-four hours ago we said good-bye to Libya as it was getting dark and headed out over the Mediterranean toward Cyprus. An RAF Hercules flew overhead. They said they were on their way to bomb Iraq. They wished us good luck and we wished them the same.

I had just tried to lie down to get some sleep when Steve shouted, "Get your parachute on—we've been told there's a very high thunderstorm ahead." Steve had lost his balloon in a similar thunderstorm over the Pacific only two months before, so he knew only too well what havoc they could wreak. By climbing, the wind would blow us over Iraq. What was worse? In the distance, we could see the traces of anti-aircraft fire. We decided to risk the thunder and pressed on. Somebody was looking over us. We not only missed the storm but also missed Iraq by 30 miles, Iran by 7 miles, and Russia by 10 miles. Right now our weatherman can do no wrong. If he gets us home for Boxing Day, the champagne is on me.

The views from where we are flying are breathtaking. We are crossing the snow-clad Armenian mountains; below us is a little village called Ararat, where—it is said—Noah landed in his Ark. Over our headsets came the crackly sound of the air-traffic controller from Armenia: "On behalf of all the Armenian people, we would like to say welcome." It was said with such genuine friendliness. If only all countries could be so welcoming.

About 2,600 miles gone—the width of the Atlantic Ocean—20,000 left to go. Everybody feeling incredibly exhilarated. I for one need to borrow somebody else's fingernails for the rest of the trip—because I no longer have any of my own left!

Day 4, 21 December 1998

We are still flying, and our voyage becomes more awesome by the minute.

We moved from Armenia through Azerbaijan, a new independent state in the former USSR, out across the Caspian Sea, through Turkmenistan and Uzbekistan (what wonderful names these states have).

We then passed over Afghanistan, where a bloody civil war has raged for years. Then early this morning a wonderful but rather frightening prospect dawned on us: the winds had unexpectedly changed, and now we would not be able to fly to the north of the largest mountain range in the world, but would have to go straight across it.

These were the awesome Himalayas, never crossed before by a balloon. We would cross Nepal, a remote kingdom between India and Tibet. Nepal is where Buddha was born, and is also known for the largest mountain on earth—Mount Everest—which soars up to nearly 30,000 feet.

This sounds wonderful, but as with everything about trying to fly a balloon around the world there was a catch. It is what's known as "the deadly curl-over." A balloon can be grabbed by the wind and literally smashed into the side of the mountain as one crosses it. To avoid this we will need to fly 1,000 feet above each mountain for every 10 mph we are traveling.

We did our calculations based on our present speed of 80 mph, and this meant we had to fly 8,000 feet above the mountain. At present we couldn't fly more than 30,000 feet, but we would have to fly 40,000 feet over Everest to avoid being smashed into the other side of it.

We couldn't do that. Can we and our team back home steer us between Everest and the next highest mountain, K2?

Well, we won't know for a few more hours. So tomorrow if we succeed I'll let you know.

Day 5, 22 December 1998

Well, I'm still here writing my diary, so we must have missed Everest and K2. In fact we steered right between them—more by luck than skill this time, since the mountains had taken control of our direction and they were not going to let us go.

We spent the last 24 hours following this spectacularly beautiful mountain range. In the day they were exquisite. At night having them a few thousand feet below was an eerie feeling. Adding to our problems were masses of ice forming on top of the balloon, blocking the helium valve.

As daytime approached, enormous clumps of it would fall down on to our capsule. It was actually very beautiful and I've made a wonderful film of our crossing of the Himalayas.

Because the winds died on us and our speed dropped, we didn't suffer "the deadly curl-over" that I had feared yesterday.

Day 6, 23 December 1998

We were three hours from crossing the Chinese border when they dropped a bombshell: "We're revoking your permission to cross China. You will not enter." We had no choice. We couldn't land in the Himalayas. That would mean certain death. But to fly into China when specifically told not to could also mean almost certain death.

The Chinese had originally given us permission to cross the south of China. Because we had been sucked into the Himalayas we were going to enter China 150 miles north of where they had asked us to.

We had three hours to try and persuade them to let us in. I knew Sir Edward Heath, who was once Prime Minister of Britain and who had excellent relations with the Chinese. So our people first contacted him and he was good enough to speak to his contacts. I got through to Saskia in my office, and asked her to contact Prime Minister Tony Blair. "But I don't have the number for Downing Street," she said. Tired out and, to be frank, pretty worried by now, I raised my voice. "Dial 192. Get it from Directory Enquiries!"

Tony Blair was good enough to write a personal letter to His Excellency Premier Zhu Rongji. I also contacted Peter Such—head of one of our rival airlines, Cathay Pacific—who was based in Hong Kong, and who was also very helpful. Our British Ambassador in Beijing and his team were enormously helpful. Finally—a half hour before we crossed the border—we got the word that we could enter as long as we stayed in the very bottom section of China. We soon realized this would be impossible. The winds would take us toward Shanghai—coincidentally a city I visited only two weeks earlier, and to which Virgin Atlantic has recently applied for permission to fly.

We then had word that the Chinese had held a press conference in Beijing and had stated that we had violated their airspace without permission—if we did not rectify this promptly the consequences could be severe.

At the same time we received a message from our base in London going through the probable sequence of actions that an escort fighter plane would adopt. We went through the sequence of events that we would try to adopt ourselves in order to comply. We then received a message from the Chinese Civil Aviation Authorities:

> **PLEASE BE INFORMED THAT YOU MUST LAND AT LHASA AIRPORT**
> **AND CANNOT CONTINUE FLYING OVER OUR AIRSPACE BECAUSE**
> **YOU CANNOT OBEY OUR REQUIREMENTS. PLEASE CONTACT LATER.**
> **YOU MUST OPERATE THE BALLOON AS REQUESTED BY LHASA ACC.**
> **THANKS FOR YOUR CO-OPERATION**
> **BEST REGARDS@OPS OF CAAC**

Well, the words "thanks for your co-operation" were the only friendly words we had heard in a while. A balloon cannot land at just any pre-determined spot, let alone a specific airport. The weather conditions were atrocious, it would be dark in two hours, we were over mountains, and we were carrying five tons of propane. We were being asked, in effect, to commit suicide. I asked Virgin ICO Global Balloon Base to contact the Chinese, explaining all our problems. We received a response one hour later:

> **PLEASE BE INFORMED YOU MUST LAND. YOU CANNOT CONTINUE**
> **OVER OUR AIRSPACE.**

We were in a catch-22 situation: to attempt to land would mean certain death, but to continue, without permission, would mean that we'd almost certainly be shot down.

I contacted the British Ambassador in Beijing and explained our predicament. He promised that he and his team would stay up all night to try to resolve it. I sent the Ambassador a note to pass on to the Chinese:

> **WE KINDLY ADVISE THAT IT IS NOT POSSIBLE TO LAND NOW**
> **WITHOUT SEVERELY ENDANGERING THE LIVES OF THE CREW AND**
> **ANY PERSONS ON THE GROUND.**

> **WE CANNOT STEER THE BALLOON, AS IT GOES WHERE THE WIND**
> **TAKES IT. WE HAVE FULL CLOUD COVER AND CANNOT SEE THE**
> **GROUND. WE CANNOT DESCEND THROUGH CLOUD, AS IT WILL**
> **CREATE ICE ON THE BALLOON RESULTING IN US CRASHING.**

> **WE KINDLY BRING TO YOUR ATTENTION THAT WE ARE DOING**
> **EVERYTHING IN OUR POWER TO RESOLVE THE SITUATION AND**
> **APOLOGIZE PROFUSELY FOR NOT BEING ABLE TO COMPLY WITH**
> **YOUR INSTRUCTIONS. WE ARE NOT BEING DISRESPECTFUL TO**
> **THE CHINESE AUTHORITIES. WE ARE JUST IN AN IMPOSSIBLE**

SITUATION THAT WE CANNOT RESOLVE AT PRESENT WITHOUT
ENDANGERING LIVES.

WE KINDLY REQUEST THAT YOU GIVE OUR TEAM MORE TIME TO
WORK ON THIS PROBLEM.

OUR PILOTS HAVE TRIED EVERY FREQUENCY THAT YOU HAVE GIVEN
TO US BUT ARE UNABLE TO CONTACT YOU. THEY WILL CONTINUE
TO TRY. PLEASE CAN YOU ADVISE SOME MORE HF OR VHF
FREQUENCIES.

WE KINDLY REQUEST A RESPONSE TO THIS MESSAGE.

We flew on nervously. After all the personal pleas from so many world
figures, we hoped the Chinese wouldn't do anything too dramatic.

In the early hours of the morning, to our great relief, the following fax
came through:

SINCE THE VIRGIN GLOBAL CHALLENGER HOT-AIR BALLOON HAS
INFRINGED THE PRINCIPLES AGREED BY THE TWO SIDES AND
THE PROMISES MADE BY THE UK SIDE AND DID NOT ENTER THE
AIRSPACE WITHIN THE DESIGNATED AREA, THE CHINESE SIDE
HAD NO OPTION BUT TO DEMAND THAT IT SHOULD LAND. IN
RESPECT OF THE APPEAL MADE BY AMBASSADOR GALSWORTHY
THE CHINESE SIDE HAVE MADE EVERY EFFORT TO OVERCOME
ALL DIFFICULTIES AND HAVE NOW DECIDED TO ALLOW THE
BALLOON TO CONTINUE ITS FLIGHT. BUT THEY REQUEST THAT
IT SHOULD LEAVE CHINESE AIRSPACE AS RAPIDLY AS POSSIBLE.
IF THE CHINESE SIDE HAVE NEW REQUESTS THEY WILL BE IN
TOUCH WITH THE BRITISH SIDE.

Phew! We cannot thank the Chinese enough. Thank you.

Day 7, 24 December 1998

A bizarre thing happened to me as we left the Chinese coast.
I received word from England:

MANY CONGRATULATIONS! VIRGIN ATLANTIC HAS BEEN GIVEN
PERMISSION TO BE THE ONLY AIRLINE TO FLY TO SHANGHAI DIRECT
FROM ENGLAND. BRITISH AIRWAYS HAS BEEN TURNED DOWN.
HURRY HOME.

It's a strange world. One minute terrified of being shot down over Shanghai in a balloon, the next being given permission to start flying a 747 there!

It would have been delightful news if we hadn't found ourselves heading for North Korea. It seems that we have a magnetic attraction to every country that does not welcome balloonists. And North Korea is one of the most closed, heavily militarist countries in the world. We had been told not even to bother to apply for overflying rights.

Bob went into overdrive to find winds to take us south through South Korea. In the meantime, Kevin Stass—who with Erin Porter had been battling back at base to get our overflight rights—thought, give it a go, and contacted the North Koreans.

To the surprise and delight of all of us, a quick response came, welcoming us to overfly. Maybe as a nation they are now ready to become part of the wider world. For whatever reason, we were extremely grateful. We now had "only" the biggest ocean in the world to cross—5,200 miles of the Pacific—then America, and then the Atlantic Ocean.

After everything that had happened, in the first five days we had only traveled a third of the way around the world.

The Pacific has claimed many other hot-air balloonists who have attempted a crossing. The day before Per and I successfully crossed the Pacific in a hot-air balloon, ten years ago, a delightful Japanese balloonist attempted it and perished. Only three months ago Steve Fossett hit a thunderstorm over the Pacific and was brought down near Fiji. We therefore all have enormous respect for the Pacific Ocean, and yet strangely we were so relieved to have gotten through the political problems of the last few days that we felt somehow we would have a drama-free trip.

It started well: We ended up crossing South Korea as it turned out, since Bob had already been working on changing our track successfully before North Korean permission came through. We then traveled on to a beautiful dawn over Mount Fuji and Kansai in Japan. We could see literally thousands of people thronging the streets looking up at the balloon as we passed overhead. Will Whitehorn, my right-hand man, who was in Kansai, contacted the balloon and said that "it was one of the most remarkable sights of my life—standing and watching the whole place come to a halt."

To our great relief, the winds began to pick up. We found speeds of between 150 and 180 mph; we were sucked into the jetstream and we needed it. We had used a lot of fuel flying over the Himalayas and had to race home. We had no more than six days' duration left, and two-thirds of the way to go. But, with these speeds, we calculated we could cross the Pacific in fewer than forty hours; a day to cross America, another to cross the Atlantic, and then home. Our spirits were high; we really thought we had a chance.

Then we received an urgent message from Bob Rice. It began: "We have a potential problem that is giving me great concern." If Bob had great concern about something then so should we. "Specifically," he went on, "there's a trough out there that will have an elongated shear line from around Hawaii, northeastward. The result of a pattern shift like that will take the balloon southeast toward Hawaii and back into the Pacific Ocean. We need to get to the trough before it starts to shear. Maximum speed is critical: more so than on any other occasion."

We knew what he meant—if we did not get through on time, we would be turned southward and end up in the water. Or, as Mike Kendrick, our base commander, said five minutes later, "This is a matter of saving you going into the drink, so, for God's sake, fly." We went as high as we could to get extra speed, but we could only find 10 knots more. Bob reran the figures to see if 10 knots was sufficient to push us through and on into America. If not, it is fortunate that the capsule was built to float. But I had no plan or wish to test it!

The diary ended there, just as things started to turn for the worse. We were too busy just trying to stay alive. I remember on that last day when we had all but crossed the Pacific and had the States ahead, with the weather forecasters saying that we would be home in two days. The winds were so strong, about 200 mph, and it looked as if we were going to cross America on Christmas Day, with Father Christmas dangling far below us, and be home for Boxing Day.

As I was going to sleep, I thought this was almost too much for one person in his lifetime, to have such fantastic experiences, and to be so fortunate. It was only when I woke up that I realized that fortune was not going to shine on us this time and that we were going to end up landing in the Pacific rather than being the first to travel around the world in a hot-air balloon.

The wall of bad weather that we had tried to beat had gotten there before us. We went as high as we could to get through it; we went as low as we could to get through it. But to no avail. It was as if a solid brick wall had been built right down the coast of America to stop us.

We were fortunate to find winds that took us back out into the Pacific, toward the only islands for thousands of miles—Hawaii. Sixty miles from them, we crashed into the sea. The balloon dragged over the waves, bouncing 300 feet each time, like the bombs in the *Dambusters* film. Pushing the dome on the roof open, we climbed out, hanging on for dear life. Finally, as the balloon hit the sea for the tenth time, we threw ourselves off, once again to be plucked out of the sea by helicopters, which just managed to reach us. No wonder Virgin funded London's helicopter ambulance service!

On Christmas Day I landed in Hawaii and decided to get to Necker Island, where all the family was. So on Boxing Day I landed to find a slightly surreal thing happening. Nobody was in the big house. All my best friends and relatives were gathered at the very far end of the island having a children's party. The reason it was surreal was that I'd written my will the day before I'd taken off in the balloon, and in it I'd instructed that, if the balloon had gone down and my body had been recovered, I was to be buried at that end of the island. I wanted my best friends and family to be at my funeral, and I wanted to remain forever in this very special place. And so it was strange to be there in person, looking around and thinking, My God, what a different kind of party this could have been.

It was at that time that I thought, I've had these incredible experiences, somebody has been kind to me, I've survived them. These ballooning exploits had helped me put Virgin on the map, put me on the map, and given me some fantastic memories to tell the grandchildren one day. But I'd pushed my luck as far as I should. Now I could see that if I could use the position in which I'd found myself—where I could pick up the phone to President Mandela or President Clinton or Prime Minister Tony Blair and get through—I might be able to do something really special. To use that power and position to try to fulfill my original dream—from when I was fifteen, starting the magazine and writing my first editorial—of trying to change the world.

What I'd always thought was that Virgin should be more than just a money-making machine, and that, as Virgin has the wealth of a small nation, we should use that wealth to tackle social issues more than we had in the past. Companies do have a responsibility to tackle them. Bill Gates, over the last few years, has invested enormous amounts of money in Africa, trying to help stamp out malaria. Despite the difficult time he's had and the bad press Microsoft has received, he's given an incredible amount back to the community. He's a tremendous example to all other entrepreneurs.

When I was last in South Africa, I visited some hospitals, particularly ones in Soweto. It was devastating to see the number of people whose lives have been destroyed by HIV/AIDS, including the millions of orphans who have become heads of households at the ripe old age of nine. After the launch of Mates in the UK, Virgin has continued to support a number of organizations in the fight against HIV/AIDS around the world—but after this trip I vowed that we would in some way do even more to help stop this disease from wiping out entire generations. I'm also a supporter of an organization that's trying to make sure that the 2 percent of Africa currently set aside for wildlife is increased to 4 or 5 percent, giving the wildlife of Africa more wild areas in which to roam—areas that are not just given over to cattle and farmers. It would be a fantastic legacy for the next generation if twice as much land as is currently used can be fenced in for wild animals, giving them a greater chance of long-term survival. Also it would encourage tourists to come and spend the foreign money that Africa desperately needs.

Another area of the world that has seen more than its fair share of trouble is Northern Ireland. Although there will always be extremists from both factions—Catholic Republicans and Protestant Unionists—by the 1990s the public was getting increasingly tired of years of sectarian bombings and killings. In May 1998 Mo Mowlam was appointed Northern Ireland Secretary—an inspired choice. Mo is a completely down-to-earth woman who could relate to the ordinary man and woman (literally—as it turned out—in the street). She decided to go above the heads of the politicians and directly to The People to hold a referendum on the future of Ireland. If she won, permanent peace was a strong possibility. If she lost, the alternative was to go back to the last thirty years in which 3,500 people had been murdered. In effect the referendum she proposed said that Northern Ireland would remain part of Great Britain, but if one day the majority of citizens of Northern Ireland wanted a unified Ireland and if they voted for it, they could have it.

Two days before the vote, the outcome looked uncertain. Mo called me and asked if I could come to Northern Ireland the next day and walk the streets with her. Perhaps in part because of my ballooning and boating ventures I was quite popular in Ireland—or she may have felt I could show how Northern Ireland could benefit from investment if peace came about, since good economic investment gives a much greater chance for healing.

The next day I set out for Heathrow with one of our PR staff, Jackie, who happened to be from Northern Ireland herself. In the lounge she turned to me and said, "Richard, I'm sorry. I just can't come with you. My dad will kill me if he sees me with you campaigning for this peace treaty." I'd never thought of her as Protestant or Catholic, just a delightful Irish girl. It brought home to me just what a difficult job Mo had ahead of her. In the end I persuaded Jackie to come. She bravely stayed with Mo and me for the rest of the day. By the end of the day Jackie was so convinced by the arguments that she decided to vote yes and persuaded her mother and sisters to vote yes as well. Unfortunately, she realized her dad was a lost cause.

That night, having walked the streets of Northern Ireland and shaken hundreds of hands, we all went back to Hillsborough Castle, the Northern Ireland Secretary's beautiful residence, for dinner and bed to await the outcome. At least I knew my trip had secured four extra votes!

The next day the good news came through—the yes vote had been won. Peace finally had come to Ireland. Since it was a peace voted by the people this time, it felt it just might hold.

11 September 2001

In my life, I've come to expect the unexpected. It sounds easy enough to say, but all the things that have happened to me, to the family, and to Virgin have taught me that you have to be prepared at all times to deal with surprises. You just develop a way of picking up your feet and getting on with it. But nothing I've ever faced made me ready for what happened on 11 September.

It was a quarter past three in the afternoon in Brussels, and I was about to stand up to address yet another European Union enquiry into competition. I've sat through dozens of meetings like this, and there was nothing out of the ordinary about that September day. The same gray suits, it seemed, sat there, ranged against us. I knew the strength of our position, so I was already thinking ahead of that meeting, about getting home, settling back into the routine at work after a summer break with the family on Necker. This time it was not about an airline, nor was it about the music business, retailing, or the railways: It was about the incredibly "interesting" subject of "block exemption" for European car manufacturers. In other words, about the fact that the people who make cars rip us all off by controlling who sells them and at what price they're sold to us. I was there because, as the years rolled on and the world of the Internet and call centers lowered the cost of distribution, it had become possible for Virgin to sell and deliver cars directly to the public at prices up to 25 percent cheaper than the dealerships.

As I was about to launch into a withering attack on the vested interests of the people who were sitting all around me in the room, someone quietly handed a note to the chairman, who looked up with an ashen face and announced to the shocked room that there had been a terrorist attack in New York, involving a number of aircraft. None of us there knew quite how serious things were; the chairman said anyone who wanted to leave could, since there was some concern that the European Union building could also be a target. As a matter of principle, I decided to carry on, deliver the speech, and answer questions from the members of the European Parliament, knowing full well that everyone's mind would be on New York.

An hour later I was about to board a Eurostar train home when I finally managed to get through to London. "It looks like Middle Eastern terrorists took over four aircraft," Will said. "The Twin Towers have just come down and there could be more than ten thousand dead. Reports are also coming in of other aircraft being hijacked. In your absence, we turned Virgin planes back; only three had passed the point of no return. Since then they've shut US airspace. I suggest we talk in more detail once you're back and all gather tomorrow morning first thing at Holland Park."

As I sat on the train with the Chief Executive of Virgin Cars, the full horror began to sink in. There was a woman sitting opposite us who was a banker and was frantically phoning friends in London and New York to find out what she could. She began to give us an account of what she knew, that the brokers Cantor Fitzgerald had been almost completely wiped out, that several French and American banks may have had severe casualties. Her distress was evident and I did what I could to help her. I still had not seen any pictures, but I could tell from her tears just how awful things were.

Only that morning, I'd run over in my mind how the businesses were going. In the run-up to 11 September, Virgin Atlantic had continued its remarkable success story. Singapore Airlines had become our partners, paying a record £600 million for a 49 percent stake in March 2000, and we had remained the only profitable airline flying across the North Atlantic in 2001. The business felt so good that year, as others struggled with out-of-control costs, unfriendly service, and aging fleets. Indeed, I felt so confident about the business that I had continued expanding by starting a new airline in Australia almost exactly a year to the day before the Twin Towers tragedy. It was called Virgin Blue. It was based on the low-cost model of Southwest Airlines. Despite the weak Australian dollar and high fuel costs, it had thrived, driving airfares down and doubling the number of people flying on its routes.

This was not the only new investment of the previous few years. We had done a lot to rationalize Virgin and its brand in the late 1990s and, by 11 September, we had a clear strategy in place, based on the concept of "branded venture capital." Instead of being a conglomerate with lots of subsidiaries, Virgin had become a diverse investor. So we'd choose business sectors carefully, trying to bring more competition to sectors that would benefit the consumer. Then we'd find good partners and managers to take the businesses forward, with the eventual aim of letting them stand on their own two feet, just as companies like Virgin Records and Virgin Radio had already done.

But we were also turning our attention to whether we could make a difference in other areas. For nearly 250 days of the year I travel around the world, trying to make Virgin the most respected brand in the world; not necessarily the biggest, but the best.

We had also built a great management team, both at UK and international levels, that could act as our eyes and ears across all the businesses, so the new investments had come at breakneck speeds over the previous couple of years. Virgin Active had become the world's third largest health-club chain; thetrainline.com, selling rail tickets via the Internet, had 5 million customers by 11 September. Virgin Mobile was Europe's fastest-growing mobile-phone company and, on that fateful day, was on the verge of doing a deal with Sprint to take our no-nonsense mobile offer to the American public.

As part of the expansion of Mobile, we had also finally consigned the Our Price brand to the dustbin of history. Since we had bought the business from WH Smith in 1998, we had rebranded it as VSHOP to sit alongside the successful Megastore chain. It, and Virgin's other presence on the high street, helped Virgin Mobile achieve nearly 2 million customers by the beginning of 2002. The success of these businesses, working together under one brand, was a huge boost to our confidence that our strategy was right.

But it was a gloomy group of us who met in my Holland Park house in West London on the morning of 12 September. Present in the sitting room were Richard Bowker, Patrick McCall, Will Whitehorn, Mark Poole, and Simon Wright. Ironically, nobody was there from Virgin Atlantic. Steve Ridgway—the managing director—and his senior team had already enacted their emergency procedures and begun an urgent seventy-two-hour review of the entire business, with a view to making recommendations by the Friday of that week as to what we should do. But all of us sitting around the table in Holland Park knew we were going to have to do something fast. With transatlantic routes closed to us, and the sudden drop in passenger numbers, Virgin Atlantic was set to lose £3 million a day. That morning I had spoken to BA's new boss—a delightful Australian named Rod Eddington—who had told me that BA could lose up to £8 million a day. I suggested that we work together in our approach to the government to see what assistance we might get once American airspace opened again. I was heartened by his straightforward reply: "Good on ya, mate! I'll call you at the start of next week."

The fact that BA may have been in even worse trouble than we were wasn't much consolation to the six of us sitting around my drawing-room table in the bright September sunshine. As we drew up lists of what we were up against, it was clear that we had enough cash in the various companies to see ourselves through the worst, but that the potential black hole at Virgin Atlantic needed to be plugged as quickly as possible. The other uncertainty was what was going to happen to our competitors. Sabena in Brussels and Ansett in Australia were going into administration, but would they survive?

One of the first things I'd checked, on hearing about the terrorist attacks, was whether anyone we knew had been involved. Frances Farrow, who had worked for us on the airline business over here and then moved to New York only that spring to marry her fiancé, lived near the Twin Towers. She was helping out on the deal with Sprint for Virgin Mobile. We lost contact with her for three days; later, we found out that she'd been driving near the World Trade Center just as the first tower started to fall. Luckily, all other relatives and friends called to let us know they were OK.

But it wasn't the same for so many others, and I had a taste of this when I was called by Howard Lutnick, the chairman of "Cantors," as they were known in the City. On Friday night, James Kyle of Cantor Fitzgerald had called Will Whitehorn. They urgently needed to fly dozens of grieving relatives to New York, but since their entire operation had been wiped out, they did not know whether they would have a business, when the markets reopened, to pay the bill. On Saturday morning we agreed to carry as many people as they needed across the Atlantic. Whatever problems we had, it was so very much worse for them.

Howard rang that afternoon to thank me personally. I couldn't begin to imagine what a hellish time he was having, facing the loss of most of his close colleagues. "Thanks for everything you're doing for us," he said. "It means a lot to everyone at Cantors." I felt embarrassed that we could do only this much, especially when I learned, after his emotional and gracious phone call, that his own brother, Gary, had died in the devastating attack.

That same weekend, the plans we'd had ready for such an emergency were used for the first time. The team at Virgin Atlantic did a fantastic job in their assessment of the "market failure" between the UK and the USA and drew up an emergency restructuring plan. There were some painful bits to this: More than 1,200 jobs would go at the airline in the UK, but they did what they could to make the thousands of others secure. Most important, they switched larger aircraft, such as the 747-400s, on to booming routes in Africa, and put the smaller airbuses into service across the North Atlantic.

On Sunday morning we pressed the button to go ahead with the restructuring and told the staff on Monday. I will not forget the good grace and professionalism with which they took the news and then got on with the job. The months that followed were sticky, but we had called it right in the first week. By Christmas it was clear that Virgin Atlantic was through the worst and would survive. This was no mean feat, given that some of our American competitors received literally billions of dollars in handouts from their government. This may be what got them through, but all we saw was that it gave them leeway to behave more anti-competitively than they usually do.

The irony of the situation was this: Not only had we built up such a fantastic team of people but, until 11 September, we'd been profitable. My biggest worry now was the impact on staff morale in the face of enforced redundancies. It was a testament to everybody involved that not only did a lot of the older and part-time staff come forward and volunteer for redundancy, but those who stayed really buckled down in the spirit that undoubtedly made Virgin Atlantic what it is today. The innovative nature of the airline— using bed-seats and in-flight masseurs to make passengers more comfortable—now meant, ironically, that we were the first to install bulletproof Kevlar cockpit doors, to further ensure passengers' safety.

It would have been harder for Virgin Atlantic's management to be as single-minded as they were if they had had to worry about short-haul operations, but under Virgin's investment model they didn't have to. We have two other airlines, Virgin Express in Brussels and Virgin Blue in Brisbane, Australia. They are separately run, and Virgin Express is even quoted on the Brussels Stock Market. The effects of 11 September on these businesses were entirely different but equally challenging. In the case of one, it faced the collapse of the main state-owned carrier (Sabena), and for the other the collapse of its main competitor (Ansett). Both have had to quickly reshape and grow their businesses, but they were able to focus completely on their own issues.

Similarly, Virgin Mobile faced growth in the UK market, a recession in Singapore, and the decision as to whether or not to expand in the US. If Virgin Mobile were one conglomerate there could have been paralysis in these decisions, but as each is under a separate joint venture structure, once again the management teams could concentrate on the job in hand. By October, the Mobile team made the momentous decision to go ahead with launching Virgin Mobile in the US in partnership with Sprint, and began a fundraising exercise to help finance the $500 million venture.

This was not as crazy as it may seem. It was clear that though the US economy was going into recession, mobile-phone sales were finally starting to boom in America following the post–11 September uncertainties. Virgin's low-cost model of prepaid phones seemed an ideal solution to help attract a youth market, one that had not warmed to mobiles and text messaging in the way that the European, African, and Asian youth markets already had.

Within another two weeks, as everyone knows, the war against the terrorists started in earnest as the bombs and cruise missiles started to rain down on their enclaves in Afghanistan. It's always hard to stay focused at times like these, as I knew from the Gulf War, but people still had jobs to go to, and so it was another shock when Virgin Rail Group's biggest supplier, Railtrack, went bust. It was a blow to the railway-using public and to Virgin, which was at the time trying to negotiate a deal to save the upgrade of the West Coast mainline. Yet again, the consequences were quickly understood by a dedicated management team, who did not have to worry about the rest of some amorphous corporations' other activities.

Another shock followed when the government hired Richard Bowker to become head of the Strategic Rail Authority. As co-chairman of Virgin Rail, he had done an excellent job in coordinating our new train orders, as was proven when the first of our Pendolinos—tilting trains—were delivered from the factory, on time and on budget, in November 2001. By way of contrast, Railtrack's cost for the upgrade had gone up fivefold, and was going to end up being years late.

It was a proud and tearful moment, standing in the Alstom factory in Birmingham in the Midlands on a cold and sunny November day, watching Joan name one of our new trains *Virgin Lady*. It was an even better moment sitting by the fire that evening watching the six o'clock news and hearing the words I had waited five years for: "Virgin has delivered on its promises." This was no mean feat, as the orders had been placed in 1998 and, despite all the technological difficulties, Virgin had produced the world's most advanced train, which tilted around corners at speeds of up to 140 mph (225 kph). Of course the irony was that the track would not be ready for 125 mph operation until 2004! Virgin Rail's finance team continued to negotiate to ensure that our trains got the track they deserve—and the public the service it deserves. The railway experts, who had predicted in 1997 that upgrading the track would be easier than the trains, were dumbfounded.

Meanwhile, in Australia, the effects of 11 September continued to be felt in the airline business. Following the collapse of Ansett, Virgin Blue suddenly found itself Australia's second-largest airline. Its chief executive, Brett Godfrey, had been steadily building the business for a year but almost overnight was running an airline that promised to be more profitable than most airlines worldwide, if only he could raise the finance. Our corporate finance director, Patrick McCall, was on a plane to Australia within three days of the Twin Towers attack. One month later Virgin Blue had announced the appointment of Goldman Sachs to prepare for a flotation in 2003 with a potential valuation being talked about of over US$2 billion.

It nearly did not turn out this way, as Ansett's parent company, Air New Zealand, had made an offer to buy Virgin Blue for US$250 million shortly before 11 September. Singapore Airlines had a 20 percent stake in ANZ, so it was the CEO, Dr. Cheong (known as CK), who telephoned me to make the offer. "Richard, I really think you should accept this offer," he said. "It is a very generous valuation and, if you don't take it, we'll put the money into Ansett instead. They will wipe out Virgin Blue within six months."

It was a difficult decision. My instinct told me that the company was worth more than that, but it wasn't an ungenerous offer. However, there was something in the desperate insistence in CK's voice on the long-distance phone line that made me hesitate. I'm not a poker player, but something made me think he was bluffing. I decided to be a little mischievous, and to call a press conference. I wanted the competition authorities to understand how strongly the public felt about the need for healthy competition. I announced, with a somber and straight face: "This is a sad day, but I've decided to sell up. This means that cheap air tickets in Australia will be a thing of the past—others won't want to follow what we tried to do. It will of course mean that our staff will be part of Ansett, and that there will be redundancies. But anyway I've done well out of it, so I'm off back to the UK right away with my $250 million profit." There was a deadly hush, and the packed room seemed in deep shock. Then I caught sight of some of our staff members across the room, who were not meant to be at the press conference. I realized they were in tears. "Only joking," I added quickly, and publicly tore up the check.

Five days later, Ansett went bust. I had called CK's poker hand correctly. Brett could barely contain himself on the phone as he outlined his plans for rapid expansion. It was then that I realized that Brett's team had built a truly Virgin business: it had revolutionized the market for Australian air travel; it had built a fantastic reputation for quality; and all this had been done as a small-scale, venture-capital start-up, with only US$5 million.

Even our newer dotcom businesses launched since 1998 seemed to go from strength to strength after 11 September, largely because they were modeled on a real brand, selling real things. Virgin Cars sold its six thousandth vehicle that winter and, despite a blip after the New York attacks, car sales actually improved in the run-up to Christmas. The same was true of thetrainline.com. Again, sales rocketed as nervous executives decided that a train from Manchester in the northwest of England or Newcastle in the northeast was a better bet than a plane. By the beginning of 2002 these and several other of our e-commerce businesses had turned cash-flow-positive. There was one exception, Virgin Wines, which, despite winning 100,000 customers, still could not get the margins it needed in a cutthroat market.

Virgin Wines was a good example of our management philosophy of giving our people the chance to become entrepreneurs in their own right. It was established as a joint venture by Virgin and Rowan Gormley, of Virgin Money, who had begun to feel by the end of 1999 that our financial-services business was maturing and needed a different sort of manager. The former venture capitalist had been bitten by the entrepreneurial bug and simply wanted to start something new. I sympathized with him and, in spite of our misgivings about entering such a different sector, we decided to back him almost as a matter of principle.

I could go on, but hopefully the point is well made. By investing in separate businesses with partners, "ring-fenced," as the bankers keep telling me, we had been able to withstand the management pressures of 11 September, spread risk and make what we hope have been a lot of good decisions. Couple these with a venture-capital private-equity model of creating individual companies with their own business cases, shareholders, and financial resources, and you have the Virgin of 2004.

It's been interesting, with the collapse of Enron, to see how people still want to build enormous companies. But if something major goes wrong the whole lot falls. What we are trying to do at Virgin is not to have one enormous company in one sector under one banner, but to have two hundred or even three hundred separate companies. Each company can stand on its own feet and, in that way, although we've got a brand that links them, if we were to have a tragedy such as that of 11 September, although it hurt the airline industry, it would not bring the whole group crashing down.

In the past, we've never let a company go: we've always paid off its debts; we've always managed to keep our reputation as an organization that honors its obligations. But, in the event of a catastrophe, we could let a company go; we could cut it out, and because of that, the rest of the group would not be affected. Obviously, our reputation would suffer and that's something we wouldn't want to happen, but at least it would avoid a disaster.

The sheer diversity of Virgin's businesses has proven the test of time and circumstance. With each management team focused on its own business and entrepreneurial goals, we could achieve just about anything, as long as it was right for the brand. I learned a lot in the late 1990s and I came to realize that sticking our name on products was not the best way to create value. Virgin Vodka might sell well on the planes and at the airports, but we did not have the worldwide distribution of firms such as United Distillers & Vintners (UDV) or Scottish Courage to back it up. However, find entrepreneurial managers, like Frank Reed and Matthew Bucknall at Virgin Active, and give them the resources, and the sky will be the limit.

The omens were not good when Virgin Active opened its first club in Preston, Lancashire in August 1999. A fire swept through the club, doing tens of thousands of pounds' worth of damage, and a distraught Frank phoned me to give me the bad news. However, when he said it gave them a chance to do one or two things differently and have longer to train the staff, I was relieved. I was also beginning to get the measure of why Frank had such a strong reputation in the leisure industry. At the same time he helped me fulfill a pledge of many years' standing to invest further in South Africa.

One of the first casualties of the stock-market decline that preceded the Twin Towers attack was a quoted South African company that happened to own the country's largest chain of health clubs. I was in the bath when Nelson Mandela called and explained that it would be a particular blow to have eighty health clubs that were owned through a black-empowerment scheme closed down with the loss of several thousand jobs. He asked whether we could rescue it. We could, and we did, so that, by 11 September 2001, Virgin Active had mushroomed through growth and acquisitions into one of the top five health-club operators in the world.

In the aftermath of the attacks of 11 September, Virgin Atlantic has completely restructured its operations while BA's main response was to wrap itself in the Union Jack and pursue the government to back yet another attempt for it to create a transatlantic monopoly with American Airlines. Instead of trying to prevent more than 60 percent of UK-US airline traffic and slots at Heathrow from falling into the hands of one monolithic structure, it was clear that the British Department of Transport was going to help!

While I was presenting our case against the deal in front of the US Senate on a warm and sunny November day in Washington, the British Embassy put out a press release supporting the merger and an attendant "Open Skies" deal—amazing considering the only beneficiaries were likely to be the two airlines creating the monopoly and equally amazing since the competition authorities were almost definitely going to rule it to be against the interests of the traveling public. With considerable pomposity, our diplomats tried to capture the pro-British mood on Capitol Hill with the words: "Two allies, united in so much else, should be able to reach agreement on something that would be to their mutual benefit." If anyone could have told me what "mutual benefit" the attempt to create a North Atlantic airline monopoly had for two allies locked in conflict with the Taliban and Osama Bin Laden, I would happily have given them free first class tickets for life.

That was not the end of it, though. In trying to defend the deal, BA made the ludicrous claim in the *Sunday Telegraph* that there was no shortage of slots at Heathrow; this was, in the immortal words of Sid Vicious, "bollocks!," and Virgin responded by offering to give £2 million to charity for every slot that Lord Marshall managed to procure for us. Naturally, he was unable to rise to the challenge, and he must have groaned when the US Department of Justice slammed the deal as anticompetitive and confirmed that its investigations concluded that the shortage of slots was a major reason why the deal should not go ahead as proposed.

It was not until late January 2002 that BA's game with American Airlines finally played itself out. The US Department of Transport announced that it would let them merge their operations if BA gave up slots to the other American carriers. The problem was the price: the US regulators realized that Heathrow was overcrowded, and they would have to give their airlines a lot of access as the price of the deal. For BA, though, the price was too high, and in the last week of January they abandoned their merger plans and went back to the drawing board on the whole "Open Skies" issue.

Since the start of their attempted merger in 1996, BA had wasted thousands of man-hours and tens of millions of pounds, on a hopeless scheme, more in tune with the 1970s view of the airline business than the modern world of deregulation, competition, and low-cost airlines. Rod Eddington wisely bit the bullet and, instead of trying to create a monopoly to get out of difficulties, he announced the "Future Size and Shape" project to restructure BA. He also urgently began to look for another partner in Europe.

Some things never change. Chief executives may come and go, but whatever the situation, you can always rely on BA to behave in exactly the same way toward Virgin as it has always done. The same is true of Camelot: Their new license to run Britain's National Lottery came into effect in January 2002, amid falling numbers of people playing.

I decided in 1999 that I would bid again with a not-for-profit consortium to take over the lottery. As before, most of my close Virgin advisers tried to persuade me not to bid because of the damage that a fight with Camelot—that few of them believed we could win—could do to the brand. Nonetheless, I felt so passionately about the good that could be done via the lottery that I decided to go ahead. My old friend Simon Burridge had spent the intervening years at the J Walter Thompson advertising agency as managing director but had lost none of his enthusiasm for either the principle of a People's Lottery or the inevitable fight with Camelot that would follow the decision. Simon was not a man to mince words: "I've been following things at Camelot very closely, Richard, and all our predictions in the 1993 bid are coming true. Sales are falling like a stone, the GTECH technology is crap, their games are unexciting, and with the right suppliers I think we can do it!"

He set to work immediately. The only exception to the previous team was Will Whitehorn, who again felt strongly that there should be a clear demarcation between Virgin and what was to become known as the People's Lottery. We were in the middle of investing in a whole new range of businesses, which, with the exception of the airline, might not see profits for the first couple of years. Will wanted to concentrate on the bigger picture—the PR for the group and the brand—and suggested using an outside PR agency for the People's Lottery. And so we assembled a new team of suppliers, agencies, and people, built around the core team from the 1993 bid. In all, we ended up with more than twenty suppliers, from Energis and Microsoft to J Walter Thompson, JP Morgan, and our previous rivals, AWI.

Freshly back from the final, failed, around-the-world balloon attempt during the Christmas of 1998, I didn't appreciate one crucial difference between the Camelot of 1993 and that of 1999. Having won the bid to run the lottery and run it for six years, Camelot was prepared to do anything to keep it. More important, because most people thought they would win it again, we ended up being the only rival bidder, which meant they (and their friends) could concentrate all their firepower against us—and me personally.

The end game played itself out in the summer of 2000, while we were on our family holiday on Necker. A fax arrived from the boss of the Lottery Commission, Dame Helena Shovelton, telling us that we had won. We were given a period of exclusivity to negotiate a deal. If we could guarantee enough money to cover any potential downside and clear up a few points, then the lottery would be ours.

If only it had been that simple. Simon and John Jackson predicted that Camelot could take a judicial review against her decision, if for no other reason than to delay the process. They did. And, what's more, they won it, which then threw the entire process into chaos that autumn. Dame Helena resigned and was replaced by Terry Burns. In a few short weeks Burns reversed Dame Helena's decision, and came to the (I felt) ludicrous conclusion that the license should go to Camelot.

None of us could believe it and, as the weeks went on into 2001, the

British public began to desert Camelot in their thousands. By the time 11 September shook the world, sales were falling at a rate of 20 percent per year. I took no satisfaction from this because, of course, it was not Camelot that suffered, but rather the many good causes—sports, the arts, charities, and other organizations—that simply got less money.

It also emerged that Camelot had managed to win the renewal of their license by pledging to raise £15 billion for good causes, but the government hadn't asked them to guarantee this. Within weeks of winning, Camelot was publicly looking for excuses as to why they wouldn't raise anything like £15 billion. "The public finds it boring," "We were distracted by the bidding process," etc. But they had their license. It was a staggering outcome and one for which I think the British government should hang their heads in shame: They had pledged at the election that the lottery would be run with all the profits going to good causes—and they'd reneged on that pledge.

Summer 2004

By the autumn of 2001, I had put the Camelot affair behind me, not only because Virgin had been incredibly busy, but also because of some big changes in family life that had kept me occupied. Holly, our daughter, sailed through her A levels and was about to fulfill her (almost) life-long ambition to go to university to study medicine. Sam had really settled down at school and reached the stage where he needed to have his dad around more and more. My son, perhaps, hasn't got the same sense of purpose at school as my daughter has, but he certainly knows how to party, and (perhaps taking after his father here) knows how to enjoy life to its fullest.

My father is about to enjoy his eighty-fifth birthday, and my mother her eightieth birthday. They are still on and off airplanes, traveling around the world. They have enormous affection for Africa, as do I, and over the last few years we have bought a beautiful game reserve called Ulusaba in South Africa, where we've built a stunning house up on the hill overlooking the jungle. We run this as a business but make sure that we all find the time to go and visit it ourselves. These are the times that you remember and cherish.

The restructuring of Virgin Atlantic after the tragedy of 11 September really began to pay off in the years that followed and the confidence of the management was if anything enhanced by the ability of the airline to withstand the shocks that followed—the aftereffects of the war in Afghanistan and the double whammy of SARS in Asia and a second war in the Gulf. Virgin Atlantic truly came of age during these events and managed to return to profitability after April 2002, despite having lost nearly £100 million in the months that followed the Twin Towers tragedy.

We also launched our secret weapon in the so-called Battle of the Beds with British Airways. In the summer of 2003, Virgin Atlantic unveiled its Upper Class Suite—the world's only truly first-class-style flat bed in a business class. It took off in every sense of the word and by the summer of 2004 we were making significant in-roads into our rivals' market share. The project to create the beds had typical Virgin characteristics. We took the brave move to design the unique product ourselves and the task fell to Jo Ferry, Virgin Atlantic's head of design. He achieved the holy grail of airline seat manufacturers in that he managed to make a comfortable seat into a genuine bed through its unique flipping mechanism. The risk paid off, and Jo's design won six of the world's biggest industrial design awards during 2004.

As Virgin Atlantic continued to recover, the fortunes of our other businesses thrived despite the terrible uncertainties that George Bush's "war on terrorism" created around the world. Virgin Blue continued to grow profitably and floated on the Australian Stock Market in December 2003. This was a remarkable achievement given the chaos in the aviation market and the tragic terrorist attack in Bali the previous year, which had dented Australians' confidence in their immunity from the problems of the rest of the world.

I myself felt a great deal of unease about the "war on terror," which had clearly become intermingled with a darker side of US foreign policy. It had long been the desire of the so-called neo-conservatives in America to conduct a more interventionist role in the Middle East and "stabilize" that region. By the autumn of 2002, it was clear that the Bush administration had made a decision to intervene in Iraq regardless of what world opinion thought of the matter and by early 2003, it was clear they would do it even if the UN did not back their decision.

I found the whole episode deeply depressing and had a real foreboding about what I believe was an unjustified invasion. Apart from the obvious human cost of a conflict, I was skeptical about the weapons of mass destruction and could not fathom why the US government would possibly find Iraq so easy to democratize when so many others had failed before. After 11 September, Will Whitehorn had counseled against public opposition to the Bush administration over the issue of Iraq on the basis that it was inevitable. George Bush continued to state on television, and at press conferences, that "War was a necessary evil"—it is my belief that most "necessary evils" are far more evil than necessary. By February 2003 I'd hatched a plan to try and persuade Saddam Hussein to stand down before war happened. With a heavy heart I called Nelson Mandela and followed this up with a letter.

Dear Madiba,

As always it was very good to talk to you. I thought I'd send you a very brief note setting out our discussion.

America and Britain have definitely decided to go to war. Inevitably there will be many civilian casualties.

I believe there may be only one way to stop a war in Iraq and I believe you may be the only person in the world to achieve it.

If Saddam Hussein could be persuaded to retire to Libya (or somewhere else) with full immunity I do not believe it would be possible for America to press ahead with war. If he were to make this sacrifice to avoid his people going through yet more suffering he would enhance his reputation considerably. The personal alternative will be the fate of Noriega, Milosevic, or worse.

Knowing your close relationship with President Qaddafi and the respect you are held in Iraq you are perhaps the only person who could organize this.

I believe that you would have the credibility to persuade Saddam Hussein to step down. By flying out with you—to say, Libya—he could leave with his head held high. It would be the best thing he could ever do for his people.

If it helps you, I would be happy to send you a plane to take you there and back (hopefully via Libya!).

I'll talk to you once you've spoken with Thabo.

Kind regards as always,
Richard

It was a bold plan that might just have worked. Nelson Mandela wanted me to get the approval of Kofi Annan, the United Nations Secretary General, and the blessing of his own president, Thabo Mbeki. I wrote to Kofi Annan and followed up with a phone call. He gave the idea his full support. On 17 March, we positioned two pilots and a Lear Jet in Johannesburg to take Mandela to Baghdad. We had managed to get the hostages out of Iraq some years before by sending Edward Heath. This time Nelson Mandela—the world's most respected person—had spoken out strongly against the upcoming US invasion. If anybody could persuade Saddam it would be him. Enormous numbers of lives could be saved and injuries avoided.

Sadly, time ran out and two days later events overtook us. On 19 March 2003 the US bombed Baghdad, and the rest is history. There is nothing in my life that I regret more.

But what I realized from the experience is that the world needs a group of elders—such as Nelson Mandela—who can step in on behalf of the world community in situations like this. Over the next couple of years we will bring together such a group to deliver a voice to the people of the world. Fortunately Mandela has agreed to be the Founding Father. Now the search is on for a special group of people who share his moral courage.

Not long after the conflict was over I saw a microcosm of Iraq first-hand when we took the first relief flight into Basra. Appropriately, it was piloted by Mike Abunalla, an Iraqi exile whose family had fled Iraq twenty-two years earlier. Our mission was to deliver more than sixty tons of generously do-nated medical supplies to the hospitals of Basra, which Saddam's army had stripped bare in their rush northward. During the flight we were all struck by the devastation of any infrastructure on the ground and the sheer empti-ness and enormity of the country.

The whole project had been a remarkable cooperation between an Iraqi exile, Luay Shakarchy, who was based in the Midlands; in Birmingham, our own Jackie McQuillan; and Air Marshal Brian Burridge. The spirit of coop-eration between the British forces on the ground in Basra and a small team of operational staff from Virgin Atlantic was remarkable; in a matter of weeks they managed to open Basra Airport for a 747 getting this much-needed aid into the country. I spent a lot of time talking to the servicemen and -women in Basra, and I could tell that many of the British forces had a strong sense of foreboding regarding the situation unfolding with their American counter-parts in the North. How true that sense of foreboding turned out to be.

Many of us were moved by what we saw and experienced during this first civilian flight into Iraq since 1990. Not least Jackie, who, joined by three Iraqi exiles who are now doctors in Britain, went downtown to visit some of the patients in Basra General Hospital. It was there she saw first-hand not only the pain and suffering inflicted on civilians during war but also that there is always hope and beauty no matter how horrific the situation. In the hospital she met a young woman of twenty who had been severely wounded in her legs and stomach by shrapnel. Despite her agony, she could not drag her eyes away from her beautiful little baby girl, who had been born by emergency cesarean section two days before. Seeing Jackie's tears of sympathy the woman said: "Please don't cry for me, God has given me the greatest gift of all and in her eyes are only innocence and love." They were some of the most poignant words relayed to me that day.

The run-up to the war and its aftermath meant that life went on in the Branson household. Joan and I were incredibly proud of how well Holly was getting on in her medical degree, so we decided to throw a big party. The weather was beautiful in Kidlington in Oxfordshire that cold November night for her twenty-first birthday, and she looked lovely in her white evening gown. Joan and I had to pinch ourselves thinking back to the little baby girl who we had brought back to our London houseboat in the Regents Canal back in 1984. It was not many months later when Sam had his eighteenth birthday, which was a considerably more "laddish" affair in the Roof Gardens in Kensington. To say that his friends' speeches were risqué would be the understatement of the year. On this occasion Joan and I had to put our fingers in our ears, rather than pinch ourselves.

Joan, Holly and I and some of the team from Virgin also had the wonderful opportunity to help, and attended Nelson Mandela's "46664" concert in South Africa in late 2003. Madiba was generous enough to use his prison number, 46664, as a symbol for hope in the fight against HIV/AIDS. Sitting next to Madiba and his wonderful wife Gracia, listening to Peter Gabriel sing "Biko" for only the second time in South Africa, was one of the most moving experiences of my life.

As the war ended, I also made a conscious decision to spend more time with my parents, in particular my father, Ted, who was the oldest. Over the previous decades, I had more and more come to appreciate his wisdom. One example had been his very wise counsel about the war, which he had also been vehemently against, but he had reinforced my own views that once the shooting started, we had to stand by and support the many brave young American and British men and women who were "following orders" in Iraq.

By the spring of 2004, Ted had fully recovered from a complex hip replacement operation a few years earlier and I took a short sabbatical from the world of Virgin to go camping with him in the Serengeti. It is an awesome place, where you can really feel nature still in charge of her destiny. Having been there, I can fully understand why so many anthropologists believe the region is where man originated as a species. We spent ten days following the wildebeest migration and the predation of the lions upon their herds. For those of you who have not spent ten days in a tent with your eighty-five-year-old father—if you are fortunate enough to be in a position to do so—I can thoroughly recommend it in every way. I think we developed an even better understanding of each other as we talked long into the evening.

More than anything, I marveled at the sense of humor of a man who had seen it all. One fantastic example of this was early one morning on his birthday. We'd all just woken up and were quite grumpy after a night in the tent, but Dad was beaming. We were all intrigued until he explained, "If I was Catholic, I'd be doing penance today. I had the most wonderful dream. It involved a girl."

"Did you misbehave with her?" I asked.

Quick as a flash Dad replied, "I don't know *what* you mean. *I* behaved. *She* was outrageously naughty!" And this from an eighty-six-year-old man!

Back in London in the spring of 2004, it was business as usual in the Virgin empire. Gordon McCallum was busy preparing Virgin Mobile for its flotation on the London Stock Market with an expected valuation of £1billion. It really had been a remarkable story. In only four years we had created the world's first virtual mobile phone network and established a base of 4 million customers who were the most satisfied in the industry. Even more exciting in some ways was the huge success of the US mobile venture, which we had started in the dark days of post–11 September America. Even by 2004, it was clear that Virgin Mobile USA could eventually be more valuable than the UK operation. It had become the fastest-growing company in the history of corporate America to reach a billion dollars in revenue. Hot on the heels of the US, other colleagues Robert Samuelson and Max Kelly were beavering away in Canada, recruiting the team for yet another mobile venture to launch there in 2005 in partnership with Bell Canada. By mid-2004, it was becoming obvious that the model really worked and we could provide a better deal for consumers, through leveraging our brand off other networks' excess capacity. As the year drew on, more and more opportunities began to pop up in places as diverse as Africa and China.

Despite 11 September, we did not ignore the airline industry where it was clear there were still opportunities to create really exciting businesses. By the summer of 2004, Fred Reid was recruited to lead Virgin's boldest move in its thirty-five-year history—an all-out assault on the bankrupt US domestic air travel market. Due to historic protectionism of its domestic market, I would have to play a relatively minor role in the creation of Virgin America as an airline, with the majority of the funding and the management coming from US institutions and companies. It was somewhat bizarre to wake up one morning in May 2004 to read that my new airline was going to be called Virgin America, but deeply satisfying. For me Virgin had come of age. We had the confidence to invest in the world's toughest aviation market and be prepared not to have full control of the company's destiny. The very rules that had made the US such a barrier to entry for us in the past, and that BA had tried to use to seal a monopoly, no longer held any fear for us. Over the years we had witnessed some of the most anti-consumer and monopolistic practices by the big US carriers. It finally appeared that the tables were turning. But for some the desire to keep the barriers up to new players within this underserved market is still great. In July 2004 I received a letter from a friend who had attended the ACTC Aviation Conference in Washington. In attendance at this event were the chief executive officers of the leading five America carriers. During the meeting one of these gentlemen was heard to remark: "All we need now is Branson and the cookies will get very burnt." This sounds vaguely familiar. If not flattering!

However, it was not the new airline but another unique aviation event that took me back to America during midsummer that year. On a cold morning on 22 June, I was fortunate enough to witness one of the most amazing sights I have ever seen, as the world's first privately funded spaceship streaked into the skies above the little town of Mohave in the Californian desert. Spaceship One was the truly remarkable brainchild of Burt Rutan, a friend I had known for many years. Burt is one of the world's true geniuses, and his designs for numerous aircraft had been groundbreaking for decades. He was indeed working with Steve Fossett and me on the Virgin Atlantic Global Flyer, a unique and beautiful aircraft that we were planning for Steve (or myself if he got ill) to attempt the world's first nonstop solo flight. The aircraft looked amazing but not as amazing as the little space plane I had seen hidden in the hangar earlier this year and was now streaking into space at 3,000 mph above our heads in the desert.

Another friend, Paul Allen, who is one of the founders of Microsoft, had funded Burt's vision of a cheap reusable space plane. Like Burt, Paul is a visionary. He was visibly excited as he watched his sci-fi dream unfold and become tomorrow's reality. Mike Melville, an incredibly brave pilot, took the little spacecraft to 328,000 feet (100 km) above the earth. I watched with awe and realized that our own vision of cheap space tourism might finally be becoming a real possibility. At dinner with Burt and Paul the night before, we discussed the future of private space flight through a partnership with each other, and I left the evening feeling uplifted. I had always felt that the government monopoly on space was a danger to mankind rather than the benefit often touted by cynical politicians and self-serving missile manufacturers. Monopolies don't work in any industry whether public or private. Here was a chance for Virgin to take on the final frontier, and I'm sure you won't be surprised to read that we had registered both the trademark rights and a company for space travel ten years earlier to be called Virgin Galactic Airways. The Virgin Group—"To Infinity and Beyond"! OK. Make that Virgin *Inter*galactic Airways!

In the summer of 2004, I also brought myself one step closer to my dream of using the strength of the brand and our people to change the world for the better by launching Virgin Unite. This new organization was built by Virgin staff around the world and will be a vehicle to pull us all together, hopefully to make a difference with some of the tougher social challenges and bring a little bit of the Virgin magic into the social space. Holly has already volunteered to spend whatever time she has during her final years at medical school to help out with sexual health issues facing young people in the UK—right back to where I started some thirty-six years ago when I opened the Student Help Centre, which I'm happy to say is still operating and providing free counseling on Portobello Road in West London.

It is with family in mind that I spend less and less time promoting the Virgin brand through dangerous world-record attempts; I think it's unlikely I will do another project on the scale of the around-the-world balloon flight. But then again . . .

I spend so much time traveling, I treasure the moments the family is together. In many ways we are closest when we are all on Necker. It has developed from being the jewel that symbolized the feelings Joan and I have for each other into being a place where the whole family feels at home and at peace. We try to go for Easter, summer, and Christmas holidays, with my parents, my sisters and their families, our closest friends, and quite a few people from all the different Virgin companies. It is like a melting pot where we all take stock of what is happening and get away from everything apart from the fax machine.

I've taught the children to play tennis there, and to swim, snorkel, and sail. When we're there we're there for each other. We make every moment count. It's a time to relax and reflect on what we're all doing, because we know that when we're back in London it's back to work.

My favorite time of day there is the early evening. By then it's midnight in London and it's virtually impossible to speak to anyone in Europe. The fax and telephone are silent, and the sun sets quickly. In an hour or so the daylight changes from brilliant, almost-white sunshine to dusk, with a deep orange blaze across the horizon. Sitting on the veranda, I can watch the last small flock of pelicans dive for fish and flap creakily away to roost. Within minutes the sky turns a velvet midnight blue, and the first handful of stars are out. The sea becomes inky black, and everything falls quiet.

We generally have supper on the terrace. Everyone is suntanned and happy. It's great to be together, and I wonder what the future holds for all the kids here. I look over at Holly and Sam and realize that I don't want to plan their lives for them. I just want them to be happy. I know that other businessmen such as Rupert Murdoch and Robert Maxwell had their children reading annual reports and financial accounts before breakfast, but I want none of that. At moments like these I am happy to forget about my notebook, with its constant burning list of things to do and people to call, and relax into being among people I love and care about.

Even as we sit here, I know that one of our brand-new jumbos is heading from Heathrow to JFK, a route that was, until recently, operated by *Maiden Voyager,* our original jumbo. She had been flying from London to New York since 1984 and had become the backbone of our airline and the linchpin of our success. Her retirement marks the end of an era but also the beginning of a new one, with the arrival of our new A340-600 in the summer of 2002. *African Queen,* one of our first A340 airbuses, is now humming through the night to Lagos, our latest destination; and *Lady in Red,* our first airbus, which was christened by Princess Diana, is heading overnight toward Hong Kong. Virgin Atlantic's offices at Crawley will be deserted save for the cleaners, and the night shift will be drinking their second or third cup of coffee at Heathrow and Gatwick. There will be queues outside Heaven nightclub, and I wonder who is performing tonight and what the future holds for them. The Japanese and Paris Megastores will be shut for the night, but late-afternoon crowds will be leafing through the racks of CDs at the New York Megastore, before buying a can of Virgin Cola from a nearby vending machine. Meanwhile, in London our team at Virgin Books will be wondering why a certain "author" is late with his manuscript!

At the outset, each of those individual ventures was a step into the unknown for the company—a bit like the loss of one's virginity. But, unlike really losing your virginity, in whatever world you make for yourself, you can keep embracing the new and the different over and over again. That's what I have always wanted for Virgin and, whether it's achieved by judgment or luck, I wouldn't have it any other way.

Index